INSPIRE / PLAN / DISCOVER / EXPERIENCE

PORTUGAL

PORTUGAL

CONTENTS

DISCOVER 6

EXPERIENCE 48

NEED TO KNOW 376

Left: Capela de Nossa Senhora da Graça, Porto Santo
Previous page: Sunset from a *miradouro*, São Miguel
Front cover: Lisbon's stunning skyline

DISCOVER

Azenhas do Mar, near Colares

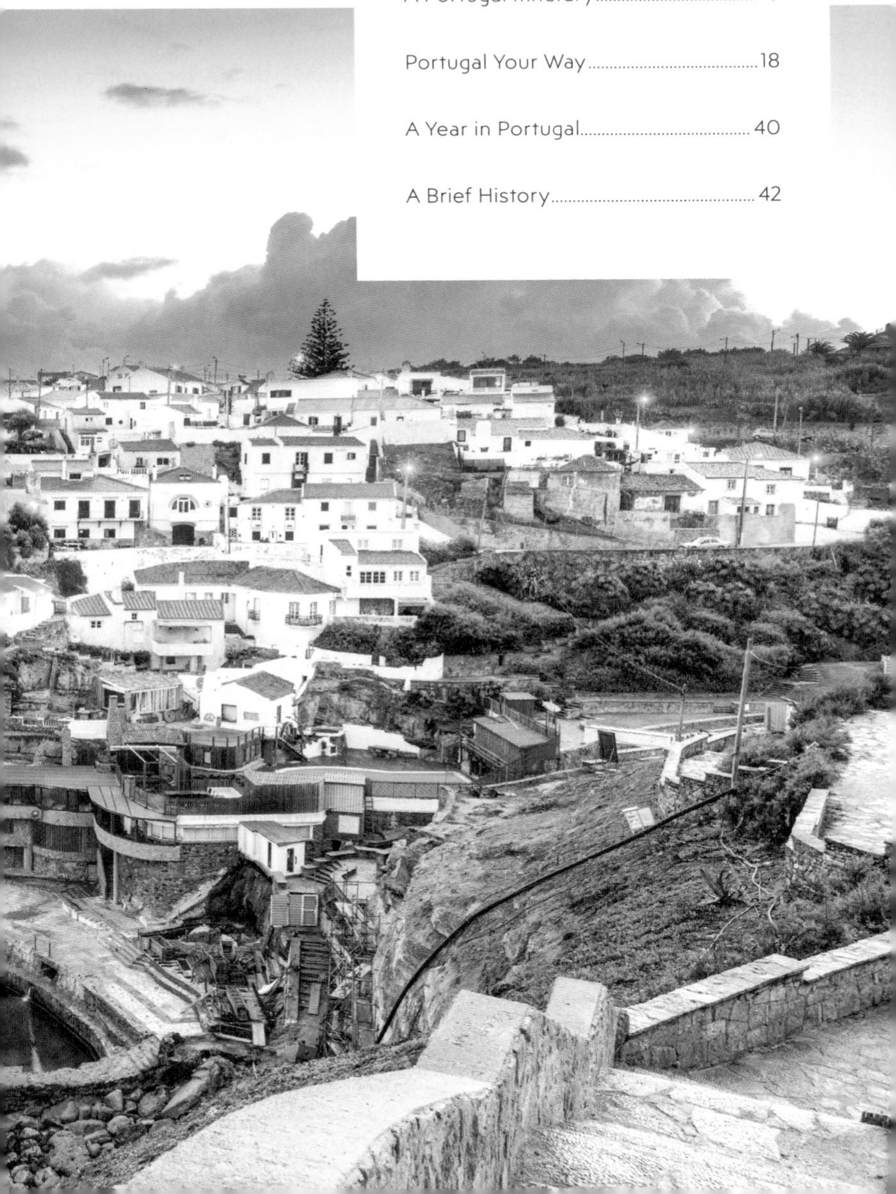

WELCOME TO
PORTUGAL

Home to world-renowned beaches, Portugal is a sunseekers' paradise. But those who venture away from the sand will be rewarded by this bountiful country: cobbled hilltop villages, verdant islands and captivating cities await exploration. Whatever your dream trip to Portugal includes, this DK Eyewitness travel guide is the perfect companion.

1 Footbridge leading to Praia do Camilo, near Lagos.

2 *Pastéis de nata* (egg custard tarts) from Lisbon.

3 Flowers blooming in front of Bom Jesus do Monte.

4 A shady *miradouro* overlooking Lisbon.

For such a small country, Portugal's regions are immensely varied. The mountainous Minho and Trás-os-Montes in the north preserve a rural way of life, while the southerly Algarve has been transformed into a holiday playground. In between these two extremes are forested hills, sun-baked plains, grape-laden valleys and buffeting waves. The landscape of the two remote archipelagos in the Atlantic Ocean differs again. Madeira is a green, subtropical paradise, while the Azores is characterized by otherworldly azure lakes and volcanic craters.

Urban Portugal is a tale of two cities. With cutting-edge art galleries and ornate Manueline monasteries, creamy custard tarts and the spine-tingling wail of traditional *fado* music, it's little wonder that Lisbon has become a firm favourite with visitors. But Porto is a serious rival to the capital city. Adorned with pretty *azulejo* tiles and tattooed with inventive street art, Portugal's northern hub is both charmingly historic and modishly cool. Trendy brunch spots stand side-by-side with ubiquitous port lodges in this foodie's haven.

With so many different things to discover and experience, Portugal can seem overwhelming. We've broken the country down into easily navigable chapters, with detailed itineraries, expert local knowledge and colourful, comprehensive maps to help you plan the perfect visit. Whether you're staying for a weekend, a week, or longer, this DK Eyewitness travel guide will ensure that you see the very best Portugal has to offer. Enjoy the book, and enjoy Portugal.

REASONS TO LOVE
PORTUGAL

Vibrant cities, natural wonders, undulating vineyards, adrenaline-inducing surfing, tasty dishes and evocative music: there are endless reasons to love Portugal. Here, we pick some of our favourites.

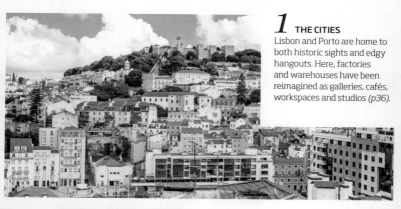

1 THE CITIES

Lisbon and Porto are home to both historic sights and edgy hangouts. Here, factories and warehouses have been reimagined as galleries, cafés, workspaces and studios *(p36)*.

STUNNING BEACHES 2

From the sheltered sandy coves of the Algarve to the wide stretches of sand that line the west coast, Portugal has some of Europe's best beaches *(p28)*.

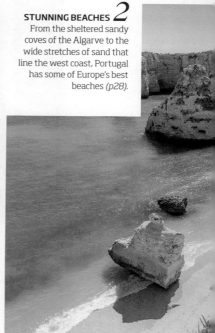

3 A NIGHT OUT IN THE BAIRRO ALTO

Bairro Alto has long been Lisbon's nightlife district, with bars and *fado* houses lining the streets; emerging international restaurants are making it a culinary hotspot too *(p89)*.

PALÁCIO DA PENA **4**

The colourful domes and turrets of this eclectic palace dominate the forested hills of Sintra. It's just as exuberant inside, with kitsch decor and over-the-top furnishings *(p152).*

WALKING THE LEVADAS OF MADEIRA **5**

Following these narrow irrigation canals takes you through some wild scenery. One of the most beautiful is the winding trail from Ribeiro Frio to Balcões *(p359).*

FESTIVALS **6**

Portugal comes alive during its summer *festas.* In the main cities, Porto celebrates São João, while Lisbon's streets fill with revellers during the Festa de Santo António *(p40).*

SURFING 7

One of Europe's top surfing spots, Portugal has waves for all abilities. With its high rolling swell, Nazaré is best for pros, while beginners should head to the Algarve's west coast *(p31)*.

LISTENING TO FADO 8

This melancholic music is unique to Portugal. Some of the best-known *fado* singers came from Lisbon's Alfama district, and it's still the best place to find a cosy *fado* bar *(p36)*.

9 AZULEJOS

Distinctive, colourful tiles can be seen on just about any street corner: on the front of churches, in metro and railway stations, or simply on the façades of houses *(p38)*.

10 PORT TASTING

Whether it's white, ruby or tawny, sip a glass of the country's eponymous fortified wine at a *quinta* (vineyard estate) in the undulating Douro Valley *(p262)*.

SAVOURING SARDINES 11

Relish sardines, caught fresh from the sea, grilled on an open-air barbecue and served with potatoes, salad and an ice-cold beer. Is there anything better?

HISTORIC TOWNS 12

With no shortage of ancient cities and fortified hilltop towns, Portugal is a joy for history buffs. Évora, with its Roman temple and medieval cathedral, is one of the best *(p296)*.

EXPLORE
PORTUGAL

This guide divides Portugal into five distinct regions: Lisbon *(p50)*, Central Portugal *(p136)*, Northern Portugal *(p220)*, Southern Portugal *(p284)* and Portugal's Islands *(p340)*. These regions have been divided into 11 colour-coded sightseeing areas, as shown on this map.

Atlantic   Ocean

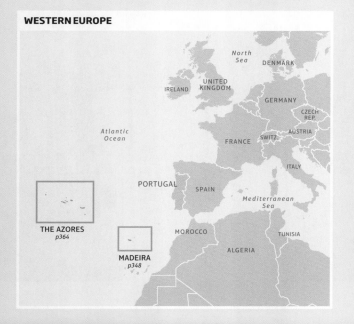

WESTERN EUROPE

North Sea

DENMARK

IRELAND

UNITED KINGDOM

GERMANY

CZECH REP.

Atlantic Ocean

AUSTRIA

FRANCE

SWITZ

ITALY

PORTUGAL

SPAIN

Mediterranean Sea

THE AZORES
p364

MOROCCO

TUNISIA

MADEIRA
p348

ALGERIA

Experience the buzzing cities of Porto and Lisbon, as well as many of the country's highlights in between, on a drive from the north to the centre of Portugal.

7 DAYS

Day 1

Morning Your journey begins in Porto, with a coffee at the Belle Epoque Majestic Café *(p36)*. Next, browse the fashionable jewellery and leather shops on the pedestrianized Rua de Santa Catarina.

Afternoon For lunch, order a *francesinha* at Café Santiago *(p37)*. Pop into São Bento Station to admire the *azulejos*, then take a trip on a *rabelo* boat from Praça Ribeira.

Evening After disembarking back at the square, enjoy a traditional Portuguese meal at Cantinho do Avillez *(p241)*, before retiring to 1872 River House *(p237)*.

Day 2

Morning Start the day admiring the Romanesque Sé *(p236)* – the city's cathedral – and the monumental Paço Episcopal, the bishop's palace *(p236)*.

Afternoon *Petiscos* (Portuguese tapas) is a good choice for lunch before walking across the magnificent Ponte de Dom Luís I to the city of Vila Nova da Gaia *(p234)*, which lies on the other side of the iconic iron bridge.

Evening Savour a glass of chilled white port at one of the city's many lodges, such as Ramos Pinto, before crossing back over to Porto for the night.

Day 3

Morning It's time to leave Portugal's second city. Drive south on the A29 to canal-latticed Aveiro *(p194)*.

Afternoon Busy Praça Humberto Delgado is the perfect spot for lunch before embarking on a one-hour trip on a colourful *moliceiro* boat.

Evening Aveiro is renowned for its seafood restaurants – our pick is Mercado do Peixe, which is found on top of the city's fish market *(p194)*. Spend the night at the Veneza Hotel *(www.venezahotel.pt/en)*.

Day 4

Morning Continue south on the N235 to the magical woodlands of Buçaco *(p202)*. There are many shaded walks to explore here. The lavish Bussaco Palace Hotel serves up excellent lunches.

1 Ornate interior of the Paço Episcopal, Porto.

2 Porto's Ponte de Dom Luís I, illuminated at night.

3 Colourful *moliceiro* boats on one of Aveiro's canals.

4 A *fado* singer at A Baiuca in Lisbon.

5 Casa das Histórias Paula Rego.

Afternoon Take the A14 to Figueira da Foz, which has an enormous beach *(p207)*. Can you think of a better way to spend the afternoon than relaxing on the sand?

Evening Spend the night at one of the resort's many beachside hotels.

Day 5

Morning Head down the A1 to the extraordinary pilgrimage town of Fátima *(p183)*. Wonder at the imposing basilica, before continuing on to Santarém *(p186)*.

Afternoon Taberna do Quinzena I *(p186)* is a good choice for lunch. After exploring the town, return to the A1 to reach Lisbon.

Evening Cervejaria Trindade *(p101)* is a sumptuous place for dinner and Hotel do Chiado has a fashionable rooftop bar to while away the rest of the day *(p98)*.

Day 6

Morning Have a coffee at the historic A Brasileira *(p101)* and then hop on the clacking tram 28 from Chiado to Alfama.

Afternoon Portas do Sol *(www.portasdo sol.pt)*, which overlooks the Tagus, is the perfect spot for an alfresco lunch. Alfama, with its impossibly narrow streets, is best explored on foot. After wandering, end up at the Castelo de São Jorge for sunset *(p64)*.

Evening Spend the evening at a *fado* house such as A Baiuca *(p71)*.

Day 7

Morning The lively seaside resort of Cascais *(p159)* has some fine beaches and plenty of restaurants for lunch – and the journey there is just as good, with the train winding from the city along the Lisbon coast.

Afternoon Explore the striking Casa das Histórias Paula Rego *(p20)*, a museum dedicated to the late contemporary visual artist who was born in Lisbon, but later left to work in London.

Evening End your trip with a cocktail at the impossibly cool Cinco Lounge *(p97)*.

Glitzy Gothic

Churches and palaces in the Gothic style date from the Middle Ages. They include Portugal's oldest surviving palace, the Palácio Nacional de Sintra *(p150)*. Despite its plain façade, the construction is anything but simple; note the distinctive conical chimneys.

Other Gothic gems are the Mosteiro de Alcobaça *(p170)* and Bragança's citadel *(p248)*.

→

The unique exterior of the Palácio Nacional de Sintra

PORTUGAL FOR
ARCHITECTURE

A riot of different architectural styles can be seen around the country. Of course, there are plenty of *azulejo*-bedecked buildings, but there are also intriguing examples of the Manueline style, which is unique to Portugal, as well as bold contemporary constructions.

ÁLVARO SIZA VIEIRA

Álvaro Siza Vieira (born 1933) is Portugal's most famous architect. He won the prestigious Pritzker Prize in 1992 for his renovation of Lisbon's Chiado district, after it was largely destroyed by a fire in 1988. Known for his Modernist clean lines and simplicity, he also worked on the Portuguese National Pavilion – famed for its huge, sagging concrete canopy – built for Expo 98. Many of his works are in his native Porto, including the remarkable sea bathing pool complex at Leça de Palmeira, just north of the city, that he created in the 1960s *(p31)*.

Modern Icons

Lisbon is home to buildings by some of the world's leading contemporary architects. In the Parque das Nações *(p132)*, you'll find Santiago Calatrava's cavernous Oriente station. The sleek MAAT *(p116)*, with its walkable wave-like roof, is a museum showcasing the best in architecture and design. Look out for Álvaro Siza Vieira's constructions in Lisbon's Chiado district and beyond the capital.

The curvaceous MAAT, ↑ designed by Amanda Levete Architects

Magnificent Manueline Marvels

The reign of Manuel I (1469-1521) was a period of enormous wealth for Portugal. The country exploited territories that were newly taken over, and lavish buildings are a reminder of this today. Funded largely by the spice and gold trade, the 16th-century Mosteiro dos Jerónimos in Lisbon is a riot of maritime-themed stone-work, including ropes and anchors *(p108)*. The style was pioneered by João de Castilho (1470-1552) and Diogo de Boitaca (1460-1528), who built the cloisters here, as well as the Torre de Belém *(p110)*.

$\longrightarrow$

The ornate, honey-coloured cloisters of the Mosteiro dos Jerónimos

Baroque Giants

Designed by João Frederico Ludovice (1673-1752), the vast Palácio de Mafra is Portugal's best example of the over-the-top Baroque style, with a 200-m- (656-ft-) long façade and some 156 staircases *(p156)*. To the north, Porto was the stomping ground of Italian Nicolau Nasoni (1691-1773), who designed the Torre and Igreja dos Clérigos *(p239)* and Paço Episcopal *(p236)*.

$\longleftarrow$

Formal courtyard garden at the Palácio de Mafra

Art Deco Gems

From railway stations such as Cais do Sodré to the A Brasileira café *(p101)*, Lisbon is full of bold early 20th-century designs. Porto's iconic Fundação de Serralves *(Rua Dom João de Castro 210; www.serralves.pt)* is partly housed in Portugal's most notable Art Deco villa. Take a tour with an architect or artist.

$\longrightarrow$

The blush exterior of the Fundação de Serralves, built in the 1930s

Modern Art

Portugal's best-known contemporary artist, Paula Rego (1935–2022), had a very distinct style. Her paintings depict muscular women, fairy tales and animals dressed in clothes to explore the themes of repression, feminism and politics. Casa das Histórias in Cascais *(p159)* hosts exhibitions of her work in a striking pyramidal building, designed by architect Eduardo Souto de Moura (b.1952). For more modern and contemporary works, check out the Museu Calouste Gulbenkian *(p122)*.

→

Admiring modern art in the Museu Calouste Gulbenkian

4,000

The number of years of art on display in the Museu Calouste Gulbenkian.

PORTUGAL FOR
ART LOVERS

With works gathered from all corners of the globe during Portugal's Age of Discovery, dynamic contemporary exhibits and the world's largest collection of original jewellery by Art Nouveau master craftsman René Lalique, Portugal is brimming with groundbreaking art. Here, we round up the highlights.

Sculpture

Named after a leading 18th-century sculptor, Porto's Museu Soares dos Reis has some great examples of António Soares dos Reis' work (1847–89; *p241*). The high-light of the collection is *O Desterrado* (1872), a brooding marble figure. Lisbon's Museu Calouste Gulbenkian houses world-class contemporary sculpture by the likes of José Maria Fernandes Marques (b.1939), whose works are rooted in both European and non-Western artistic traditions.

←

António Teixeira Lopes's *Childhood of Cain* (1890) at the Museu Soares dos Reis

↑ Exhibition of Chinese pottery at the Museu Nacional de Arte Antiga

Portuguese Colonial Art

During the 15th and 16th centuries, Portugal acquired bounty from across the globe. Admire delicate Chinese porcelain, intricate inlaid Indian cabinets and ivory hunting horns from Africa at Lisbon's Museu Nacional de Arte Antiga *(p92)*. Many of the treasures were brought over from Brazil and Africa by spice merchants for their wealthy patrons.

Sacred Art

In the 15th and 16th centuries, Flemish sacred art was highly fashionable among wealthy sugar traders in Madeira, who bought and commissioned paintings, triptychs and sculptures for their private chapels and grandiose houses. You can see these works at Funchal's Museu de Arte Sacra *(p352)* and Lisbon's Museu Nacional de Arte Antiga.

→

A painting on display in the Museu de Arte Sacra

Art Nouveau and Art Deco

Jewellery, glassware and furnishings, many intertwined with René Lalique's (1860-1945) signature ornate serpents and peacocks, can be seen at Lisbon's Museu Calouste Gulbenkian. Highlights include a spectacular dragonfly brooch, an orchid comb and the sublime *Cats Choker* (1906-8), crafted from rock crystal.

← Jewellery by René Lalique at the Museu Calouste Gulbenkian

Island Cuisine

Portugal's islands have their own specialities. On Madeiran menus you'll find succulent scabbard fish often accompanied by native bananas. Of course, Madeira wine is the top tipple here *(p360)*. The greener Azores are known for their creamy cheeses and the signature *cozido das Furnas*, a meat stew which is cooked in pots underground and overnight in the hot volcanic soil.

→

Barbecuing fresh fish at a seafood restaurant in Funchal, Madeira

PORTUGAL FOR
FOODIES

Portuguese cuisine has been underrated for years, but the country's abundance of fresh fish, seafood and lush vegetables is finally being recognized and it's now firmly on the culinary map. Each region has its own must-eat and must-drink; here, we tell you what to order and where.

Southern Style

Restaurants on the southern coast serve up fish and seafood dishes, such as *cataplana* (a tasty, tomatoey seafood stew) and barbecued sardines. You will also find plenty of restaurants specializing in the ubiquitous spicy chicken piri-piri, which originated in Portugal's former African colonies. Moving inland, the rural south is known for its pork, olives and oranges, with the region's signature dish *carne de porco à Alentejana* featuring two of its best ingredients in an unusual but tasty combination of cubes of pork, fried with clams, garlic and coriander.

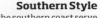

→

Carne de porco à Alentejana, served in a stylish copper dish with bread

The Varied Centre

Roast suckling pig accompanied by red sparkling wine, a rich choice of seafood and comforting stews: central Portugal's cuisine is as diverse as its landscape. The granite Serra da Estrela mountain range is home to Portugal's most famous cheese, the distinctive and buttery Serra, while the Dão region produces some of Portugal's finest full-bodied and fruity red wines.

A board featuring a selection of cheeses from Portugal

The Hearty North

The cuisine here is heavier than in the south, with menus dominated by grilled meats, game and tripe. Porto's signature dish is the gut-busting *francesinha* – doorstop slices of bread filled with steak, sausage, ham and melted cheese, and covered in a thick tomato-and-beer sauce. Iconic wines include light *vinho verde (p281)* and full-bodied port *(p262)*.

$\longrightarrow$

Tucking into a *francesinha*, the speciality of Porto

Foodie Capital

In Lisbon, chefs such as José Avillez are revitalizing the culinary scene by producing innovative dishes from traditional ingredients. But the city offers plenty of tasty traditional stalwarts too, including *ginjinha*, a sweet cherry liqueur sold from street stalls. And what trip to Portugal is complete without a bite of crispy, flaky custard tart that simply melts in the mouth? Antiga Confeitaria de Belém is the birthplace of the *pastéis de nata (p115)*.

José Avillez serving up a dish at Belcanto, one of his restaurants in Lisbon

EAT

Belcanto

José Avillez's restaurant has been awarded two Michelin stars.

🚇 M7 🏠 Rua Serpa Pinto 10A, Lisbon 🌐 belcanto.pt

—————————

Il Gallo d'Oro

This restaurant was the first in Madeira to be awarded a Michelin star.

🏠 B7 🏠 Estrada Monumental 147, Funchal 🌐 portobay.com

Hilltop Homes

Many of Portugal's villages are found along the mountainous border with Spain. Built in high, isolated locations for protection, the villages enjoy amazing 360-degree panoramas over the surrounding countryside. One of the most dramatic examples is Marvão *(p302)*, where you can walk along the crumbling walls that surround the village's picturesque white-washed houses. From the fortifications you will be granted far-reaching vistas over olive groves, woods and plains into Spain.

→

Marvão's dramatic stone fortifications

PORTUGAL FOR
VILLAGE LIFE

A world away from the buzzing cities and bustling beach resorts, Portugal's hilltop villages are remote, preserving a slower pace of life and traditional rural outlook. Make the journey inland for dramatic locations and stunning views.

Stays Away

Experience local life by spending the night in a Portuguese village. Marvão, Óbidos *(p179)* and Estremoz *(p306)* have *pousadas* *(www.pousadas.pt)* – historic buildings now run as small hotels – while others, such as Monsaraz *(p308)* and Castelo de Vide *(p303)*, offer small rural guesthouses. For a unique stay, book a room that seems straight out of *The Hobbit*. Sun Set House in Monsanto *(www.sun-set-house.com.es)* and Casa da Lagariça in Sortelha *(p215)* are both traditional and atmospheric examples.

←

Lunch with a view at Marvão's *pousada*

TOP 3 VILLAGE FESTIVALS

Easter
On Easter Sunday, a crucifix is paraded through the streets for parishioners to kiss Jesus's feet, before rockets illuminate the skies in celebration.

Romarias
A religious festival where saints' statues are brought from the church and paraded through the streets.

Christmas
Between Christmas and Epiphany, boys in the Trás-os-Montes area dress as tricksters in colourful fringed suits.

Take a Tour

With pretty villages scattered across the length of the country, why not take a tour? Start at Cacela Velha *(p338)* in the south, then head into the Alentejo, to the whitewashed village of Serpa *(p310)*. Next stop is Monsaraz en route to Marvão on the Spanish border. Finish your tour at Monsanto *(p216)*.

→

The whitewashed village of Monsaraz

Party Time!

Most villages have their own annual festivals, and many of these celebrate a local harvest. Marvão, for example, has a Chestnut Festival in November. Though every festival has its own character – think colourful religious processions, parades, rodeos and even *pauliteiros* (stick dancing) – one thing always guaranteed is lots of food and drink. Join a picnic or barbecue and enjoy the celebrations.

←

Paper flowers in Campo Maior's Festas do Povo·

Soaring Mountains

Portugal's highest mountain, Pico, is the summit of the Mid-Atlantic Ridge *(p373)*. The top of a vast underwater volcano, Pico dominates the island in the Azores to which it lends its name. The strenuous 9-hour climb to the summit is only for the energetic.

→

Scaling the narrow track to Pico's summit

PORTUGAL FOR
NATURAL
WONDERS

For such a small country, mainland Portugal has a surprising variety of dramatic scenery. Head out to its islands, far out in the Atlantic, and you'll find even more stunning examples of why Portugal is a land of natural wonders.

Vibrant Wetlands

Covering some 56 km (35 miles) of coastline, the Algarve's Parque Natural da Ria Formosa is an important wetland area of marshes, saltpans and islets *(p335)*. The park is protected from the sea by a series of sandbars lined with long sandy beaches, making it the ideal spot for sunbathing, swimming, walking and bird-watching.

A wooden bridge crossing the river in the Parque Natural da Ria Formosa

Wonderful Waterfalls

Portugal's only national park, the Parque Nacional da Peneda-Gerês covers some 700 sq km (270 sq miles) of wild mountainous and wooded scenery *(p270)*. Remote villages and deep reservoirs are the only reminders of life here. Take a walk through the park to reach the Arado Falls, a series of dramatic waterfalls gushing from the mountainside – the pools are a perfect place to bathe on a hot day.

→

The Arado Falls thundering into the pool below in the Parque Nacional da Peneda-Gerês

Amazing Caves

Journey deep underground into the cavernous Grutas de Mira de Aire, near Porto do Mós *(p182)*. Only 600 m (656 yards) of the whopping 11-km- (7-mile-) long network of caves can be visited, but on your tour you will traverse a series of tunnels and walkways, where you can see stalactites, stalagmites and weird rock formations. The visit culminates at a lake filled with fountains.

←

Exploring Grutas de Mira de Aire

Fantastic Forests

Swathes of Madeira are covered in laurel forests so ancient that they are UNESCO World Heritage Sites. To explore them, walk along the *levadas* from Ribeiro Frio to Portela *(p359)* or take the shorter walk to Balcões, which overlooks the wooded valleys.

→

A family walking along a trail through one of Madeira's laurel forests

Family Fun

Almost completely enclosed in a scallop-shell-shaped bay, calm waters lap onto soft sand at São Martinho do Porto *(p180)*. There are pedalos for hire, a great ice cream parlour and huge sand dunes, which make great places to play, on the other side of the bay.

←

Kids boogie boarding on a Portuguese beach

PORTUGAL FOR
BREATHTAKING BEACHES

At more than 1,610 km (1,000 miles) long, with family-friendly stretches, surfing hot spots buffeted by rolling Atlantic breakers and nightly parties on the sand, Portugal's coastline offers something for everyone.

Escape the Crowds

Between Praia da Rocha's lively party scene and Praia do Alvor, which is usually packed with summer holidaymakers, you'll find a secluded hideaway. Prainha, meaning "tiny beach" in Portuguese, is a pretty beach near Alvor *(p330)*. Explore the little grottoes among the rocks here, which are inscribed with love messages.

→

Secluded Prainha, near Alvor, enclosed by rock formations

393

The number of Blue
Flags awarded
to Portugal's
cleanest beaches
in 2022.

Sandy Strolls

The southern Alentejan
coast is great for walking. The
Trilho dos Pescadores – a long-
distance route – follows fishers'
paths along the coast from
Porto Covo *(p315)* to Odeceixe
(p326), taking in dramatic
clifftops, the wide sandy beach
of Zambujeira do Mar *(p315)*
and plenty of sheltered coves.

$\longrightarrow$

Walking on a
sandy path to a sea

Late 'n' Lively

If you want more from your beach
after dark, Figueira da Foz is
the spot for you *(p207)*. At this
bustling cosmopolitan resort,
locals party late into the night.
As well as a long, wide stretch
of sand, the town has a marina,
casino and no shortage of bars
and restaurants.

$\longleftarrow$

Revellers dancing
on a beach on a warm
summer evening

Seafood Spots

Pretty much any beach
in Portugal will have a
simple joint cooking grilled
sardines, but for a choice of
restaurants head to the
former fishing village of
Nazaré *(p181)*. Pick from
fresh fish, lobster, crab and
other shellfish and watch
the surfers riding Nazaré's
famed waves while you eat.

$\longrightarrow$

Goose barnacles, a
Portuguese delicacy,
and huge prawns

▷ Take a Hike

The Parque Natural Peneda-Gerês is a great place for hiking (p270). The signposted 10-km (6-mile) PR3 trail takes in the stunning Pedra Bela viewpoint. For more of a challenge, walk the seven-day Caminho Português da Costa from Valença to Porto.

▷ On Par

Portugal is one of the world's top golfing destinations, with many courses on offer, particularly around the Lisbon coast and in the Algarve (see *www.portugalgolf.pt* for a full list). Our pick is Dom Pedro Victoria in Vilamoura, acclaimed as one of the best courses in Europe within a year of opening.

PORTUGAL FOR
OUTDOOR
ACTIVITIES

With an average of 300 days of sunshine a year, Portugal offers plenty of reason to get outdoors. Swim, surf, hike, cycle – the list of activities is endless. Here, we round up some of the best.

▷ Wheelie Good Fun

Based in Lagos (p329), the Mountain Bike Adventure (*www.themountainbike adventure.com*) runs great off-road guided bike trips along little-known coastal trails. As well as mountain biking, Portugal Bike Tours (*www.portugalbike.com*) offers road cycling and hybrid tours, and self-guided routes, all around the mainland for between 7 and 14 days.

▷ On the Rocks

All around the rocky island of Madeira, swimming pools have been blasted into the sea edge. Porto Moniz is one of the best, with crystal-clear salt water enclosed by volcanic walls *(p362)*. On the mainland, 10 km (6 miles) from Porto you can swim in the Leça de Palmeira sea pools, designed by the respected architect Álvaro Siza Vieira.

◁ Down to the Wire

Take the small ferry from Alcoutim *(p339)* over the Guadiana river to Sanlucar in Spain, then whizz back at about 64 km/h (40 mph) on the world's only cross-border zipwire, LimiteZero *(www.limitezero.com)*. The fun, adrenaline-inducing ride is perfect for daredevils. During the 720 m (2,360 ft) ride you'll soar over rugged mountains, farms and the boats on the river. Bear in mind when booking that LimiteZero operates on Spanish time, meaning it's one hour ahead of Portugal.

TOP 5 SURF BEACHES IN PORTUGAL

Sagres
Perfect for both learners and pros *(p328)*.

The Ericeira Coast
Europe's first World Surfing Reserve *(p157)*.

Peniche and Baleal
Year-round surfing, with over 30 breaks *(p178)*.

Nazaré
Tackle the world's highest waves *(p181)*.

Figueira da Foz
Home to one of the longest right-hand breaks in Europe *(p207)*.

△ Walk this Way

Madeira's *levada* walks follow small irrigation channels cut into the island's steep hillsides. One of the best is the Vereda dos Balcões, an hour-and-a-half round trip from Ribeiro Frio that leads to a viewpoint overlooking the mountains. Another favourite is the demanding two- to three-hour walk to the beauty spot known as Vinte e Cinco Fontes (25 Springs).

PORTUGAL FOR
FAMILIES

**Beautiful beaches aside, Portugal is a great place for kids.
The people are friendly, the food familiar and there are
plenty of things to do to give kids a holiday to remember.**

Get Outside

Small children will enjoy wandering around
Coimbra's Portugal dos Pequenitos *(p199)*, with
its recreations of some of Portugal's best-
known monuments, including an impressive
replica of Tomar's Convento de Cristo *(p176)*,
and regional houses, all in miniature. For
thrill-seekers, Madeira's Monte Toboggan
is a hair-raising ride down a steep
hillside in a wicker basket *(p357)*. The
descent is made safe by the *carreiros*
(toboggan-drivers), dressed in white with
straw boaters, who use their rubber-soled
shoes to control the speed and direction
of the basket. A fun way to get from A to B!

→

A mother and son
enjoying a ride on
the Monte Toboggan

Rainy-Day Activities

Parque das Nações *(p132)*, in Lisbon, has plenty of child-friendly attractions, including water fountains to play in, a cable car and the Oceanário de Lisboa. Here you'll find a vast array of fish, as well as puffins, penguins and sea otters. For kids who love cars and trains, a visit to Lisbon's Museu da Carris *(p131)* includes a trip around the huge site in a traditional tram, as well as the chance to climb into old buses, horse-drawn trams, coaches and trucks. No football fan will want to miss Funchal's Museu CR7 – better known as the Cristiano Ronaldo Museum *(p355)*. Inside is a huge array of trophies, golden boots, video clips showing some of Ronaldo's best goals and plenty of correspondence from his fans.

← Admiring all things aquatic at Oceanário de Lisboa

> **INSIDER TIP**
> **Go Halves**
>
> Few restaurants in Portugal have children's menus, but almost all will serve a *meia dose* (half portion) of a dish on request. Ordering *petiscos* (tapas) is a great way to encourage fussy eaters to try different foods.

Bodyboarding on a gentle ocean wave ↑

Fun on the Water

Portugal's beaches have more to offer than sun and sand *(p28)*. Pedalos and inflatables can be hired and watersports centres rent out paddleboards, kayaks and windsurfing equipment for older kids. Setúbal, on the Lisbon Coast, is the best place to go dolphin watching *(p162)*. The pod of wild bottlenose dolphins are so friendly that they often swim alongside the boats.

A boat trip watching a pod of bottlenose dolphins swimming ↑

Tram-Spotting

Porto's historic trams are fantastically photogenic. Head to Praça de Parada Leitão, where you can snap tram 22 in front of Igreja do Carmo and Carmelitas *(p240)*. No budding photographer should leave Lisbon without a shot of the iconic tram 28. A great place to catch the bright yellow tram as it trundles through cobbled alleys is along the narrow Rua das Escola Gerais.

←

Lisbon's tram 28 trundling through Alfama's cobbled alleys

PORTUGAL FOR
PHOTOGRAPHY

With its soft Atlantic light, bright sun and blue skies, Portugal is great for photographers. As well as dramatic landscapes and lively street scenes, around the country you'll find dramatic *miradouros*, or viewpoints, many with traditional tiles, all of which make for great photo opportunities.

TOP 3 LISBON MIRADOUROS

Santa Luzia
This viewpoint offers a charming tiled terrace overlooking the Alfama district.

São Pedro de Alcântara
This *miradouro* in Bairro Alto features views of the Castelo de São Jorge and can be accessed on foot or via a funicular.

Miradouro da Graça
The neighbourhood of Graça gives its name to this shaded *miradouro* and the church on site.

Sensational Seascape

Praia de Bordeira, near Sagres *(p328)*, is a wide, sandy stretch lapped by rolling Atlantic breakers. Take the road that runs alongside Ribeira da Carrapateira to the south of the beach and park on the cliff top. From here, wooden walkways lead down over the cliff to give fantastic vistas along the unspoiled coastline.

→

Ponta da Piedade on Portugal's Atlantic coast as the sun rises

↑ The trail between Pico do Arieiro and Pico Ruivo, and *(inset)* the summit of Pico Ruivo

Marvellous Mountainscape

The walk from Pico do Arieiro to Pico Ruivo in Madeira is one of the most spectacular on the island *(p359)*. There are wonderful photo opportunities all along the walk, culminating at the summit, where the panorama stretches over the north and east coasts of this lush island. Try to make the hike in the morning for the clearest uninterrupted views from the top of the mountain.

📷 PICTURE PERFECT
Dusky Lisbon

At dusk, head across the Ponte 25 de Abril to Cacilhas. From here you can take a great photo of the bridge illuminated against the twinkling lights of Lisbon.

Village Vistas

The pretty Alentejan village of Serpa *(p310)* offers plenty of opportunities to capture the quintessential image of traditional Portuguese life. For the best photos, walk along the crenellated castle walls from which you can look down across the village's narrow, cobbled alleys and red-tiled roofs to the surrounding countryside. This is a land of patchwork fields and groves growing olives, oranges and cork, making for a fabulous photograph of rural life.

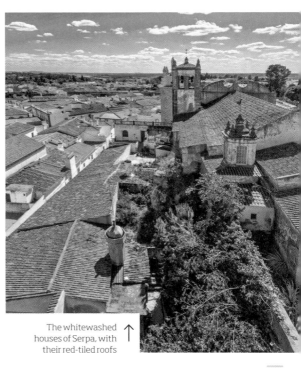

The whitewashed houses of Serpa, with their red-tiled roofs ↑

Espresso Yourself

Lisbon's Art Deco A Brasileira café has been serving the city's literary greats for more than 100 years *(p101)*. Over in Porto, high society and intellectuals have been flocking to the far more ornate Majestic Café, with its decorative stone cherubs, since it opened in 1921 *(www.cafemajestic.com)*.

←

Statue of poet Fernando Pessoa outside A Brasileira

PORTUGAL FOR
CAPTIVATING CITIES

Urban Portugal is a tale of two cities. The traditional saying "Porto works, while Lisbon plays" no longer holds true, with both cities having much to offer.

FADO

Like blues music, *fado* is an expression of longing and sorrow. Literally meaning "fate", the music owes much to the concept known as *saudade*, meaning a longing both for what has been lost, and for what has never been attained. The people of Lisbon have nurtured this poignant music in backstreet cafés and restaurants for over 150 years, and it has altered little in that time. Fado is sung as often by women as men and is always accompanied by a *guitarra* (a Portuguese guitar) and a *viola* (an acoustic Spanish guitar). Alfama is the best place to hear it; we love A Baiuca *(p71)*.

Rhythm of the Night

Both cities have a lively nightlife, with traditional bars sitting side by side with trendy clubs. But, with its myriad drinking holes spilling out into narrow cobbled streets, Lisbon's Bairro Alto *(p89)* is an unbeatable party destination. For a change of pace, no trip to the capital would be complete without a visit to an atmospheric *fado* bar.

→

Electronic band performing at festival Rock in Rio Lisboa

Retail Therapy

There are plenty of places to shop in Lisbon and Porto, and they both have some standout spots. Lisbon's Time Out Market is the place for foodies *(p101)*. Alongside traditional produce stalls, kiosks serve a variety of gourmet treats from some of Portugal's top chefs. Porto's must-visit shop is the fabulous Art Deco Livraria Lello.

→

The Livraria Lello, said to have inspired the fictional Hogwarts

Staple Dishes

Pastéis de nata – the deliciously flaky custard tarts – are ubiquitous in Lisbon. Head to Antiga Confeitaria de Belém to sample them *(p115)*. Porto's culinary staple, the *francesinha* or "little Frenchie", requires a bigger appetite. The retro Café Santiago is regularly victorious in competitions to find the best doorstop-sized sandwich *(www.cafesantiago.pt)*.

←

Pastéis de nata at Antiga Confeitaria de Belém

Charming Streets

Tumbling down steep hillsides, Lisbon's Alfama and Porto's Ribeira districts have much in common. Both are working-class areas that have been gentrified in recent years and their narrow streets remain atmospheric places to get lost in. While Alfama *(p60)* is full of red-tiled roofs and always decked in colourful garlands, Ribeira *(p232)* has higgledy-piggledy houses, tiled in different colours. Wander through each area listening out for the sounds of local life through the open windows strung with washing.

→

Everyday life in the narrow streets of Lisbon's Alfama

TOP 5 DECORATED LISBON METRO STATIONS

Metro do Oriente
Maritime-themed *azulejos* are found here.

Jardim Zoológico
Contemporary tiles on an animal theme adorn the walls.

Alvalade
Don't miss Maria Keil's colourful panels of women and monkeys.

Campo Grande
Home to some unusual 18th-century figures by Eduardo Nery.

Cais do Sodré
A huge illustration of Alice in Wonderland's white rabbit hangs here.

A Chegança by Luiz Ventura (1994) in Restauradores station ↑

PORTUGAL FOR
AZULEJOS

Decorative tiles were first brought to Portugal by the Moors in the 8th century, but became an art form as the uniquely Portuguese *azulejos* under Manuel I in the 16th century. Today, ceramic designs adorn the walls of everything from historic palaces to modern-day metro stations.

Painted Palaces

As a sign of wealth, is it any wonder that *azulejos* adorn former royal homes? The Palácio Nacional de Sintra's Sala dos Árabes is decorated with green geometric tiles, while the flamboyant Sala dos Brasões houses 18th-century blue Delft examples *(p150)*. In Lisbon, the Palácio Fronteira is home to both 17th-century Delft and Portuguese tiles *(p134)*.

→

Blue tiles providing a backdrop to the Palácio Fronteira's gardens

Sacred Adornment

Many churches are decorated with *azulejos* depicting biblical scenes. In Lisbon's São Vicente de Fora, 38 tiles illustrate the fables of La Fontaine *(p66)*. Meanwhile, Igreja Matriz de São Lourenço in Almancil is covered in tiles *(p333)*. Porto's Igreja do Carmo, however, is the church you're most likely to recognize – it's featured on many Instagram feeds *(p240)*.

↑ The blue-and-white exterior of the Igreja do Carmo

Above their Station

People generally just pass through train stations, but some of Portugal's transport hubs are destinations in themselves. Porto's São Bento station is home to some 20,000 *azulejos (p237)*, rural Pinhão's station depicts the port industry *(p263)* and some of Lisbon's most fantastic contemporary tiles adorn its metro stops.

Eat Beautiful

For dining with a difference, head to one of Lisbon's tiled restaurants. Cervejaria Trindade occupies several rooms lined with beautiful tiles *(p101)*, while Casa de Alentejo *(p84)* houses Moorish-style tiles and 20th-century hand-painted panels amid a riot of decorative stucco-work.

Dining in Lisbon's ornate Cervejaria Trindade

Tiles and Styles

Housed in the beautiful former Madre de Deus convent, Lisbon's Museu Nacional do Azulejo provides an overview of the history behind this unique artform, from the Moors to the 20th century *(p126)*. The museum also gives visitors the chance to see some of the country's most stunning examples of *azulejos*.

↑ Seventeenth-century *azulejos* depicting a hunt in the Museu Nacional do Azulejo

A YEAR IN
PORTUGAL

JANUARY

△ **Epiphany** *(6 Jan)*. The day is celebrated by eating the traditional Epiphany cake, *bolo rei* (king's cake).

Festa de São Gonçalinho *(2nd week)*. A crowd gathers around Aveiro's Capela de São Gonçalinho, with nets and umbrellas, to catch loaves of bread thrown from the roof.

FEBRUARY

Fantasporto *(late Feb–early Mar)*. Porto's international film festival shows many science fiction, horror and fantasy flicks by new directors.

△ **Carnival** *(Shrove Tuesday; exact date varies)*. Parades, spectacular costumes and floats flood Portugal's streets in a final hurrah before the sombre days of Lent.

MAY

△ **Fátima Pilgrimage** *(13 May)*. Thousands of pilgrims gather to commemorate the appearance of the Virgin to three shepherd children in 1917.

Madeira Flower Festival *(mid-May)*. Funchal's shops and houses bloom with flowers during this annual festival, which culminates in an enchanting parade.

JUNE

Santo António *(12 and 13 June)*. Lisbon's Alfama district comes alive in this riotous celebration.

São João *(23 and 24 Jun)*. Watch out for people with plastic hammers during Porto's street party.

△ **Lisbon Pride** *(last weekend)*. A series of LGBTQ+ events take place throughout the capital, including club nights and a jubilant parade.

SEPTEMBER

Romaria de Nossa Senhora dos Remédios *(1st week)*. Three days of processions conclude with a pilgrimage to Lamego's famous shrine.

△ **Feiras Novas** *(early to mid-Sep)*. Ponte de Lima hosts a huge market with a fairground, fireworks, carnival costumes and a brass band competition.

OCTOBER

△ **Doclisboa** *(mid–late-Oct)*. Documentaries take over the capital's independent cinemas during this annual film festival that has been running since 2002.

Festival Nacional de Gastronomia de Santarém *(late Oct–early Nov)*. Santarém plays host to food stalls, wine tastings and cookery demonstrations.

MARCH

△ **Moda Lisboa** *(mid-Mar)*. The first of two annual fashion weeks (the second takes place in October) where cutting-edge garments are paraded down Lisbon's runways.

EDP Lisbon Half Marathon *(mid-Mar)*. In one of the capital's most popular sporting events, runners from all over the world cross the Ponte 25 Abril to finish at the Mosteiro dos Jerónimos in Belém.

APRIL

Semana Santa *(Easter week; exact date varies)*. The city of Braga is illuminated during Holy Week by solemn torch-lit processions of barefoot, hooded believers spinning eerie rattles.

IndieLisboa *(late Apr)*. Features and shorts of renowned and up-and-coming directors are screened at this independent film festival.

△ **Dia da Revolução** *(25 Apr)*. A military parade, political speeches and festivities celebrate the Carnation Revolution of 1974, when 48 years of dictatorship were ended without bloodshed.

JULY

Festa dos Tabuleiros *(early Jul; every 4 years; next in 2027)*. Tomar's "Festival of the Trays" sees women carrying *tabuleiros* – 30 flowered loaves of bread topped with a crown– on their heads.

△ **NOS Alive** *(mid-Jul)*. World-renowned indie, rock and alternative music festival in Lisbon.

AUGUST

△ **Semana do Mar** *(1st week)*. Food, music, crafts, watersports and lively competitions are on the agenda at Horta's Festival of the Sea on Faial in the Azores.

Festas Gualterianas *(1st weekend)*. A torch-lit procession through the streets, a medieval parade and lots of dancing are the highlights at this festival in Guimarães.

NOVEMBER

△ **All Saints' Day** *(1 Nov)*. Throughout the country, candles are lit and flowers placed on graves to honour the dead.

Feira Nacional do Cavalo *(first two weeks)*. Golegã – the Portuguese capital of the horse – is taken over with races and parades as owners showcase their thoroughbreds.

Festa de São Martinho *(11 Nov)*. St Martin's Day is celebrated in Madeira with roasted chestnuts and tastings of the year's new wine.

DECEMBER

Christmas *(25 Dec)*. Midnight Mass is followed by a traditional meal of *bacalhau* (salted cod).

△ **New Year's Eve** *(31 Dec)*. Fireworks illuminate the major cities, with Funchal having one of the biggest displays.

A BRIEF
HISTORY

Portugal is one of the oldest nation states in Europe. During the 15th and 16th centuries, early explorers traversed the Atlantic Ocean and made Portugal the nexus of a global empire. The country was later beleaguered by invasions, revolutions and economic crises.

The Stone Age to Roman Lusitania

From about 2000 BCE, the Iberians and Celts supplanted Portugal's Stone Age communities. When Rome swept into the area in 218 BCE, they met with fierce resistance from one of the tribes – the Lusitanians – who were only defeated when their leader Viriato was poisoned by undercover Roman agents in 139 BCE. The Romans named the province Lusitania in the tribe's honour. Romanization led to four centuries of stability, but as the Empire collapsed, Lusitania was overrun by Germanic tribes.

Did You Know?

Granite statues of pigs found in Northern Portugal were probably used in Celtic fertility rites.

Timeline of events

2000 BCE
Iberian tribes arrive in the area.

700 BCE
Celtic invaders settle in Portugal.

218 BCE
The Romans arrive in the Iberian Peninsula.

200 CE
Christianity becomes established in Roman-ruled Lusitania.

409
Invasion by "barbarian" tribes: the Vandals, the Alani and the Suevi.

42

Birth of a Nation

Infighting between the Visigoths paved the way for the country's next invaders: armies from North Africa known as the Moors. After being asked to help a Visigoth faction in 711 CE, they quickly occupied huge swathes of Portugal's southern coast. In 756, Adb al-Rahman established the independent kingdom of Al-Andalus, stretching from the south of the Iberian Peninsula as far north as modern-day Coimbra. The Moors called the southwest part of this region Al-Gharb (Algarve), which means "the west" in Arabic.

While there was peace in the south, small, agitating Christian kingdoms were gaining in strength in the north and, in the 11th century, they began the Reconquista (reconquest). Following a series of successful skirmishes against the Moors, "Portucale" – a small area around the Douro, which was part of the kingdom of Léon – began to grow in stature. In 1139, their ruler Afonso Henriques was victorious at Ourique and declared himself Dom – king of Portugal. The Algarve remained under Moorish rule until 1249, when Faro was finally taken by Afonso III. Portugal's borders have remained largely unchanged ever since.

1 Historical map showing the regions of Portugal in 1762.

2 Stone Age megaliths found near Évora in the Alentejo.

3 *The Death of Viriatus, Chief of the Lusitanians* by José de Madrazo (1807).

4 An 18th-century engraving showing Afonso Henriques' victory at Ourique.

585
Visigoths take over the northern Suevian kingdom.

1139
Afonso Henriques declares himself king of Portugal.

1249
Afonso III conquers the Algarve.

415
Visigoths invade and drive out the Vandals and the Alani.

711
A large Moorish army of Berbers and Arabs conquers the Iberian Peninsula following disputes over Visigothic succession.

The Age of Discovery

After overcoming Castilian competition for the crown *(p173)*, the reign of João I saw the beginning of Portuguese imperialism, with the capture of the North African city of Ceuta in 1415. João's third son, who became known as Henry the Navigator, financed expeditions along the West African coast. Vast profits were made from gold and enslaved people taken from the Gulf of Guinea. This wealth was hugely amplified under Manuel I when, in 1498, Vasco da Gama *(p114)* reached India. In 1500, as he sought out favourable winds by sailing west into the Atlantic, Pedro Álvares Cabral landed in Brazil and enforced rule there.

Spanish Rule

The age of expansion ended with an unsuccessful expedition to Morocco in 1578, led by Sebastião I. When the Cardinal-King Henrique died without an heir in 1580, Philip II of Spain successfully claimed the Portuguese throne through his mother, who was a daughter of Manuel I. Under Spanish rule, Portuguese nobility held influential positions, but a common foreign policy led to the steady loss of Portugal's colonies to the Dutch. In

1 An 18th-century *azulejo* panel depicting the capture of Ceuta.

2 Painting depicting Pedro Álvares Cabral landing in Porto Seguro, Brazil.

3 *The Earthquake in Lisbon* (c.1760) by João Glama Ströberle.

4 Depiction of the Battle of Bussaco (1810), where Wellington fought Napoleon's forces.

Timeline of events

1385

João I defeats the invading Castilian army at the Battle of Albujarotta.

1418

Henry the Navigator is made governor of the Algarve and commissions expeditions to Africa.

1498

Vasco da Gama finds a sea route to India.

1578

King Sebastião's expedition to Morocco ends with defeat at the Battle of Alcácer-Quibir.

1580

Philip II becomes king of Portugal and the country is ruled by Spain.

1640, Lisbon revolted and the duke of Bragança was chosen to become King João IV. Spain retaliated and the ensuing War of Restoration continued until 1668, when Portugal's independence was finally recognized.

The Age of Absolutism

The 18th century was a period of mixed fortune for Portugal. Despite vast revenues from Brazilian gold and diamonds, João V almost bankrupted the country with his extravagance. In 1755, an earthquake devastated Lisbon, killing more than 10 per cent of the city's population. The Marquês de Pombal helped to rebuild the capital and applied the ideals of the Enlightenment by reforming commerce, education and the government and, in 1761, abolishing Portugal's trade of enslaved people.

In 1807, Napoleon's seemingly unstoppable French army invaded Portugal, bringing the country into the Peninsular War. The royal family were forced to flee to Brazil and Rio de Janeiro briefly became capital of the Portuguese empire. It was left to British generals Beresford and Wellington to drive out Napoleon in 1811, but the royal family did not return to Portugal until 1821.

MARQUÊS DE POMBAL

Chief minister to José I, Sebastião José de Carvalho e Melo (1699–1782) is better known as the Marquês de Pombal. While philosophers moralized, Pombal's response to the 1755 earthquake was "bury the dead and feed the living".

1640
Duke of Bragança crowned King João IV after an uprising against Spanish rule.

1756
Douro Valley becomes world's first demarcated wine region.

1807
The royal family flees to Brazil as Napoleon's forces invade.

1588
The Spanish Armada sets sail from Lisbon to invade England.

1755
The Great Earthquake devastates Lisbon and much of the south of Portugal.

The Route to a Republic

Portugal suffered many depredations during the Peninsular War, and as a result of losing mineral-rich Brazil, which was granted independence in 1822. A decade-long period of chaos culminated in civil war between the Liberal Pedro IV and the Absolutist Miguel, in what became known as the War of the Two Brothers. Pedro IV was ultimately victorious and the second half of the 19th century saw a period of economic revival.

Increased mechanization resulted in growing unemployment and discontentment among the urban poor. Republicanism swept through the middle class and, in 1908, King Carlos was assassinated in Lisbon's Praça do Comércio. Two years later, an uprising by military officers forced Manuel II – later known as "the Unfortunate" – into exile and a republic was declared.

The New State

The early years of the Republic were marked by political and economic crises until a military coup in 1926 paved the way for the so-called *Estado Novo* (New State) of 1933. This was in effect a dictatorship under António Salazar, who banned strikes, censored

↑ The assassination of King Carlos depicted on the cover of *Le Petit Parisien*

Timeline of events

1822
Brazil declares independence from Portugal.

1832–4
War of the Two Brothers culminates in the defeat of Absolutist Miguel.

1910
A republic is declared in Lisbon.

1932
Conservative António Salazar becomes prime minister.

4

the press and crushed opposition through a brutal secret police force – the Polícia Internacional e de Defesa do Estado (PIDE). Although Portugal was freed of its debts, it suffered from growing poverty and unemployment. It became reliant on its African colonies but many of these agitated for independence, leading to costly wars and unrest in the army. On 25 April 1974, officers carried out a bloodless coup, known as the Carnation Revolution after the soldiers put flowers in their rifles as a symbol of peace.

Portugal Today

In 1986, Portugal joined the European Communities, bringing investment. In 1992, EC trade barriers fell and Portugal suddenly faced competition. Corruption and rising inflation meant that the country suffered badly from the 2008 financial crisis and it soon requested a bailout.

Portugal has since recovered from the economic crash, mainly thanks to tourism and investment in alternative forms of energy. In 2019, the country welcomed a record number of 24.6 million tourists. Meanwhile, new visa policies continue to make Portugal a popular base for remote workers.

1 Miguel attacking his sister during the War of the Two Brothers.

2 Blindfolded soldiers in the 1926 military coup.

3 Soldiers during the Carnation Revolution.

4 Modern-day Lisbon.

Did You Know?
——
In May 2016, Portugal ran solely on renewable energy sources for a straight 107 hours.

1974
The Carnation Revolution sees the end of the *Estado Novo* regime.

1986
Portugal joins the European Communities.

2007
The Lisbon Treaty establishes a draft EU constitution.

2013
Ryanair begin flights to Lisbon airport, kick-starting a tourism boom.

2022
Portugal wins "Best Tourist Destination in Europe" for the fifth year in a row.

EXPERIENCE

Rabelo boats on the Douro in Porto

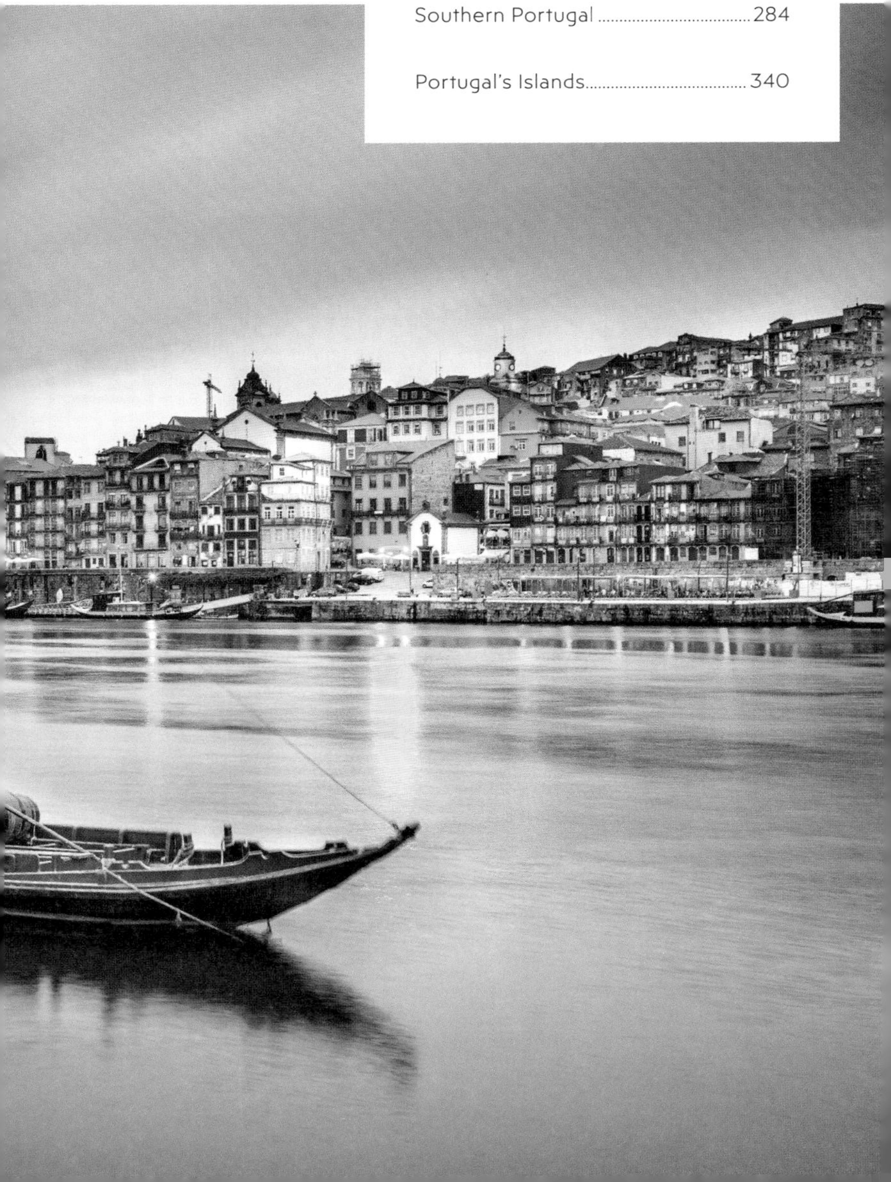

LISBON

The curved Museu de Arte, Arquitetura e Tecnologia, Belém

EXPLORE
LISBON

This section divides Lisbon into four sightseeing areas, as shown below, and an area beyond the city. Find out more about each area on the following pages.

Palácio Fronteira

Parque Florestal de Monsanto

Aqueduto das Águas Livres

CASELAS

CARAMÃO

BAIRRO DA AJUDA

Parque da Tapada da Ajuda

Cemitério dos Prazeres

ALTO DA AJUDA

RESTELO

Jardim Botânico da Ajuda

Palácio Nacional da Ajuda

Igreja da Memória

AJUDA

SANTO AMARO

Fundação Oriente Museu

ALCÂNTARA

Ermida de São Jerónimo

BELÉM

BELÉM
p104

Museu de Marinha

Mosteiro dos Jerónimos

Museu Nacional dos Coches

Centro Cultural de Belém

MAAT – Museu de Arte, Arquitetura e Tecnologia

Padrão dos Descobrimentos

Torre de Belém

Ponte 25 de Abril

Tejo (Tagus)

0 metres 800 N
0 yards 800 ↑

PORTO BRANDÃO

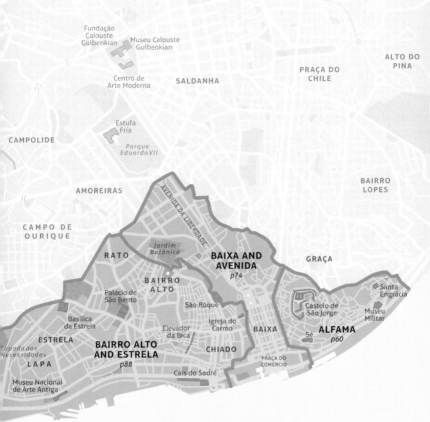

CAMPO PEQUENO

Fundação
Calouste
Gulbenkian
Museu Calouste
Gulbenkian

Centro de
Arte Moderna

SALDANHA

PRAÇA DO
CHILE

ALTO DO
PINA

Estufa
Fría

CAMPOLIDE

Parque
Eduardo VII

AMOREIRAS

BAIRRO
LOPES

CAMPO DE
OURIQUE

AVENIDA DA LIBERDADE

RATO

Jardim
Botânico

BAIXA AND
AVENIDA
p74

GRAÇA

BAIRRO
ALTO

Palácio de
São Bento

São Roque

Santa
Engrácia

Castelo de
São Jorge

Museu
Militar

Basílica
da Estrela

Elevador
da Bica

Igreja do
Carmo

BAIXA

ALFAMA
p60

Sé

ESTRELA

Tapada das
Necessidades

LAPA

BAIRRO ALTO
AND ESTRELA
p88

CHIADO

Museu Nacional
de Arte Antiga

Cais do Sodré

PRAÇA DO
COMÉRCIO

Tejo (Tagus)

CACILHAS

ARIALVA

ALMADA

WESTERN EUROPE

Atlantic

Ocean

FRANCE

Porto •

PORTUGAL

SPAIN

LISBON •

Mediterranean
Sea

Faro •

ALGERIA

GETTING TO KNOW
LISBON

One of Europe's oldest and most attractive capitals, Lisbon has arrived into the 21st century in style; across the city, tradition jostles with cutting-edge architecture, contemporary galleries and innovative restaurants. Some familiarity with each district will help when planning your trip.

PAGE 60

ALFAMA

Lisbon's oldest district, the labyrinthine Alfama tumbles downhill towards the river, hiding tiny bars, secret squares and a traditional way of life amid its narrow streets. This is the birthplace of *fado*, Portugal's mournful style of music, and the neighbourhood still hosts the Feira da Ladra, a twice-weekly street market packed with everything from postcards to antiques. Some of Lisbon's best viewpoints can also be found in the Alfama, with both the castle's ramparts and the Miradouro de Santa Luzia offering sweeping panoramas over the rest of the city.

Best for
Getting lost amid winding alleys and drinking in the city's atmosphere

Home to
The towering Castelo de São Jorge

Experience
Great views from the dome of Santa Engrácia, or an evening of music at a fado house

BAIXA AND AVENIDA

PAGE 74

The Baixa (lower town) is the heart of the city, comprising a grid of streets dotted with shops, cafés and boutiques, and culminating in the wide Praça do Comércio waterfront. Running through the centre of the district is the pedestrianized Rua Augusta, where throngs of visitors and locals alike gather to shop, graze and gossip. Also in this area is the imposing Avenida da Liberdade, a wide avenue lined with Art Deco buildings that stretches all the way to Parque Eduardo VII.

Best for
Shopping and grand squares

Home to
The quirky Elevador de Santa Justa and the Praça do Comércio

Experience
Coffee and cakes at the Confeitaria Nacional, one of Lisbon's historic cafés

BAIRRO ALTO AND ESTRELA

PAGE 88

The Bairro Alto is Lisbon's nightlife district. By day it's relatively tranquil, but at night the neighbourhood comes alive with restaurants, cafés and bars that spill revellers out into the streets until the early hours. In Cais do Sodré you'll find the literally named Pink Street: once Lisbon's red light district, but now populated with stylish cocktail bars and clubs. The area offers culture, too, from Estrela's grand domed basilica to the impressive Museu Nacional de Arte Antiga in Lapa, home of Portugal's national art collection.

Best for
Lively restaurants and late-night bars

Home to
The Museu Nacional de Arte Antiga

Experience
Some of Lisbon's finest street food – from traditional to experimental – at the Time Out Market

$\rightarrow$

PAGE 104

BELÉM

Once the embarkation point for Portugal's intrepid seafaring explorers, this scenic waterfront suburb is perhaps best known for its dramatic Manueline monuments from that period. Belém also features more modern attractions – such as the Berardo Collection of contemporary art and the imposing Padrão dos Descobrimentos – which combine with the neighbourhood's spacious streets and well-maintained, leafy parks to make it a pleasant place to wander.

Best for
Awe-inspiring architecture

Home to
The ornate Mosteiro dos Jerónimos and the Torre de Belém

Experience
A pastel de nata fresh out of the ovens at the original Belém bakery

BEYOND THE CENTRE

Outside the city centre, there are still an impressive number of sights. Parque Eduardo VII, with its sharply edged hedges and expansive *miradouro*, is a welcome green space, while the astounding collections of Museu Calouste Gulbenkian make for a rewarding visit. Virtually under the arches of the Ponte 25 de Abril bridge, which stretches dramatically across the Tagus, is LX Factory, one of the city's hippest spots: a reclaimed industrial area packed with studios, workshops, cafés and bars.

Best for
*Wide parks and a break
from the city's bustle*

Home to
*The Museu Calouste Gulbenkian
and the colourful Museu
Nacional do Azulejo*

Experience
*Panoramic vistas from
the viewing platform
atop the Ponte 25 de Abril*

1 Torre de Belém.

2 Museu Calouste Gulbenkian.

3 Perfectly baked *pastéis de nata*.

4 Time Out Market Lisbon.

2 DAYS

Day 1

Morning Start your day with breakfast at one of the cafés on Praça da Figueira (p84) or neighbouring Rossio (p83) – Confeitaria Nacional (www.confeitaria nacional.com) has a great pastry selection. Once fully fuelled, wander through the Baixa's pedestrianized streets to the quirky, Gothic-style Elevador de Santa Justa (p80). Follow the backstreets or take the lift up to the hilltop Museu do Carmo (p96), an archaeological museum housed in a Carmelite church, whose graceful ruined arches stand out against the city skyline. Browse among the boutiques before heading through the elegant Chiado district towards the waterfront.

Afternoon Here, the Time Out Market (p101) in Cais do Sodré is a great place for a pick-and-mix lunch. The selection on offer is huge – just pick your stall, choose a dish (or two) and snag a seat at one of the tables. After lunch, hop on the metro to the Museu Calouste Gulbenkian (p122), where exploring the sprawling collection of artworks will eat up the rest of your afternoon.

Evening Head back towards the city centre and spend the evening in lively Bairro Alto. Book a table at The Insólito (Rua de São Pedro de Alcântara 83) where you can dine against the stunning backdrop of Lisbon's skyline. This rooftop bar overlooks the river, with tasty contemporary Portuguese dishes on the menu and a strong line of signature cocktails.

Day 2

Morning Aim for a bright and early start in order to make the most of Belém, one of Lisbon's prettiest suburbs. Take a short tram ride or the train along the waterfront, and head first to the Mosteiro dos Jerónimos (p108). This elaborately decorated monastery demands at least an hour or two to explore properly – the refectory's azulejo panels and the cloister are particularly spectacular. Next, cross through the gardens to the towering 52-m- (170-ft-) high Padrão dos Descobrimentos (p114), and take the high-speed lift to the top for great views over the monastery and river.

Afternoon Nearby, the colourful Rua Vieira Portuense is home to a number of excellent restaurants where you can lunch at outdoor tables. Skip pudding here and cross the road to the Antiga Confeitaria de Belém bakery (p115) – where better to sample Portugal's iconic tarts than the café in which they were first created? Walk off your sweet treat along the waterfront to reach the Torre de Belém (p110), worth a visit to admire its intricate stonework.

Evening Next, take a look round the impressive Museu Colecção Berardo (p115), where the modern art on display includes pieces by the likes of Dalí, Picasso and Andy Warhol. End your evening in Taberna dos Ferreiros, a cosy restaurant tucked away in Travessa Ferreiros a Belém, offering traditional Portuguese options alongside international recipes.

ALFAMA

Humble Alfama, the oldest and most atmospheric of Lisbon's neighbourhoods, was once the city's most desirable quarter, and today it is creeping back into vogue. It was first settled by the Romans but flourished in Moorish times, when the tightly packed *becos* (alleyways) and tiny squares comprised the whole city. The Moors took advantage of Alfama's slopes, building the fortified Castelo de São Jorge on the crown of the hill and turning the city into a defensive stronghold.

But even that couldn't hold off the crusaders forever. The city was captured by Afonso Henriques in 1147, and the seeds of Alfama's decline were sown in the Middle Ages when wealthy residents moved west for fear of earthquakes, leaving the quarter to fishers and paupers. Many of its buildings survived the 1755 earthquake – although no Moorish houses still stand – and the quarter retains its kasbah-like layout. Compact houses line steep streets and stairways, their façades strung with washing, and daily life still revolves around local grocery stores and small, cellar-like taverns.

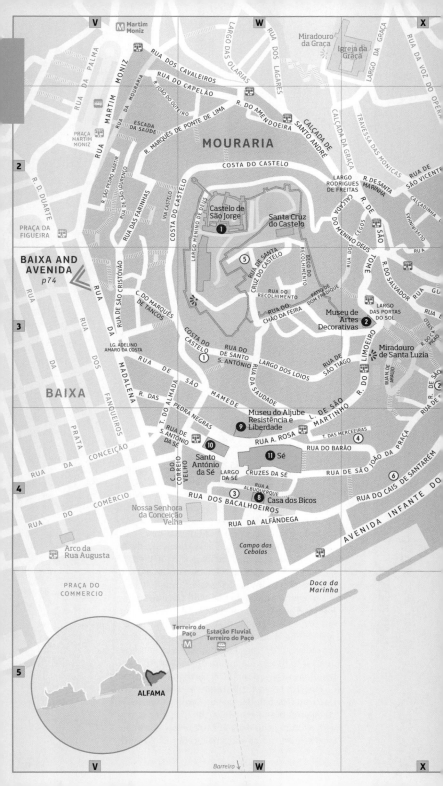

ALFAMA

Must See

1 Castelo de São Jorge

Experience More

2 Museu de Artes Decorativas
3 São Vicente de Fora
4 Feira da Ladra
5 Santa Engrácia
6 Museu do Fado
7 Museu Militar
8 Casa dos Bicos
9 Museu do Aljube – Resistência e Liberdade
10 Santo António da Sé
11 Sé

Eat

1 Chapitô à Mesa
2 A Baiuca
3 Taberna Moderna

Stay

4 Memmo Alfama
5 Solar do Castelo
6 Palacete Chafariz del Rei

①

CASTELO DE SÃO JORGE

Torre de Ulisses

🅦 W2 🅐 Porta de São Jorge (entrance on Rua de Santa Cruz do Castelo) 🚌 737 🚋 28 🕐 Mar-Oct: 9am-9pm daily; Nov-Feb: 9am-7pm daily (check website for further details) 🆆 castelodesaojorge.pt

Towering above central Lisbon, this Moorish citadel is one of the city's most recognizable landmarks. Though much of the present castle dates from a 1930s restoration, visitors still flock to the top of the hill to seek out traces of the city's history and enjoy the spectacular views laid out below.

Following the recapture of Lisbon from the Moors in 1147, Dom Afonso Henriques transformed their hilltop citadel into the residence of the Portuguese kings. In 1511, Manuel I built a more lavish palace in what is now the Praça do Comércio and the citadel castle was used variously as a theatre, prison and arms depot. After the 1755 earthquake, the ramparts remained in ruins until 1938, when António Salazar *(p46)* began a complete renovation, rebuilding the "medieval" walls and adding gardens and wildfowl. The gardens and the narrow streets of the Santa Cruz district within the walls make a pleasant stroll, and views from the observation terrace are some of the finest in Lisbon. Other attractions on site include the city's only camera obscura and the Torre da Igreja, a formerly closed church tower that reopened to visitors in 2018. A separate ticket gives access to the top where incredible views of the city await.

The Museu do Castelo, which displays artifacts from the archaeological site and charts the history of the city.

① The citadel is set on a hilltop location above Lisbon's colourful rooftops.

② Visitors can climb the towers and walk along the reconstructed ramparts of the castle walls.

③ The castle's Observation Terrace is a large shaded square offering spectacular views over the city.

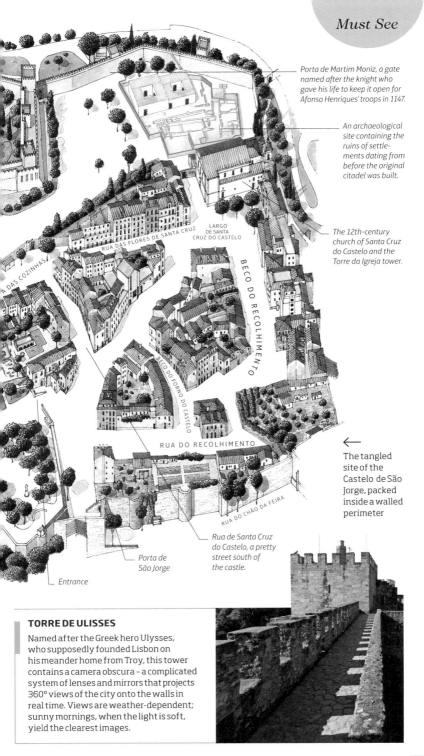

Porta de Martim Moniz, a gate named after the knight who gave his life to keep it open for Afonso Henriques' troops in 1147.

An archaeological site containing the ruins of settlements dating from before the original citadel was built.

The 12th-century church of Santa Cruz do Castelo and the Torre da Igreja tower.

LARGO DE SANTA CRUZ DO CASTELO

RUA DAS FLORES DE SANTA CRUZ

A DAS COZINHAS

BECO DO RECOLHIMENTO

BECO DO FORNO DO CASTELO

RUA DO RECOLHIMENTO

← The tangled site of the Castelo de São Jorge, packed inside a walled perimeter

RUA DO CHÃO DA FEIRA

Rua de Santa Cruz do Castelo, a pretty street south of the castle.

Porta de São Jorge

Entrance

TORRE DE ULISSES

Named after the Greek hero Ulysses, who supposedly founded Lisbon on his meander home from Troy, this tower contains a camera obscura – a complicated system of lenses and mirrors that projects 360° views of the city onto the walls in real time. Views are weather-dependent; sunny mornings, when the light is soft, yield the clearest images.

EXPERIENCE MORE

2

Museu de Artes Decorativas

📍X3 🏛Largo Portas
do Sol 2 🚌737 🚋12, 28
🕐10am–5pm Wed–Mon
🚫1 Jan, 1 May, 25 Dec
🌐fress.pt

Also known as the Ricardo do Espírito Santo Silva Foundation, the museum was set up in 1953 to preserve the traditions and increase public awareness of the Portuguese decorative arts. The foundation was named after a banker who bought the 17th-century Palácio Azurara in 1947 to house his fine collection of furniture, textiles, silver and ceramics. Among the 17th- and 18th-century antiques displayed in this handsome four-storey mansion are many pieces made from various kinds of wood, including an 18th-century rosewood back-gammon and chess table. Also of note are the collections of 18th-century silver and Chinese porcelain, and hand-embroidered wool carpets from Arraiolos. The spacious rooms still retain some original ceilings and *azulejo* panels.

In the adjoining building are workshops where artisans preserve the techniques of cabinet-making, gilding, book-binding, wood-carving and other traditional crafts. Temporary exhibitions, lectures and concerts are also held in the museum.

3

São Vicente de Fora

📍Y2 🏛Largo de São Vicente
🚌712, 734 🚋28 🕐10am–
6pm Tue–Sun (last adm 5pm)
🚫Public hols 🌐mosteiro
desaovicentedefora.com

St Vincent was proclaimed Lisbon's patron saint in 1173, when his relics were transferred from the Algarve to a church on this site outside *(fora)* the city walls. Designed by Italian architect Filippo Terzi, and completed in 1627, the sober, off-white façade is in Italian Renaissance style, with towers either side and three arches leading to the entrance hall. Statues of saints Augustine, Sebastian and Vincent can be seen over the entrance. The adjoining former Augustinian monastery, reached via the nave, retains its 16th-century cistern and vestiges of the former cloister, but it is visited mainly for its 18th-century *azulejos*. Among the panels in the entrance hall off the first cloister there are lively, though historically inaccurate, tile scenes of Afonso

→
Intricate marble inlays adorning São Vicente de Fora

Henriques attacking Lisbon and Santarém. A passageway leads behind the church to the old refectory, transformed into the Bragança Pantheon in 1885. The stone sarcophagi of almost every king and queen are here, from João I, who died in 1656, to Manuel II, the last king of Portugal. Only Maria I and Pedro IV are not buried here. A stone mourner kneels at the tomb of Carlos I and his son Luís Filipe, assassinated in Praça do Comércio in 1908. The church now operates as a museum, with access to the Bragança Pantheon.

4

Feira da Ladra

📍Y2 🏛Campo de Santa
Clara 🚌712 🚋28
🕐9am–5pm Tue & Sat

The stalls of the so-called "Thieves' Market" have occupied this site on the edge of the Alfama for over a century, and are still laid out under the shade of trees or canopies. As the fame of this

↑ Ornate carriage on display at Museu de Artes Decorativas

flea market has grown over the years, bargains are increasingly hard to find among the mass of bric-a-brac, but a few of the vendors have interesting wrought-iron work, prints and tiles, as well as second-hand clothes. (Note, however, that some of the tiles sold here might have been illegally taken from the city's buildings, which is an ongoing problem.) Evidence of the country's colonial past is reflected in the stalls selling African statuary, masks and jewellery.

← A bric-a-brac stall at the Feira da Ladra flea market

5

Santa Engrácia

📍 Y2 🏛 Campo de Santa Clara 🚌 712 🚋 28 🕐 10am–5pm Tue–Sun (Apr–Sep: to 6pm) 🚫 1 Jan, 1 May, Easter Sun, 13 Jun, 24 & 25 Dec 🌐 panteaonacional.gov.pt

One of Lisbon's most striking landmarks, the soaring dome of Santa Engrácia (officially known as Panteão Nacional) punctuates the skyline in the east of the city. The original church collapsed in a storm in 1681. The first stone of the Baroque monument, laid in 1682, marked the beginning of a 284-year saga that led to the invention of a saying that a Santa Engrácia job was never done. The church was not completed until 1966.

The interior is paved with coloured marble and crowned by a giant cupola. As the

GREAT VIEW
Miradouro de Santa Luzia

The terrace by the church of Santa Luzia provides a sweeping view over the Alfama and the River Tagus. Landmarks, from left to right, are the cupola of Santa Engrácia, the church of Santo Estêvão and the white towers of São Miguel. While tourists admire the views, older residents play cards under the bougainvillea-clad pergola.

National Pantheon, it houses cenotaphs of Portuguese figures, such as Vasco da Gama (p114) and Afonso de Albuquerque, Viceroy of India (1502–15) on the left, and on the right Henry the Navigator (p328). More contemporary tombs include that of the fadista Amália Rodrigues. A small lift and some steps up to the dome offer a magnificent panorama of the city.

↑ José Malhoa's *O Fado*, a haunting portrait hanging at the Museu do Fado

Museu do Fado

Q Y3 **A** Largo do Chafariz de Dentro 1 🚌 728, 735, 759, 794 🕐 10am-6pm Tue-Sun 🌐 museudofado.pt

Alfama is considered the true home of *fado* and this museum portrays the influence that this ever-popular and intensely heartfelt genre of music has had on the city over the past two centuries. A permanent display traces the genre's history from its origins in the early 19th century to the present day, from Maria Severa, the first *fado* diva, to more contemporary singers such as Mariza and Amália Rodrigues. Regular temporary exhibitions take place during the year on a range of musical themes, with the occasional live *fado* concert.

Museu Militar

Q Y3 **A** Largo do Museu da Artilharia 🚌 728, 735, 759 🚋 28 🕐 10am-5pm Tue-Sun 🏛 Public hols 🌐 exercito.pt

Located on the site of a 16th-century cannon foundry and arms depot, visits here begin in the Vasco da Gama Room, with cannons and modern murals depicting the discovery of the sea route to India. The Salas da Grande Guerra display exhibits related to World War I. Other rooms focus on the evolution of weapons in Portugal, from flints to spears to rifles. The courtyard, flanked by cannons, tells the story of Portugal in tiled panels, from the Christian Reconquest to World War I. The Portuguese artillery section displays the wagon used to transport the triumphal arch to Rua Augusta *(p84)*.

Casa dos Bicos

Q W4 **A** Rua dos Bacalhoeiros 🚌 728, 735, 759 🚋 15, 25 🕐 10am-6pm Mon-Sat 🌐 jose saramago.org

Faced with diamond-shaped stones *(bicos)*, Casa dos Bicos (House of Spikes) looks rather

> ### MONUMENT TO THE ENSLAVED PEOPLE
> More than 200 years after slavery was abolished in Portugal, Lisbon is planning a Monument to the Enslaved People at Campo das Cebolas, near the Museu do Fado. The chosen design, "Plantation - Prosperity and Nightmare", a work by Angolan artist Kiluanji Kia Henda, depicts sugar cane, one of the goods traded during the Portuguese Age of Discovery.

↑ Monumental portico at the entrance to the Museu Militar

↑ Street café in front of the 16th-century Casa dos Bicos

conspicuous among the other buildings in the Alfama area. It was built in 1523 for Brás de Albuquerque, illegitimate son of Afonso, Viceroy of India and conqueror of Goa and Malacca. The façade is an adaptation of a style that was popular across Europe during the 16th century. The top two storeys, ruined in the earthquake of 1755, were restored in the 1980s, recreating the original from old views of Lisbon in tile panels and engravings. In the interim the building was used for salting fish (Rua dos Bacalhoeiros means street of the cod fishers).

Following an extensive renovation in the 20th century, Casa dos Biscos now plays host to the headquarters of the José Saramago Foundation. It is also home to a permanent exhibition dedicated to the life and works of this Nobel Prize-winning author, who died in 2010. A variety of cultural events often take place here; these include concerts, plays and book releases, along with a range of seminars, debates and lively talks.

9

Museu do Aljube – Resistência e Liberdade

📍W4 🏛Rua Augusto Rosa 42 🕐10am–6pm Tue–Sun 🚫1 Jan, 1 May, 25 Dec 🌐museudoaljube.pt

This fascinating museum was once used by António Salazar – who ruled Portugal as a dictator from 1926 until his passing in 1970 – to imprison his political opponents. It is dedicated to those who were prepared to fight for democracy, both in Portugal and in its former colonies. Three floors are filled with evocative photos, posters and radio broadcasts, with labelling in English. There are also harrowing personal accounts from people who were incarcerated and often tortured for views that were considered contrary to those of the state; many of these inmates were later deported to Madeira or the Azores. Their cramped, windowless cells can still be visited.

The basement houses archaeological finds from beneath the building, which date back to Moorish times, while the top-floor often hosts temporary exhibits.

Santo António da Sé

📍W4 📍Largo Santo
António da Sé 24 📞218
869145 🚍737 🚋12, 28
🕐8am-7pm daily (to
8pm Sat & Sun); Museu
Antoniano: 10am-6pm
Tue-Sun

The popular little church of Santo António allegedly stands on the site of the house in which St Anthony was born. The crypt, reached via the tiled sacristy on the left of the church, is all that remains of the original church destroyed by the earthquake of 1755. Work began on the new church in 1757, headed by Mateus Vicente, architect of the Basílica da Estrela (p100), and was partially funded by donations collected by local children with the cry "a small coin for St Anthony". Even today the floor of the tiny chapel in the crypt is strewn with coins and the walls are scrawled with devotional messages from worshippers.

The church's façade blends the undulating curves of the Baroque style with Neo-Classical Ionic columns on either side of the main portal. Inside, on the way down to the crypt, a modern *azulejo* panel commemorates the visit of Pope John Paul II in 1982. In 1995 the church was given a face-lift for the saint's eighth centenary. It is traditional for young couples to visit the church on their wedding day and leave flowers for St Anthony, who is believed to bring good luck to new marriages. Next door, in the building thought to be where St Anthony was born, the small Museu Antoniano houses artifacts relating to the saint, along with gold- and silverware that used to decorate the church. The most charming exhibit is a 17th-century tiled panel of St Anthony preaching to the fish.

↑ The impressive Baroque façade of Santo António da Sé

Sé

📍W4 📍Largo da Sé 🚍737
🚋12, 28 🕐May-Oct:
9:30am-7pm Mon, Tue,
Thu & Fri, 10am-6pm Wed
& Sat; Nov-Apr: 10am-6pm
Mon-Sat 🌐sedelisboa.pt

In 1150, three years after Afonso Henriques recaptured Lisbon from the Moors, he built a cathedral for the first bishop of Lisbon, the English crusader Gilbert of Hastings, on the site of the old mosque. Sé is short for Sede Episcopal, the seat (or see) of a bishop. Devastated by three earth tremors in the 14th century, as well as the earthquake of 1755, and renovated over the centuries, the cathedral you see today blends a variety of architectural styles. The façade, with twin castellated bell towers and a splendid rose window, retains its solid Romanesque aspect. The gloomy interior is simple and austere, and little remains of the embellishment lavished upon it by King João V in the first half of the 18th century. Beyond the renovated Romanesque nave,

---

SANTO ANTÓNIO (C 1195-1231)

The best-loved saint of the Lisboetas is St Anthony of Padua. Although born and raised in Lisbon, he spent the last months of his life in Padua, Italy. St Anthony joined the Franciscan Order in 1220, impressed by some crusading friars he had met at Coimbra. The friar was a learned and passionate preacher, known for his devotion to the poor and his ability to convert heretics. Many statues and paintings of St Anthony depict him carrying the Infant Jesus on a book, while others show him preaching to fish, as St Francis preached to birds. In 1934, Pope Pius XI declared St Anthony a patron saint of Portugal.

the ambulatory has nine Gothic chapels. The Capela de Santo Ildefonso contains the 14th-century sarcophagi of Lopo Fernandes Pacheco, companion in arms to King Afonso IV, and his wife, Maria Vilalobos. The bearded figure of the nobleman, who is holding a sword in his hand, and his wife, clutching a prayer book, are carved onto the tombs with their dogs sitting faithfully at their feet. In the adjacent chancel are the tombs of Afonso IV and his wife Dona Beatriz.

The Gothic cloister (closed for renovation until further notice) has elegant double arches with some finely carved capitals. One of the chapels is still fitted with its 13th-century wrought-iron gate. Ongoing archaeological excavations in the cloister have unearthed various Roman and other remains. To the left of the cathedral entrance, the Franciscan chapel contains the font where St Anthony was baptized in 1195 and is decorated with a tiled scene of him preaching to the fish. The adjacent chapel contains a Baroque Nativity scene made of cork, wood and terracotta by Machado de Castro (1766).

The treasury is at the top of the staircase on the right. It houses silver, ecclesiastical robes, statuary, illustrated manuscripts and a few relics associated with St Vincent, which were transferred to Lisbon from Cabo de São Vicente in southern Portugal in 1173. Legend has it that two sacred ravens kept a vigil over the boat that transported the relics. The ravens and the boat became a symbol of the city of Lisbon, still very much in use today. It is also said that the raven's descendants used to dwell in the cloisters of the cathedral.

Interior of the city's cathedral, and *(inset)* its stunning stained glass

EAT

Chapitô à Mesa
For a meal with a view, the terrace here has jaw-dropping vistas.

📍W3 🏠Costa do Castelo 7 📞218 875 077

€€€

A Baiuca
This tiny *tasca* has a good menu but even better *fado vadio* (amateur *fado*).

📍X3 🏠Rua de São Miguel 20 📞939 457 098

€€€

Taberna Moderna
Elegant and laid-back, with a modern tapas-style take on tradition.

📍W4 🏠Rua dos Bacalhoeiros 18A 📞218 865 039 🕐Sun & L Mon-Fri

€€€

A SHORT WALK
ALFAMA

Distance 600 m (0.4 miles)   **Nearest station** Portas do Sol tram
and bus stop   **Time** 15 minutes

A fascinating quarter at any time of day, the Alfama comes to life in the late afternoon and early evening; time your walk for these hours, when the locals emerge at their doorways and the small taverns start to fill. Given the steep streets and steps of the neighbourhood, the least strenuous approach is to start at the top

and work your way down. A wander through the maze of winding alleyways will reveal picturesque corners and crumbling churches, plus panoramic views from shady terraces, such as the Miradouro de Santa Luzia. A new generation of younger residents has also resulted in a small number of trendy shops and bars.

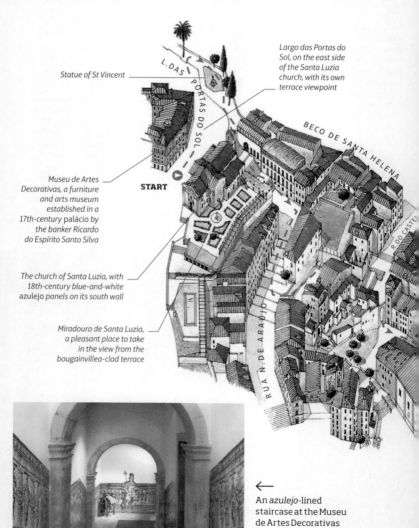

Statue of St Vincent

Largo das Portas do Sol, on the east side of the Santa Luzia church, with its own terrace viewpoint

L. DAS PORTAS DO SOL

BECO DE SANTA HELENA

R. DO CASTE

START

Museu de Artes Decorativas, a furniture and arts museum established in a 17th-century palácio by the banker Ricardo do Espírito Santo Silva

The church of Santa Luzia, with 18th-century blue-and-white azulejo panels on its south wall

Miradouro de Santa Luzia, a pleasant place to take in the view from the bougainvillea-clad terrace

RUA N. DE ARAÚJO

← An *azulejo*-lined staircase at the Museu de Artes Decorativas

↑ The spectacular cityscape, as seen from the Miradouro de Santa Luzia

Locator Map
For more detail see p62

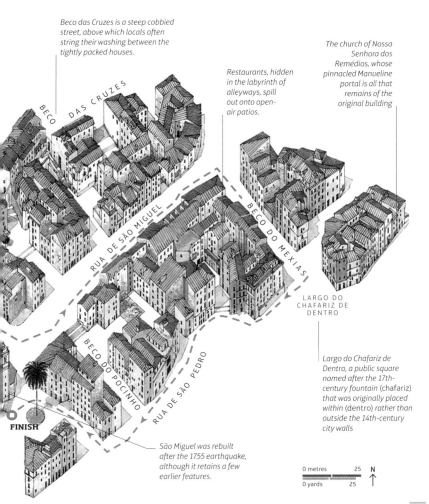

Beco das Cruzes is a steep cobbled street, above which locals often string their washing between the tightly packed houses.

BECO DAS CRUZES

Restaurants, hidden in the labyrinth of alleyways, spill out onto open-air patios.

The church of Nossa Senhora dos Remédios, whose pinnacled Manueline portal is all that remains of the original building

RUA DE SÃO MIGUEL

BECO DO MEXIAS

LARGO DO CHAFARIZ DE DENTRO

BECO DO POCINHO

RUA DE SÃO PEDRO

Largo do Chafariz de Dentro, a public square named after the 17th-century fountain (chafariz) that was originally placed within (dentro) rather than outside the 14th-century city walls

FINISH

São Miguel was rebuilt after the 1755 earthquake, although it retains a few earlier features.

0 metres   25
0 yards   25

N ↑

The wide Rua Augusta cutting through Lisbon's Baixa district

BAIXA AND AVENIDA

It was the Baixa that felt the full force of the 1755 earthquake, which destroyed much of the neighbourhood. From its ruins, the Marquês de Pombal created an entirely new centre, using a grid layout of streets and linking the riverfront Praça do Comércio with the busy Rossio square. The streets were flanked by uniform Neo-Classical buildings and named according to the shopkeepers and crafters who traded there – Rua do Ouro was the goldsmiths' street and Rua dos Sapateiros that of the shoemakers.

Some 80 years later, the Arco da Rua Augusta was built to celebrate the Baixa's reconstruction. The Avenida da Liberdade followed shortly afterwards, laid out in 1882 as the city's main avenue between the Baixa and Parque Eduardo VII. Fashioned on Paris's Champs-Élysées, it is still the city's most upmarket area, lined with grand 19th-century mansions and a tree-dotted central strip.

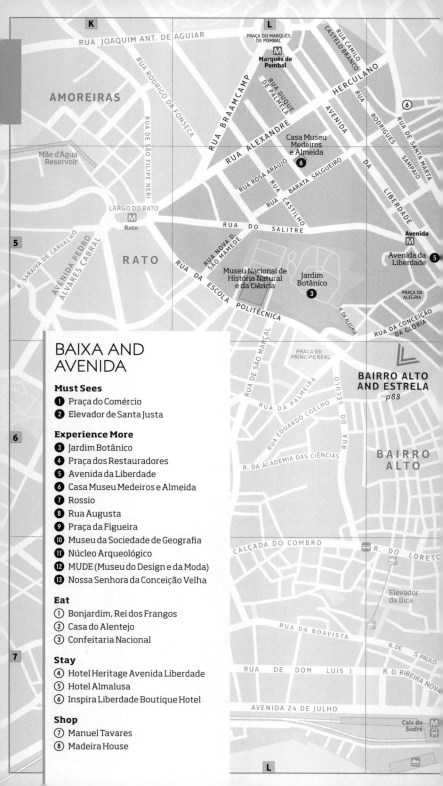

BAIXA AND AVENIDA

Must Sees
1 Praça do Comércio
2 Elevador de Santa Justa

Experience More
3 Jardim Botânico
4 Praça dos Restauradores
5 Avenida da Liberdade
6 Casa Museu Medeiros e Almeida
7 Rossio
8 Rua Augusta
9 Praça da Figueira
10 Museu da Sociedade de Geografia
11 Núcleo Arqueológico
12 MUDE (Museu do Design e da Moda)
13 Nossa Senhora da Conceição Velha

Eat
1 Bonjardim, Rei dos Frangos
2 Casa do Alentejo
3 Confeitaria Nacional

Stay
4 Hotel Heritage Avenida Liberdade
5 Hotel Almalusa
6 Inspira Liberdade Boutique Hotel

Shop
7 Manuel Tavares
8 Madeira House

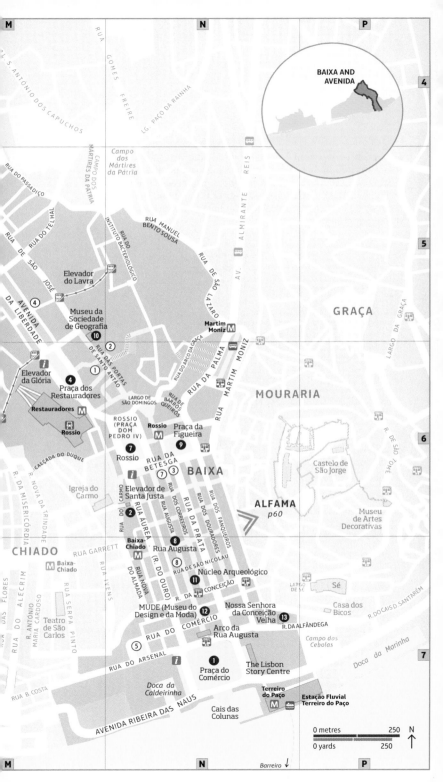

BAIXA AND AVENIDA

M · **N** · **P**

4

RUA DOS S. ANTONIO DOS CAPUCHOS

RUA GOMES FREIRE

LG. PAÇO DA RAINHA

RUA DO PASSADIÇO

RUA DE SÃO JOSÉ

RUA DO TE HAL

CAMPO DOS MÁRTIRES DA PATRIA

Campo dos Mártires da Pátria

RUA MANUEL BENTO SOUSA

RUA DO INSTITUTO BACTERIOLÓGICO

AV. ALMIRANTE REIS

5

Elevador do Lavra

Museu da Sociedade de Geografia ⑩

RUA DAS PORTAS DE SANTO ANTÃO

② ①

RUA DE SÃO LAZARO

Martim Moniz Ⓜ

GRAÇA

LARGO DA GRAÇA

④ **AVENIDA DA LIBERDADE**

Elevador da Glória ℹ

④ **Praça dos Restauradores**

Restauradores Ⓜ

Rossio 🚉

LARGO DE SÃO DOMINGOS

RUA DO ARCO DA GRAÇA

RUA DE BARROS QUEIROS

RUA DA PALMA

RUA MARTIM MONIZ

MOURARIA

R. DE SÃO TOMÉ

6

CALÇADA DO DUQUE

R. DA MISERICÓRDIA

R. NOVA DA TRINDADE

ROSSIO (PRAÇA DOM PEDRO IV)

Rossio Ⓜ

Praça da Figueira ⑨

⑦ **Rossio**

RUA DA BETESGA

ℹ ⑦ ③ **BAIXA**

Castelo de São Jorge

ALFAMA p60

CHIADO

Igreja do Carmo

Elevador de Santa Justa ②

RUA DO CARMO

RUA AUREA

RUA DOS CORREEIROS

RUA DA PRATA

RUA DOS DOURADORES

RUA DOS FANQUEIROS

Museu de Artes Decorativas

Ⓜ **Baixa-Chiado**

RUA GARRETT

RUA IVENS

Baixa-Chiado Ⓜ

RUA NOVA DO ALMADA

Rua Augusta ⑧

⑧

RUA DE SÃO NICOLAU

Núcleo Arqueológico ⑪

R. DA CONCEIÇÃO

LARGO DE SÉ

Sé

RUA DAS FLORES

RUA DO ALECRIM

R. ANTONIO MARIA CARDOSO

RUA SERPA PINTO

Teatro de São Carlos

MUDE (Museu do Design e da Moda) ⑫

Nossa Senhora da Conceição Velha ⑬

R. DA ALFÂNDEGA

Casa dos Bicos

R. DO CAIS DE SANTARÉM

RUA NOVA DO OURO

RUA DO COMÉRCIO

Arco da Rua Augusta 🚉

Campo das Cebolas

Doca da Marinha

7

RUA DA B. COSTA

⑤

ℹ

RUA DO ARSENAL

Praça do Comércio ❶

The Lisbon Story Centre

Doca da Caldeirinha

Terreiro do Paço Ⓜ

Estação Fluvial Terreiro do Paço

Cais das Colunas

AVENIDA RIBEIRA DAS NAUS

| 0 metres | | 250 |
| 0 yards | | 250 |

N ↑

M · **N** · **P**

Barreiro ↓

❶ 〔🍴〕〔🖥〕〔🛍〕

PRAÇA DO COMÉRCIO

📍N7 🚌711, 714, 759, 794 & many other routes 🚋15, 18, 25

The beautiful riverfront Praça do Comércio is a vast square with shady arcades on three sides and the wide expanse of the Tagus lapping at its southern edge. It was the centrepiece of the Marquês de Pombal's post-earthquake redesign of the city, and today it remains a lively gathering place that hosts cultural events throughout the year.

Known to locals as *Terreiro do Paço* (Palace Square), this huge open space was the site of the royal palace for 400 years. Manuel I transferred the royal residence from Castelo de São Jorge to this more convenient spot by the river in 1511. When the original palace was destroyed in the 1755 earthquake, Pombal housed the new palace in spacious arcaded buildings around three sides of the square. On the fourth side, grand marble steps stretch down to the water's edge.

Highlights of the square include a huge bronze statue of King José I, the impressive Arco da Rua Augusta on the north side and the Lisbon Story Centre, an interactive museum exploring events in the city's history.

HISTORY IN THE MAKING

The Praça do Comércio has been the scene of major events throughout Lisbon's history. On 1 February 1908, King Carlos and his son Luís Filipe were assassinated as they passed through the square, an event that eventually led to the abolition of the monarchy and the declaration of the Republic two years later. Then in 1974, the square saw the first uprising of the Armed Forces Movement, whose soldiers – sporting carnations in their rifles – overthrew the Caetano regime in a bloodless revolution.

① Locals gather on the square's stone steps leading down to the wide Tagus river.

② Museum-goers take in an unusual exhibit at the Lisbon Story Centre.

③ The colonnade and archways around the square's edges provide a cool place to stroll.

Did You Know?

The Martinho da Arcada, set in a corner of the square, is Lisbon's oldest café.

↑ Busy Praça do Comércio, dominated by a huge statue of King José I

Lisbon's historic centre unfurling beneath the viewing gallery at the top of the lift ↑

2

ELEVADOR DE SANTA JUSTA

📍N6 🏠Rua de Santa Justa and Largo do Carmo
📞213 613 000 🕐7:30am–9pm daily (May–Sep: to 11pm)

Sandwiched between pale stone buildings, this arresting iron structure is a vertical link between Lisbon's lowest and highest neighbourhoods. A platform at the top provides spectacular city views.

Also known as the Elevador do Carmo, this Neo-Gothic lift was built at the turn of the 20th century by French architect Raoul Mesnier du Ponsard, a student of Alexandre Gustave Eiffel. Made of iron and embellished with filigree, it is one of the more eccentric features of the Baixa. The ticket office is located at the foot of the lift, and from here passengers can travel up and down inside the tower in one of two smart wood-panelled cabins with brass fittings; at the top is a walkway linking the Baixa with Largo do Carmo in the Bairro Alto, 32 m (105 ft) above. The apex of the tower, reached via an extremely tight spiral stairway, is given over to a viewing gallery. This high vantage point commands splendid views of Rossio, the Baixa, the castle on the opposite hill, the river and the nearby ruins of the Carmo church. The fire that gutted the Chiado district (p97) was extinguished close to the lift.

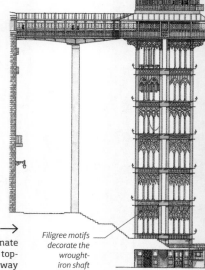

A stunning panorama of the Baixa's grid pattern can be seen from the platform

→ The ornate lift shaft and top-level walkway

Filigree motifs decorate the wrought-iron shaft

Must See

EXPERIENCE MORE

3

Jardim Botânico

L5 Rua da Escola Politécnica 56-58 758 Rato Gardens: 10am-8pm daily (Oct-Mar: to 5pm); MUHNAC: 10am-5pm Tue-Sun Public hols museus.ulisboa.pt

This complex comprises a museum and (10 acres) 4 ha of gardens. The botanical gardens are well kept, and it is worth paying the entrance fee to wander among the different types of trees and dense paths as the gardens descend from the main entrance towards Rua da Alegria. A magnificent, verdant avenue of lofty palms connects the two levels.

The Museu Nacional de História Natural e da Ciência, or MUHNAC (National Museum of Natural History and Science), has collections on botany, zoology, anthropology, geology and palaeontology, as well as hosting temporary exhibitions on themes such as dinosaurs. The museum also exhibits scientific instruments dating from the 16th to the 20th century and holds popular child-friendly programmes that demonstrate basic scientific principles.

↑ Steps leading up to the impressive Elevador de Santa Justa

> 💬 INSIDER TIP
> **Upwardly Mobile**
>
> The Santa Justa lift (or Carmo lift) is technically part of Lisbon's public transport system – and therefore a ride is covered by the 24-hour public transport tickets that can be purchased from any metro station.

STAY

Hotel Heritage Avenida Liberdade
Tastefully converted mansion with slick decor.

M5 Avenida da Liberdade 28 heritageav liberdade.com

€€€

Hotel Almalusa
Beautiful 18th-century building on a historic square. Many rooms have original features.

N7 Praça do Município 21 almalusahotels.com

€€€

Inspira Liberdade Boutique Hotel
Eco-friendly hotel with contemporary feng-shui inspired decor.

M4 Rua de Santa Marta 48 inspirahotels.com

€€€

↑ Shaded path descending among dense foliage, Jardim Botânico

Praça dos Restauradores

M6 709, 711, 736 & many other routes
M Restauradores

This square, distinguished by its soaring obelisk erected in 1886, commemorates the country's liberation from the Spanish yoke in 1640 *(p45)*. The bronze figures on the pedestal depict Victory, holding a palm and a crown, and Freedom. The names and dates that are inscribed on the sides of the obelisk are those of the battles of the War of Restoration.

On the west side, the Palácio Foz now houses a tourist office and other businesses. It was built by Francesco Saverio Fabri in 1755–77 for the Marquês de Castelo-Melhor and renamed after the Marquês de Foz, who lived here in the 19th century. The smart Avenida Palace Hotel on the southwest side of the square was designed by José Luís Monteiro (1848–1942), who also built Rossio railway station.

Avenida da Liberdade

M5 709, 711, 736 & many other routes
M Restauradores, Avenida

After the earthquake of 1755, the Marquês de Pombal created the Passeio Público (public promenade) in the area now occupied by the lower part of Avenida da Liberdade and Praça dos Restauradores. Despite its name, enjoyment of the park was restricted to Lisbon's high society and walls and gates ensured the exclusion of the lower classes. In 1821, when the Liberals came to power, the barriers were pulled down and the Avenida and square became open to all.

The Avenida da Liberdade you see today was built in 1879–82 to replicate the sophistication and style of the Champs-Elysées in Paris. The wide, tree-lined avenue became a focus for pageants, festivities and demonstrations. A war memorial stands as a tribute to those who died in World War I. The avenue still retains a certain elegance, with fountains and café tables shaded by trees; however, it no longer makes for a peaceful stroll. The once majestic thoroughfare, 90 m (295 ft) wide and decorated with abstract pavement patterns, is now divided by seven lanes of traffic linking Praça dos Restauradores and Praça Marquês de Pombal to the north. Many of the Art Nouveau façades have given way to modern ones occupied by offices, hotels or shopping complexes, though some of the original mansions have been preserved. Look out for the Neo-Classical Tivoli theatre at No 188, with an original 1920s kiosk outside, and Casa Lambertini with its colourful mosaic decoration at No 166.

> **The Avenida da Liberdade you see today was built in 1879–82 to replicate the sophistication and style of the Champs-Elysées in Paris.**

The soaring obelisk dominating Praça dos Restauradores ↑

↑ Rossio, featuring wavy paving, and *(inset)* a fountain that is illuminated at night

6
Casa Museu Medeiros e Almeida

☷ L5 **⌂ Rua Rosa Araújo 41** **☉ 10am–5pm Mon–Sat** **ⓦ museumedeirose almeida.pt**

This little-known museum off the Avenida is in the former home of António Medeiros e Almeida, an industrialist who amassed an astonishing collection of international arts and crafts before bequeathing it to the nation in the 1970s.

Today the collection sprawls across 27 galleries – housed partly in Medeiros e Almeida's 19th-century mansion and partly in a modern wing. It includes paintings by Rubens, Pieter Bruegel II and Jacob Huysman, with a self-portrait by Rembrandt as one of the highlights. Other notable items include a tea set that belonged to Napoleon, some of the earliest Chinese porcelain to reach Europe and a collection of ornate watches and clocks.

7
Rossio

☷ N6 **🚌 709, 711, 736 & many other routes** **Ⓜ Rossio**

Formally called Praça Dom Pedro IV, this large square has been Lisbon's nerve centre for six centuries: the stage of bullfights, festivals, military parades and gruesome *autos da fé* (acts of faith). The sober Pombaline buildings are now occupied by shops and cafés. Centre stage is a statue of Dom Pedro IV, the first emperor of independent Brazil.

In the mid-19th century, the square was paved with wave-patterned mosaics that gave it the nickname of "Rolling Motion Square". The grey and white stone cubes were the first such designs to decorate the city's pavements.

On the north side of Rossio is the Teatro Nacional Dona Maria II, named after Dom Pedro's daughter. The Neo-Classical structure was built in the 1840s by the Italian architect Fortunato Lodi. The interior was destroyed by fire in 1964 and reconstructed in the 1970s. Atop the pediment is Gil Vicente (1465–1536), the founder of Portuguese theatre.

Café Nicola on the west side of the square was a favourite meeting place among writers, including the poet Manuel du Bocage (1765–1805), who was notorious for his satires.

SHOP

Manuel Tavares
This 19th-century shop is partly a deli – selling local cheeses, nuts and preserves – and partly a wine store, with a large selection of port and Madeira wine.

☷ N6 **⌂ Rua da Betesga 1a** **☉ Sun** **ⓦ manueltavares.com**

Madeira House
A traditional shop selling quality embroidery and linen from Madeira, as well as beautiful ceramics, decorative tiles and handicrafts from mainland Portugal.

☷ N7 **⌂ Rua Augusta 133** **ⓦ madeira-house.com**

↑ Cafés lining the grand Rua Augusta, framed by the triumphal arch

8

Rua Augusta

 N7 🚌 711, 714, 732, 736, 759 & many other routes Ⓜ Baixa-Chiado

A lively pedestrianized street decorated with mosaic pavements and lined with boutiques and cafés, Rua Augusta is the main tourist thoroughfare and the smartest in the Baixa. Street performers provide entertainment, while vendors sell souvenirs. The triumphal Arco da Rua Augusta, built to commemorate the city's recovery from the earthquake, was completed only in 1873. There are great views from the top of the arch, which is accessed by an elevator.

The other main thoroughfares of the Baixa are Rua da Prata (silversmiths' street) and Rua do Ouro or Rua Áurea (goldsmiths' street). Cutting across these main streets are smaller streets that give glimpses up to the Bairro Alto to the west and Castelo de São Jorge (p64) to the east. Many streets retain shops that gave them their name: jewellers in Rua da Prata and Rua do Ouro and banks in Rua do Comércio.

In the heart of the Baixa is a small section of the Roman baths, located within the Banco Comercial Português in Rua dos Correeiros. The ruins and mosaics can be seen from the window at the back of the bank; alternatively you can book ahead to visit the "museum" on 211 131 070.

9

Praça da Figueira

 N6 🚌 714, 759, 760 & many other routes 🚊 12, 15 Ⓜ Rossio

Before the 1755 earthquake, the square next to Rossio was the site of the Hospital de Todos-os-Santos (All Saints). In Pombal's design for the

EAT

Bonjardim, Rei dos Frangos
On a side street, this is the ideal place to sample Portugal's spit-roast chicken – with or without fiery piri-piri sauce.

 M6 🏠 Travessa de Santo Antão 11–18 📞 213 424 389

€€€

Casa do Alentejo
Set in an *azulejo*-adorned building of Moorish influence; dine in lavish halls, or feast on heartier fare in an intimate courtyard outside.

 N6 🏠 Rua das Portas de Santo Antão 58 🌐 casadoalentejo.pt

€€€

Confeitaria Nacional
This historic café opened in 1829 and still serves a tempting array of pastries, teas and strong coffee.

 N6 🏠 Praça da Figueira 18 📞 213 424 470

€€€

Baixa, the square took on the role of the city's central marketplace. In 1885 a covered market was built, but this was pulled down in the 1950s. Today, the four-storey buildings are given over to hotels, shops and cafés; the square is occasionally used as a marketplace. Perhaps its most eye-catching feature is the multitude of pigeons that perch on the pedestal supporting Leopoldo de Almeida's bronze equestrian statue of João I, erected in 1971.

→ Equestrian statue of João I standing in Praça da Figueira

DAS REGRAS, POVO DE LISBOA E CORTES DA NAÇÃO

Museu da Sociedade de Geografia

📍 M5 🏛 Rua das Portas de Santo Antão 100 📞 213 425 401 🚌 709, 711, 736 Ⓜ Restauradores 🕐 10am–12:45pm & 2–4:45pm

This museum houses an idiosyncratic ethnographical collection brought back from Portugal's former colonies. On display are circumcision masks from Guinea Bissau, musical instruments and snake spears. From Angola there are neck rests to sustain coiffures and the original *padrão* – the pillar erected by the Portuguese in 1482 to mark their sovereignty over the colony.

Núcleo Arqueológico

📍 N7 🏛 Rua dos Correeiros 21 📞 211 131 070 🕐 Four tours: 10am–noon & 2–5pm Mon–Sat

Late 20th-century renovation works on this site uncovered archaeological finds, many dating back over 2,500 years. These have been preserved, often under glass flooring, and today can be visited in situ as part of a free and interesting guided tour. The cramped underground walkways provide a fascinating insight into Lisbon's history, from pre-Roman times to the 18th century. Displays range from the remains of Roman fish-preserving tanks to wooden pillars used to prop up Baixa's buildings when it was rebuilt on waterlogged land after the earthquake of 1755.

MUDE (Museu do Design e da Moda)

📍 N7 🏛 Rua Augusta 24 🕐 10am–6pm Tue–Sun (closed for renovation until further notice, check website for updates) 🌐 mude.pt

Anyone with an interest in design or fashion will want to linger at this tremendous collection of 20th-century classics from around the world, which traces the evolution of design from the 1930s onwards. The bulk of the pieces on display are from the private collection of Francisco Capelo, which the wealthy economist bequeathed to the state in 2003.

Exhibits are overhauled regularly, but usually feature the likes of "Marilyn's lips" (Bocca's iconic mouth-shaped sofa), furniture by Philippe Starck or Charles and Ray Eames, and wonderful haute couture from Vivienne Westwood, Jean-Paul Gaultier and Alexander McQueen.

Nossa Senhora da Conceição Velha

📍 N7 🏛 Rua da Alfândega 📞 218 870 202 🚌 759, 794 🚊 15, 25 🕐 Times vary, call ahead

The elaborate Manueline doorway of the church is the only surviving feature from the original 16th-century Nossa Senhora da Misericórdia, which stood here until the 1755 earthquake. The portal is decorated with a profusion of Manueline detail including angels, beasts, flowers and the cross of the Order of Christ. In the tympanum, the Virgin Mary spreads her protective mantle over various contemporary figures. These include Pope Leo X, Manuel I and his sister, Queen Leonor, widow of João II. It was Leonor who founded the original Misericórdia (almshouse) on the site of a former synagogue.

 HIDDEN GEM
Elevador do Lavra

Seek out the Elevador do Lavra, one of the city's lesser-known street lifts located at the end of Largo da Anunciada. Dating back to 1884, it climbs up to the pretty Jardim do Torel gardens.

↓ MUDE, with the Arco da Rua Augusta in the background

A SHORT WALK
RESTAURADORES

Distance 1.3 km (0.8 miles) **Nearest station**
Restauradores metro **Time** 20 minutes

This is the busiest part of Lisbon,
especially the central squares of Rossio
and Praça da Figueira. Totally rebuilt
after the earthquake of 1755, the area
was one of Europe's first examples of
town planning. Stroll the wide streets
to admire the large Neo-Classical
buildings, before absorbing more
of the atmosphere and surroundings
from one of the bustling pavement
cafés. Nearby Rua das Portas de
Santo Antão, a pedestrianized
street with an array of seafood
restaurants, allows for
a more leisurely pace.

*The Elevador da Glória funicular
goes up the hill towards the Bairro
Alto, as far as the Miradouro de
São Pedro de Alcântara (p99).*

*Built by Italian architect
Francesco Fabri, the
magnificent 18th-century
Palácio Foz is now home to
a tourist office.*

*This large tree- and café-lined
square was named after the
soldiers who gave their lives
during the War of Restoration.*

START

PRAÇA DOS
RESTAURADORES

FINISH

Restauradores

0 metres	50
0 yards	50

N ↑

*The Neo-Manueline
Rossio station has an
eye-catching façade
featuring two Moorish-
style horseshoe arches.*

← The ornate
façade of Rossio
railway station

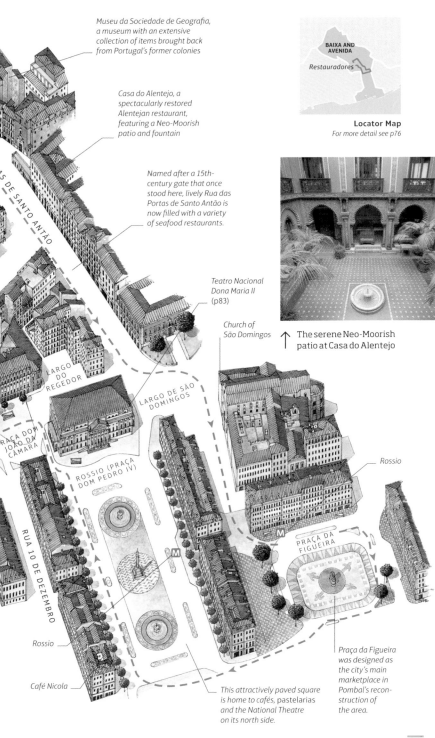

Museu da Sociedade de Geografia, a museum with an extensive collection of items brought back from Portugal's former colonies

Casa do Alentejo, a spectacularly restored Alentejan restaurant, featuring a Neo-Moorish patio and fountain

Named after a 15th-century gate that once stood here, lively Rua das Portas de Santo Antão is now filled with a variety of seafood restaurants.

Teatro Nacional Dona Maria II (p83)

Church of São Domingos

AS DE SANTO ANTÃO

LARGO DO REGEDOR

LARGO DE SÃO DOMINGOS

PRAÇA DOM JOÃO DA CAMARA

ROSSIO (PRAÇA DOM PEDRO IV)

RUA 10 DE DEZEMBRO

Rossio

Rossio

Café Nicola

PRAÇA DA FIGUEIRA

↑ The serene Neo-Moorish patio at Casa do Alentejo

This attractively paved square is home to cafés, pastelarias and the National Theatre on its north side.

Praça da Figueira was designed as the city's main marketplace in Pombal's reconstruction of the area.

BAIRRO ALTO AND ESTRELA

Laid out in a grid pattern in the late 16th century, the hilltop Bairro Alto was first settled by rich citizens who moved out of the disreputable Alfama. By the 19th century it had become the centre of a more liberal and free-thinking Lisbon, attracting writers and artists, journalists, sex workers and *fadistas*. Small shops, family-run *tascas* (cheap restaurants) and bars moved in to form a district that today really comes alive at night.

In contrast, the nearby elegant commercial district known as the Chiado is home to some of the city's oldest shops and cafés. Many of the area's original Belle Époque buildings were destroyed by a fire in 1988, but cleverly restored by architect Álvaro Siza Vieira around the turn of the century. To the northwest, the Estrela quarter is centred on a huge domed basilica, built in 1790, while the smart district of Lapa, to the southwest, was laid out in the mid-18th century.

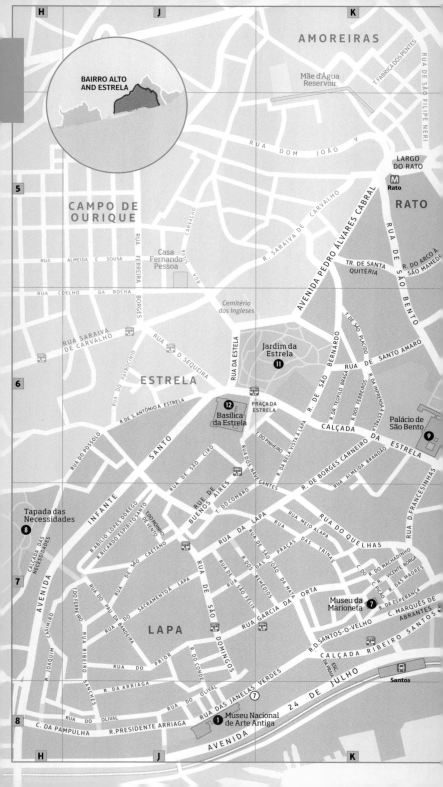

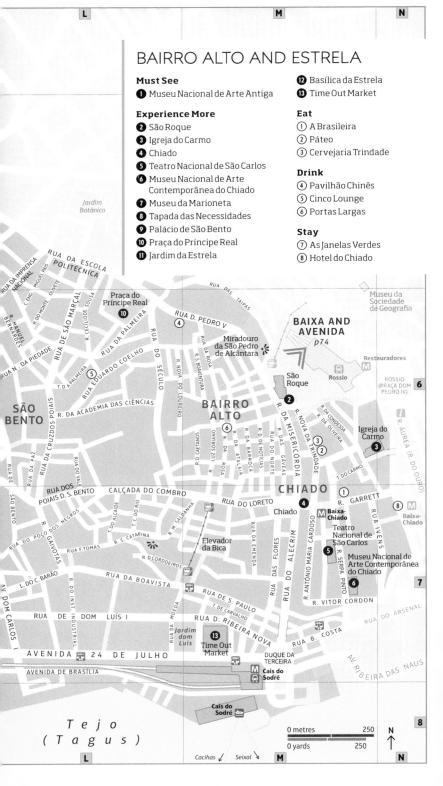

BAIRRO ALTO AND ESTRELA

Must See
❶ Museu Nacional de Arte Antiga

Experience More
❷ São Roque
❸ Igreja do Carmo
❹ Chiado
❺ Teatro Nacional de São Carlos
❻ Museu Nacional de Arte Contemporânea do Chiado
❼ Museu da Marioneta
❽ Tapada das Necessidades
❾ Palácio de São Bento
❿ Praça do Príncipe Real
⓫ Jardim da Estrela

⓬ Basílica da Estrela
⓭ Time Out Market

Eat
① A Brasileira
② Páteo
③ Cervejaria Trindade

Drink
④ Pavilhão Chinês
⑤ Cinco Lounge
⑥ Portas Largas

Stay
⑦ As Janelas Verdes
⑧ Hotel do Chiado

① 🏷 🍴 🍽

MUSEU NACIONAL DE ARTE ANTIGA

📍 J8 🏠 Rua das Janelas Verdes 🚌 713, 714, 727 🚊 15, 18 🕙 10am-6pm Tue-Sun
🚫 1 Jan, Easter, 1 May, 13 Jun, 25 Dec 🌐 museudearteantiga.pt

Portugal's national art collection is housed in a lemon-yellow 17th-century palace, originally built for the counts of Alvor. Among the exhibits are more state-designated "national treasures" than anywhere else in the country.

Inaugurated in 1884, the museum is known locally as the Museu das Janelas Verdes, a nod to the former green windows of the palace. In 1940, an annexe (including the main façade) was built on the site of the St Albert Carmelite monastery, which was partially demolished between 1910 and 1920. All that survived was a chapel, now integrated into the museum and gradually being restored. After an afternoon's culture, the magnificent garden overlooking the Tagus offers an oasis of calm, plus an adjoining restaurant that serves delicious coffee and pastries. The museum's collection emphasizes Portuguese works, as well as paintings, artifacts and an extensive collection of jewellery from around the world. Highlights of the permanent collection include the exquisite 16th-century Namban screens, which depict contemporary Japanese trade with Portugal.

> 💬 INSIDER TIP
> **Into the Gardens**
>
> Once you've had your fill of culture amid the galleries, head for the sun-dappled gardens, where sculptures and river views create a relaxing and pleasant place to unwind.

→ The museum's walls and pretty gardens, and *(inset)* its alfresco café

1 The gallery of Portuguese painting and sculpture displays its exhibits in a sparse, dramatic arrangement.

2 This statue of St Leonard is by the renowned Florentine sculptor Andrea della Robbia (1435–1525).

3 Visitors admire *The Temptation of St Anthony*, a depiction of spiritual torment by the Dutch master of fantasy, Hieronymus Bosch (1450–1516).

40,000

The number of works of art housed in the museum.

The museum's bright, wide galleries lined with priceless paintings ↑

Exploring the Collections

The museum has the largest collection of paintings in Portugal, including an extensive treasury of early religious works by Portuguese artists. The majority of exhibits came from convents and monasteries following the suppression of religious orders in 1834. There are also wide-ranging displays of sculpture, silverware, porcelain and applied arts, giving an overview of Portuguese art from the Middle Ages to the 19th century, complemented by fine European and Eastern pieces. The theme of the Age of Discovery is ever-present, illustrating Portugal's links with Brazil, Africa, India, China and Japan.

Did You Know?

Hieronymus Bosch never dated his works, so we can't be exactly sure when they were painted.

Visitors admiring the *São Vicente de Fora* polyptych, one of the museum's most important pieces ↑

European Art

▶ Paintings by European artists, dating from the 14th to the 19th century, hang chronologically on the first floor. Most of the works in this section were donated from private collections, contributing to the great diversity of works on display. Among the most notable works are *Salomé* by Lucus Cranach the Elder (1472-1553) and *The Temptations of St Anthony* by Hieronymus Bosch (1450-1516).

Portuguese Painting and Sculpture

Many of the earliest works of art are by the Portuguese primitive painters, who were influenced by a Flemish trend of realistic detail. Thought to be by Nuno Gonçalves, the invaluable *São Vicente de Fora* polyptych is currently undergoing restoration - visitors can observe the process from behind protective glass. The sculpture collection includes many Gothic polychrome stone and wood statues.

Portuguese and Chinese Ceramics

The collection of Chinese porcelain and Portuguese faïence showcases the reciprocal influence between Eastern and Portuguese potters. From the 16th century, Portuguese ceramics show a marked influence of Ming, and conversely, Chinese pieces bear Portuguese motifs such as coats of arms. By the mid-18th century, an increasingly personalized European style emerged among Portuguese potters, using popular, rustic designs.

Asian and African Art

The collection of ivories and furniture, with their European motifs, further illustrates the exchange of influences of Portugal and its colonies. The 16th-century gave rise to a huge demand for items such as carved ivory hunting horns from Africa. The 16th- and 17th-century Japanese Namban screens show the Portuguese trading in Japan. *Namban-jin* (barbarians from the south) is the name the Japanese gave to the Portuguese.

Silver, Gold and Jewellery

◀ Among the ecclesiastical treasures are King Sancho I's 1214 gold cross and the 1506 Belém monstrance. The collection of jewels came from convents, originally donated by wealthy novices on entering religious orders.

Decorative Arts

Furniture, tapestries and textiles, liturgical vestments and bishops' mitres are among the wide range of objects on display. The furniture collection includes many pieces from Portuguese and other European royal courts. Among the textiles are 17th-century bedspreads, tapestries (many of Flemish origin, such as the 16th-century Baptism of Christ), embroidered rugs and Arraiolos carpets.

TOP 5 UNMISSABLE EXHIBITS

Ivory Salt Cellar
Portuguese dignitaries are carved in ivory on this 16th-century West African salt shaker.

The Chapel of St Albert
Admire the Baroque interior, covered in blue-and-white *azulejos*.

Faïence Violin
Portraits of Italian composers decorate this ceramic piece.

Salomé
Lucus Cranach the Elder's study of virtue or seductive perversion.

The Temptations of St Anthony
A fantastical oil-on-oak triptych.

EXPERIENCE MORE

2
São Roque

📍M6 🏛Largo Trindade Coelho 📞213 235 444 🚌758 🕐10am–6pm Tue–Sun 🚫Public hols

São Roque's plain façade belies a rich interior. The church was founded at the end of the 16th century by the Jesuit Order, which was then at the peak of its power. In 1742, the Chapel of St John the Baptist was commissioned by the prodigal João V from Italian architects Luigi Vanvitelli and Nicola Salvi. Constructed in Rome and embellished with jewels, precious marbles, gold, silver and mosaics, the ornate chapel was given the pope's blessing in the church of Sant'Antonio dei Portoghesi in Rome, dismantled and then sent to Lisbon in three ships.

Among the church's many tiles, the oldest and most interesting are those in the third chapel on the right, dating from the 16th century and dedicated to São Roque (St Roch), protector against the plague. Other notable features of the church are the scenes of the Apocalypse painted on the ceiling.

3
Igreja do Carmo

📍M6 🏛Largo do Carmo 📞213 460 473 🚌758 🚈28 Ⓜ Baixa-Chiado 🕐10am–6pm Mon-Sat (May–Oct: to 7pm) 🚫1 Jan, 1 May, 25 Dec

The Gothic ruins of this Carmelite church, built on a slope overlooking the Baixa, are evocative reminders of the devastation left by the earthquake of 1755. The church collapsed during Mass, depositing tons of masonry onto the people below. Founded in the late 14th century by Nuno Álvares Pereira, the

↓ Interior of São Roque, the earliest Jesuit church in Lisbon

> **Did You Know?**
>
> Fernando Pessoa liked to write under distinct literary personas, which he called "heteronyms".

commander who became a member of the Carmelite Order, the church was at one time the biggest in Lisbon. Today, the main body of the church and the chancel, whose roof withstood the earthquake, houses the Museu do Carmo, with a small, heterogeneous collection of sarcophagi, statuary, ceramics and mosaics.

Among more ancient finds from Europe are a remnant of a Visigothic pillar and a Roman tomb carved with reliefs depicting the Muses. There are also pieces from Mexico and South America, including ancient mummies.

↑ Statue of Fernando Pessoa outside the café A Brasileira

 4

Chiado

M7 **758** **28**
M Baixa-Chiado

Statues of literary figures can be found in this area, known for its intellectual associations. A bronze statue by sculptor Lagoa Henriques

---

💬 **INSIDER TIP**
African Lisbon Tours

Uncover traces of African history in Lisbon on this walking tour *(www.africanlisbontour. com)* led by Naki Gaglo, who exposes Portugal's colonial history and its connection with human enslavement. The tour passes through many statues and sites in the Bairro Alto and Estrela districts, all linked to the city's African community, and ends with a meal at a traditional restaurant.

---

depicts Fernando Pessoa, Portugal's great Modernist poet, writer and literary critic, sitting at a table outside the café A Brasileira, which was once a favourite rendezvous of the city's intellectuals.

Rua Garrett, named after the author and poet João Almeida Garrett (1799–1854), descending from Largo do Chiado towards the Baixa, is known for its cafés and shops. Devastated by fire in 1988, the former elegance of this quarter has now been restored.

 5

Teatro Nacional de São Carlos

M7 **Rua Serpa Pinto 9**
758 **28** **M** Baixa-Chiado **W** tnsc.pt

Replacing a former opera house that was ruined by the earthquake of 1755, the Teatro de São Carlos was built in 1792–5 by Portuguese architect José da Costa e Silva. Inspired by the design of great Italian theatres such as La Scala in Milan and the San Carlo in Naples, the building has a beautifully proportioned yellow façade and an enchanting Rococo interior.

The opera season lasts from September to June, but concerts and ballets are also staged here at other times of the year. The opera house is also home to the Portuguese Symphonic Orchestra.

Pavilhão Chinês
This quirky bar is packed with a bizarre array of collector's items, from dolls to model planes, and also features a strong cocktail list.

L6 **Rua Dom Pedro V 89**
213 424 729

Cinco Lounge
Credited with making cocktails cool in Lisbon, this smart and very chic bar offers over 100 options, ranging from classics to the more experimental.

L6 **Rua Ruben A. Leitão 17a**
W cincolounge.com

Portas Largas
A buzzy, traditional tavern with live music and well-priced drinks where the revelry spills out onto the street.

M6 **Rua da Atalaia 103-105**
213 466 379

↑ Paintings and sculpture at Museu Nacional de Arte Contemporânea do Chiado

6 🎨 🏛

Museu Nacional de Arte Contemporânea do Chiado

📍M7 🏛Rua Serpa Pinto 4-6 🚌758 🚋28 Ⓜ Baixa-Chiado 🕙10am–1pm & 2-6pm Tue-Fri, 10am-2pm & 3-6pm Sat & Sun 🚫1 Jan, Easter, 1 May, 13 Jun, 25 Dec 🌐museuarte contemporanea.gov.pt

The National Museum of Contemporary Art moved to this stylishly restored warehouse in 1994. The paintings and sculpture are arranged over three floors in seven rooms. Each room has a different theme illustrating the development from Romanticism to Modernism. The majority are Portuguese works, often showing a marked influence from other European countries – this is particularly noticeable in the 19th-century landscape painters who had contact with artists from the French Barbizon School. The few international works of art on display are mainly French sculpture from the late 19th century, including one by Rodin (1840–1917). There are also temporary exhibitions, which are held for new artists.

7 🎨

Museu da Marioneta

📍K7 🏛Convento das Bernardas, Rua da Esperança 146 🚌713, 727, 760 🚋15, 25 Ⓜ Cais do Sodré 🚉Santos 🕙10am–6pm Tue-Sun 🚫1 Jan, 1 May, 24 & 25 Dec, 31 Dec 🌐museudamarioneta.pt

This small puppet museum, housed in an elegantly refurbished convent building, includes characters from 17th- and 18th-century theatre and opera, including devils, knights, jesters and satirical figures. Many of the puppets possess gruesome, contorted features that may not always appeal to small children. The museum explains the history of the art form and runs videos of puppet shows. Check the website

↑ Puppets from the collection at Museu da Marioneta

to see if a live performance is being held on the small stage. There is also a space for children's entertainment and learning.

Miradouro de São Pedro de Alcântara

This *miradouro* features a sweeping vista of eastern Lisbon. A tiled map, placed against the balustrade, helps you locate the landmarks. The view is most attractive at sunset and by night, when the castle is floodlit and the terrace becomes a meeting point for young Lisboetas.

8

Tapada das Necessidades

 H7 North Entrance: Rua do Borja; South Entrance: Largo das Necessidades 712, 714, 727, 773 Alcântara Apr-Sep: 8am-8pm Mon-Fri, 10am-7pm Sat & Sun; Oct-Mar: 8am-7pm Mon-Fri, 10am-6pm Sat & Sun

For centuries, only Portuguese royalty could wander through Tapada das Necessidades, a former hunting ground which then became a picnic spot for kings and queens in the 19th century. Today, visitors come here to enjoy the quiet, stroll through the cactus garden and relish the river views. Dotted around are a few abandoned buildings, including a glass-house and the Casa de Regalo, where Queen Amélia used to paint. There are two entrances to the park. To be greeted by peacocks, enter through the south. It's around here you'll find the Palácio das Necessidades, the residence of the last Portuguese king before the monarchy ended. The building now houses the Ministry of Foreign Affairs.

9

Palácio de São Bento

 K6 Praça da Constituição de 1976 213 910 843 773 28 By appt 11:15am Tue & Fri, 3:15pm Wed Aug: for tours on Wed parlamento.pt

Also known as the Assembleia da República, this massive white Neo-Classical building started life in the late 1500s as the Benedictine monastery of São Bento. After the dissolution of the religious orders in 1834, the building became the seat of parliament, known as the Palácio das Cortes. The interior is grand, with marble pillars and Neo-Classical statues.

10

Praça do Príncipe Real

 L6 758

Originally laid out in 1860 as a residential neighbourhood, Praça do Príncipe Real still retains its air of affluence. Smart mansions surround a park with a café, statuary and some robinia, magnolia and Judas trees. In 2017, a monument to Lisbon's LGBTQ+ community was erected here, showing a man and woman stepping out of a closet. On the large square, at No 26, the white Neo-Moorish building has a shopping gallery.

> **Originally laid out in 1860 as a residential neighbourhood, Praça do Príncipe Real still retains its air of affluence.**

↑ Tree-shaded park at the heart of Praça do Príncipe Real

↑ The wrought-iron bandstand at the centre of Jardim da Estrela

months. The bandstand was built in 1884 and originally stood on the Passeio Público, before the creation of Avenida da Liberdade (p82).

The English Cemetery to the north of the gardens is best known as the burial place of Henry Fielding (1707–54), the English novelist and playwright who died in Lisbon at the age of 47. The *Journal of a Voyage to Lisbon*, published posthumously in 1775, recounts his last voyage to Portugal, made in a fruitless attempt to recover his failing health.

⑪
Jardim da Estrela

🚩K6 🚏Praça da Estrela
🚌720, 738 🚋25, 28
🕐7am-midnight daily

Laid out in the middle of the 19th century, opposite the Basílica da Estrela, the popular gardens are a focal part of the Estrela quarter. Picturesque and serene, they provide an oasis from the hustle and bustle of the city.

Local families congregate here at weekends to feed the ducks and carp in the lake, sit at the waterside café or wander among the flowerbeds, plants and trees. The formal gardens are planted with herbaceous borders and shrubs surrounding plane trees and elms. The central feature of the park is a green wrought-iron bandstand, decorated with elegant filigree, where musicians strike up in the summer

⑫
Basílica da Estrela

🚩J6 🚏Praça da Estrela
📞213 960 915 🚌720, 738
🚋25, 28 🕐9am-1pm,
3-6:45pm Mon-Sun

In the second half of the 18th century Maria I (p155), daughter of José I, vowed she would build a church if she bore a son and heir to the throne. Her wish was granted and construction of the basilica began in 1779. Her son José, however, died of smallpox two years before the completion of the church in 1790.

The huge domed Basílica da Estrela, which is proudly set on a hill overlooking the west of the city, is one of Lisbon's most remarkable landmarks. A simpler version of the basilica at Mafra (p156), this church was built by architects from the Mafra School in late-Baroque and Neo-Classical style. The façade is flanked by twin bell towers and decorated with an array of statues of saints and allegorical figures.

The spacious, awe-inspiring interior, where light streams down from the pierced dome, is clad in grey, pink and yellow marble. The elaborate Empire-style tomb of Queen Maria I, who died in Brazil, lies in the right transept. Locked in a room nearby is Machado de

---

CONTEMPORARY PORTUGUESE CUISINE

Exploding olives and acorn ice cream are some of the unusual offerings now found at Lisbon's innovative new restaurants. Spearheaded by the likes of José Avillez *(right)*, creator of Belcanto, the first Lisbon restaurant to earn two Michelin stars, contemporary Portuguese dining focuses on finding unexpected, top-quality local ingredients to lift traditional recipes into something unforgettable.

> **The huge domed Basílica da Estrela, which is proudly set on a hill overlooking the west of the city, is one of Lisbon's most remarkable landmarks.**

Castro's extraordinary Nativity scene, composed of over 500 cork-and-terracotta figures. To see it, ask the sacristan.

Be sure to climb the dome's steep stone steps to access the flat roof above the Basílica, where you'll find breathtaking views of the western city – and down into the church below.

Time Out Market (Mercado da Ribeira)

📍 M7 🏛 Avenida 24 de Julho 🕐 10am-midnight Mon-Sun; fish, fruit and vegetable market: 6am-2pm Mon-Sat 🌐 timeout market.com

Lisbon's historic Mercado da Ribeira opened for business in 1930, and has served as the city's main fruit and vegetable market ever since. It was rejuvenated in 2014, by incorporating the many food and drink stalls of the world's first Time Out Market, which now occupy most of the cavernous central hall.

Stake your claim on one of the benches and sample the diverse array of produce on offer from some of Lisbon's best-known food outlets (including Henrique Sá Pessoa from Michelin-starred restaurant Alma). You can enjoy anything from burgers and sushi to fine cheeses, *pastéis de nata* and ice cream, while champagne bars and wine, beer or juice stalls cater to the thirsty.

There are further bars and restaurants around the outside of the market and on the first floor, which has a music venue for concerts. The concept has proved overwhelmingly successful – attracting over three million visitors a year – and Time Out has subsequently opened similar markets in the US.

↓ The Time Out Market's cavernous food court, thronging with visitors

---

EAT

A Brasileira
The intellectuals who made this 1905 café famous are gone, but its Art Deco interior and bar filled with tempting pastries remain a draw.

📍 M6 🏛 Rua Garrett 120 📞 213 469 541

Páteo
Occupying a covered patio inside a former monastery, this lovely space specializes in quality fish and seafood, prepared by chef José Avillez.

📍 M6 🏛 Bairro do Avillez, 18 Rua Nova da Trindade 📞 215 830 290

Cervejaria Trindade
Famed for its beautiful *azulejos,* this 1830s beer hall serves tasty seafood and steak.

📍 M6 🏛 Rua Nova da Trindade 20 📞 213 423 506

A SHORT WALK
BAIRRO ALTO AND CHIADO

Distance 1 km (0.5 miles) **Nearest station** Baixa-Chiado metro **Time** 15 minutes

The Bairro Alto (high quarter) is a fascinating plot of cobbled streets adjacent to the Carmo and Chiado areas. Since the 1980s, this has been Lisbon's best-known nightlife zone, with countless small bars and restaurants alongside the older *casas de fado*. While more modern buildings have also sprung up in recent years, the quarter remains a lively part of the city to wander. In contrast, the Chiado presents a more manicured façade, filled as it is with elegant shops and old-style cafés that extend down from Praça Luís de Camões towards Rua do Carmo and the Baixa. Climb from Chiado up to Bairro Alto to experience Lisbon's traditional and cosmopolitan sides.

Manteigaria, a bakery which serves some of the best pastéis de nata in town and is open late into the night.

Praça Luís de Camões

This statue of realist novelist Eça de Queirós (1845–1900), by Teixeira Lopes, was erected in 1903.

RUA DO NORTE

RUA DAS GÁVEAS

RUA DO ALECRIM

Largo do Chiado, flanked by the churches of Loreto and Nossa Senhora da Encarnação

L. DO CHIADO

RUA GARRETT

Chiado

A Brasileira, a historic café on Largo do Chiado adorned with gilded mirrors

Rua Garrett, the Chiado's main shopping street

← Shaded café tables on the patterned cobbles of Largo do Chiado

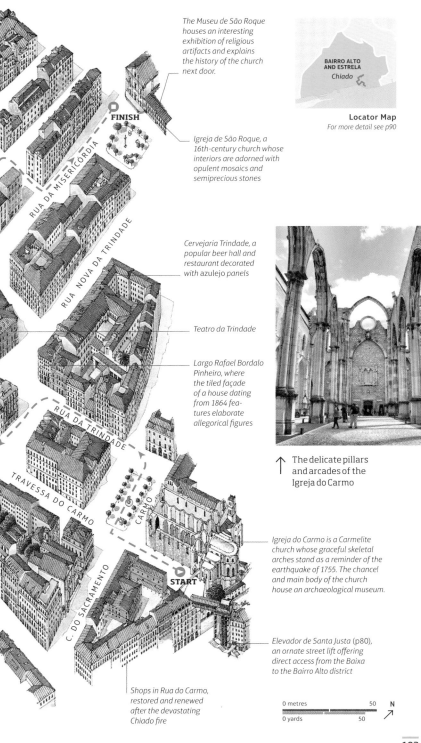

The Museu de São Roque houses an interesting exhibition of religious artifacts and explains the history of the church next door.

Locator Map
For more detail see p90

BAIRRO ALTO AND ESTRELA
Chiado

FINISH

Igreja de São Roque, a 16th-century church whose interiors are adorned with opulent mosaics and semiprecious stones

RUA DA MISERICORDIA

RUA NOVA DA TRINDADE

Cervejaria Trindade, a popular beer hall and restaurant decorated with azulejo panels

Teatro da Trindade

Largo Rafael Bordalo Pinheiro, where the tiled façade of a house dating from 1864 features elaborate allegorical figures

RUA DA TRINDADE

TRAVESSA DO CARMO

C. DO SACRAMENTO

CARMO

START

↑ The delicate pillars and arcades of the Igreja do Carmo

Igreja do Carmo is a Carmelite church whose graceful skeletal arches stand as a reminder of the earthquake of 1755. The chancel and main body of the church house an archaeological museum.

Elevador de Santa Justa (p80), an ornate street lift offering direct access from the Baixa to the Bairro Alto district

Shops in Rua do Carmo, restored and renewed after the devastating Chiado fire

0 metres   50
0 yards   50

N ↗

BELÉM

Perched as it is at the mouth of the Tejo river, where the caravels set sail on their voyages, Belém is inextricably linked with Portugal's Age of Discovery. When Manuel I came to power in 1495 he reaped the profits of colonial expansion, using them to build grandiose monuments and churches that mirrored the spirit of the time. Two of the finest examples of this exuberant Manueline style of architecture are the Mosteiro dos Jerónimos and the Torre de Belém.

Following the earthquake of 1775, José I installed his court in a series of tents in Belém's hills, the site of the Palácio Nacional da Ajuda, where it would remain for nearly three decades. This move attracted commerce to the area and Belém continued to thrive. The 19th-century main street has largely resisted modernization, and the Antiga Confeitaria de Belém, celebrated as the birthplace of Lisbon's iconic custard tart, can still be visited at its original site.

BELÉM

Must Sees
1. Mosteiro dos Jerónimos
2. Torre de Belém

Experience More
3. Museu Nacional dos Coches
4. Jardim Botânico Tropical
5. Palácio de Belém
6. Museu Nacional de Arqueologia
7. Planetário de Marinha
8. Museu de Marinha
9. Centro Cultural de Belém
10. Padrão dos Descobrimentos
11. Museu Colecção Berardo
12. MAAT – Museu de Arte, Arquitetura e Tecnologia
13. Ermida de São Jerónimo
14. Igreja da Memória
15. Jardim Botânico da Ajuda
16. Palácio Nacional da Ajuda

Eat
1. Antiga Confeitaria de Belém

Stay
2. Jerónimos 8
3. Altis Belém
4. Pestana Palace

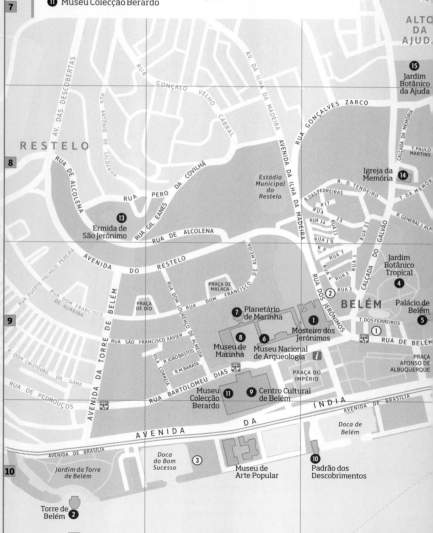

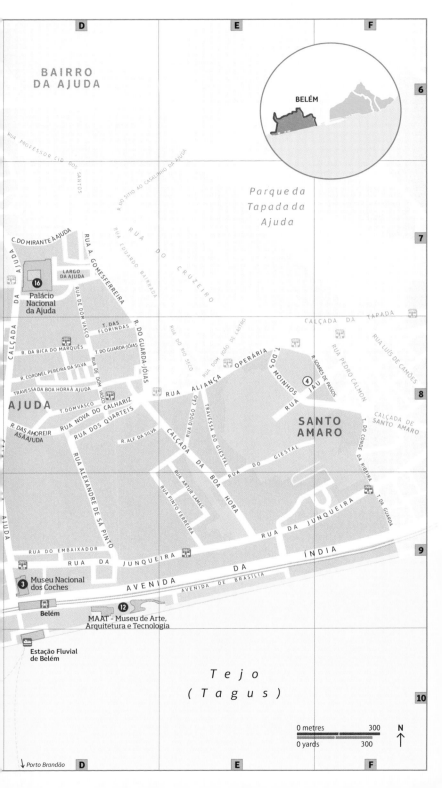

① ✍

MOSTEIRO DOS JERÓNIMOS

📍C9 🏛Praça do Império (combined ticket for monastery and Torre de Belém available) 🚌714, 727, 728, 729, 751 🚊15 🚇Belém 🕙9:30am-6pm Tue-Sun (last adm 5pm) ☒Public hols 🌐mosteirojeronimos.gov.pt

Transformed from a humble hermitage into a magnificent monastery, complete with twisted columns and maritime motifs, the Mosteiro dos Jerónimos is a symbol of Portugal's colonial conquests and imperial ambitions.

A monument to the wealth of the Age of Discovery (p44), the monastery was commissioned by Manuel I around 1501, and was financed largely by "pepper money" – a tax levied on spices, precious stones and gold. The monastery was cared for by the Order of St Jerome (Hieronymites) until 1834, when all religious orders were disbanded. Great figures from Portugal's history are entombed here – but one tomb stands empty: that of the "longed for" Dom Sebastião, the young king who never returned from battle in 1578.

The walls of the refectory are tiled with 18th-century azulejos.

↑ The monastery's exterior, designed to emphasize the Portuguese empire's wealth

→
The decorated exterior and interior of the Mosteiro dos Jerónimos

The modern wing, built in 1850 in Neo-Manueline style, houses the Museu Nacional de Arqueologia (p113).

The west portal, designed by the French sculptor Nicolau Chanterène

1 Slender pillars rise like palm trees to the spectacular vaulted roof in the church of Santa Maria.

2 The 19th-century tomb of navigator Vasco da Gama is festooned with seafaring symbols.

3 João de Castilho's pure Manueline cloisters are adorned with delicate tracery and richly carved arches.

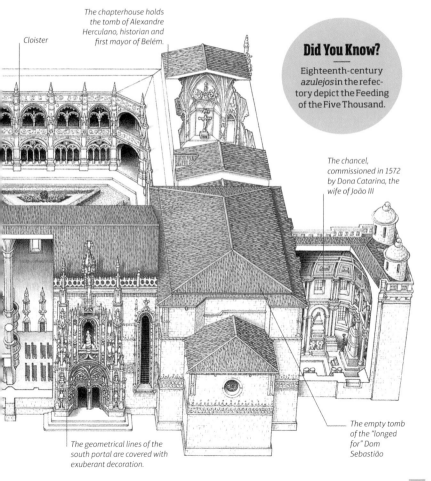

Cloister

The chapterhouse holds the tomb of Alexandre Herculano, historian and first mayor of Belém.

The chancel, commissioned in 1572 by Dona Catarina, the wife of João III

The geometrical lines of the south portal are covered with exuberant decoration.

The empty tomb of the "longed for" Dom Sebastião

2 ⊘

TORRE DE BELÉM

📍 A10 🏛 Avenida de Brasilia 🚌 727, 728, 729, 751
🚋 15 🚉 Belém 🕐 9:30am–6pm Tue–Sun (last adm 5pm) 🚫 1 Jan, Easter Sun, 1 May, 13 Jun, 25 Dec
🌐 torrebelem.gov.pt

Set like a giant stone rook at the edge of the Tagus, this elaborate tower showcases some of Belém's best Manueline architecture. Be sure to climb its narrow spiral staircase for breathtaking views.

Commissioned by Manuel I, the tower was built as a fortress in 1514–20 and soon became a symbol of Portugal's era of expansion. The real beauty of this Manueline gem lies in the intricate decoration of the exterior. Adorned with rope carved in stone, it has openwork balconies, Moorish-style watchtowers and distinctive battlements in the shape of shields. The Gothic interior below the terrace, which served as a storeroom for arms and a prison, is very austere, but the private quarters in the tower are worth visiting for the loggia and the panorama.

Did You Know?

The tower's real name is the Torre de São Vicente, after the city's patron saint.

Battlements, decorated with the cross of the Order of Christ

The Italian-inspired arcaded loggia is a light touch along the battlements.

→ The stone fortress, a symbol of Portugal's seafaring power

Sentry posts

King's room

The vaulted dungeon was used as a prison until the 19th century.

Statue of the Virgin Mary, a symbol of protection for sailors

↑ The Torre de Belém, sitting at the edge of the Tagus river

↑ Open cloister in the tower, designed to dispel cannon smoke

Entrance

Gangway to shore

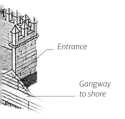

💬 **INSIDER TIP**
Aim High

Head to the former royal residences at the top of the tower to glimpse the most ornate carvings. Simple carvings adorn the old ammunitions store and prison rooms on the lower floors.

EXPERIENCE MORE

3

Museu Nacional dos Coches

📍D9 🏛 Avenida da Índia 136
🚌714, 727, 728, 729, 751 🚋15
🚃Belém ⏰10am-6pm Tue-Sun ⏰1 Jan, Easter, 1 May, 13 Jun, 24 & 25 Dec 🌐museudoscoches.gov.pt

The museum's collection of coaches is arguably the finest in Europe. First established in the old Royal Riding School, the museum showcases a unique and opulent collection of coaches, carriages and sedan chairs dating from the 17th, 18th and 19th centuries. The collection was moved to a new, modern building by the Brazilian architect Paulo Mendes da Rocha, winner of the 2006 Pritzker Prize, in 2015.

The extra space enabled more modern vehicles to be added to the display. However, for most visitors the historic royal carriages still steal the show. Made in Portugal, Italy, France, Austria and Spain, carriages range from the plain to the preposterous. One of the earliest is the comparatively simple 17th-century leather and wood coach of Philip II of Spain. As time goes by, the coaches become more sumptuous, the interiors lined with red velvet and gold, the exteriors carved and decorated with allegories and royal coats of arms. Three huge Baroque coaches made in Rome for the Portuguese ambassador to the Vatican Dom Rodrigo Almeida e Menezes, Marquês de Abrantes, are the epitome of pomp, embellished with life-size gilded statues.

Further examples of royal carriages include two-wheeled cabriolets, landaus and pony-drawn chaises used by young members of the royal family. The 18th-century Eyeglass Chaise, whose black leather hood is pierced by sinister eye-like windows, was made during the Pombal era *(p128)* when lavish decoration was discouraged. The museology, installed in 2017, presents interactive displays that give context to the collection.

> **Made in Portugal, Italy, France, Austria and Spain, carriages range from the plain to the preposterous.**

↑ Opulent carriages exhibited at the Museu Nacional dos Coches

STAY

Jerónimos 8

This sleek, modern hotel is at odds with its location in historic Belém, close to the monastery.

📍C9 🏠Rua dos Jerónimos 8
🌐jeronimos8.com

€€€

Altis Belém

Beside the Tagus river, this ultra-modern hotel has a Michelin-starred restaurant and rooftop pool with city views.

📍B10 🏠Doca do Bom Sucesso
🌐altishotels.com

€€€

Pestana Palace

The sumptuous interiors of this ornate palace are matched by lovely gardens with a pool and Chinese pavilion.

📍E8 🏠Rua Jau 54
🌐pestanapalace lisbon.com

€€€

Jardim Botânico Tropical

📍C9 🏠Largo do Jerónimos
📞213 921 808 🚌714, 727, 728, 729, 751 🚊15 🚇Belém
🕐10am-8pm daily (Oct-Mar: to 5pm) 🚫1 Jan, 24 & 25 Dec

Also known as the Jardim do Ultramar, this peaceful park with ponds, waterfowl and peacocks attracts surprisingly few visitors. Designed at the beginning of the 20th century as the research centre of the Institute for Tropical Sciences, it is more of an arboretum than a flower garden. The emphasis is on rare and endangered tropical and subtropical trees and plants. Among the most striking are dragon trees, native to the Canary Islands and Madeira, monkey puzzle trees from South America and a splendid avenue of Washington palms. A number of structures within the garden, including the large Chinese-style gateway and several sculptures by Manuel de Oliveira, date back to the Exhibition of the Portuguese World in 1940 (p118).

The research buildings are located in the neighbouring Palácio dos Condes da Calheta, whose interior walls are covered with *azulejos* that span

Did You Know?

Most of Belém's museums and historic buildings were built for the 1940 Lisbon Expo.

three centuries. Temporary exhibitions are held in the palace (closed for renovations).

Palácio de Belém

📍C9 🏠Praça Afonso de Albuquerque 🚌714, 727, 728, 729, 751 🚊15
🚇Belém 🕐Museu da Presidência da República: 10am-6pm Tue-Fri, 10am-1pm & 2-6pm Sat & Sun
🚫1 Jan, Easter, 1 May, 24 & 25 Dec; Palácio de Belém closed until further notice
🌐museu.presidencia.pt

Built by the Conde de Aveiras in 1559, before the Tagus had receded, this palace once had gardens bordering the river. In the 1700s it was bought by

Manicured gardens of the Palácio de Belém

João V, who made it suitably lavish for his amorous liaisons. When the 1755 earthquake struck, the king, José I, and his family were staying here and thus survived the devastation of central Lisbon. Fearing another tremor, the royal family temporarily set up camp in tents in the palace grounds, while the interior was used as a hospital. Today the elegant pink building is the official residence of the President of Portugal.

The Museu da Presidência da República holds personal items and state gifts of former presidents, as well as the official portrait gallery.

 6 🖉

Museu Nacional de Arqueologia

📍 B9 🏛 Praça do Império
🚌 714, 727, 728, 729, 751
🚊 15 🚉 Belém ⏰ For renovation until 2025
🌐 museunacional arqueologia.gov.pt

The west wing of the Mosteiro dos Jerónimos (p108), which was formerly the monks' dormitory, has been the National Archaeological Museum since 1906. Reconstructed in the middle of the 19th century, the building is a poor imitation of the Manueline original. The museum houses Portugal's main archaeological research centre and the exhibits, from sites all over the country, include a gold Iron Age bracelet, Visigothic jewellery found in the Alentejo in southern Portugal, Roman ornaments, fine Roman mosaics and early 8th-century Moorish artifacts.

The main Egyptian section, the biggest in Portugal, is particularly strong on funerary art, featuring figurines, masks, terracotta amulets and tombstones inscribed with hieroglyphics, dating from 6000 BCE.

In a dimly lit room, the exhibition "Treasures of Portuguese Archaeology" is full of exquisite gold and silver artifacts, including coins, necklaces, bracelets and other jewellery dating from 1800 BCE-5 DC. This room has been refurbished to allow more of the magnificent jewellery, unseen by the public for decades, to be displayed. In addition, the museum holds temporary exhibitions from time to time.

↑ The entrance to the Planetário de Marinha

 7 🖉

Planetário de Marinha

📍 B9 🏛 Praça do Império
🚌 727, 728, 751 🚊 15
🚉 Belém ⏰ Times vary, check website 🌐 ccm. marinha.pt/pt/planetario

Originally financed by the Gulbenkian Foundation (p122) and built in 1965, this modern building sits incongruously beside the Jerónimos monastery. Since 2021, it's been run by the Portuguese Navy, but there's still a wing dedicated to Gulbenkian's legacy. Inside, the planetarium reveals the mysteries of the cosmos. There are shows in Portuguese, English, Spanish and French explaining our solar system, as well as presentations on the constellations or the Star of Bethlehem (Belém). The Hubble Vision show includes stunning images provided by the orbital telescope.

> **The west wing of the Mosteiro dos Jerónimos, which was formerly the monks' dormitory, has been the National Archaeological Museum since 1906.**

8 🎫

Museu de Marinha

📍B9 🏛Praça do Império
🚌714, 727, 728, 729, 751
🚊15 🚋Belém ⏰10am–
6pm daily (Oct–Apr: to
5pm) 🚫1 Jan, Easter, 1 May,
25 Dec 🌐ccm.marinha.pt/
pt/museu

The Maritime Museum was
inaugurated in 1962 in the
west wing of the Jerónimos
monastery *(p108)*. It was here,
in the chapel built by Henry
the Navigator *(p328)*, that
mariners took Mass before
embarking on their voyages. A
hall devoted to the Discoveries
illustrates the progress in
shipbuilding from the mid-
15th century, capitalizing
on the experience of long-
distance explorers. Small
replicas show the transition
from the barque to the lateen-
rigged caravel, through the
faster square-rigged caravel,
to the Portuguese *nau.*

Also here are navigational
instruments, astrolabes
and replicas of 16th-century
maps showing the world
as it was known then. The
stone pillars, carved with
the Cross of the Knights of
Christ, are replicas of the
types of *padrão* set up as

Fine models of old
sailing ships on display
at the Museu de Marinha

monuments to Portuguese
sovereignty on the lands
they laid claim to.

A series of rooms
displaying models of mod-
ern Portuguese ships leads
on to the Royal Quarters,
where you can see the
exquisitely furnished wood-
panelled cabin of King Carlos
and Queen Amélia from the
royal yacht *Amélia*, built in
Scotland in 1900.

The modern, incongruous
pavilion opposite houses
original royal barges, the
most extravagant of which
is the royal brig built in 1780
for Maria I. The collection
ends with an exhibition
of seaplanes, including the
Santa Clara, which made
the first crossing of the
South Atlantic, from Lisbon
to Rio de Janeiro, in 1922.

MUSEU DOS DESCOBRIMENTOS

In 2017, the Museum of
Discoveries was pledged
as an addition to Lisbon's
existing monuments
dedicated to Portugal's
seafaring history. The
plan, proposed by mayor
Fernando Medina,
sparked debate among
locals and academics
alike, who feared
Portugal's role in the
trade of enslaved people
would not be covered
proportionally. Despite
the controversy over
the museum's name and
components, the project
is still set to go ahead.

9 🎫 🍴 💻 🛍

Centro Cultural de Belém

📍B9 🏛Praça do Império
🚌714, 727, 728, 729, 751
🚊15 🚋Belém ⏰8am–8pm
Mon–Fri, 10am–6pm Sat,
Sun & public hols 🌐ccb.pt

Standing between the Tagus
and the Jerónimos monastery,

this stark, modern building
was erected as the head-
quarters of the Portuguese
presidency of the European
Community. In 1993, it opened
as a cultural centre offering
performing arts, music and
photography. An exhibition
centre houses the Museu
Colecção Berardo *(p115)*.

Both the restaurant
and café spill out onto the
ramparts of the building,
whose peaceful gardens
look out over the quay
and the river.

10 🎫

Padrão dos Descobrimentos

📍C10 🏛Avenida de
Brasília 🚌727, 728
🚊15 🚋Belém ⏰10am–
7pm daily (Oct–Feb: to
6pm) 🚫1 Jan, 1 May, 24,
25 & 31 Dec 🌐padraodos
descobrimentos.pt

Standing prominently
on the Belém waterfront,
this huge angular struc-
ture, the Padrão dos
Descobrimentos (Monument
to the Discoveries), was built
in 1960 to mark the 500th
anniversary of the death
of Henry the Navigator.

The 52-m- (170-ft-) high monument, commissioned by the Salazar regime, commemorates the mariners, royal patrons and all those who took part in the development of the Portuguese Age of Discovery. The monument is designed in the shape of a caravel, with Portugal's coat of arms on the sides and the sword of the Royal House of Avis rising above the entrance. Henry the Navigator stands at the prow with a caravel in hand. In two sloping lines either side of the monument are stone statues of famous Portuguese people linked with the Age of Discovery, such as Dom Manuel I holding an armillary sphere, the poet Camões with a copy of *Os Lusíadas* and the painter Nuno Gonçalves. On the monument's north side, the huge mariner's compass cut into the paving stone was a gift from South Africa in 1960. The central map, dotted with mermaids and galleons, shows the routes of the sailors in the 15th and 16th centuries. Inside the monument a lift (there is a fee) whisks you up to the sixth floor where steps then lead to the top for a splendid panorama of Belém. The basement level is used for temporary exhibitions.

The Padrão is not to everyone's taste but the setting is undeniably splendid and the caravel design is imaginative. The monument looks particularly dramatic when viewed from the west in the light of the late afternoon sun.

11

Museu Colecção Berardo

📍 B9 🏛 Praça do Império
🚌 727, 728, 729, 751 🚋 15
🚇 Belém 🕐 10am–7pm daily 🌐 museuberardo.pt

The brainchild of business mogul and art collector José Manuel Rodrigues Berardo, this fascinating gallery, in the Centro Cultural de Belém, features around 1,000 works by more than 500 artists. The Museu Colecção Berardo provides a rich compendium of a century of modern and contemporary art through a variety of media, from canvas to sculpture and from photography to video installations.

Highlights include Pablo Picasso's *Tête de Femme* (1909), a good example of the Spanish artist's Cubist style; variants of Andy Warhol's famous *Brillo Box* (1964–8); and Jeff Koons' *Poodle* (1991). Other artists on show include Francis Bacon, Willem de Kooning and Henry Moore. Notable Portuguese art on display includes Alberto Carneiro's sculptures and etchings by Paula Rego.

← Padrão dos Descobrimentos, inaugurated in 1960

MAAT – Museu de Arte, Arquitetura e Tecnologia

🗺 D9 🏛 Avenida Brasília 🚌 727, 728, 729 🚋 15 🚈 Belém 🕐 10am-7pm Wed-Mon 🚫 1 Jan, 1 May, 24 & 25 Dec 🌐 maat.pt

With riverside views, the stylish Museu de Arte, Arquitetura e Tecnologia is operated by the EDP Foundation, and is dedicated to contemporary art, primarily Portuguese, along with modern architecture and technology. Popularly known as MAAT, the exhibits are housed in an award-winning building designed by the London-based architect Amanda Levete. Its structure is a sharp contrast to the well-known Lisbon power station, which stands next door and forms an integral part of this building complex. Visits to the MAAT can include a tour of the iconic power station, and access to the building's undulating pedestrian roof which affords stunning views of Lisbon and the Tagus river.

As well as cutting-edge temporary exhibitions, the museum also features the Pedro Cabrita Reis Collection, which consists of some 400 works by over 70 artists from the end of the 20th century.

 Colourful stained glass gracing the chapel of Ermida de São Jerónimo

Ermida de São Jerónimo

🗺 A8 🏛 Praça de Itália 📞 210 966 989 🚌 714, 728, 732, 751 🕐 Mon-Sat (by appt only)

Also known as the Capela de São Jerónimo, this little chapel was constructed in 1514 when Diogo Boitac was working on the Jerónimos monastery (p108). Although a far simpler building, it is also Manueline in style and may have been built to a design by Boitac. The only decorative elements on the monolithic chapel are the four pinnacles, corner gargoyles and Manueline portal. Perched on a quiet hill above Belém, the chapel has fine views.

Igreja da Memória

🗺 C8 🏛 Calçada do Galvão, Ajuda 📞 213 635 295 🚌 728, 732 🚋 18 🕐 For Mass: 6pm Mon-Sat, 10am Sun

Built in 1760, this church was founded by King José I in gratitude for his escape from an assassination plot on the site in 1758. The king was returning from a secret liaison with a lady of the noble Távora family when his carriage was attacked and a bullet hit him in the arm. Pombal (p128) used this as an excuse to get rid of his enemies in the Távora family, accusing them of conspiracy. In 1759 they were savagely tortured

 MAAT, housed in an innovative building beside the Tagus river

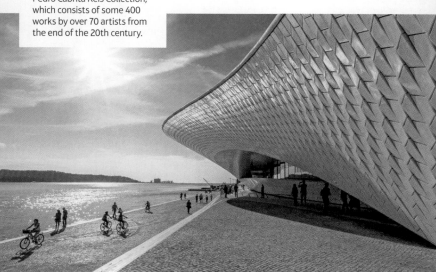

↑ Manicured formal gardens of the Jardim Botânico da Ajuda

and executed. Their deaths are commemorated by a pillar in Beco do Chão Salgado, off Rua de Belém.

The Neo-Classical domed church has a marble-clad interior and a small chapel, on the right, containing the tomb of Pombal, who died at the age of 83, a year after being banished from Lisbon.

15

Jardim Botânico da Ajuda

📍 C7 📍 Calçada da Ajuda
🚌 714, 727, 728, 729, 732
🚊 18 📅 Apr-Oct: 10am-5pm daily (to 6pm Sat & Sun), May-Sep: 10am-6pm daily (to 8pm Sat & Sun) 🚫 1 Jan, 25 Dec 🌐 isa.ulisboa.pt/jba

Laid out on two levels by Pombal in 1768, these Italian-

💬 INSIDER TIP
Plan(t) Ahead

To view a variety of plant specimens in the Jardim Botânico da Ajuda, head straight for the upper level. Here you can delight at the ancient dragon tree from Madeira and a sprawling *Schotia afra*.

style gardens provide a pleasant respite from the noisy suburbs of Belém. The entrance on Calçada da Ajuda (wrought-iron gates in a pink wall) is easy to miss. The park comprises 5,000 plant species from Africa, Asia and America. Notable features are the 400-year-old dragon tree, native of Madeira, and the flamboyant 18th-century fountain decorated with serpents, winged fish, sea horses and mythical creatures. A majestic terrace looks out over the lower level of the gardens.

16

Palácio Nacional da Ajuda

📍 D7 📍 Largo da Ajuda
🚌 732, 742, 760 🚊 18
📅 10am-6pm Fri-Wed (last adm 5:30pm) 🚫 1 Jan, Easter, 1 May, 13 Jun, 25 Dec
🌐 patrimoniocultural.gov.pt

The royal palace, which was in fact destroyed by fire in 1795, was replaced in the early 19th century by this magnificent Neo-Classical building set around a large quadrangle. It was left incomplete when the royal family was forced into exile in Brazil in 1807, following the invasion of Portugal.

Did You Know?

In the Palácio Nacional da Ajuda's collection are 2,000 household objects, from kitchen- to picnic-ware.

The palace only became a permanent residence of the royal family when Luís I became king in 1861 and married an Italian Princess, Maria Pia di Savoia. No expense was spared in furnishing the apartments, which are decorated with silk wallpaper, Sèvres porcelain and crystal chandeliers.

A prime example of regal excess is the extraordinary Saxe Room in which every piece of furniture is decorated with Meissen porcelain. On the first floor the huge Banqueting Hall, with an allegory of the birth of João VI on the frescoed ceiling, is truly impressive. At the other end of the palace, Luís I's Neo-Gothic painting studio is a more intimate display of intricately carved furniture. Meanwhile, the renovated west wing is home to the Museu do Tesouro Real, a museum which showcases a collection of Portugal's crown jewels.

A SHORT WALK
BELÉM

Distance 1.5 km (1 mile) **Nearest station** Mosteiro dos Jerónimos tram stop **Time** 25 minutes

Portugal's former maritime glory, expressed in imposing, exuberant buildings such as the Jerónimos monastery, is evident everywhere in Belém. Silted up since the days of the caravels, this picturesque area along the waterfront was restructured at Salazar's (p46) insistence, in an attempt to revive awareness of and celebrate the country's prosperity. A stroll here is consequently littered with historically significant sights: Praça do Império was laid out for the 1940 Exhibition of the Portuguese World, while Praça Afonso de Albuquerque was dedicated to Portugal's first viceroy of India. The Palácio de Belém, restored in the 18th century, briefly housed the royal family after the earthquake of 1755.

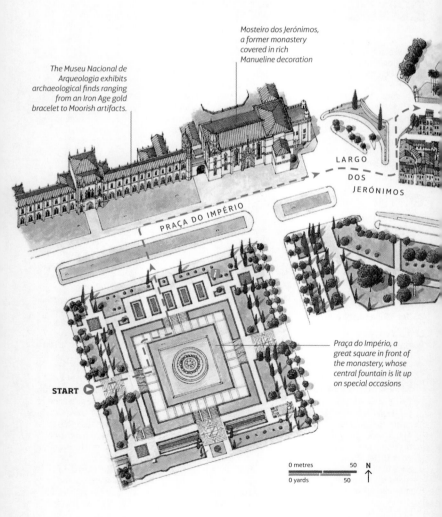

The Museu Nacional de Arqueologia exhibits archaeological finds ranging from an Iron Age gold bracelet to Moorish artifacts.

Mosteiro dos Jerónimos, a former monastery covered in rich Manueline decoration

LARGO DOS JERÓNIMOS

PRAÇA DO IMPÉRIO

Praça do Império, a great square in front of the monastery, whose central fountain is lit up on special occasions

START

0 metres   50
0 yards   50
N

Locator Map
For more detail see p106

↑ The vaulted arcades
of the Manueline cloister of
Mosteiro dos Jerónimos

*Jardim Botânico Tropical,
peaceful gardens filled
with plants and trees
gathered from Portugal's
former colonies*

*The Museu da Presidência, set
inside a former royal palace,
houses a collection of items
related to the country's past
presidents, whose official
residence is attached to
the museum.*

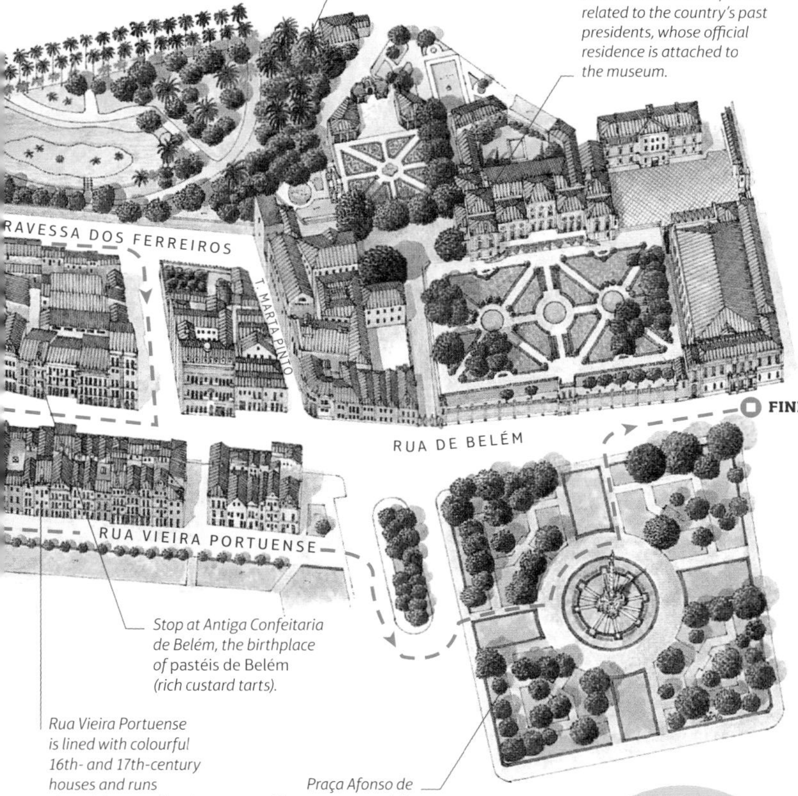

○ **FINISH**

*Stop at Antiga Confeitaria
de Belém, the birthplace
of pastéis de Belém
(rich custard tarts).*

*Rua Vieira Portuense
is lined with colourful
16th- and 17th-century
houses and runs
alongside a small park.*

*Praça Afonso de
Albuquerque, a public
square with a central
Neo-Manueline statue of
the first Portuguese
viceroy of India, after
whom the space is named*

Did You Know?

Manuel I granted the
Mosteiro dos Jerónimos
to the Hieronymite
order, said to protect
kings after death.

The Cristo Rei sculpture glimpsed through the red towers of the Ponte 25 de Abril

BEYOND
THE CENTRE

Away from the city centre, Lisbon unfolds in a blend of residential sprawl, industrial parks and the remnants of ancient villages. Older sights include the manicured Parque Eduardo VII to the north, and the 16th-century, tile-fronted Palácio Fronteira to the northwest.

Most of Lisbon's outlying suburbs originated much later, however, with several Salazar-era buildings and structures – such as the vast Cristo Rei – springing up during the mid-20th century.

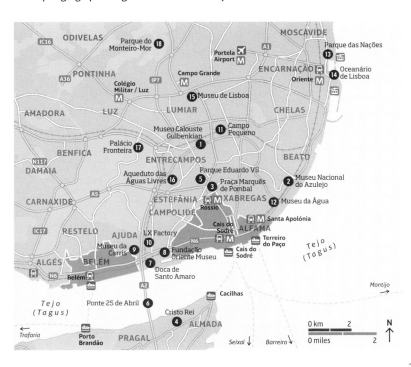

① 🎨 🍴 🖥 🛍

MUSEU CALOUSTE GULBENKIAN

📍 Avenida de Berna 45A 🚌 713, 716, 726, 742, 746, 756 Ⓜ Praça de Espanha or São Sebastião 🕐 10am–6pm Wed–Mon (free Sun after 2pm) 🚫 1 Jan, Easter, 1 May, 24 & 25 Dec; Modern Collection closed for renovations 🌐 gulbenkian.pt/museu

Thanks to wealthy Armenian oil magnate Calouste Gulbenkian's wide-ranging tastes and his eye for a masterpiece, this museum has one of the finest collections of art in Europe.

The museum's works are split across two separately housed collections, linked by a serene stretch of urban park. The Founder's Collection – Gulbenkian's personal pieces – sits within a purpose-built museum dating from 1969, with varied exhibits ranging from ancient Egyptian statuettes to an astonishing array of René Lalique Art Nouveau jewellery. South of the gardens stands the Modern Collection, widely considered to be the world's most complete collection of modern Portuguese art. Standard tickets allow access to both collections, while the sculpture-dotted gardens can be explored free of charge.

CALOUSTE GULBENKIAN

Born in Scutari in 1869, Gulbenkian started his art collection at the age of 14, when he bought some ancient coins in a bazaar. In 1928, he was granted a 5 per cent stake in four major oil companies, earning himself the nickname "Mr Five Percent". With the wealth he accumulated, Gulbenkian was able to indulge his love of fine art. During World War II, he went to live in neutral Portugal, and bequeathed his estate to his adopted nation upon his death in 1955.

6,000

Artworks were amassed by Gulbenkian in his personal collection.

1 The blocky concrete building in which the Founder's Collection is housed.

2 This fine marble statue of Diana, goddess of the hunt, is part of the Founder's Collection.

3 The spacious galleries of the Founder's Collection.

↑ Exhibits within the museum's extensive Modern Collection

FOUNDER'S COLLECTION

Ranking alongside the Museu de Arte Antiga (p92) as the finest museum in Lisbon, the Founder's Collection exhibits are displayed in spacious and well-lit galleries, many overlooking the gardens or courtyards. The exhibits span over 4,000 years from ancient Egyptian figurines, through translucent Islamic glassware, to Art Nouveau brooches. Although the museum is not large, each work of art is worthy of attention.

In the Egyptian, Classical and Mesopotamian gallery priceless treasures chart the evolution of Egyptian art from the Old Kingdom (c.2700 BCE)

to the Roman period (from the 1st century BCE). Outstanding pieces in the Classical art section include a magnificent red-figure Greek vase and a Roman satyr's head from the 2nd century CE.

The museum's Eastern art is also remarkable. Being Armenian, Gulbenkian had a keen interest in works from the Near and Middle East, resulting in a fine collection of Persian and Turkish carpets, textiles, costumes and ceramics in the Eastern Islamic gallery. In terms of Eastern pieces, there is a large collection of Chinese porcelain acquired by Gulbenkian between 1907 and 1947. One of the rarest pieces is a small blue-glazed bowl from the Yuan Dynasty (1271–1368).

The carefully plotted route around the

↑ Rembrandt's *Portrait of an Old Man* (1645), a masterclass in light and shade

museum ends with a room filled with the flamboyant Art Nouveau creations of French jeweller René Lalique (1860–1945). Gulbenkian was a close friend of Lalique's and acquired many of the pieces on display directly from the artist. Inlaid with semiprecious stones and covered with enamel or gold leaf, the ornate collection constitutes a spectacular finish to this unique and incredibly diverse museum.

← Porcelain vases on display within the Founder's Collection

↑ Visitor wandering the galleries of the Founder's Collection

FOUNDER'S COLLECTION PIECES

St Catherine
A serene 15th-century bust painted by the Flemish artist Rogier van der Weyden.

Boy Blowing Bubbles
Édouard Manet's 1867 painting considers the transience of life and art.

Yuan Dynasty Stem Cup
This blue-glazed piece is decorated with delicate reliefs of Taoist figures under bamboo leaves.

Diana Statue
A graceful marble statue (p123) once owned by Catherine the Great and considered too obscene to exhibit.

Ancient Greek Vase
This 5th-century BCE vase is adorned with mythological motifs.

Busts on display in the Modern Collection ↑

MODERN COLLECTION

The Modern Collection lies across the gardens from the Founder's Collection and is part of the same cultural foundation. It is housed in a large, light-filled building designed by architect Sir Leslie Martin in 1983.

The permanent collection features over 10,000 works, with an emphasis on paintings and sculpture by Portuguese artists from the turn of the 20th century to the present day. Perhaps the most famous painting is the striking portrait of poet Fernando Pessoa in the Café Irmãos Unidos (1964) by José de Almada Negreiros (1893–1970), a leading exponent of Portuguese Modernism. The oil painting was com-missioned by the Calouste Gulbenkian Foundation, and intended to replicate a similar portrait that Almada had produced for the café itself.

Also of interest are paintings by Eduardo Viana (1881–1967), Amadeo de Sousa Cardoso (1887–1910) and contemporary artists such as Rui Sanches, Graça Morais, Teresa Magalhães

and – perhaps the best known – Paula Rego (1935–2022). Rego settled in London in the mid-1970s, but she was hailed in Portugal as one of the nation's greatest artists. Her work often contained elements of magical realism, although later works have gradually tended towards more realistic renderings.

Within the international collection are works by big hitters such as David Hockney and British sculptor Antony Gormley (renowned for his *Angel of the North* sculpture in Gateshead, England).

As well as the exhibition space, which comprises three linked galleries, there is also an events area, a busy café and a museum bookshop.

Did You Know?

Paula Rego's pieces have fetched up to £1.1 million at auction, a record for a Portuguese artist.

PICTURE PERFECT
Manueline Cloister

Set around a central courtyard, the cloister is a serene spot. Its delicate columns and carved vaulted walkways are the perfect place to point your lens.

MUSEU NACIONAL DO AZULEJO

🏠 Rua da Madre de Deus 4 🚌 718, 728, 742, 759, 794 🕐 10am–1pm & 2–6pm Tue–Sun 🚫 Mon, public hols 🌐 patrimoniocultural.gov.pt

Housed in a beautiful 16th-century convent, the National Tile Museum offers an unmatched display of this uniquely Portuguese art form, with *azulejos* dating from the 15th century right through to the present day.

Dona Leonor, widow of King João II, founded the Convento da Madre de Deus in 1509. Built in Manueline style, restorations of the church under João III and João V added its simple Renaissance designs and striking Baroque decoration. The stunning convent cloisters are now home to the National Tile Museum. Decorative panels and individual tiles trace the evolution of tile-making from its Moorish roots, up to the current Portuguese art form. The walls of the restaurant are lined with 19th-century tiles depicting hanging game, from wild boar and pheasants to fish.

Did You Know?

The word *azulejo* has Arabic roots – it means "small polished stone".

↑ Fine 17th-century tiles
patterning the cloister,
from the original convent

1 The church's Manueline
portal was recreated from
a 16th-century painting.

2 The 16th-century church
of Madre de Deus acquired
its sumptuous interiors
under João V. The Rococo
altarpiece was added after
the earthquake of 1755.

3 On the top floor, a striking
18th-century panorama
depicts Lisbon before the
1755 earthquake.

EXPERIENCE MORE

❸
Praça Marquês de Pombal

 711, 712, 720 & many other routes Ⓜ Marquês de Pombal

At the top of Avenida da Liberdade (p82), traffic thunders round the "Rotunda" (roundabout), as the *praça* is also known. At the centre is a lofty 1934 monument to Pombal. The despotic states-man, who virtually ruled Portugal from 1750 to 1777, stands on the top of the column, his hand on a lion (a symbol of power) and his eyes directed down to the Baixa, whose creation he masterminded. Allegorical images depicting Pombal's political, educational and agricultural reforms decorate the base of the monument. Although greatly feared, this controversial politician propelled the country into the Age of Enlightenment. Broken blocks of stone at the foot of the monument and tidal waves flooding the city are an allegory of the destruction caused by the 1755 earthquake.

Nearby, the well-tended Parque Eduardo VII extends northwards behind the square. The paving stones around the Rotunda are dec-orated with a mosaic of Lisbon's coat of arms. Many of the city's sightseeing operators have their main pick-up located at the bottom of Parque Eduardo VII. There is also a multilingual booth where visitors can buy tickets and plan excursions.

❹
Cristo Rei

🏠 Santuário Nacional do Cristo Rei, Alto do Pragal, Almada 🚢 from Cais do Sodré to Cacilhas, then 🚌 101 🕐 10am-7pm daily (winter: to 6pm) 🌐 cristorei.pt

Modelled on the Cristo Redentor in Rio de Janeiro, Brazil, this giant-sized statue stands with arms outstretched on the south bank of the Tagus river. The impressive 28-m- (92-ft-) tall figure of Christ, mounted on an 82-m (269-ft) pedestal, was sculpted by Francisco Franco in 1949–59 at the instigation of Prime Minister Salazar.

You can see the monument from various viewpoints in the city, but it is fun to take a ferry from Cais do Sodré to the Margem Sul (the south bank, which until recently was usually simply known as the Outra Banda, or "other bank"), then a bus or taxi to the monument. A lift, plus some

⛰ GREAT VIEW
River Vistas

Take the passenger ferry from Cais do Sodré across the Tagus to the little port of Cacilhas, where you'll find many riverfront seafood restaurants and great views of Lisbon back across the water.

↑ The mammoth Cristo Rei statue, soaring high into the sky

↑ Expansive views of the city from the *miradouro* of Parque Eduardo VII

steps take you up 82 m (269 ft) to the top of the pedestal, affording fine views of the city and river below.

5

Parque Eduardo VII

Praça Marquês de Pombal
218 170 996 711, 712, 720 Marquês de Pombal
Estufa Fria: 10am-7pm daily (Nov-Mar: 9am-5pm)
1 Jan, 1 May, 25 Dec

Central Lisbon's largest park was named in honour of King Edward VII of the United Kingdom, who came to Lisbon in 1902 to reaffirm the Anglo-Portuguese alliance.

The wide, grassy slope, which extends for 62 acres (25 ha), was laid out as Parque da Liberdade, a continuation of Avenida da Liberdade *(p82)* in the late 19th century. Neatly clipped box hedging, flanked by mosaic-patterned walkways, stretches uphill from the Praça Marquês de Pombal to a belvedere at the top. Here you will find a flower-filled garden dedicated to the memory of renowned Portuguese *fado* singer Amália Rodrigues, and a pleasant

café. The vantage point at the summit of the park offers fine, sweeping views of the city. On clear days you can see as far as the Serra da Arrábida, a nature reserve located 40 km (25 miles) from the city centre *(p161)*.

Situated in the northwest corner, the most inspiring feature of this park is the jungle-like Estufa Fria, or greenhouse, where tropical plants, streams and waterfalls provide serene respite from the city streets. At this urban oasis there are in fact three greenhouses: in the Estufa Fria (cold greenhouse), palms push through the slatted bamboo roof and paths wind through a forest of ferns, fuchsias, flowering shrubs and banana trees; the warmer Estufa Quente and Estufa Doce are filled with tropical plants, water-lily ponds and impressive cactuses.

Near the *estufas* a pond with large carp and a galleon-shaped play area are popular with children. On the east side, the Pavilhão Carlos Lopes, named after the 1984 Olympic marathon winner, was extensively refurbished in 2016 and is now used for concerts, exhibitions and conferences.

↑ Ponte 25 de Abril illuminated at night, with the city lights behind

6
Ponte 25 de Abril

 For Pillar 7: tram 15, bus 714, 727, 732, 751, 756

Once called the Ponte Salazar after the dictator who had it built in 1966, Lisbon's suspension bridge was renamed to commemorate the revolution of 25 April 1974 that restored democracy to Portugal (p47).

Inspired by San Francisco's Golden Gate Bridge in the US, this steel construction stretches for 2 km (1 mile). The lower tier was modified in 1999 to accommodate the Fertagus, a railway across the Tagus. The bridge's notorious traffic

congestion has been partly resolved by the opening of the 11-km (7-mile) Vasco da Gama bridge, which spans the Tagus river from Montijo to Sacavém, north of the Parque das Nações.

7
Doca de Santo Amaro

714, 727, 732, 751, 756
15 Alcântara-Mar

In the early 1930s, Lisbon's docks at Alcântara were the city's main access point. As the importance of the docks declined, the once-industrial riverside has been opened up.

One of the best places to head for is the Doca de Santo Amaro, a largely enclosed dock that sits below the humming traffic of the dramatic Ponte 25 de Abril. The inner edge of the docks is lined with former warehouses, converted in the 1990s and now housing cafés, restaurants and bars with fine views over the water. These tend to be popular, and tables on the outside terraces get snapped up quickly.

Beneath the bridge to the west of the docks is a strange,

 GREAT VIEW
Ponte 25 de Abril

For a unique experience take the lift up Pillar 7 of this landmark bridge, which offers unbroken views across the river and the city's south bank from 80 m (262 ft) above the waves. Tickets cost around €5.

Brisé fan from China in the Fundação Oriente Museu

boomerang-shaped structure, designed to stop falling debris. Continue past this and it's a nice 20-minute walk to Belém.

Fundação Oriente Museu

📍 Avenida Brasília, Doca de Alcântara Norte 🚌 712, 714, 728, 738, 742 🕙 10am-6pm Tue-Sun (to 8pm Fri) 🌐 museudooriente.pt

This museum and cultural centre is dedicated to showing the historical and cultural links between Portugal and its former colonies in the East.

The permanent exhibition is split into two collections. The Portuguese Presence in Asia has a selection of exhibits ranging from furniture and jewellery to porcelain, paintings and textiles. Highlights include 17th- and 18th-century Chinese and Japanese folding screens and some rare examples of Namban art – Portuguese-influenced Japanese art of the 16th and 17th centuries.

The second exhibition is the Kwok On Collection, which features the performing arts of a vast geographic area extending from Turkey to Japan. It includes fine masks from Asia and a section on shadow theatre and puppetry from India, China and Indonesia.

Museu da Carris

📍 Rua 1 de Maio 🚌 714, 727, 732 🕙 10am-1pm & 2-6pm Mon-Sat 🌐 museu.carris.pt

Carris is the company that runs Lisbon's surface public transport and this engaging museum details the history of a system that has had to negotiate a broad river estuary and some serious hills since 1872.

Set in a sprawling former tram depot, the museum is divided into three zones. The first uses various exhibits to trace the development of Lisbon's public transport. You can then take a fun trip on a tram to the other two zones, which are filled with historic trams and buses, including early horse-drawn varieties.

Down by the river at the bottom of the site, a collection of old shipping containers and double-decker buses make up Village Underground, an innovative work space for Lisbon's creative set.

LX Factory

📍 Rua Rodrigues Faria 103 🚌 742, 751, 756, 760 🌐 lxfactory.com

Virtually beneath the Ponte 25 de Abril in a slightly shabby part of town, LX Factory is one of the hippest places in Lisbon. The complex is inside a huge former textiles plant, with the warehouses, factory spaces and courtyards transformed into studios and workshops for the arts, fashion and creative media. Woven among them are innovative cafés, bars, restaurants and shops. Visit on Sunday morning when a lively flea market takes place.

Shelves stacked to the ceiling at a book-shop in LX Factory ↑

Neo-Moorish façade
of the bullring in
Campo Pequeno ↑

Campo Pequeno

🚌727, 736 Ⓜ Campo
🕐Shopping centre:
10am–11pm daily

This square is dominated by
the red-brick Neo-Moorish
bullring built in the late 19th
century. The building has
undergone development, and
a car park and leisure centre
have been added. Much of
the bullring's distinctive
architecture, such as keyhole-
shaped windows and double
cupolas, have been retained.

Museu da Água

🏛Rua do Alviela 12 ☎218
100 215 🚌735 🕐10am–
12:30pm & 1:30–5:30pm
Tue–Sun 🔒Public hols

Dedicated to the history of
Lisbon's water supply, this
informative museum was
imaginatively created around
the city's first steam pumping
station. It commemorates
Manuel da Maia, the 18th-
century engineer behind the
Águas Livres aqueduct (p134).

Pride of place goes to four
lovingly preserved steam
engines, one of which still
functions (by electricity). The
development of technology

relating to the city's water
supply is documented with
photographs. Particularly interesting is the exhibit on the
Alfama's 17th-century Chafariz
d'El Rei, one of Lisbon's first
fountains. Locals used to queue
at one of six founts, depending on their social status.

Parque das Nações

🏛Avenida Dom João ll
🚌705, 725, 728, 744, 750,
782 Ⓜ Oriente 🚆Oriente
🕐Park: 24 hours daily;
Pavilhão do Conhecimento:
10am–6pm Tue–Fri, 10am–
7pm Sat & Sun 🔒1 Jan, 24,
25 & 31 Dec 🌐portaldas
nacoes.pt

Originally the site of Expo 98,
Parque das Nações is now a
Lisbon hub. With its contemporary architecture and
family-oriented attractions,
the area has renewed the
eastern waterfront, which was
once an industrial wasteland.
The soaring geometry of
the platform canopies over
Santiago Calatrava's Oriente
Station set the architectural
tone. The Portugal Pavillion
has a large reinforced concrete
roof suspended like a sailcloth
above its forecourt.

Pavilhão do Conhecimento –
Ciencia Viva is a fascinating

Did You Know?

The Vasco da Gama
bridge (near the Parque
das Nações) is Europe's
longest, stretching
17 km (11 miles).

modern museum of science
and technology that houses
several interactive exhibitions.

Spectacular views can be
had from the cable car that
links the Torre Vasco da Gama
with the marina. The promenade along the river also offers
delightful views, including of
the Vasco da Gama bridge. Also
in the area is the Altice Arena, a
multi-purpose venue that
was built for Expo 98.

Oceanário de Lisboa

🏛Esplanada D Carlos 1,
Parque das Nações 🚌705,
725, 728, 744, 750, 782
Ⓜ Oriente 🚆Oriente
🕐10am–8pm daily
🌐oceanario.pt

The main attraction at Parque
das Nações, the oceanarium
was designed by American
architect Peter Chermayeff and

> **The aquarium's central tank has a variety of fish, large and small. Sharks co-exist peaceably with bream in the softly lit waters.**

is perched on the end of a pier. It holds an impressive array of species – birds and some mammals as well as fish and other underwater dwellers.

Landscapes represent the habitats of the Atlantic, Pacific, Indian and Antarctic oceans, with suitable fauna and flora. The aquarium's central tank has a variety of fish, large and small. Sharks coexist peaceably with bream in the softly lit waters.

---

 ⑮

Museu de Lisboa

🏛 Campo Grande 245
🚌 701, 736, 750 Ⓜ Campo Grande ◷ 10am-6pm Tue-Sun ◷ 1 Jan, 1 May, 25 Dec
🌐 museudelisboa.pt

The Museum of Lisbon is set in a summer palace, which is framed by the remains of an old manor farm. The palace was built between 1734 and 1746, at the request of Diogo de Sousa Mexia; the architect

Visitors watching the fish in the central tank at Oceanário de Lisboa ↓

is unknown. When the mansion was built, it occupied a quiet site outside the city. Today it has to contend with the traffic of Campo Grande. The house itself retains its period charm.

The displays follow the development of the city, from prehistoric times through the Romans, Visigoths and Moors, traced by means of drawings, tiles, paintings, models and historical documents. Notable exhibits are those depicting the city before the earthquake of 1755, including a highly detailed model made in the 1950s and an impressive 17th-century oil painting by Dirk Stoop (1610–86) of *Terreiro do Paço*, as Praça do Comércio was known then (*p78*). There are also pictures of the city amid the devastation and various plans for its reconstruction.

One room is devoted to the Águas Livres aqueduct (*p134*), with architectural plans as well as prints and watercolours of the completed aqueduct.

Another room represents the 20th century with a large colour poster celebrating the Revolution of 1910 and the proclamation of the new republic (*p47*).

EAT

Eleven
Michelin-star dining and stunning city views are on offer at this airy, modern restaurant. Opt for an à la carte or a tasting menu. The "Eleven Menu", which features the chef's signature creations, is a popular choice.

🏛 Rua Marquês da Fronteira, Jardim Amália Rodrigues ◷ Sun 🌐 restaurant eleven.com

 €€€

Restaurante Farol
This centuries-old establishment is the best-known seafood restaurant in Cacilhas. Foodies seek out this spot for its tasty lobsters, great views across the Tagus river and fine-tasting beer.

🏛 Largo Alfredo Dinis 1, Cacilhas 🌐 restaurante farol.com

 €€€

Pastelaria Versailles
A wonderful array of cakes and pastries are on offer at this traditional café, which dates from the early 1920s. Good-value lunches are also served, while the decadent, cream-topped hot chocolate makes a tasty treat on chilly afternoons.

🏛 Avenida da República 15a, Saldanha 📞 213 546 340

 €€€

Imposing arches of ↑
the Aqueduto das
Águas Livres

Aqueduto das Águas Livres

📍 Best seen from Calçada da Quintinha 🚌 774, 783
🕐 10am–5:30pm Tue–Sun; Mãe d'Água das Amoreiras: 10am–1:30pm Tue–Sun
🚫 Public hols

Considered the most beautiful sight in Lisbon at the turn of the 20th century, the impressive structure of the Aqueduto das Águas Livres looms over the Alcântara valley northwest of the city. The construction of an aqueduct gave João V (p45) an opportunity to indulge his passion for grandiose building schemes, as the only area of Lisbon with fresh drinking water was the Alfama. A tax on meat, wine, olive oil and other comestibles funded the project, and although not complete until the 19th century, it was already supplying the city with water by 1748. The main pipeline measures 19 km (12 miles), but the total length, including all the secondary channels, is 58 km (36 miles). The most visible part of this imposing structure is the 35 arches crossing the Alcântara valley, the tallest of which rise 65 m (213 ft) above the city.

It is possible to take guided tours over the Alcântara arches. There are also tours of the Mãe d'Água reservoir and trips to the Mãe d'Água springs. Contact the Museu da Água (p132) for details of the trips.

At the end of the aqueduct, the Mãe d'Água das Amoreiras is a castle-like building that served as a reservoir for the water supplied from the aqueduct. Today the space is used for art exhibitions, fashion shows and other events.

Did You Know?

Aqueduto das Águas Livres only stopped supplying water for human consumption in the 1960s.

visible in the distance, it still occupies a quiet spot, by the Parque Florestal de Monsanto. Both house and garden have *azulejo* decoration whose subjects include battle scenes and trumpet-blowing monkeys.

Although the palace is still occupied by the 13th marquis, some of the living rooms and the library, as well as the formal gardens, are included in the tour. The Battles Room has tiled panels depicting scenes of the War of Restoration (1640–68), with a detail of João de Fronteira fighting a Spanish general. It was his loyalty to Pedro II in this war that earned him the title of Marquês. Interesting comparisons can be made between these naive 17th-century Portuguese tiles and the Delft ones from the same period in the dining room, depicting naturalistic scenes. The dining room is also decorated with frescoed panels and portraits of Portuguese nobility.

The late 16th-century chapel is the oldest part of the house. The façade is adorned with stones, shells, broken glass and bits of china. These fragments of crockery are believed to have been used

Palácio Fronteira

📍 Largo São Domingos de Benfica 1 🚌 770 Ⓜ Jardim Zoológico 🚃 Benfica
🕐 Palace by tour only Jun–Sep: 10:30am, 11am, 11:30am, noon; Oct–May: 11am, noon; Gardens: 10am–5pm Mon–Fri (to 1pm Sat; last adm 12:30pm)
🚫 Sun, public hols
🌐 fronteira-alorna.pt

This country manor house was built as a hunting pavilion for João de Mascarenhas, the first Marquês de Fronteira, in 1640. Although skyscrapers are

INSIDER TIP
Catch a Match

Two of Europe's leading football clubs play in Lisbon: Sporting Lisbon launched the career of Cristiano Ronaldo, while Benfica have two European Cups to their name. Buy tickets at the stadiums or online.

at the feast inaugurating the palace and then smashed to ensure no one else could sup off the same set. Visits to the garden start at the chapel terrace, where tiled niches are decorated with figures personifying the arts and mythological creatures.

In the formal Italian garden the immaculate box hedges are cut into shapes to represent the seasons of the year. To one end, tiled scenes of dashing knights on horseback, representing ancestors of the Fronteira family, are reflected in the waters of a large tank. On either side of the water, a grand staircase leads to a terrace above. Here, decorative niches contain the busts of

Portuguese kings and colourful majolica reliefs adorn the arcades. More blue-and-white tiled scenes, realistic and allegorical, decorate the wall at the far end of the garden.

18

Parque do Monteiro-Mor

Largo Júlio Castilho ☎217 567 620 🚌703, 736, 796 Ⓜ Lumiar ⏰Park: 10am–1pm & 2–6pm Tue–Sun

Monteiro-Mor park was sold to the state in 1975 and the 18th-century palace buildings were converted to museums. The gardens are attractive; Much of the land is wooded, though the area around the museums has gardens with flowering shrubs, duck ponds and tropical trees.

The slightly old-fashioned **Museu Nacional do Traje** (Costume Museum) has a

vast collection of textiles, accessories and costumes worn by people of note.

The **Museu Nacional do Teatro** has two buildings, one devoted to temporary exhibitions, the other containing a small permanent collection. Photographs, posters and cartoons feature famous 20th-century Portuguese actors – one section is focused on famous *fado* singer Amália Rodrigues (*p36*).

Museu Nacional do Traje
⏰10am–1pm & 2–6pm 🚫1 Jan, Easter, 1 May, 13 Jun, 25 Dec 🌐patrimoniocultural.gov.pt

Museu Nacional do Teatro
⏰10am–1pm & 2–6pm Tue–Sun 🚫1 Jan, Easter, 1 May, 13 Jun, 25 Dec 🌐patrimoniocultural.gov.pt

Tiled terrace of the Palácio Fronteira's chapel, and *(inset)* its beautiful sculptures ↓

CENTRAL
PORTUGAL

The town of Coimbra, dominated by its hilltop university

EXPLORE
CENTRAL
PORTUGAL

This section divides Central Portugal into three colour-coded
sightseeing areas, as shown on this map. Find out more
about each area on the following pages.

Atlantic
Ocean

Praia de Mira

Monten
o-Velh

Figueira da Foz

São Pedro de Muel

LEIRIA

Leiria

Batalha

Nazaré

São Martinho
do Porto

Alcobaça

Peniche

ESTREMADURA
AND RIBATEJO
p166

Óbidos

Rio Maior

Lourinhã

Santarém

Torres
Vedras

Alenquer

Ericeira

Mafra

Alverca

Vila Franca
de Xira

Tejo (Tag)

LISBOA

Colares

Sintra

Alcochete

LISBON

THE
LISBON COAST
p144

Costa da
Caparica

Setúbal

Tróia

Sesimbra

Baía de
Setúbal

PORTUGAL

GETTING TO KNOW
CENTRAL
PORTUGAL

A varied landscape lies between Portugal's capital and Porto. Forested hills overlook wild waves on the Lisbon coast, while Estremadura and the Ribatejo mix empty beaches and quaint fishing villages with lush farmland. Further north, the Beiras is home to the vine-clad valleys of the Dão wine region, bleak highlands and fortress towns.

PAGE 144

THE LISBON COAST

Breathtaking beaches and fairy-tale castles seem a world away from the hustle and bustle of the capital, but it is only an hour's drive to the Lisbon Coast. The resorts of Costa da Caparica and Sesimbra, sheltered by the verdant Serra da Arrábida, lie to the south, while to the north you'll find the wooded slopes of Sintra, dotted with stunning summer palaces. It is not hard to see how the town inspired Hans Christian Andersen's fairy tales or why Lord Byron proclaimed it a "glorious Eden". The coast is also a surfers' paradise as fierce Atlantic waves batter the area around Ericeira.

Best for
Hilltop palaces and fashionable resorts

Home to
Palácio Nacional da Pena, Palácio Nacional de Queluz, Palácio Nacional de Sintra

Experience
Arroz de marisco, a flavoursome seafood rice, at a seafront restaurant

ESTREMADURA AND RIBATEJO

Between the Tagus and the coast lie the rolling hills, rugged cliffs and sandy beaches of Estremadura. In contrast, vineyard-strewn Ribatejo is a vast alluvial plain lying along the riverbanks. Here, Portugal's finest medieval monasteries bear witness to an illustrious, if turbulent, past. Ancient Tomar and picture-perfect Óbidos are congenial bases from which to visit the great abbey at Batalha or the modern shrine at Fátima. There are beach resorts aplenty, too.

Best for
Historic buildings and buffeted beaches

Home to
Alcobaça, Batalha's Mosteiro de Santa Maria da Vitória, Tomar's Convento de Cristo

Experience
A surfing lesson at Baleal, the ideal spot for beginners

THE BEIRAS

Ranging from the Spanish frontier to the sea, the Beiras is a bulwark between the cool green north and the parched south. Here you'll find the country's highest mountains in the Serra da Estrela, the flat salt marshes of the Ria de Aveiro and the busy seaside resort of Figueira da Foz. Use the stately old university city of Coimbra as a base for visiting the Roman ruins of Conímbriga and the magical forest of Buçaco, with its crumbling grottoes. Inland, the charming town of Viseu is an ideal stopover on the way to the medieval strongholds of Guarda, Almeida and Monsanto.

Best for
Unspoiled, mountainous terrain

Home to
Aveiro, Coimbra and its university, Buçaco, Serra da Estrela

Experience
A boat trip in a colourful moliceiro on Aveiro's atmospheric waterways

With palaces, beaches and traditional villages to see, journey out from the captivating capital to explore the heart of Central Portugal.

7 DAYS

In Central Portugal

Day 1

Morning From Lisbon, head north on the A37 to hilltop Sintra *(p148)*. The conical chimneys of the 14th-century Palácio Nacional de Sintra *(p150)* herald the pastel-hued old town, which is surrounded by dewy forests.

Afternoon Enjoy a light lunch at Saudade *(p159)*. The jungle-like gardens of Monserrate *(p158)* on the N247 were immortalized in Lord Byron's *Childe Harold's Pilgrimage*. It's not hard to see why he was inspired by them. Return to Sintra to spend the night at the modern Moon Hill Hostel *(p157)*.

Day 2

Morning Start the day with a visit to the amazing 19th-century Palácio Nacional da Pena *(p152)*, the bizarre former summer retreat of Portuguese royalty. Don't forget to explore Parque da Pena *(p149)* – the romantic woodlands – which is home to quaint little grottoes. Your next stop is the former fishing village of Ericeira *(p157)*, which is a 40-minute drive away on the N247.

Afternoon Have lunch at one of Ericeira's fine fish restaurants before spending the rest of the day relaxing on the beach. The Praça da Rebública is always buzzing with the sounds of revelry in the evening.

Day 3

Morning After exploring the winding alleys of whitewashed Ericeira, drive the coastal N247 north to Baleal, a lovely islet village with a beach on either side of the spit *(p178)*.

Afternoon Lunch on the beach, then take the IP6 to picturesque Óbidos, which was famously once gifted to the bride of a Portuguese king *(p179)*. Spend a night at the Pousada Castelo Óbidos hotel, housed in the town's medieval castle *(p179)*.

Day 4

Morning Take the scenic route north to Coimbra via the historic abbeys of Alcobaça *(p170)* and Santa Maria da Vitória *(p172)*, and the bustling resort of Nazaré *(p181)*.

1 The view from the cloisters of Santa Maria da Vitória.

2 The pretty town of Ericeira.

3 Sintra's Palácio da Pena.

4 A dam in the Parque Natural da Serra da Estrela.

5 Miradouro de Santa Luzia.

Afternoon After watching the waves crashing on the beach, visit the Baroque church of Nossa Senhora da Nazaré. Join the A1 to continue your journey to Coimbra *(p196)*. There are plenty of busy bars in this historic city, but for a truly unique experience head to a *fado* club.

Day 5

Morning Coimbra's ancient university was founded in 1290, making it one of the oldest in Europe *(p200)*. Don't miss its Baroque library, the Biblioteca Joanina.

Afternoon Pick up all you need for a picnic and spend the afternoon admiring the impressive nearby ruins of Conímbriga *(p209)*. It's hard not to imagine Roman life as you explore the country's most important Roman site. Return to Coimbra for the evening.

Day 6

Morning Inland Portugal has some magnificent wild terrain, such as the Parque Natural da Serra da Estrela. Take the IC6 to the park, where you can drive right to the top of the mainland's highest summit, Torre *(p204)*.

Afternoon After hiking one of the many trails that crisscross the mountains, taking in waterfalls, otherworldly granite formations and medieval castles, spend the night in sleepy Linhares in the heart of the park *(p205)*.

Day 7

Morning Head back to Lisbon on the A13 via the lovely riverside town of Tomar, stopping to explore the mighty Convento de Cristo, a fortress convent dating from the 12th century *(p176)*.

Afternoon Back in the capital, take the clacking tram 28 up to Alfama and watch the sunset from the Miradouro de Santa Luzia *(p67)*. End the day – and your trip – at A Baiuca, where sorrowful *fado* singers entertain you as you dine *(p71)*.

THE LISBON COAST

Within an hour's drive northwest of Lisbon you can reach Portugal's rocky Atlantic coast. Traders and invaders, from the Phoenicians to the Spanish, have left their mark on this region – in particular the Moors, whose forts and castles, rebuilt many times over the centuries, can be found all along the coast. After Lisbon became the country's capital in 1256, Portuguese kings and nobles built summer palaces and villas in the countryside west of the city, and on the cool, green heights of the Serra de Sintra. Along the "Portuguese Riviera", wealthy Lisboetas have been building holiday villas in the seaside resort of Cascais as far back as the late 19th century.

Neighbouring Estoril became fashionable when exiled European royalty moved there during World War II; in its heyday, the town became a hotbed of spies, including Ian Fleming, who recreated Estoril's casino in his first James Bond novel. Across the Tagus, the less fashionable southern shore could be reached only by ferry until the Ponte 25 de Abril was built in 1966. This swiftly opened up the long sandy beaches of the Costa da Caparica, the coast around the fishing town of Sesimbra, and even the remote Tróia peninsula as popular summer resorts.

THE LISBON COAST

Must Sees
1 Sintra
2 Palácio Nacional de Queluz

Experience More
3 Palácio de Mafra
4 Colares
5 Ericeira
6 Monserrate
7 Estoril
8 Cascais
9 Alcochete
10 Costa da Caparica
11 Sesimbra
12 Cabo Espichel
13 Palmela
14 Serra da Arrábida
15 Península de Tróia
16 Setúbal
17 Alcácer do Sal

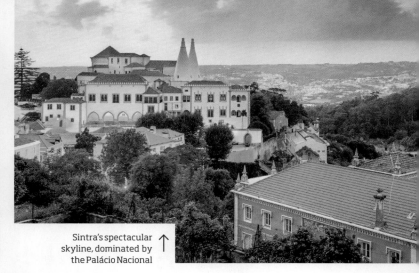

Sintra's spectacular skyline, dominated by the Palácio Nacional ↑

❶
SINTRA

🅰D5 🚗29 km (18 miles) NW of Lisbon 🚉🚌Avenida Dr Miguel Bombarda; bus 434 runs from station to all the major sights ℹ️ Praça da República 23; 219 231 157

Sintra's stunning setting on the north slopes of the granite Serra made it a favourite summer retreat for the kings of Portugal – resulting in the construction of a number of quirkily spectacular palaces. Today, the town (recognized as a UNESCO Cultural Landscape Site in 1995) draws thousands of visitors all through the year. Nevertheless, many quiet walks can be found in the beautiful surrounding wooded hills.

❶
Palácio Biester

🏠 Avenida Almeida Garrett 1A 🕐10am-8pm (Nov-Mar: to 6:30pm) 🚫1 Jan, 25 Dec 🌐biester.pt

Built as a private residence for the merchant and playwright Ernesto Biester and his family, this 19th-century palace opened to the public in 2022. In its lifetime, it's also been a guesthouse and a movie location for Roman Polanski's *The Ninth Gate* (1999). The surrounding park offers privileged views of Sintra's top attractions.

❷
Museu das Artes de Sintra

🏠 Avenida Heliodoro Salgado 📞219 236 106 🕐10am-6pm Tue-Fri, 12-6pm Sat & Sun 🚫Public hols

This museum displays Portuguese and international artworks, including sculptures, paintings and photography pieces. The permanent exhibition features the private collections of Emílio Paula Campos and Dórita Castel-Branco, and several landscapes of Sintra dating from the mid-18th century.

❸
Quinta da Regaleira

🏠 Rua Barbosa du Bocage 🚌435 🕐10am-5:30pm daily 🌐regaleira.pt

Built between 1904 and 1910, this palace and its extensive gardens are a feast of historical and religious references, occult symbols and mystery. The brainchild of eccentric millionaire António Augusto Carvalho Monteiro, the grounds are riddled with secret passages and hidden tunnels. Sintra's local government reclaimed the site as a national monument in 1997 and opened it to the public shortly afterwards.

↑ Spiral Initiation Wells at the Quinta da Regaleira

④ Parque da Pena

🏠 Estrada da Pena
🕐 9am–7pm daily 🚫 1 Jan,
25 Dec 🌐 parquesde
sintra.pt

A huge park surrounds the Palácio Nacional da Pena (*p152*), and hidden among the foliage are gazebos, follies and fountains, as well as a chalet built by Fernando II for his second wife, the Countess of Edla, in 1869. Cruz Alta, the highest point of the Serra at 529 m (1,740 ft), commands spectacular views of the Serra and surrounding plain. On a nearby crag is a striking statue known as "The Warrior", which supposedly symbolizes the king watching over his park and palace.

⑤ Castelo dos Mouros

🏠 Estrada da Pena
🕐 9am–6:30pm daily
(last adm 30 mins before closing) 🚫 1 Jan, 25 Dec
🌐 parquesdesintra.pt

Above the old town, the ramparts of the 10th-century Moorish castle taken by Afonso Henriques in 1147 snake over the top of the Serra like scales on a dragon's back. On a fine day, there are great views from the castle walls over the old town to the multicoloured Palácio Nacional da Pena and along the coast. Hidden inside the walls is an ancient Moorish cistern. Look out for the carved monogram ("DFII") on the gateway, which is a reminder that Fernando II restored the castle in the 19th century.

Must See

STAY

Lawrence's
Spend the night at Lawrence's, Sintra's oldest hotel, famously patronized by Lord Byron in the early 1800s. It's located in an 18th-century mansion, within which visitors can expect charmingly decorated rooms and an elegant restaurant.

🏠 Rua Consiglieri Pedroso 38, 2710-550 Sintra 🌐 lawrences hotel.com

€€€

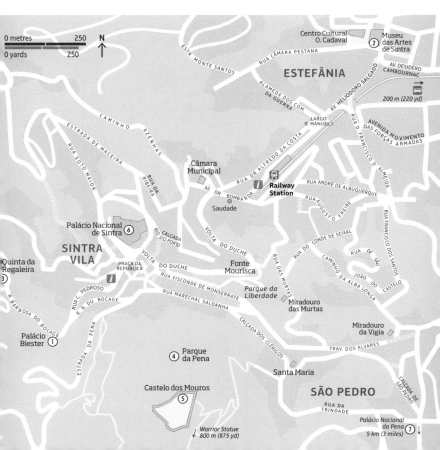

PALÁCIO NACIONAL DE SINTRA

📍 Largo Rainha Dona Amélia 🕐 9:30am–6:30pm daily (last adm 30 mins before closing) 🚫 1 Jan, 25 Dec 🌐 parquesdesintra.pt

One of the best-preserved royal palaces in Portugal, the striking white exterior of Sintra's National Palace is made up of a fascinating mix of Moorish and Manueline architecture. Inside, the lavishly decorated, whimsically themed rooms are a delight to explore.

At the heart of the old town of Sintra (Sintra Vila), a pair of strange conical chimneys rise above the Royal Palace. The main part of the palace, including this central block with its plain Gothic façade, was built by João I in the late 14th century, on a site once occupied by the Moorish rulers. The Paço Real, as it is also known, soon became the favourite summer retreat for the court, and continued as a residence for Portuguese royalty until 1910. Additions to the building by Manuel I, in the early 16th century, echo the Moorish style. The palace stretches across a number of levels, in acquiescence to the mountain on which it sits.

The Sala dos Brasões, one of Europe's most impressive heraldry rooms

Did You Know?

Afonso VI was imprisoned by his brother, Pedro II, in the palace for nine years.

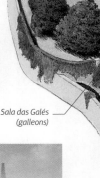

Sala das Galés (galleons)

Jardim da Preta, a walled garden

Quarto de Dom Sebastião, the bedroom of the young king

← The white walls and distinctive chimneys of the Palácio Nacional de Sintra

① The domed ceiling of the Sala dos Brasões is decorated with stags holding the coats of arms (*brasões*) of 72 noble Portuguese families. The lower walls are lined with 18th-century Delft-like tiled panels.

② The magnificent ceiling of the former banqueting hall is divided into octagonal panels decorated with swans *(cisnes)*, each wearing an elegant golden collar.

③ The Ala Manuelina (Manuel's Wing) was built between 1497 and 1530 and the rooms are adorned with tiles from Seville.

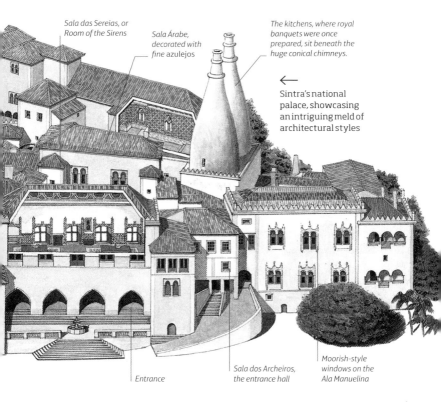

Sala das Sereias, or Room of the Sirens

Sala Árabe, once decorated with fine azulejos

The kitchens, where royal banquets were once prepared, sit beneath the huge conical chimneys.

← Sintra's national palace, showcasing an intriguing meld of architectural styles

Moorish-style windows on the Ala Manuelina

Sala dos Archeiros, the entrance hall

Entrance

Timeline

8th Century	1147	1495	1755	1910
First palace established here by the Moors.	Christian reconquest; Afonso Henriques takes over palace.	Reign of Manuel I begins; major palace restoration and additions.	Parts of palace damaged in great earthquake.	Palace becomes a national monument.

151

⑦ 🛠 🍴

PALÁCIO NACIONAL DA PENA

Manuel II's bedroom, an oval-shaped room decorated with a stuccoed ceiling

🏠 Estrada da Pena, 5 km (3 miles) S of Sintra 🚌 434 from Avenida Dr Miguel Bombarda, Sintra ⏰ Park: 9am–7pm daily; palace: 9:30am–6:30pm daily 🚫 1 Jan, 25 Dec 🌐 parquesdesintra.pt

On the highest peaks of the Serra de Sintra stands the spectacular palace of Pena. Built in the 19th century for Queen Maria II's flamboyantly creative husband, Ferdinand Saxe-Coburg and Gotha, it comprises an eclectic medley of architectural styles.

The bright pink-and-yellow walls of the palace stand over the ruins of a Hieronymite monastery, founded here in the 15th century. Ferdinand appointed a German architect, Baron Von Eschwege, to build his dream summer palace, filled with international oddities and surrounded by a park. Construction started in 1840, and the extravagant project would ultimately last 45 years – the rest of the king's life. With the declaration of the Republic in 1910, the palace became a museum, preserved as it was when the royal family lived here.

Kitchen, where the dinner service still bears Ferdinand's coat of arms

1 The brightly painted hilltop palace is a UNESCO World Heritage Site.

2 Trompe-l'oeil frescoes cover the walls and ceiling of the Arab Room, one of the loveliest in the palace.

3 The exterior is adorned with intricate architecture, heavily inspired by European Romanticism.

152

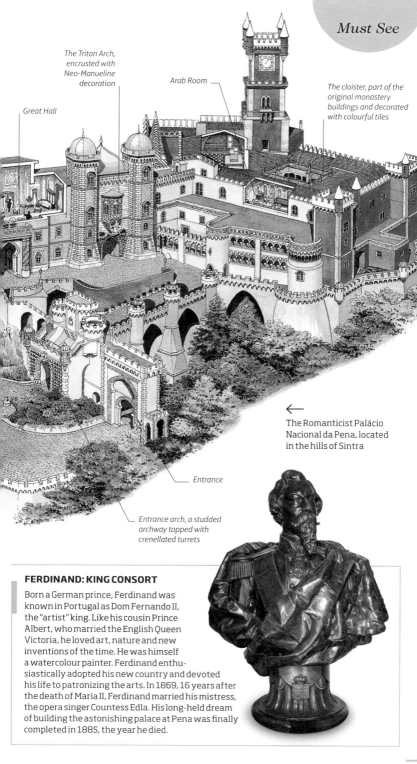

The Triton Arch, encrusted with Neo-Manueline decoration

Arab Room

The cloister, part of the original monastery buildings and decorated with colourful tiles

Great Hall

← The Romanticist Palácio Nacional da Pena, located in the hills of Sintra

Entrance

Entrance arch, a studded archway topped with crenellated turrets

FERDINAND: KING CONSORT

Born a German prince, Ferdinand was known in Portugal as Dom Fernando II, the "artist" king. Like his cousin Prince Albert, who married the English Queen Victoria, he loved art, nature and new inventions of the time. He was himself a watercolour painter. Ferdinand enthusiastically adopted his new country and devoted his life to patronizing the arts. In 1869, 16 years after the death of Maria II, Ferdinand married his mistress, the opera singer Countess Edla. His long-held dream of building the astonishing palace at Pena was finally completed in 1885, the year he died.

② ✍ 🖥 🍴

PALÁCIO NACIONAL DE QUELUZ

🅐 D5 🏠 Largo do Palácio, Queluz; 14 km (9 miles) NW of Lisbon 🚌 From Lisbon (Colégio Militar) 🚊 Queluz-Belas 🕐 Palace: 9am–6pm daily; gardens: 9am–6:30pm daily (last adm 5:30pm) 🚫 1 Jan, 25 Dec 🌐 parquesdesintra.pt

Often referred to as Lisbon's Versailles, this palace is an excellent example of 18th-century Portuguese architecture. Initially intended as a summer residence, it became the royal family's permanent home from 1794 until their departure for Brazil in 1807.

In 1747, Pedro, younger son of João V, commissioned Mateus Vicente to transform his 17th-century hunting lodge into a Rococo summer palace. The central section, including a music room and chapel, was built first, and after Pedro's marriage in 1760 to the future Maria I, the palace was again extended. The French architect Jean-Baptiste Robillion added the sumptuous Robillion Pavilion and gardens, cleared space for the throne room and redesigned the music room. During Maria's reign, the royal family kept a menagerie and went boating on the *azulejo*-lined canal.

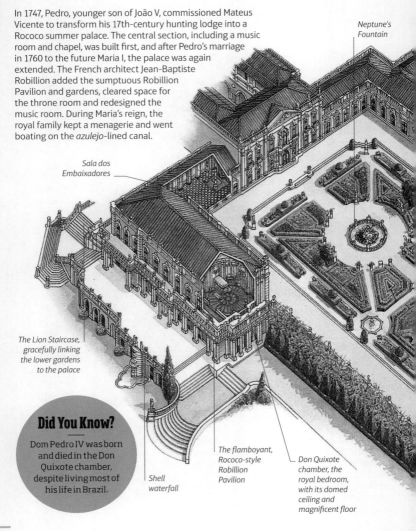

Neptune's Fountain

Sala dos Embaixadores

The Lion Staircase, gracefully linking the lower gardens to the palace

Did You Know?

Dom Pedro IV was born and died in the Don Quixote chamber, despite living most of his life in Brazil.

Shell waterfall

The flamboyant, Rococo-style Robillion Pavilion

Don Quixote chamber, the royal bedroom, with its domed ceiling and magnificent floor

1. The ornate palace façade overlooks the spectacular Neptune's Fountain.

2. The formal gardens, adorned with statues, fountains and topiary, were often used for entertaining.

3. The Sala dos Embaixadores was a stately room built by Robillon and used for both diplomatic audiences and concerts.

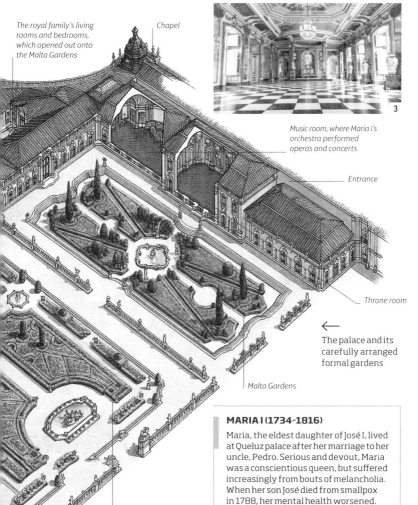

The royal family's living rooms and bedrooms, which opened out onto the Malta Gardens

Chapel

Music room, where Maria i's orchestra performed operas and concerts

Entrance

Throne room

← The palace and its carefully arranged formal gardens

Malta Gardens

The Hanging Gardens, elaborately designed by Robillion and built over arches

MARIA I (1734–1816)

Maria, the eldest daughter of José I, lived at Queluz palace after her marriage to her uncle, Pedro. Serious and devout, Maria was a conscientious queen, but suffered increasingly from bouts of melancholia. When her son José died from smallpox in 1788, her mental health worsened. Visitors to Queluz were dismayed by her agonizing shrieks as she had visions and hallucinations. After the 1807 invasion, her younger son João took Maria to Brazil.

EXPERIENCE MORE

3

Palácio de Mafra

🅐D5 🏛Terreiro de Dom João V, Mafra ➐From Lisbon Ⓜ Campo Grande, then ➐Ericeira ◷9:30am-5:30pm Wed-Mon (last adm 4:45pm) 🚫1 Jan, Easter, 1 May, 25 Dec 🌐cm-mafra.pt

This massive Baroque palace and monastery were built during the reign of João V, and began with a vow by the young king to build a new monastery and basilica, supposedly in return for an heir. Work began in 1717 on a modest project but, as wealth began to pour into the royal coffers from Brazil, the king and his Italian-trained architect, Johann Friedrich Ludwig (1670–1752), made ever more extravagant plans. No expense was spared: the finished project housed 330 friars, a royal palace and one of the finest libraries in Europe, decorated with precious marble, fine wood and countless works of art. The magnificent basilica was consecrated on the king's 41st birthday, 22 October 1730.

The palace was only popular with those members of the royal family who enjoyed hunting deer and wild boar. Most of the finest furniture

→
A narrow street in the fishing village of Ericeira

1717

Construction of the Palácio de Mafra began, a project so ambitious it almost bankrupted the state.

and art works were taken to Brazil when the royal family escaped the French invasion in 1807. The monastery was abandoned in 1834 following the dissolution of all religious orders, and the palace itself was abandoned in 1910.

The tour starts in the rooms of the monastery, through the pharmacy, with some alarming medical instruments, to the infirmary, where patients could see and hear Mass in the adjoining chapel from their beds.

Upstairs, the sumptuous state rooms extend across the whole of the west façade, with the king's apartments at one end and the queen's apartments at the other. Midway, the long, imposing façade is relieved by the twin towers of the domed basilica. The church's interior is decorated in contrasting colours of marble and furnished with six early 19th-century organs. Mafra's greatest treasure, however, is its library, with its Rococo-style wooden bookcases and a collection of over 40,000 books in

gold-embossed leather bindings, including a prized first edition of *Os Lusíadas* (1572) by the Portuguese poet Luís de Camões (1524–80).

4

Colares

🅐D5 ➐ ℹCabo da Roca; 219 238 543

On the lower slopes of the Serra de Sintra, this lovely village faces the sea over a green valley. A leafy avenue winds its way up to the village. Small quantities of the famous Colares wine are still made.

The hardy vines grow in sandy soil, with the roots set deep in

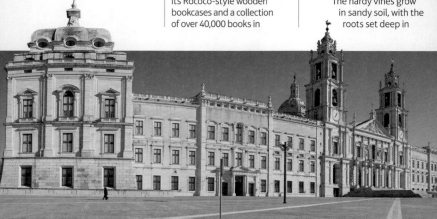

clay; these were among the few vines in Europe to survive the disastrous phylloxera epidemic brought from America in the late 19th century. The insect ate the vines' roots but could not penetrate the dense sandy soil of the Atlantic coast. The Adega Regional de Colares on Alameda de Coronel Linhares de Lima offers wine tastings.

There are several popular beach resorts west of Colares. Just north of Praia das Maçãs is the picturesque village of Azenhas do Mar, clinging to the cliffs; to the south is the larger resort of Praia Grande.

5

Ericeira

 D5   Praça da República 17; 261 863 122

Ericeira is an old fishing village that keeps its traditions despite an ever-increasing influx of summer visitors who enjoy the

The impressive Baroque façade of the Palácio de Mafra

bracing climate, clean, sandy beaches and fresh seafood. In July and August, pavement cafés, restaurants and bars around the Praça da República are busy late into the night. During the daytime, attractions include Santa Marta park and the parish church.

The unspoiled old town, a maze of whitewashed houses and narrow, cobbled streets, is perched high above the ocean. From Largo das Ribas, at the top of a 30-m (100-ft) stone-faced cliff, there is a bird's-eye view over the busy fishing harbour below, where tractors haul the boats out of reach of the tide. In mid-August, the annual fishers' festival is celebrated with a candlelit procession to the harbour at the foot of the cliffs for the blessing of the boats.

On 5 October 1910, Manuel II, the last king of Portugal, sailed into exile from Ericeira as the Republic was declared in Lisbon; a tiled panel in the fishers' chapel of Santo António above the harbour records the event. The banished king settled in Twickenham, southwest London, where he died in 1932.

STAY

Fortaleza do Guincho

Housed in a 17th-century fortress, this luxury hotel offers posh rooms with ocean views, and is home to a Michelin-starred restaurant. It's only a few steps from the Praia do Guincho and the cycling lane to Cascais.

 D5 ⚐ Estrada do Guincho 2750-642, Cascais Ⓦ fortaleza doguincho.com

€€€

Moon Hill Hostel

Tucked in a quiet corner of hilltop Sintra, this modern hostel offers stylish double rooms as well as contemporary dorms. There's a communal lounge, kitchen and pretty patio garden.

 D5 ⚐ Rua Guilherme Gomes Fernandes 17, Sintra Ⓦ moonhill hostel.com

€€€

← The Palace of Monserrate's beautifully wrought Romantic architecture, and *(inset)* its lavish interior

Estoril from Cascais, besides a pleasant beach promenade of 3 km (2 miles) and a mansion-covered ridge known as Monte Estoril, is its sense of place. The heart of Estoril is immediately accessible from the train station. On one side of the tracks is the riviera-like, but relaxed beach; on the other, a palm-lined park flanked by grand buildings stretches up past fountains to a casino. Dwarfing the casino is the Estoril Congress Centre, a vast multipurpose edifice that speaks confidently of Estoril's contemporary role.

6 Monserrate

🅐D5 🏠 Rua Barbosa du Bocage 🚃 To Sintra then bus 435 or taxi ⏰ Park: 9am–7pm daily; Palace: 9:30am–6:30pm daily; last adm 6pm 🌐 parquesdesintra.pt

The wild, romantic garden of this estate is a jungle of tropical trees and flowering shrubs. Among the subtropical foliage and valley of tree ferns are a waterfall, a small lake and a chapel, which was built as a ruin, tangled in the roots of a giant *Ficus* tree. Its history dates back to the

Moors, but it takes its name from a small 16th-century chapel dedicated to Our Lady of Montserrat in Catalonia, Spain. The gardens were landscaped in the late 1700s by a wealthy young Englishman, William Beckford. They were later immortalized by Lord Byron in *Childe Harold's Pilgrimage* (1812).

In 1856, the abandoned estate was bought by another Englishman, Sir Francis Cook, who built a fantastic Moorish-style palace (which has been restored) and transformed the gardens with a sweeping lawn, camellias and subtropical trees from all over the world.

INSIDER TIP
Fonte da Telha

Take the beach train from Caparica to the end of the line at Fonte da Telha. This is a popular family destination, but keep walking and you'll quickly find a patch of golden sands that you can have all to yourself.

7 Estoril

🅐D5 🚃 *i* Praça 5 de Outubro, Cascais; 912 034 214

The lovely resort town of Estoril is a tourist and business resort, and a place for comfortable retirement. What separates

→ Bathers enjoying the clear blue waters and sandy beach at Cascais

8
Cascais

A D5 **B** **B** **i** Praça 5 de
Outubro; 912 034 214

A holiday resort for well over
a century, Cascais possesses a
certain illustriousness that
younger resorts lack. Its history
is visible in its villas, summer
residences of wealthy Lisboetas
who followed King Luís I's lead
during the late 19th century.

Cascais today is a favoured
suburb of Lisbon, a place of
seaside apartments and pine-
studded plots by golf courses.
But the beautiful coastline
beyond the town has been
left largely undeveloped.

Housed in a castle-like villa,
the **Museu Condes de Castro
Guimarães** is the best place to
get a taste of Cascais's history.

The **Casa das Histórias
Paula Rego** is dedicated to
the work of the late painter,
illustrator and printmaker.

Museu Condes de
Castro Guimarães

⊘ **A** Avenida Rei Humberto
de Itália **C** 214 815 303
O 10am-1pm, 2-6pm Tue-Sun

Casa das Histórias
Paula Rego

⊘ **A** Avenida da República 300
O 10am-6pm Tue-Sun **C** 1 Jan,
Easter, 1 May & 25 Dec **W** casa
dashistoriaspaularego.com

9
Alcochete

A D5 **B** **i** Largo Barão
Samora Correia; 212 348 655

This delightful old town
overlooks the Tagus estuary
from the southern shore. Salt
has long been one of the main
industries here, and saltpans
can still be seen north and
south of the town, while in the
town centre a large statue of a
muscular salt worker has the
inscription: "Do Sal a Revolta
e a Esperança" (From Salt
to Rebellion and Hope). The
Reserva Natural do Estuário do
Tejo covers a vast area of estuary water, salt marshes and
small islands around Alcochete,
and is a very important breeding ground for water birds.

10
Costa da Caparica

A D5 **B** To Cacilhas or
Trafaria then bus **B** To
Pragal, then 194 bus
i Frente Urbana de
Praias; 212 900 071

Long beaches backed by sand
dunes make this a popular
holiday resort for Lisboetas
who come to swim, sunbathe
and enjoy the seafood restaurants and beach cafés. A
railway, with open carriages,
runs 10 km (6 miles) along the
coast in summer months. The
first beaches reached from
the town are popular with
families with children, while
the furthest beaches suit
those seeking quiet isolation.

EAT

O Pescador

This nautical-themed
restaurant is lined with
wooden tables and
fishing paraphernalia.
Diners can sit on the
pleasant outdoor terrace
and enjoy the menu's
emphasis on fresh fish.

A D5 **A** Rua das Flores
10b, Cascais **C** Wed
W restaurante
pescador.com

€€€

O Rodinhas

Running since 1992,
this popular seafood
restaurant plates up
everything from stuffed
crab to fried cuttlefish. It
only takes cash.

A D5 **A** Rua Marquês de
Pombal 25, Sesimbra
C Wed & Thu
W marisqueirao
rodinhas.pt

€€€

Sesimbra

⚠D5 🚌 ℹ Rua da Fortaleza de Santiago; 212 288 540

Protected from north winds by the slopes of the Serra da Arrábida, this busy fishing village has become a popular holiday resort. The old town is a maze of steep, narrow streets, with the Santiago Fort (now a customs post) in the centre overlooking the sea. From the terrace there are views of the town, the Atlantic and the wide sandy beach that stretches out on either side. Sesimbra is fast developing as a resort, with plentiful pavement cafés and bars that are always busy on sunny days.

The fishing fleet is moored in the Porto de Abrigo to the west of the main town. The harbour is reached by taking Avenida dos Náufragos, a sweeping promenade that follows the beach out of town. When the fishing boats return from a day at sea, a colourful, noisy fish auction takes place on the quayside.

↓ Brightly painted fishing boats moored in the harbour at Sesimbra

The day's catch can be tasted in the town's excellent fish restaurants along the shore.

High above the town is the Moorish castle, greatly restored in the 18th century when a church and a small, flower-filled cemetery were added inside the walls. There are wonderful views from the ramparts, especially at sunset.

Cabo Espichel

⚠D5 🚌 From Sesimbra

Sheer cliffs drop straight into the sea on this windswept promontory. The Romans named it Promontorium Barbaricum, alluding to its dangerous location, and a lighthouse warns sailors of the treacherous rocks below. Stunning views of the ocean and the coast can be enjoyed from this bleak outcrop of land, but beware of the strong gusts of wind on the cliff edge.

In this desolate setting is the impressive Santuário de Nossa Senhora do Cabo, a late 17th-century church with its back to the sea. On either side of the church a long line of pilgrims' lodgings facing inwards form an open courtyard. Baroque paintings, *ex votos* and a frescoed ceiling decorate the church's interior. Nearby, a domed chapel has tiled blue-and-white *azulejo* panels depicting fishing scenes. The site became a popular place of pilgrimage in the 13th century when a local man had a vision of the Madonna rising from the sea on a mule. Legend has it that the tracks of the mule can be seen embedded in the rock.

Palmela

⚠D5 🚌🚌 ℹ Castelo de Palmela; 212 332 122

The formidable castle at Palmela stands over the small hill town, high on a north-eastern spur of the wooded Serra da Arrábida. Its strategic position dominates the plain for miles around, especially when floodlit at night. Heavily defended by the Moors, it was finally overthrown in the 12th century and given by Sancho I to the Knights of the Order of Santiago. In 1423, João I transformed the castle into a monastery for the Order. It has since been restored and converted into a splendid

 The castle at Palmela with views over the Serra da Arrábida

pousada, with a restaurant in the monks' refectory and a swimming pool for residents, hidden inside the castle walls.

From the castle terraces and the top of the 14th-century keep there are fantastic views over the Serra da Arrábida to the south, and on a clear day across the Tagus to Lisbon. In the town square below, the church of São Pedro contains 8th-century tiles of scenes from the life of St Peter.

The annual wine festival, the Festa das Vindimas, is held on the first weekend of September in front of the 17th-century Paços do Concelho (town hall). Traditionally dressed villagers press the wine barefoot and on the final day of celebrations there is a spectacular fireworks display from the castle walls.

---

⑭
Serra da Arrábida

🅰D5 🚍Setúbal 🅸Parque Natural da Arrábida, Praça da República, Setúbal; 265 541 140

The Serra da Arrábida Natural Park covers the range of limestone mountains that stretch east–west along the coast between Sesimbra and Setúbal. It was established to protect the wild, beautiful landscape and rich variety of birds and wildlife, including wildcats and badgers.

The sheltered, south-facing slopes are thickly covered with aromatic and evergreen shrubs and trees such as pine and cypress, more typical of the Mediterranean. Vineyards also thrive on the sheltered slopes and the town of Vila Nogueira de Azeitão is particularly known for its wine, Moscatel de Setúbal.

The Estrada de Escarpa (the N379-1) snakes across the top of the ridge, with astounding views. A hair-raisingly narrow road winds down to Portinho da Arrábida, a sheltered cove with a beach of fine white sand and crystal-clear sea, popular with underwater fishers. The sandy beaches of Galapos and Figueirinha are a little further east along the coast road towards Setúbal. Just east of Sesimbra, the Serra da Arrábida drops to the sea in the sheer 380-m (1,250-ft) cliffs of Risco, the highest in mainland Portugal.

> **From the castle terraces and the top of the 14th-century keep, there are fantastic views over the Serra da Arrábida to the south, and on a clear day across the Tagus to Lisbon.**

EAT

O Barbas Catedral

This renowned restaurant, which overlooks the breakers of Caparica beach, is usually packed at weekends thanks to its delicious seafood dishes.

🅐D5 🅐Apoio de Praia 13, Caparica 📞212 900 163 🅚Wed

€€€

O Farol

Expect sparkling sea views from the terrace and fresh seafood at this family-friendly restaurant above the water.

🅐D5 🅐Portinho da Arrábida 📞212 181 177 🅚Mon

€€€

Ribamar

This upmarket restaurant is right on the seafront and has been serving tasty seafood dishes for over 60 years.

🅐D5 🅐Avenida dos Náufragos 29, Sesimbra 🅦restauranteribamar.pt

€€€

🔟⑤ Península de Tróia

🅐D5 🚆🚌Tróia 🅘Tróia Resort; 265 499 400 🅞Cetóbriga: 10am–1pm & 2:30–6pm Wed–Sat (Jul & Aug: Tue also) 🅦troia resort.pt

Holiday apartments dominate the tip of the Tróia peninsula, easily accessible from Setúbal by ferry. The Atlantic coast, stretching south for 18 km (11 miles) of untouched sandy beaches, is now the haunt of sun-seekers in the summer.

Near Tróia, in the sheltered lagoon, the Roman town of Cetóbriga was the site of a thriving fish-salting business. The stone tanks and ruined buildings are open to visit.

Further on, Carrasqueira is an old fishing community where you can still see traditional reed houses.

🔟⑥ Setúbal

🅐D5 🚆🚌🚌 🅘Casa da Baía, Avenida Luísa Todi 468; 265 545 010

An important industrial town and the third-largest port in Portugal (after Lisbon and Porto), Setúbal makes a good base from which to explore the Lisbon Coast. To the south of the town's central gardens and

> ### Did You Know?
>
> One of the most famous people to be born in Setúbal is football manager José Mourinho.

fountains are the fishing harbour, marina and ferry port, as well as a lively covered market. North of the gardens is the old town, with attractive pedestrian streets and squares full of cafés.

The 16th-century cathedral, dedicated to Santa Maria da Graça, has glorious 18th-century tiled panels, and gilded altar decoration. Street names commemorate two famous Setúbal residents: Manuel Barbosa du Bocage (1765–1805), whose satirical poetry landed him in prison, and Luísa Todi (1753–1833), a celebrated opera singer.

In Roman times, fish-salting was the most important industry here. Rectangular stone tanks used for this process can still be seen on Travessa Frei Gaspar.

To the north of the old town, the striking Igreja de Jesus is one of Setúbal's treasures. Designed by the architect Diogo Boitac in 1494, the lofty interior is adorned with twisted columns of pinkish Arrábida

←

Jetty with fishing boats moored on the mud flats at Carrasqueira

limestone, and rope-like stone ribs, recognized as the first examples of the distinctive Manueline style.

On Rua do Balneário, in the old monastic quarters, a museum houses 14 remarkable paintings of the life of Christ. The works are attributed to followers of the Renaissance painter Jorge Afonso (1520–30).

The **Museu de Arquelogia e Etnografia** displays a wealth of finds from digs around Setúbal, including Bronze Age pots and Roman coins. The ethnography display shows local arts, crafts and industries, including the processing of salt and cork over the centuries.

The **Castelo de São Filipe** was built in 1595 by Philip II of Spain, during the period of Spanish rule, to keep a wary eye on pirates, English invaders and the local population. It now houses a boutique hotel, but the battlements and ramparts are open to the public and offer marvellous views over the city and the Sado estuary.

Setúbal is an ideal starting point for a tour by car of the unspoiled Reserva Natural do Estuário do Sado, a vast stretch of mud flats, shallow lagoons and salt marshes, which has been explored and inhabited since 3500 BCE.

Museu de Arquelogia e Etnografia
🅰 Avenida Luísa Todi 162 🕘 9am–12:30pm, 2–5:30pm Tue–Sat 🚫 Public hols, Aug: Sat 🌐 maeds.amrs.pt

Castelo de São Filipe
🔅 🅰 Estrada de São Filipe 🚫 For renovation until further notice

17

Alcácer do Sal

🅰 E5 🚆🚌 ℹ Largo Luís de Camões; 911 794 685

Bypassed by the main road, the ancient town of Alcácer do Sal (al-kasr from the Arabic for castle, and do sal from its trade in salt) sits on the north bank of the Sado river. The imposing castle was a hillfort as early as the 6th century BCE. The Phoenicians made an inland trading port here, and the castle later became a Roman stronghold. Rebuilt by the Moors, it was taken by Afonso II in 1217. The buildings have now taken on a new life as a pousada. Also here is the **Cripta Arqueológica do Castelo**, an archaeological museum holding locally excavated items. The collections include artifacts from the Iron Age, as well as from the Roman, Moorish and medieval periods.

There are pleasant cafés along the riverside promenade and several historic churches.

Cripta Arqueológica do Castelo
♿ 🅰 Castelo de Alcácer do Sal 📞 265 612 058 🕘 Sep–Jun: 9am–12:30pm & 2–5:30pm Tue–Sun; Jul & Aug: 9:30am–1pm & 3–6:30pm Tue–Sun 🚫 1 Jan, Easter Sun, 1 May, 25 Dec

Tiled chapel in Castelo de São Filipe, Setúbal ↑

A DRIVING TOUR
SERRA DE SINTRA

Length 36 km (22 miles) **Stopping-off points** Cabo da Roca; Colares **Terrain** Mountainous in places, with steep, narrow roads

This round trip from Sintra follows a dramatic route over the top of the wooded Serra. The first part is a challenging drive with hazardous hairpin bends on steep, narrow roads that are at times poorly surfaced. It passes through dense forest and a surreal landscape of giant moss-covered boulders, with breathtaking views over the Atlantic coast, the Tagus estuary and beyond. After dropping down to the rugged, windswept coast, the route returns to small country roads, passing through hill villages and large estates on the cool, green northern slopes of the Serra de Sintra.

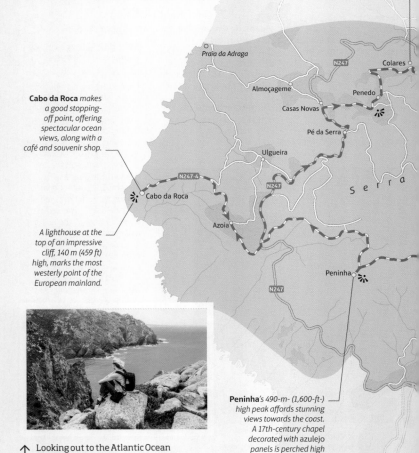

The village of **Colares** *rests on the lower slopes of the wooded Serra, surrounded by gardens and vineyards (p156). There are several delightful bars and restaurants here too.*

Cabo da Roca *makes a good stopping-off point, offering spectacular ocean views, along with a café and souvenir shop.*

Praia da Adraga

Almoçageme

Colares

N247

Penedo

Casas Novas

Pé da Serra

Ulgueira

N247

Cabo da Roca

N247-4

S e r r a

Azoia

A lighthouse at the top of an impressive cliff, 140 m (459 ft) high, marks the most westerly point of the European mainland.

Peninha

N247

Peninha's 490-m- (1,600-ft-) high peak affords stunning views towards the coast. A 17th-century chapel decorated with azulejo panels is perched high on the grey rocks.

↑ Looking out to the Atlantic Ocean from Cabo da Roca's windswept cliffs

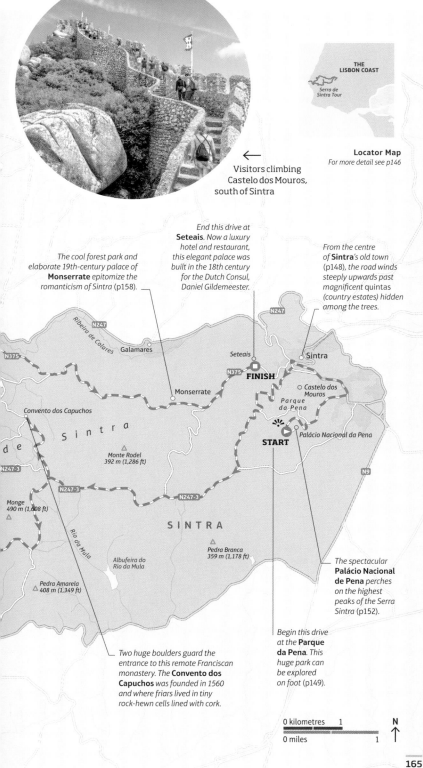

Visitors climbing
Castelo dos Mouros,
south of Sintra

Locator Map
For more detail see p146

End this drive at
Seteais. *Now a luxury
hotel and restaurant,
this elegant palace was
built in the 18th century
for the Dutch Consul,
Daniel Gildemeester.*

*The cool forest park and
elaborate 19th-century palace of*
Monserrate *epitomize the
romanticism of Sintra (p158).*

*From the centre
of* **Sintra**'s *old town
(p148), the road winds
steeply upwards past
magnificent* quintas
*(country estates) hidden
among the trees.*

The spectacular
**Palácio Nacional
de Pena** *perches
on the highest
peaks of the Serra
Sintra (p152).*

*Begin this drive
at the* **Parque
da Pena**. *This
huge park can
be explored
on foot (p149).*

*Two huge boulders guard the
entrance to this remote Franciscan
monastery. The* **Convento dos
Capuchos** *was founded in 1560
and where friars lived in tiny
rock-hewn cells lined with cork.*

0 kilometres   1
0 miles   1

N

ESTREMADURA AND RIBATEJO

The name Estremadura comes from the Latin *Extrema Durii*, "beyond the Douro". This was once the border of the Christian kingdoms in the north. As Portugal expanded southwards in the 12th century, land taken from the Moors was given to the religious orders. The Cistercian abbey at Alcobaça celebrates Afonso Henriques' capture of the town of Santarém in 1147, after which the Knights Templar began constructing their citadel at Tomar. Overthrowing the Moors did not signal lasting peace in the region, however, as Spanish claims to the Portuguese throne brought more fighting. João I was victorious over the Castilians at the Battle of Aljubarrota in 1385, and he built Batalha's magnificent abbey near the site to celebrate Portuguese independence.

In 1808–10, Napoleonic forces sacked many towns in the region, but were stopped by Wellington's formidable defences, the Lines of Torres Vedras. Christianity remains as important here as it was in the Middle Ages and, in the 20th century, Fátima became an important pilgrimage destination following celebrated visions of the Virgin Mary in 1917. The region is not out of touch with the modern world, however, and the building of the dam at Castelo de Bode in the 1940s heralded a new era of hydroelectric power.

ESTREMADURA AND RIBATEJO

MOSTEIRO DE SANTA MARIA DE ALCOBAÇA

⊠D4 ⊠Praça 25 de Abril, Alcobaça ⊟From Lisbon, Coimbra & Leiria ⊙Apr–Sep: 9am–7pm daily; Oct–Mar: 9am–6pm daily (last adm 30 mins before closing) ⊠1 Jan, Easter, 1 May, 20 Aug, 25 Dec ⊠mosteiroalcobaca.pt

Portugal's largest church, the monastery at Alcobaça is renowned for its simple medieval architecture and its illustrious history.

Founded in 1153, this UNESCO World Heritage Site is closely linked to the arrival of the Cistercian order in Portugal 15 years earlier, as well as the birth of the nation. To commemorate his victory over the Moorish stronghold of Santarém in March 1147, King Afonso Henriques vowed to build a monastery for the Cistercians. Originally, the monks lived in wooden houses on the site until the vast stone building was habitable in 1223. The monastery was further endowed by other monarchs, notably King Dinis, who built the main cloister. Among those buried here are the tragic lovers King Pedro and his murdered mistress Inês.

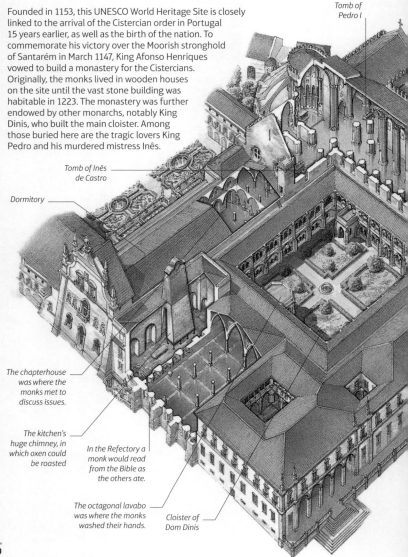

Tomb of Pedro I

Tomb of Inês de Castro

Dormitory

The chapterhouse was where the monks met to discuss issues.

The kitchen's huge chimney, in which oxen could be roasted

In the Refectory a monk would read from the Bible as the others ate.

The octagonal lavabo was where the monks washed their hands.

Cloister of Dom Dinis

Central nave

The Gothic portal and rose window on this façade are the only original 13th-century elements.

Main entrance

In the Sala dos Reis, tiles from the 18th century depict the founding of the abbey and statues of Portuguese kings adorn the walls.

↑ The grand exterior and interior of the Mosteiro de Santa Maria de Alcobaça

① The façade is a richly decorated 18th-century addition, with marble statues of St Benedict and St Bernard flanking the main doorway of the church.

② The vaulted roof and soaring columns of the central nave create an impression of harmony and austere simplicity.

③ The tomb of Pedro I, with his statue attended by angels, lies opposite that of his mistress, Inês de Castro. Popular legend says that the king insisted that they face each other so that his first sight on Judgement Day would be of her.

THE MURDER OF INÊS DE CASTRO

Reasons of state obliged Pedro, son and heir of Afonso IV, to marry Costanza, Infanta of Castile. On her death, Pedro went to live with Inês de Castro, a lady at court with whom he had fallen in love, in Coimbra. Persuaded that Inês's family was dangerous, Afonso IV had her murdered on 7 January 1355. On Afonso's death, Pedro took revenge on two of the killers by having their hearts torn out. Claiming that he had been married to Inês, Pedro had her corpse exhumed and crowned.

INÊS DE CASTRO

2 ⚜

MOSTEIRO DE SANTA MARIA DA VITÓRIA

🅐 D4 🏠 Batalha 🚌 From Lisbon, Leiria, Porto de Mós & Fátima 🕐 Apr-mid-Oct: 9am-6:30pm daily; mid-Oct-Mar: 9am-6pm daily (last adm 30 mins before closing) 🚫 1 Jan, Easter, 1 May, 24 & 25 Dec 🌐 mosteirobatalha.pt

This pale limestone monastery celebrates João I's 1385 victory over Castile at Aljubarrota. As well as being João's final resting place, two unknown World War I soldiers lie in the chapterhouse, making the monastery a monument to fortitude.

The Dominican monastery of Santa Maria da Vitória at Batalha is a masterpiece of Portuguese Gothic architecture, notable for its Manueline elements. The monastery was begun in 1388 under master builder Afonso Domingues (1330–1402), who was succeeded on his death by David Huguet in 1406. Over the next two centuries successive kings left their mark on the monastery. João I's son, King Duarte, ordered a royal pantheon to be built behind the apse. Unfortunately, he died before it was completed and the octagonal mausoleum was abandoned by Manuel I in favour of the Mosteiro dos Jerónimos *(p108)*, although many Manueline decorations remain.

Did You Know?

João I's motto, *"por bem"* (for good), is inscribed on his tomb.

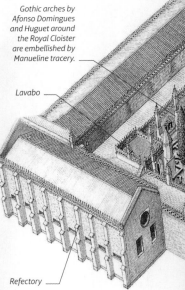

Gothic arches by Afonso Domingues and Huguet around the Royal Cloister are embellished by Manueline tracery.

Lavabo

Refectory

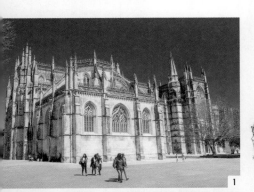

① The pale exterior of the monastery is a fine example of late Gothic architecture.

② The portal was decorated by Huguet with intricate statues of the Apostles.

③ The lavabo, where friars washed their hands before and after meals, contains a fish-filled fountain built around 1450.

THE BATTLE OF ALJUBARROTA

In 1383, Portugal's direct male line of descent ended with the death of Fernando I. Dom João, the illegitimate son of Fernando's father, was proclaimed king, ending the regency of Leonor Teles, but his claim was opposed by Juan I of Castile. On 14 August 1385, João I's greatly outnumbered forces, commanded by Nuno Álvares Pereira *(left)*, faced the Castilians on a small plateau near Aljubarrota, 3 km (2 miles) south of Batalha. João's victory ensured 200 years of independence from Spain and cemented the power of the house of Avis.

Guards keep watch by the Tomb of the Unknown Soldiers in the chapterhouse.

The stained-glass window behind the choir dates from 1514.

Unfinished chapels

Lofty nave by Afonso Domingues

The chapel is topped by an octagonal lantern.

The tomb of João I and his English wife Philippa of Lancaster, lying hand in hand in the Founder's Chapel, was begun in 1426 by Huguet.

Main entrance

← The ornate Gothic Mosteiro de Santa Maria da Vitória

3

TOMAR

 E4 ⬛ Tomar 🚌 From Lisbon, Coimbra & Leiria
ℹ️ Avenida Dr Cândido Madureira; www.visit-tomar.com

Founded in 1157 by Gualdim Pais, the first Grand Master of the Order of the Templars in Portugal, Tomar is dominated by the Convento de Cristo. The heart of this charming town is a neat grid of narrow streets.

①

Nossa Senhora da Conceição

📍 Ermida da Imaculada Conceição 📞 249 315 089

On the slopes of the hill leading up to the Convento do Cristo is the Renaissance basilica Nossa Senhora da Conceição. Built between 1530 and 1550, it was conceived as a funerary pantheon. Its simple exterior contrasts with the delicately carved Corinthian columns of the interior. The ceiling of the transept is decorated with geometric and floral designs.

The architect is believed to have been Francisco de Holanda (1517–84), who worked for King João III.

②

Sinagoga e Núcleo Interpretativo da Sinagoga de Tomar

📍 Rua Dr Joaquim Jacinto 73 📞 249 329 823 🕐 Apr-Sep: 10am-1pm & 2-6pm Tue-Sun; Oct-Mar: 10am-noon & 2-5pm Tue-Sun 🚫 1 Jan, 1 May, 25 Dec

Built in 1430–60, with four tall columns and a vaulted ceiling, this is one of the oldest synagogues in Portugal. The building was last used as a place of worship in 1497, after which Manuel I banished all Jews who refused to convert to Christianity. It has since had a varied existence, serving as a prison, a hay loft and a warehouse. Today, it has a Jewish museum named after Abraham Zacuto, a 15th-century astronomer and mathematician.

← The ornately decorated interior of Nossa Senhora da Conceição

← The Convento de Cristo overlooking Tomar, on the Nabão river

Manueline portal, complete with the coat of arms of the Order of the Templars, and is capped by an octagonal-spired belfry with a clock. Inside, there is a carved stone pulpit and 16th-century paintings including a depiction of the Last Supper by Gregório Lopes (1490–1550). A particularly gory painting of the beheading of John the Baptist hanging here is also attributed to Lopes.

The area outside the church is the focus of the spectacular Festa dos Tabuleiros *(p41)*, a festival with pagan origins held in July, every four years. During the celebrations, girls dressed in white carry towering platters of bread and flowers on their heads. The festival has similar roots to the Festa do Espírito Santo, which is popular in the Azores.

MATA NACIONAL DOS SETE MONTES

Originally the Convento de Cristo's gardens, the Mata Nacional dos Sete Montes (National Forest of the Seven Hills) is the perfect place for a walk. Local families descend on the green space at weekends for picnics in the sunshine and strolls in the extensive woodlands. There are various marked woodland trails to explore, as well as a more formal landscaped area by the park entrance.

③
Museu dos Fósforos

🏛 Av General Bernardo Faria 🕐 Apr-Sep: 10am-1pm & 2-6pm Tue-Sun; Oct-Mar: 10am-noon & 2-5pm Tue-Sun 🚫 1 Jan, 1 May, 25 Dec

The former cloisters of the 17th-century church of São Francisco now house the Museu dos Fósforos. This museum features the largest collection of matches in Europe, with over 43,000 matchboxes from 104 countries of the world on display. The boxes depict everything from dinosaurs to Nazi propaganda. You don't have to be a phillumenist to appreciate this curious museum.

④
São João Baptista

🏛 Praça da República 📞 249 312 611

The lively shopping street Rua Serpa Pinto leads to the Gothic church of São João Baptista on Praça da República, the town's main square. The late 15th-century church has an elegant

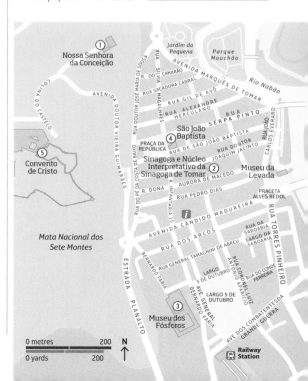

⑤ 🏛️

CONVENTO DE CRISTO

🅰E4 🚶15-minute walk from Tomar centre 🚉Tomar 🚌From Lisbon, Coimbra, Leiria ⏰Jun-Sep: 9am-6:30pm daily (Oct-May: to 5:30pm) 📅1 Jan, 1 Mar, Easter, 1 May, 24 & 25 Dec 🌐conventocristo.pt

Crowning the wooded hill that overlooks Tomar, the Convento de Cristo is a magnificent complex of chapels, cloisters and a medieval castle, showing the wealth and importance of the Order of Christ.

Founded in 1160 by the Grand Master of the Templars, the Convent of Christ still retains some reminders of these monk-knights and the inheritors of their mantle, the Order of Christ. Under Henry the Navigator, the governor of the order from 1418, cloisters were built between the Charola (the Templars' church) and the fortress, but it was the reign of João III (1521–57) that saw the greatest changes. Architects such as João de Castilho and Diogo de Arruda, engaged to express the order's power and royal patronage in stone, built the church and cloisters with dazzling Manueline flourishes, which reached a crescendo with the window in the west front of the church.

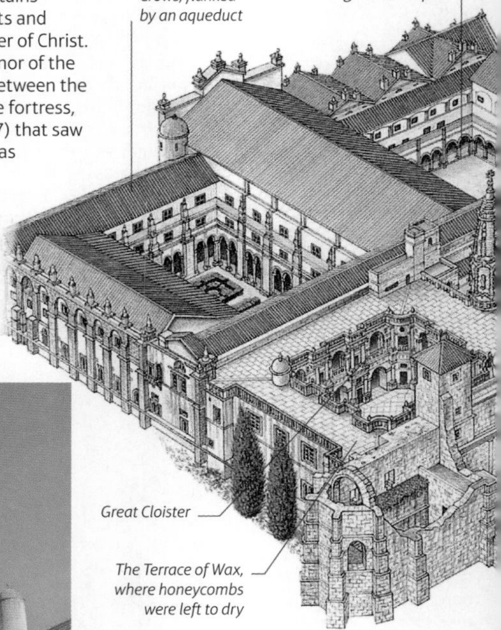

Cloister of the Crows, flanked by an aqueduct

The "Bread" Cloister, where loaves were given to the poor

Great Cloister

The Terrace of Wax, where honeycombs were left to dry

↑ The Charola on the south side of the Convento de Cristo

THE ORDER OF CHRIST

During the 12th and 13th centuries, the crusading Order of the Knights Templar helped the Portuguese in their battle against the Moors. In return they were rewarded with extensive lands and political power. In 1314, Pope Clement V was forced to suppress the order but, in Portugal, King Dinis renamed it the Order of Christ, and it inherited the Templar's properties. In 1356, Tomar became the order's headquarters.

1 Begun in the 1550s, probably by Diogo de Torralva, the Great Cloister reflects João III's passion for Italian art.

2 Expressive carvings are found throughout the Convento de Cristo.

3 The original 12th-century Templar church, the Charola – sometimes called the Rotunda – was built in the shape of a 16-sided drum.

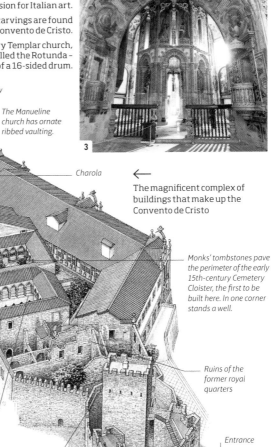

Manueline window

The Manueline church has ornate ribbed vaulting.

Charola ←

The magnificent complex of buildings that make up the Convento de Cristo

Monks' tombstones pave the perimeter of the early 15th-century Cemetery Cloister, the first to be built here. In one corner stands a well.

The south portal is initialled by João de Castilho.

Ruins of the former royal quarters

The Washing Cloister was built around a pair of large reservoirs, today planted with flowers.

Entrance

In 1160, the Templars' Grand Master built this castle on land given to the order for services in battle.

EXPERIENCE MORE

④ Berlenga Islands

🅰C4 🚢From Peniche ℹRua Alexandre Herculano, Peniche; 262 789 571

Monks, a lighthouse keeper, fishers and biologists have inhabited this rocky archipelago that juts out from the Atlantic Ocean 12 km (7 miles) from the mainland. Berlenga Grande, the biggest island, can be reached by ferry in about an hour. This island is a nature reserve with nesting sites for sea birds. On the southeast side of the island is the 17th-century pentagonal Forte de São João Baptista. This stark stone fort suffered repeated assaults from pirates and foreign armies. Today it is a basic hostel.

Small boats can be hired from the jetty to explore the marine grottoes around the island. Furado Grande is the most spectacular of these: a 70-m (230-ft) tunnel, opening into the Cova do Sonho (Dream Cove), framed by imposing red granite cliffs.

Stone fortress of São João on Berlenga Grande ↑

⑤ Peniche

🅰D4 🚌 ℹRua Alexandre Herculano; 262 789 571

Set on a peninsula, this small, pleasant town is partly enclosed by 16th-century walls. Dependent on its port, Peniche has good fish restaurants and deep-sea fishing facilities. At the water's edge on the south side of town stands the 16th-century Fortaleza, used as a prison during the Salazar regime. The fortress was made famous by the escape in 1960 of the Communist leader Álvaro Cunhal. Inside, the **Museu Nacional da Resistência e Liberdade** has an exhibit on the anti-New State resistance movement and offers a tour that includes a look into the prison cells. On Largo 5 de Outubro, the Igreja da Misericórdia has 17th-century painted ceiling panels depicting the Life of Christ.

On the peninsula's western headland, 2 km (1 mile) from Peniche, Cabo Carvoeiro affords grand views of the strange-shaped rocks along the eroded coastline. Here, the interior of the chapel of Nossa Senhora dos Remédios is adorned with 18th-century tiles on the Life of the Virgin attributed to the workshop of António de Oliveira Bernardes.

Museu Nacional da Resistência e Liberdade

◉ ◉ 🅒Campo da República
🅒For renovation until 2024
🆆museunacionalresistencia
liberdade-peniche.gov.pt

⑥ Baleal

🅰D4 🚗3 km (2 miles) north of Peniche

This picturesque village, which bustles with water-front cafés, bars and restaurants, is squeezed on to a little islet on the coast. Baleal is connected to the mainland by a narrow causeway, with superb sandy beaches on either side. One side of the causeway is sheltered, making it the chosen spot for bathers, while the other, with its good breakers, is a surfers' haunt. Unsurprisingly, Baleal is home to several surf schools offering lessons to beginners and organizing trips to nearby swells for more experienced practitioners. Vehicles are best left at the car parks on the mainland side of the causeway, from where it is an easy walk to the islet.

7

Óbidos

 D4 🚌 🚐 ℹ️ Rua da Porta da Vila (Parque do Estacionamento Grande); 262 959 231

This enchanting hill town with whitewashed houses is enclosed within 14th-century walls. From the 13th century, Óbidos was an important port, but by the 16th century the river had silted up. The town has since been restored and preserved.

The entrance into the town is through the southern gate, Porta da Vila, whose interior is embellished with 18th-century tiles. Rua Direita, the main shopping street, leads to Praça de Santa Maria. Here, a Manueline *pelourinho* (pillory)

is decorated with a fishing net, the emblem of Dona Leonor, wife of João II. She chose this emblem in honour of the fishers who tried in vain to save her son from drowning.

Opposite the pillory is the church of Santa Maria, with a simple Renaissance portal. The future Afonso V was married to his cousin Isabel here in 1441. He was ten years old, she eight. The interior of the church retains a simple clarity, with a painted wooden ceiling and 17th-century tiles. In the chancel, a retable depicting the *Mystic Marriage of St Catherine* (1661) is by Josefa de Óbidos. The artist lived most of her life in Óbidos and is buried in the church of São Pedro on Largo de São Pedro. Her work is also on display in the **Museu Municipal**.

Dominating Óbidos is the castle, rebuilt by Afonso Henriques after he took the town from the Moors in 1148. Today it is a charming *pousada*. The path along the battlements affords fine views.

Southeast of town is the Baroque Santuário do Senhor da Pedra, a church begun in 1740 to a hexagonal plan.

Museu Municipal
🖼️ 🏛️ Solar da Praça de Santa Maria, Rua Direita 📞 262 955 500 🕐 10am–1pm, 2–5pm Tue–Sun

→ Perched on the hilltop, the enchanting walled town of Óbidos

A pretty street in Caldas da Rainha, and *(inset)* colourful local ceramics on display

8 São Martinho do Porto

D4 🚌 ℹ️ Rua Vasco da Gama; 302 044 067

This pleasant little resort, with its safe waters, is an exception to most of the others along this stretch of the coast, which are only recommended for surfers. Connected to the Atlantic Ocean by a small passage between the hills, São Martinho do Porto sits on a curving, almost landlocked bay, making its soft sands both safe and extremely appealing, especially for families. If you head south along the beach, it doesn't take long to find a patch of sand to yourself, even in the height of summer.

Most of the largely modern resort buildings sit at the northern end of the bay, where you can hire kayaks and pedalos. Don't miss the lift ride from the tourist office, which takes you up to a little viewpoint in the old part of São Martinho do Porto.

> ⛰️ GREAT VIEW
> ## To the Lighthouse
>
> Walk up the steep path above the quayside to the lighthouse for sublime views across São Martinho do Porto and the bay.

---

9 Caldas da Rainha

D4 🚌🚃 ℹ️ Rua do Provedor Frei Jorge de São Paulo 5A; 262 240 005

The "queen's hot springs", a sprawling spa town, owes its prosperity to three different fields: thermal cures, ceramics and fruit farming. The town is named after Dona Leonor, founder of the Misericórdia hospital on Largo Rainha Dona Leonor. The original hospital chapel later became the impressive Manueline Igreja do Populo, built by Diogo Boitac. Inside is the 15th-century chapel of São Sebastião, decorated with 18th-century *azulejos*.

The shops on Rua da Liberdade sell ceramics, including the local green majolica ware. Examples of the work of the potter Rafael Bordalo Pinheiro (1846–1905) can be seen in the **Museu de Cerâmica**. The Museu José Malhoa is dedicated to the eponymous artist (1855–1933), known as "the painter of Portuguese sun and light".

Saltwater Lagoa de Óbidos, 15 km (9 miles) west of Caldas da Rainha, is a calm, sheltered lagoon that is popular for sailing and fishing.

Museu de Cerâmica

♿ 🚌 Rua Dr Ilídio Amado
📞 262 840 280 🕐 Apr-Sep: 10am-12:30pm & 2-6pm Tue-Sun; Oct-Mar: 10am-12:30pm & 2-5:30pm Tue-Sun 🚫 1 Jan, Easter Sun, 1 & 15 May, 25 Dec

---

10 Bacalhôa Buddha Eden Gardens

D4 🚗 Quinta dos Loridos, Carvalhal Bombarral
🕐 9am-6pm daily (May-Sep: to 7pm) 🚫 1 Jan, 25 Dec 🌐 bacalhoa.pt

Eastern statues stand out against the quintessential Portuguese landscape of cork and olive trees in these beautiful gardens. Disturbed by the destruction of the

> Explore the charmingly landscaped lawns, deeply wooded areas and a central lake, while admiring over 200 Eastern-inspired sculptures, statues and modern art.

Bamiyan Buddha statues by the Taliban in Afghanistan in 2001, José Berardo – a wealthy philanthropist – designated the Bacalhôa Buddha Eden Gardens as a place for everyone to enjoy regardless of their wealth, ethnicity, religion or sexual orientation.

Explore the charmingly landscaped lawns, deeply wooded areas and a central lake, while admiring over 200 Eastern-inspired sculptures, statues and modern art at every turn. Many of these are of the Buddha, including a 21-m- (69-ft-) high "Giant Buddha" and an enormous reclining figure. You'll also encounter cobalt blue replicas of the Xi'an Terracotta Warriors from China, as well as a fascinating separate section for imaginative contemporary and African sculptures.

You could easily spend half a day wandering around the spacious gardens, but there's also a land train which beetles through the gardens. Don't miss trying the estate's wine.

---

⑪ Nazaré

🅰 D4 🚌 **ℹ Avenida Vieira Guimarães 54, Mercado Municipal; 262 561 194**

Beside a glorious beach in a sweeping bay backed by steep cliffs, this fishing village is a popular summer resort that has maintained some of its traditional character. Fishers dressed in checked shirts and black stocking caps, and fishwives wearing several layers of petticoats can still be seen mending nets and drying fish on wire racks on the beach. The bright boats with tall prows that were once hauled from the sea by oxen are still used, although now they have a proper anchorage south of the beach. According to legend, the name Nazaré comes from a statue of the Virgin Mary brought to the town by a monk from Nazareth in the 4th century. High on the cliff above the

town is Sítio, reached by a funicular that climbs 110 m (360 ft). At the cliff edge stands the tiny Ermida da Memória. This is said to be where the Virgin Mary saved Dom Fuas Roupinho, a local dignitary, and his horse from following a deer that leapt off the cliff in a sea mist in 1182. Across the square from this chapel, the 17th-century church of Nossa Senhora da Nazaré, with two Baroque belfries and 18th-century tiles inside, contains an anonymous painting of the miraculous rescue. The church also contains the revered image of Our Lady of Nazaré. In September this statue is borne down to the sea in a traditional procession.

The Visigothic church of São Gião, 5 km (3 miles) south of Nazaré, has fine sculpting and well-proportioned arches.

Did You Know?

Sebastian Steudtner mastered the largest wave ever surfed, 26.2 m (86 ft) high, at Nazaré in 2022.

A fisherman hanging out his nets to dry on the beach at Nazaré ↓

Porto de Mós castle, towering over the town's red roofs ↑

⑫

Porto de Mós

△D4 ⊞ 🅹Jardim Municipal; 244 499 656

Originally a Moorish fort, and rebuilt over the centuries by successive Christian kings, a rather fanciful castle perches on a hill above the small town of Porto de Mós. Its present appearance, with green cone-shaped turrets and an exquisite loggia, was the inspired work of King Afonso IV's master builders in 1420.

In the town below, the 13th-century church of São João Baptista retains its original Romanesque portal. In the public gardens is the richly decorated Baroque church of São Pedro. Just off the Praça da República, the **Museu Municipal** displays a varied collection of local finds dating back to Roman remains and dinosaur bones. More modern exhibits include the local *mós* (millstones), as well as present-day ceramics and woven rugs.

The area south of Porto de Mós is dotted with vast and spectacular underground caverns with odd rock formations and festoons of stalactites and stalagmites. The **Grutas de Mira de Aire**, 17 km (11 miles) southeast,

are the biggest, descending 110 m (360 ft) into tunnels and walkways around subterranean lakes. A tour through caverns with names such as the "Jewel Room", past bizarre rocks dubbed "Chinese Hat" or "Jellyfish", ends in a theatrical light-and-water show.

Museu Municipal

🏠Travessa de São Pedro 🅲244 499 652 🕒9am-12:30pm, 2-5:30pm Tue-Sat 🅲Public hols

Grutas de Mira de Aire

 🏠Av Dr Luciano Justo Ramos 🕒Daily 🆆grutas miradaire.com

⑬

Leiria

△D4 🚉⊞ 🅹Jardim Luís de Camões; www.turismo docentro.pt

An episcopal city since 1545, Leiria is set in attractive countryside on the banks of the Lis river. Originally the Roman town of Collipo, it was recaptured from the Moors by Afonso Henriques in the 12th century. In 1254, Afonso III held a *cortes* here, the first parliament attended by common laypeople.

The resplendent hilltop **Castelo de Leiria** was part of the defence system of central Portugal. In the early 1300s, King Dinis turned the castle into a royal residence for himself and his queen, Isabel of Aragon. Within the battlements is the Gothic church of Nossa Senhora da Pena. The view from the castle loggia overlooks the Pinhal de Leiria and the town below.

The old town is full of charm, with graceful arcades and the small 12th-century church of São Pedro on Largo de São Pedro. The muted 16th-century Sé above Praça Rodrigues Lobo has an altarpiece in the chancel painted in 1605 by Simão Rodrigues. From Avenida Marquês de Pombal, opposite the castle, an 18th-century stairway ascends to the elaborate 16th-century Santuário de Nossa Senhora da Encarnação. The small Baroque interior is tightly packed with colourful geometric *azulejo* panels and 17th-century paintings of the Life of the Virgin.

Castelo de Leiria

⊗ 🏠Largo de São Pedro 🅲244 839 670 🕒Apr-Sep: 9:30am-6:30pm; Oct-Mar: 9:30am-5:30pm 🅲1 Jan, Easter, 25 Dec

⑭ Pombal

🅐D3 🚌🚃 ⓘ Rua do Castelo; 236 210 556

This small town of white-washed houses is overlooked by the stately castle, founded in 1161 by the Knights Templar *(p176)*. The town is closely associated with the Marquês de Pombal *(p45)*. In Praça Marquês de Pombal, the old prison and the *celeiro* (granary) are adorned with the Pombal family crest. The Museu Marquês de Pombal features a collection of documents and artworks focusing on the Marquis.

⑮ Fátima

🅐D4 🚌 ⓘ Avenida Dom José Alves Correia da Silva; www.turismodocentro.pt

The sanctuary of Fátima is a pilgrim destination on a par with Lourdes in France. The Neo-Baroque limestone basilica, flanked by statues of saints, has a huge tower and an esplanade twice the size of St Peter's Square in Rome.

On 12 and 13 of May and October, vast crowds of pilgrims arrive to commemorate appearances of the Virgin to three shepherd children (the three *pastorinhos*). On 13 May 1917, 10-year-old Lucia Santos and her young cousins, Jacinta and Francisco Marto, saw a shining figure in a holm oak tree. The apparition ordered the children to return to the tree on the same day for six months and by 13 October, 70,000 pilgrims were with the children by the tree. Only Lucia heard the "Secret of Fátima", spoken on her last appearance. The first part of the secret was a vision of hell; the second was of a war more devastating than World War I. The third part, a vision of papal assassination, was finally revealed by pope John Paul II on the occasion of the millennium. The Pope beatified Jacinta and Francisco in 2000. Their tombs are inside the basilica. Lucia became a nun, and died in 2005.

Stained-glass windows show scenes of the sightings. In the esplanade, the Capela das Aparições marks the site of the apparition. But for many the most memorable aspect is the emotion and faith of the penitents who approach the shrine on their knees. Wax limbs are burned as offerings for miracles performed by the Virgin and candles light the esplanade during the night-time Masses.

Fátima's basilica, and *(inset)* its lovely stained-glass windows

⑯ Ourém

🅐D4 🏠 10 km (6 miles) northeast of Fátima

The medieval town of Ourém is a walled citadel dominated by the 15th-century castle of Ourém, built by Afonso, grandson of Nuno Álvares Pereira *(p173)*. His magnificent tomb is in the 15th-century Igreja Matriz. The town's name is said to derive from Oureana, a Moorish girl who, before she fell in love with a Christian knight and converted, was called Fátima.

LUÍS VAZ DE CAMÕES (1524–80)

The author of Portugal's celebrated epic poem, *Os Lusíadas*, had a passionate nature. Banished from court, he enlisted in 1547 and set sail for North Africa, where he lost an eye in a fight. Imprisoned after another brawl, he agreed to serve his country in India, but his was the only ship from the fleet to survive the stormy seas. This experience gave his poem, published in 1572, its vibrant power.

CAMOENS

Né à Lisbonne en 1525
Mort à Lisbonne en 1580

Pegadas dos Dinossáurios

D4 🚗 Estrada de Fátima, Bairro ⏰ 10am–12:30pm, 2–6pm Tue–Sun (21 Mar–22 Sep: to 8pm Sat & Sun) 🚫 1 Jan, 25 Dec 🌐 pegadas dedinossaurios.org

In a former quarry in the heart of the Parque Natural das Serras de Aire, you will find these superbly preserved dinosaur footprints. Discovered in 1994, they belong to sauropods that, at 30 m (98 ft) in length, were some of the largest land animals to have ever lived.

In the late Triassic Period, the area was a shallow lagoon. As the dinosaurs made their way through the sediments, they left prints, which then solidified into limestone.

There are hundreds of tracks to follow, including one set of prints that is 147 m (482 ft) in length – by studying the tracks experts can estimate the size of the animals. Take a tour or follow the walkway around the open-air museum and watch an informative film at the ticket office, which explains more about these herbivorous giants that once lived here some 200 million years ago.

Barragem do Castelo de Bode

E4 🚌 To dam 🚌 From Castanheira ⏰ By appt (249 362 239) 🏛 Avenida Dr Cândido Madureira, Tomar; 249 329 823

Perhaps there once was a "Castle of the Billygoat", but today the name refers to a large dam *(barragem)* that blocks the flow of the Zêzere river 10 km (6 miles) upstream from its confluence with the Tagus. Construction

of the dam began in 1946 to serve the first of Portugal's hydroelectric power stations. Above it, a long, sprawling lake nestles between hills covered in pine and eucalyptus forests. Between the trees lie small, isolated villages. The valley is a secluded area popular for boating, fishing and watersports and it is possible to hire equipment from centres along the lake shore. Canoes, windsurf boards and water-skis can be found at the Centro Naútico do Zêzere, in Castanheira on the western side of the lake, and the Centro Naútico de Castelo do Bode. Yachting facilities are usually available from the lakeside hotels, such as the peaceful Lago Azul Eco Hotel *(www.lagoazul ecohotel.com)*. A cruise can also be taken from the hotel, stopping at the sandy beaches and small islands. There are some great spots for swimming, including the so-called river beaches of Alverangel, Montes and Castanheira, locally known as the Lago Azul because of its deep blue colour.

Castelo de Bode, the dam that controls the flow of the Zêzere river ↓

→

Walking trail near the village of Constância, running beside the Zêzere river

⑲ Abrantes

 E4 🚌 ℹ️ Esplanada 1° de Maio; 241 330 100

Grandly situated above the Tagus river, the town of Abrantes was once of strategic importance. It had a vital role in the Reconquista, and during the Peninsular War both the French General Junot and the British Duke of Wellington made it a base. The defensive walls of the early 13th-century ruined fortress that overlooks the town and the surrounding flatlands are a reminder of its important status.

The 15th-century church of Santa Maria do Castelo, within the castle walls, is now the small **Museu Dom Lopo de Almeida**. Besides an extensive collection of local archaeological finds, sculpture, vestments, ethnography and sacred art, it has the tombs of the Almeida family, counts of Abrantes, and the richest and most remarkable nucleus of Sevillian dry-stone tiles in the country.

On Rua da República, the Misericórdia church, constructed in 1584, has six magnificent religious panels attributed to Gregório Lopes (1490–1550).

The 16th-century church of São Tiago e São Mateus, located in the town of Sardoal, 8 km (5 miles) north of Abrantes, holds a compelling thorn-crowned Christ by the 16th-century painter the Master of Sardoal. An 18th-century tile panel on the façade of the Capela do Espírito Santo, in Praça da República, honours Gil Vicente, the 16th-century playwright who was born here.

Museu Dom Lopo de Almeida

🏠 Rua Dom Francisco de Almeida ☎️ 241 371 724 ⏰ Tue–Sun

⑳ Constância

 E4 🚗 12 km (7 miles) west of Abrantes

The pretty whitewashed town of Constância nurtures the memory of the poet Luís Vaz de Camões, who lived here for three years before he was banished from court in 1546 for writing a love sonnet to a lady who was also favoured by King João III. The riverside gardens seen today were influenced by those described in his poem Os Lusíadas.

The town sits on the confluence of the Tagus and Zêzere rivers, and there are lovely local walks along their shores.

㉑ Castelo de Almourol

 E4 ☎️ 927 228 354 🚌 To Barquinha then taxi and ferry ⏰ Tue–Sun during daylight hours

Set in a dramatic location on a tiny island in the Tagus, this enchanting castle was constructed over a Roman fortress in 1171 by Gualdim Pais. Legends of this magical place abound. A 16th-century verse romance called Palmeirim de Inglaterra weaves an intricate tale of giants and knights, as well as the fight of the crusader Palmeirim for the lovely Polinarda. Some say the castle is haunted by the ghost of a princess sighing for the love of her Moorish slave.

🏔️ GREAT VIEW
Capture the Castle

With a car, head to Bar do Castelo, off the M1191. This little bar is on the opposite bank of the Tagus to Castelo de Almourol, making it a great spot to enjoy a refreshing drink with a view.

---

22 Santarém

Ⓐ D4 🚌 ℹ️ Rua Capelo Ivens 63; 243 304 437

The lively district capital of the Ribatejo, overlooking the Tagus, has an illustrious past. To Julius Caesar it was an important bureaucratic centre, Praesidium Julium. To the Moors it was the stronghold of Xantarim. To the Portuguese kings, Santarém was the site of many gatherings of the *cortes* (parliaments).

At the centre of the old town, in Praça Sá da Bandeira, is the vast Igreja do Seminário, a multi-windowed Baroque edifice built by João IV for the Jesuits in 1640 on the site of a royal palace. The huge interior has a painted wooden ceiling and marble and gilt ornamentation. From here, Rua Serpa Pinto runs southeast past a cluster of older buildings.

↑ Praça Sá da Bandeira, a square at the heart of Santarém's old town

The lofty Igreja de Marvila, built in the 12th century and later altered, has a Manueline portal and is lined with dazzling early 17th-century diamond-patterned *azulejo* panels. The medieval 22-m- (72-ft-) high Torre das Cabaças was once a clock tower and now houses a small museum of time. Opposite the tower, the Museu Arqueológico was formerly the Romanesque church of São João de Alporão.

Rua Serpa Pinto leads into Rua 5 de Outubro and up to the Jardim das Portas do Sol, built on the site of a Moorish castle. The gardens are enclosed by the city's medieval walls.

Returning into town, on Largo Pedro Álvares Cabral, the 14th-century Igreja da Graça has a spectacular rose window carved from a single stone. Further south, the 14th-century Igreja do Santíssimo Milagre, on Largo do Milagre, has a Renaissance interior and 16th-century *azulejos*.

12th-century fortress now enclose a garden. Just below the castle is the 16th-century Misericórdia church with a Renaissance portal and an interior lined with colourful "carpet" *azulejos* from 1674. The Igreja de Santiago, on Largo do Paço, was probably built in 1203, although a gilded retable with a wood carving of the young Jesus assisting Joseph in his carpentry is a 17th-century addition.

In the centre of town is the **Museu Municipal de Carlos Reis**, named after the painter Carlos Reis (1863–1940), who was born here. The museum contains paintings by 19th- and early 20th-century artists and a 15th-century Gothic figure of Nossa Senhora do Ó.

Museu Municipal de Carlos Reis

🏛️ Rua do Salvador 🕐 9am– 12:30pm & 2–5:30pm Tue–Fri, 2–6pm Sat & Sun 🚫 Public hols 🌐 museu.cm-torresnovas.pt

---

24 Golegã

Ⓐ E4 🚌 ℹ️ Rua de D Afonso Henriques, Largo da Imaculada Conceição; 249 979 002

Usually a quiet town, Golegã is overrun during the first two weeks of November by horse enthusiasts who throng to the annual Feira Nacional do Cavalo. This horse fair coincides with the tasting of the year's new wine on

23 Torres Novas

Ⓐ E4 🚌 ℹ️ Largo dos Combatentes 4–5; 249 813 019

Animated streets and fine churches cluster beneath the castle walls of this handsome town. The ruins of the

St Martin's Day (11 November). On this day, revellers drink the young wine, known as *agua-pé* (literally, "foot water").

In the centre of town, the 16th-century Igreja Matriz, attributed to Diogo Boitac, has an exquisite Manueline portal and an interior rich in *azulejos*. The small **Casa-Estúdio Carlos Relvas** is housed in the elegant Art Nouveau house and studio of the photographer (1838–94).

Casa-Estúdio Carlos Relvas

 🏛 Largo Dom Manuel I ⏰ For tours only: 10am, 11am, noon, 2:30pm & 3:30pm 🚫 Public hols 🌐 casarelvas.com/site/pt

---

㉕

Alpiarça

🅰 E4 🚍 🛈 Rua Dr Queirós Vaz Guedes (Jardim Municipal); 243 556 000

Set in the vast, fertile plain known as the Lezíria, which stretches east of the Tagus and is famous for horse breeding, Alpiarça is a small, neat town. The fine twin-towered parish church, on Rua José Relvas, is dedicated to Santo Eustáquio, patron saint of the town. Built in the late 19th century, it houses paintings from the 17th century, including a charming *Divine Shepherdess* in the sacristy in which the young Jesus is shown conversing with a sheep.

On the southern outskirts of town is the striking **Casa Museu dos Patudos**, surrounded by vineyards. This was the residence of the wealthy and cultivated José Relvas (1858–1929), an art collector and – briefly – premier of the Republic. The exterior of this eye-catching country house, built for him by Raúl Lino in 1905–9, has simple whitewashed walls and a green-and-white striped spire. The colonnaded loggia, reached via an outside staircase, is lined with *azulejo* panels. The museum contains Relvas's personal collection of fine and decorative art. Renaissance paintings include *Virgin with Child and St John* by the school of Leonardo da Vinci and *Christ in the Tomb* by the German school. There are also paintings by Delacroix and Zurbarán as well as many works by 19th-century Portuguese artists, including 30 by Relvas's friend José Malhôa. Relvas also collected exquisite porcelain, bronzes, furniture and Eastern rugs, as well as early Portuguese Arraiolos carpets, including a particularly fine one in silk.

Casa Museu dos Patudos

 🏛 2 km (1 mile) S of Alpiarça on N118 ☎ 243 558 321 ⏰ Tue–Sun 🚫 Public hols

---

TOP 5

CENTRAL PORTUGUESE DISHES

Feijoada
Paprika-spiced stew of beans and vegetables, with cured meat.

Caldeirada de Peixe
A stew of fish, peppers, tomatoes and potatoes.

Favas à Portuguesa
Fava beans combined with *morcela* (blood sausage) and pork ribs.

Arroz Doce
Lemon zest-scented rice pudding with cinnamon.

Magusto
A purée of dry maize and white bread blended with water and kale, served with *bacalhau*.

↑ Horses and riders parading at the annual Feira Nacional do Cavalo in Golegã

Admiring the collection in the Museu do Neo-Realismo, Vila Franca de Xira

Museu do Neo-Realismo

 Rua Alves Redol 45
🕐 10am–6pm Tue–Fri & Sun (to 7pm Sat) 🚫 Public hols
🌐 museudoneorealismo.pt

㉗

Coruche

🅰E5 🚉🚌 *i* Galeria do Mercado Municipal; 243 619 072

Coruche is an attractive little town in the heart of bullfighting country with a riverside location overlooking the Lezíria, the wide open plain that stretches east of the Tagus river. The town, inhabited since Palaeolithic times, was razed to the ground in 1180 by the Moors as reprisal against the reconquering Christians.

A short walk up the street stands the tiny church of São Pedro. Inside, the church is completely covered with 17th-century blue-and-yellow carpet tiles. An *azulejo* panel on the altar front shows St Peter surrounded by birds and animals. Above the town stands the simple 12th-century blue-and-white church of Nossa Senhora do Castelo. From here there are excellent views over the fertile agricultural land and cork oaks of the Sorraia valley and the Lezíria.

㉖

Vila Franca de Xira

🅰D5 🚉🚌 *i* Rua Alves Redol 5; 263 285 605

Sitting beside the Tagus, this small town has a reputation larger than its modest appearance suggests. Traditionally the area has been the centre for Portugal's bull-and-horse rearing communities. Twice a year, people come here to participate in the bull-running through the streets and watch the *tourada* (bullfighting) and traditional horsemanship. The animated and gaudy Festa do Colete Encarnado (named after the red waistcoat worn by *campinos*, the Ribatejo herders) takes place over several days in early July. The festival is a lively occasion with folk dancing, boat races on the Tagus and sardines grilled in the street, so it's not all about bullfighting. A similar festival, the Feira de Outubro, takes place in October.

Whatever your opinion on bullfighting, Vila Franca de Xira is worth visiting outside the festivals. Archaeological exhibits and artifacts relating to regional history are on display in the **Museu Municipal**. A collection of Neo-Realist literature and art dating from the early 20th century, meanwhile, is found in the **Museu do Neo-Realismo**, which comprises a library and exhibition space.

The town centre retains an exuberantly tile-covered market dating from the 1920s. Further east, on Largo da Misericórdia, striking 18th-century *azulejos* adorn the chancel of the Misericórdia church. South of town, the Ponte Marechal Carmona, built in 1951, is the only bridge across the Tagus between Santarém to the north and Lisbon to the south.

Museu Municipal

 Rua Serpa Pinto 65
🕐 9:30am–12:30pm, 2–5:30pm Tue–Sun 🚫 Public hols, 1–15 Aug 🌐 museu municipalvfxira.pt

㉘

Alenquer

🅰D5 🚌 *i* Parque Vaz Monteiro; 263 711 433

Vila Alta, the old part of town, climbs steeply up the slopes of the hillside, high above the newer town by the river. In the central Travessa de São Pedro, the 15th-century church of São Pedro contains the tomb of the Humanist chronicler and native son Damião de Góis (1502–74). Pêro de Alenquer, a navigator for the explorers Bartolomeu Dias in 1488 and Vasco da Gama in 1497 (p114), was also born here. Uphill, near the ruins of a 13th-century castle, the monastery church of São Francisco retains a Manueline cloister and a 13th-century portal. Founded in 1222, this was Portugal's first Franciscan monastery.

 29

Torres Vedras

D5 🚌🚋 **f** Praça do Município, Edifício dos Paços do Concelho; 261 310 483

The town is closely linked with the Lines of Torres Vedras, fortified defences built by the Duke of Wellington to repel

Napoleon's troops during the Peninsular War. North of the town, near the restored fort of São Vicente, traces of trenches and bastions are still visible, but along most of the lines the forts and earthworks have gone, buried by time and rapid change.

Above the town, the restored walls of the 13th-century castle embrace a shady garden and the church of Santa Maria do Castelo. Down in the town, on Praça 25 de Abril, a memorial to those who died in the Peninsular War stands in front of the 16th-century Convento da Graça. Today the convent houses the well-lit **Museu Municipal**. A room devoted to the Peninsular War displays a model of the lines; other interesting exhibits include a 15th-century Flemish School *Retábulo da Vida da Virgem*.

Open for Mass at weekends, the monastery church, Igreja da Graça, has a 17th-century gilded altarpiece. In a niche in the chancel is the tomb of São Gonçalo de Lagos.

Beyond the pedestrian Rua 9 de Abril, the Manueline church of São Pedro greets visitors with a winged dragon on the portal. The interior has a painted wooden ceiling and walls adorned with colourful 18th-century *azulejo* panels depicting scenes of

↑ Traditional tiles decorating the Convento da Graça, Torres Vedras

daily life. Behind the church, on Rua Cândido dos Reis, stands a pretty 16th-century water fountain that is worth seeing, the Chafariz dos Canos (Fountain of the Pipes).

Museu Municipal

♿ 🏛 Praça 25 de Abril 📞 261 310 485 🕐 Tue–Sun 🚫 1 Jan, Easter, 1 May, 24 & 25 Dec

Vineyard at Alenquer, an area known for its wine production ↑

THE BEIRAS

The three provinces of the Beiras may not be a tourist hub, but their past commercial and defensive significance has left its mark. In Beira Litoral, the prows of Aveiro's seaweed boats are a legacy of trade with the Phoenicians, while Viseu – Beira Alta's capital – grew up at a crossroads of Roman trading routes. The Romans were never as firmly entrenched here as further south, but the ruins of Conímbriga speak eloquently of the elegant city that once stood here. It gave its name to Coimbra, which temporarily became the country's capital from 1139 until 1260. Conscious of Spain's proximity and claim on their land, successive Portuguese kings constructed a great defensive chain of forts along the vulnerable eastern border. These fortresses continued to prove vital in the fight for independence from Spain in the 17th century, and again against Napoleon's forces. Even Buçaco, revered for the peace and sanctity of its forest, is known as the site of Wellington's successful stand against Masséna.

Despite the unforgiving terrain, the Beiras are famed as the source of some gastronomic treats: Portugal's favourite cheese is made in the Serra da Estrela, while the region's red wines are among Portugal's best known.

THE BEIRAS

Atlantic Ocean

Trofa
Santo Tirso
Mindelo
Coronado
Francisco
Sá Carneiro
Airport
PORTO
Penafiel
Matosinhos
Valongo
Porto
A41
Melres
Espinho
Santa Maria da Feira
São João
da Madeira
Vale de
Cambra
OVAR **8**
Oliveira
Torreira
Estarreja
AVEIRO
N327
Albergaria-
a-Velha
São
Jacinto
Rio Vouga
Talhadas
AVEIRO **1**
Ílhavo
Águeda
Vagos
Sangalhos
PRAIA DE
MIRA **6**
Curia
Mira
LUSO **14**
Mealhada
Cantanhede
3
Tocha
Portunhos
BUÇACO
Penacova
MONTEMOR-
O-VELHO
FIGUEIRA
DA FOZ
10
2 COIMBRA
9
COIMBRA
Condeixa-
a-Nova
LOUSÃ
Lavos
13 CONÍMBRIGA
Soure
12 PENEL
Rabaçal
Guia
Monte Redondo
ESTREMADURA
AND RIBATEJO
LEIRIA
p166
Leiria
Freixianda
Cardosos
Beira Baixa
Batalha
Ferreira
do Zêzere
Ourém
Tomar
SANTARÉM
Constância
Alcanena

↑ Brightly coloured *moliceiros* on the Canal Central

AVEIRO

⚐ D3 **🚉 Avenida Dr Lourenço Peixinho** **🚌 Avenida Dr Lourenço Peixinho** **⛴ Forte da Barra-São Jacinto: daily** **ℹ Rua João Mendonça 8; 234 420 760**

This little city, once a great sea port, has a long history, with its salt pans featuring in a will in 959 CE. By the 16th century, Aveiro was a considerable town, rich from salt and the *bacalhoeiros* fishing for cod off Newfoundland. When storms silted up the harbour in 1575 this wealth vanished, and the town languished beside its lagoon, the *ria*. Only in the 19th century did Aveiro regain its prosperity and it is now ringed with industry.

① Old Quarter

Tucked in between the Canal das Pirâmides, which was named after the salt pyramids that once lined this waterway, and the Canal de São Roque, the old quarter of the city was once home to salt warehouses. Although no longer lined with industry, this area is still home to the neat, whitewashed houses of Aveiro's fishers. In the early morning, the focus of activity is the Mercado do Peixe at the end of the Canal das Pirâmides, where the fish from the night's catch is auctioned to local restaurants. Although it was remodelled in the early 21st century, there has been a bustling market hall on this site since the late 18th century, making it a historic part of local life.

Skirting the Canal Central, along Rua João de Mendonça, are Art Nouveau mansions and some of the many *pastelarias* selling Aveiro's speciality: *ovos moles*. Literally "soft eggs", these are a rich confection of sweetened egg yolk in candied casings shaped like fish or barrels. As so often in Portugal, the original recipe is credited to nuns. *Ovos moles* are sold by weight or in little barrels.

② Across the Canal Central

South of the Canal Central and the bustling Praça General Humberto Delgado are the principal historic buildings of Aveiro. The Misericórdia church in the Praça da República dates from the 16th century, its façade of *azulejos* framing a splendid Mannerist portal. In the same square stands the stately 18th-century Paços do Concelho, or town hall, with its distinctive Tuscan-style pillars.

Nearby is Aveiro's modest 15th-century cathedral of São Domingos. The figures of the Three Graces over the door on the Baroque façade were added in 1719. A short walk south lies the Igreja das

> 💬 **INSIDER TIP**
> **Fish Food**
>
> The upper floor of the Mercado do Peixe is now a buzzing restaurant, populated by students and locals. Of course, the menu uses fresh fish from the market below. While you eat, look out of the huge windows on to the Canal de São Roque.

→

Decorated buildings, one an Art Nouveau marvel, in the Old Quarter

Carmelitas, its nave and chancel decorated with paintings of the life of the Carmelite reformer, St Teresa.

---

③

Museu de Aveiro

⌂ Ave Santa Joana ☏ 234 423297 🕐 10am-12:30pm & 1:30-6pm Tue-Sun 🚫 1 Jan, 1 May, Easter Sun, 25 Dec

The former Mosteiro de Jesus is full of mementos of Santa Joana, who died here in 1490. The daughter of Afonso V, Joana retreated to the convent in 1472 and spent the rest of her life here. She was beatified in 1693 and her ornamental Baroque marble tomb is in the lower choir. The 18th-century paintings in the chapel show scenes of her life. This was once the needlework room where Santa Joana died. Among the Portuguese primitive paintings is a 15th-century full-face portrait of the princess in court dress.

Other interesting things to see in this museum include the superb gilded chancel (1725-9), the 15th-century cloisters and the refectory, which is decorated in local Coimbra tiles. Between the refectory and chapterhouse lies the Gothic tomb of an armoured knight, Dom João de Albuquerque.

---

④

Ria de Aveiro

Old maritime charts do not show a lagoon here, but in 1575 a terrible storm raised a sand bar that blocked the harbour to create the lagoon. Denied access to the sea, Aveiro declined, its population cut down by the fever bred in the stagnant waters. It was not until 1808 that the *barra nova* was created, linking Aveiro once more to the sea.

The lagoon that remains covers some 65 sq km (25 sq miles), and is nearly 50 km (30 miles) long, from Furadouro south past Aveiro's salt pans and the Reserva Natural das Dunas de São Jacinto (Nature Reserve of São Jacinto) to Costa Nova. The reserve includes beaches, dunes and woods as well as the lagoon, and is home to a large and varied bird population, including pin-tails and goshawks. Of the boats seen here, the most elegant is the *moliceiro*. Despite the bright, often humorous decoration on its high, curving prow, this is a working boat, harvesting *moliço* (seaweed) for fertilizer. Chemical fertilizers have drastically cut demand for *moliço*, but the boats have survived as a star attraction. Visitors can hop aboard these vessels and enjoy a 45-minute tour along the city's canals.

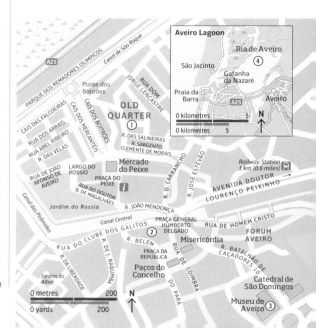

A boat on the Mondego river passing the town of Coimbra ↑

COIMBRA

 E3 🚉 Coimbra A, Av Emídio Navarro; Coimbra B, N of city, on N11 🚌 Av Fernão de Magalhães 🛈 Praça da República (239 857 186); Universidade de Coimbra (239 242 744); Largo da Portagem (239 488 120)

The birthplace of six kings and the seat of Portugal's oldest university, Coimbra arouses an affection shared by no other city. Afonso Henriques, the first king of Portugal, moved his capital here in 1139, an honour it retained until 1256. For the Portuguese, Coimbra holds the roots of nationhood and, for visitors, a wealth of fascinating historic associations.

①
Santa Cruz

🏛 Praça 8 de Maio 📞 239 822 941 🕒 9:30am–4:30pm Mon-Sat, 1–5pm Sun 🚫 1 Jan, Easter, Corpus Christi, University Festivities, 24 Oct am, 24 Dec

Founded by the canons of St Augustine in 1131, the church and monastery of Santa Cruz are rich in examples of the city's early 16th-century school of sculpture. Carvings by Nicolau Chanterène and Jean de Rouen adorn the church's Portal da Majestade, designed by Diogo de Castilho in 1523. The chapterhouse by Diogo Boitac

is Manueline in style, as are the Claustro do Silêncio (which has an admission fee) and the choir stalls, carved in 1518 with a frieze about exploration. Portugal's first two kings, Afonso Henriques and Sancho I, were reinterred here in 1520.

②
Sé Velha

🏛 Largo da Sé Velha 📞 239 825 273 🕒 9:30am–5:30pm Mon-Sat, 11am–5pm Sun & religious holidays (Aug: to 6pm daily)

The fortress-style Old Cathedral is widely regarded as the finest

Romanesque building in Portugal, a celebration in stone of the triumph over the Moors in 1064. Sancho I was crowned here in 1185, soon after the cathedral was completed.

Inside, square piers lead the eye up the nave to the flamboyant retable over the altar. The work of Flemish woodcarvers in about 1502, this depicts the birth of Christ, the Assumption and many saints. A 16th-century

---

COIMBRA FADO

While Lisbon's music is melancholy and sombre, Coimbra's is boisterous and romantic. Sung by male students or alumni of Coimbra's university, *fado* in this city ranges from serenades to drinking songs. Remember to cough rather than clap the singers.

→ Admiring a sculpture in the Museu Nacional Machado de Castro

altarpiece in the south transept is also highly decorated, as is the Manueline font, thought to be by Diogo Pires the Younger. In contrast is the quiet restraint of the cloister, built in 1218.

The tomb of the city's first Christian governor, Sisinando (a Muslim convert who died in 1091), lies in the chapterhouse.

---

③ ✎

Museu Nacional Machado de Castro

⌖ Largo Dr José Rodrigues
⌚ 10am–6pm Tue–Sun
🚫 1 Jan, Easter, 1 May, 4 Jul, 24 & 25 Dec ⌨ patrimonio cultural.gov.pt

The elegant 16th-century loggias of the former bishop's palace are the setting for a display of some of Portugal's finest sculpture. The museum is named after master sculptor Joaquim Machado de Castro (1731–1822).

Among the medieval pieces on display here is an endearing stone knight holding a mace dating from the 14th century. Also in the collection, along with furnishings and vestments, are paintings from the 12th to 20th centuries, including the *Assumption of the Virgin* by the Master of Sardoal. Look for Queen Leonor's coat of arms, which she had painted into the work.

An intriguing feature of the museum is the Criptoportico de Aeminium, a maze of underground passages holding a collection of Roman sculpture and stelae and Visigothic artifacts.

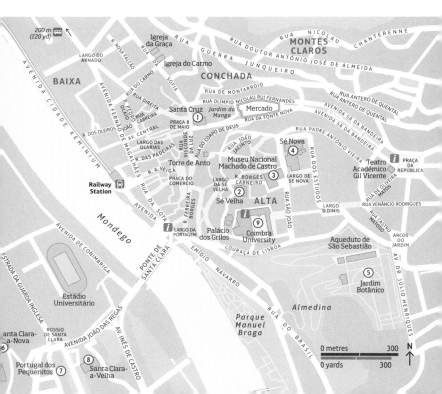

Sé Nova

🏛 Largo da Sé Nova
📞 239 823 138 🕐 9am–6pm Mon, Tue, Thu & Sat (to 6:30pm Wed & Fri), 9am–11am & 12:30–6pm Sun
🚫 1 Jan, Easter, 25 Dec

Nova, or new, is a relative term, as this church was founded by the Jesuits in 1598. Located a short walk from the university, their adjacent Colégio das Onze Mil Virgens is today part of the sciences faculty. The Jesuit Order was banned by the Marquês de Pombal in 1759 but their church became the episcopal seat in 1772. Jesuit saints still look out from the façade.

The interior is barrel-vaulted, with a dome over the crossing. To the left of the entrance is a Manueline-style octagonal font brought, with the choir stalls, from the Sé Velha. The paintings above the stalls are copies of Italian masters. The altarpiece in the 17th-century chancel, featuring more Jesuit saints, is flanked by a pair of 18th-century organs.

↑ Paths leading up to an ornate stone fountain in the Jardim Botânico

Jardim Botânico

🏛 Calçada Martim de Freitas 🕐 Apr–Sep: 9am–8pm daily; Oct–Mar: 9am–5:30pm daily
🚫 1 Jan, 25 Dec 🌐 uc.pt/jardimbotanico

These, Portugal's largest botanical gardens, were created in 1772 when the reforming Marquês de

Pombal (p45) introduced the study of natural history at the University of Coimbra. The university is still a centre for the study of flora.

The entrance, near the 16th-century aqueduct of São Sebastião, leads into 50 acres (20 ha) devoted to a remarkable collection of some 1,200 plants, including many rare species. The gardens are used for research, but are laid out as pleasure gardens, with green-houses and a wild area over-looking the Mondego river.

Santa Clara-a-Nova

🏛 Alto de Santa Clara
📞 239 441 674 🕐 Apr–Sep: 10am–7pm daily (Oct–Mar: to 6pm)

The vast "new" convent of the Poor Clares was built between 1649 and 1677 to house the nuns from Santa Clara-a-Velha on drier land uphill. The building was designed by a mathematics professor, João Turriano, and now serves in part as a barracks for the army.

← A 17th-century gilt-and-wood sculpture of a saint on the Sé Nova's altarpiece

In the richly Baroque church, pride of place is given to the silver tomb of Santa Isabel, installed in 1696 and paid for by the people of Coimbra. The saint's original tomb, a single stone, lies in the lower choir and polychrome wooden panels in the aisles tell the story of her life.

The convent's large cloister, built by the Hungarian Carlos Mardel, was contributed in 1733 by João V, a generous benefactor who was well-known for his charity to nuns.

Portugal dos Pequenitos

🏛 Santa Clara ⏰ Jan, Feb & mid-Oct-Dec: 10am-5pm daily (Mar-Oct: to 7pm daily) 🚫 25 Dec 🌐 portugaldos pequenitos.pt

At this world in miniature, you can explore scaled-down versions of Portugal's finest national buildings, whole villages of typical regional architecture, and pagodas and temples representing the furthest reaches of the former Portuguese empire. Parts of Africa, from Angola to Mozambique, South America and Asia that were once colonized by Portugal are all represented here among their native vegetation.

The park also includes a reconstruction of Coimbra itself, complete with its famed university, but the real highlight is a magnificent replica of the Convento de Cristo in Tomar (p176).

Santa Clara-a-Velha

🏛 Santa Clara 📞 239 801 160 🚫 For renovation until further notice

Founded in the late 13th century, the first monastery on this site was dissolved in 1311. In 1314, Santa Isabel, the widow of King Dinis, who was admired for her charity, had the convent of Santa Clara rebuilt because she had a palace nearby. She died in 1336 in Estremoz (p306) but was buried here in an elaborate tomb, attesting to her affinity with the monastery. Inês de Castro was also laid to rest here 20 years later, but was re-entombed at Alcobaça (p170).

INSIDER TIP
Kayak the Mondego

The Mondego river offers some of the country's best opportunities for kayaking. Follow the 18-km- (11-mile-) long stretch from Penacova to Coimbra, which passes through beautiful scenery. The many river beaches en route make for pleasant stopping-off points.

Almost from the day it was built, Santa Clara suffered from flooding and it was finally abandoned in 1677. In 1696, Santa Isabel's remains were moved to the Convent of Santa Clara-a-Nova, which sits on higher ground.

The original Gothic church, in silted ruins since the late 17th century, has at last been restored. Beneath the mud and water, the monastery was preserved in excellent condition and the site gives a fascinating insight into the everyday lives of the monastic community who once lived here.

↑ Exploring miniature regional houses at Portugal dos Pequenitos

⑨ 🔖 Ⓜ 🖥

COIMBRA UNIVERSITY

🅰 E3 🏛 Paço das Escolas 🚌 103 from train station A 🕙 10am–7pm daily (late Oct–early May: 9am–5pm daily) 🚫 Some areas close for lunch (1–2pm); 1 Jan, 22 May, 24, 25 & 31 Dec 🌐 visit.uc.pt

A trip to Coimbra would not be complete without a visit to the historic university, which dominates the city. The complex is home to graceful buildings, hallowed halls and quirky traditions.

In 1290, King Dinis founded a university in Lisbon, which became one of the world's oldest and most illustrious institutions. In 1537, it was transferred to Coimbra and located in what used to be King Afonso's palace. Study was mostly of canon and civil law, medicine and letters (grammar and philosophy) until reforms by the Marquês de Pombal in the 1770s broadened the curriculum. Several 19th-century literary figures, including Eça de Queirós, were alumni of Coimbra. Many buildings were replaced after the 1940s, but the halls around the Pátio das Escolas echo with 700 years of learning. It will come as no surprise that the university is a UNESCO World Heritage Site.

↑ Students outside the Via Latina

The Sala do Exame Privado is the private examination hall.

As well as works of art on religious themes, the Museu de Arte Sacra has vestments, chalices and books of early sacred music.

Portrait of João V (c.1730)

The 16th-century portal of Capela de São Miguel, by Marcos Pires, is Manueline in style.

Capela de São Miguel

Biblioteca Joanina

① The Sala Grande dos Actos is lined with dons' benches and portraits of Portuguese monarchs.

② Named after its benefactor, João V, the 18th-century Biblioteca Joanina holds over 300,000 books under a painted ceiling.

③ The Capela de São Miguel has an impressive Mannerist altar surrounded by *azulejos*.

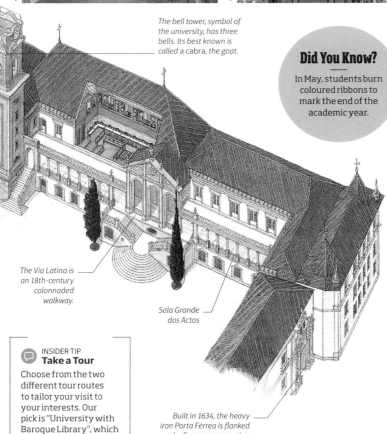

The bell tower, symbol of the university, has three bells. Its best known is called a cabra, *the goat.*

Did You Know?

In May, students burn coloured ribbons to mark the end of the academic year.

The Via Latina is an 18th-century colonnaded walkway.

Sala Grande dos Actos

INSIDER TIP
Take a Tour

Choose from the two different tour routes to tailor your visit to your interests. Our pick is "University with Baroque Library", which takes in the Biblioteca Joanina and the Capela de São Miguel.

Built in 1634, the heavy iron Porta Férrea is flanked by figures representing canon and civil law, medicine and letters.

↑ The grand Coimbra University, with its iconic bell tower

BUÇACO

📍 E3 🏠 3 km (2 miles) SE of Luso 📞 231 937 000 📠
🕐 9am–6pm daily (last adm 5pm) 🌐 fmb.pt

Part-ancient woodland, part-arboretum, the National Forest of Buçaco is a magical place, with its shady walks, hermits' grottoes and the astonishing Bussaco Palace Hotel at its centre.

As early as the 6th century, this 260-acre (105-ha) park was a monastic retreat, and in 1628 the Carmelites built a monastery here, walling in the forest to keep the world at bay. In their secluded forest the monks established contemplative walks and chapels. The trees, added to by Portuguese explorers, gained papal protection in 1632, and there are some 700 species here, including the venerable "Buçaco cedar". The peace of the forest was disturbed in 1810 as British and Portuguese troops fought the French on Buçaco ridge.

King Carlos, who commissioned this extravaganza in 1888, never lived to see his creation. Completed in 1907, the Neo-Manueline folly of a hunting lodge built by Luigi Manini includes murals and tiles by prominent artists. *Azulejos* in the hall feature scenes of the Battle of Buçaco.

The palace's rebirth as a luxury hotel in 1917, serving its own wines, was the inspiration of the royal chef and it became a fashionable rendezvous for socialites. Much of the decor inside still echoes that era.

The exterior of the Bussaco Palace Hotel, and *(inset)* its grand hall with *azulejos* featuring scenes from the Battle of Buçaco

[1] The Bussaco Palace Hotel has a light and airy restaurant, serving a delightful breakfast buffet. With such a lavish interior, it is not hard to see why Manuel II is said to have brought the French actress Gaby Deslys here for a romantic interlude.

[2] The park is great for walkers and there are many shaded paths through the forest to choose from.

[3] Only the cloisters, chapel and a few monks' cells of the Carmelite Monastery remain.

Did You Know?

During World War II, the hotel was rumoured to be frequented by spies.

TOP 5 FOREST FEATURES

Fonte Fria
This impressive stepped cascade, fed by a forest spring, tumbles down to a magnolia-fringed pool.

Vale dos Fetos
Leading down to a small lake, the Valley of Ferns is lined with specimens from around the world.

Via Sacra
Installed by the Bishop of Coimbra in 1693, chapels containing life-size figures mark the Stations of the Cross along this winding path.

Cruz Alta
The forest's highest point has glorious views as far as the sea.

The Buçaco Cedar
Now 28 m (92 ft) high, this tree is said to have been planted in 1644.

Autumn foliage gilding the Serra da Estrela mountains ↑

4

SERRA DA ESTRELA

🅰 F3 🚉 Covilhã, Guarda 🚌 To Covilhã, Seia & Guarda; limited local service within park
ℹ Mercado Municipal, Rua Pintor Lucas Marrão, Seia (238 317 762); Covilhã (275 330 635); Gouveia (238 083 930); Manteigas (275 981 129)

A designated nature reserve, the Serra da Estrela's long-distance paths and stunning flora attract walkers and nature enthusiasts, while a winter snowfall brings skiers to the slopes around Torre.

These "star mountains" are the tallest range on mainland Portugal. The highest point rises to 1,993 m (6,539 ft) but is topped by a small stone tower – the Torre – to "stretch" it to 2,000 m (6,561 ft) above the Zêzere river. The exposed granite of the upper slopes is good for little but grazing sheep, and stone shepherds' huts, with thatched roofs, form part of the landscape. Sheep have shaped the fortunes of the area, providing wool for a textile industry and milk for Portugal's best-known cheese.

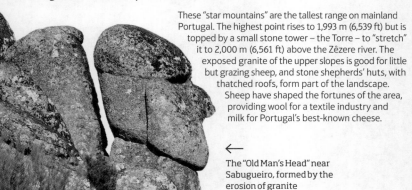

←

The "Old Man's Head" near Sabugueiro, formed by the erosion of granite

GREAT VIEW
Torre Tour

Climb up mainland Portugal's highest mountain for amazing views of the Zêzere valley. There are 1950s radar stations at the top, which make an interesting contrast with the natural scene set out below.

Did You Know?

Serra da Estrela sheepdogs are reputed to have some wolf blood in their ancestry.

① Intelligent, loyal and brave, the Serra da Estrela sheepdog embodies all the qualities required in this wild region. Its heavy, shaggy coat helps it survive the bitter high-altitude winters and in the past its strength was called upon to defend the flock from wolves.

② The Zêzere flows through a classic glacier-cut valley. The golden broom growing here is used to thatch mountain huts.

③ Linhares, a town on the western slopes of the Serra da Estrela, is like a living museum, with many fine houses dating from its 15th-century heyday.

EXPERIENCE MORE

Paiva Walkways

⚑E2 ⚐Start at Areinho or Espiunca ⏰Apr & Oct: 9am–7pm daily, May–Sep: 8am–8pm daily, Nov–Mar: 9am–5pm daily; last adm 3 hours before closing ⬡reservas. passadicosdopaiva.pt

This 8.7-km (5.4-mile) walkway has a wooden boardwalk that weaves its way along the contours of the Paiva river valley. Parts of the trail are stepped and extremely steep. The area is prone to summer fires and visitor numbers are restricted, so advance booking is essential. It's best to start the walk from Areinho, as the end point at Espiunca is largely downhill. On the south end of the walkways is the 516 Arouca Bridge, one of the world's longest pedestrian suspended bridges.

↑ Hikers taking the walkway through the Paiva river valley

Praia de Mira

⚑D3 ⬛ ℹAv da Barrinha; 924 473 751

This unspoiled stretch of coast is backed by a wooded reserve, the Mata Nacional das Dunas de Mira. Praia de Mira, with the dunes and Atlantic on one side and the peaceful lagoon of Barrinha de Mira on the other, is a pretty fishing village developing as a resort. Fishing boats are still drawn by oxen up the spectacular beach but leisure craft now cruise the shore and inland waterways, and the fishers' striped *palheiros*, popular as seaside cottages, are fast vanishing amid bars and cafés.

HIKING AND CYCLING ROUTES

The relatively flat coastline makes the area around Praia de Mira ideal for hiking and cycling. Visit the tourist office to pick up leaflets detailing the marked trails around local lakes and watermills. Our choice is the 25-km (15-mile) Pista Ciclo-Pedonal de Mira, which follows inland canals towards Aveiro via dunes, lakes and pine woods *(www.cm-mira.pt/node/139)*.

Arouca

⚑E2 ⬛ ℹRua Abel Botelho 4; 256 940 258

This small town in a green valley owes its main attraction, the great **Mosteiro de Arouca**, to its saintly royal benefactor, Mafalda. Princess Mafalda was born in 1195, the daughter of Sancho I. She was betrothed to the teenage Prince Enrique of Castile, but when he died in an accident, Mafalda took the veil in Arouca. Under her, the convent became Cistercian and Mafalda's wealth and dedication made the house highly influential. She died in 1256, and her incorrupt corpse was discovered in 1616, leading to her beatification in 1793. For over a thousand years the convent has stood beside Arouca's church on the cobbled main square. In the early 18th century the church underwent costly redecoration: 104 carved choir stalls are surmounted by paintings in sumptuous gilded panels, and the organ and chancel retable are also heavily gilded. Honoured with its own altar is a recumbent effigy of Santa Mafalda in a silver and ebony casket; her mummified remains lie below the casket.

Guided tours take visitors round the convent's museum, in which are displayed some exquisite silver monstrances, furniture and religious works of art, including two paintings by 18th-century artist André Gonçalves, showing Mafalda saving the monastery from fire. The Neo-Classical double cloister, begun in 1781, the large refectory and kitchen, and a chapterhouse covered with cheerful Coimbra tiles of rural scenes can also be visited.

Mosteiro de Arouca
 ⚑Largo de Santa Mafalda 📞256 943 321 ⏰Tue–Sun ⚑Public hols

8

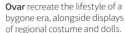

Ovar

E2 🚌🚃 ℹ️ **Largo Família Soares Pinto; 256 572 215**

This small town once earned its living from the Ria de Aveiro (*p195*). Industry has arrived in the shape of foundries and steel mills, but oxen still plod along the roads. Gleaming tiles cover many of the small houses, as well as the twin-towered 17th-century Igreja Matriz in Avenida do Bom Reitor. In the town centre the Calvary chapel of the 18th-century Capela dos Passos is adorned with wood carvings carrying a shell motif. Tableaux in the **Museu de Ovar** recreate the lifestyle of a bygone era, alongside displays of regional costume and dolls.

Located 6.5 km (4 miles) from Ovar, the church at Válega has a stunning façade covered in *azulejos*.

Museu de Ovar

♿ 🏠 Rua Heliodoro Salgado 11 📞 256 572 822 🕐 Tue–Sat 🔒 Public hols

9

Figueira da Foz

D3 🚌🚃 ℹ️ **Esplanada Silva Guimarães, Castelo Engenheiro Silva; 233 209 500**

Lively and cosmopolitan, this popular resort has a marina, a casino and a wide beach with breakers that attract surfers.

The town is not just a playground for holiday-makers, however, and the **Museu Municipal Dr Santos Rocha** has archaeological artifacts and an eclectic display, from Arraiolos carpets and religious art to Indo-Portuguese furniture.

Museu Municipal Dr Santos Rocha

🏠 Rua Calouste Gulbenkian 📞 233 402 840 🕐 Jul–mid-Sep: 9:30am–6pm Tue–Fri, 2–7pm Sat & Sun; mid-Sep–Jun: 9:30am–5pm Tue–Fri, 2–7pm Sat 🔒 1 Jan, Easter, 1 May, 25 Dec

HIDDEN GEM
Perfect Picnics

From Figueira da Foz, it's a short drive to the Parque Florestal da Serra da Boa Viagem. This beautiful wooded hilltop reserve offers woodland walks and picnic and children's play areas, as well as the Parque Aventura - a high-rope adventure course with zip wires.

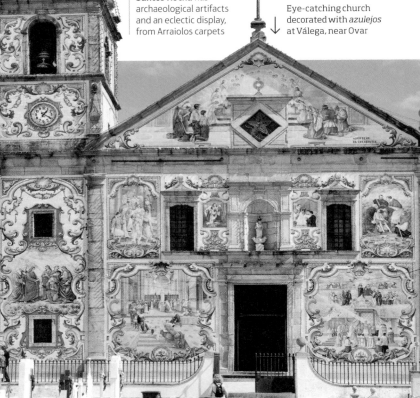

Eye-catching church decorated with *azulejos* at Válega, near Ovar

🔟 Montemor-o-Velho

🅐 D3 🚌 ℹ️ Castelo de Montemor-o-Velho; 239 680 380

This attractive and historic hillside town rises out of fields of rice and maize beside the Mondego river. Its castle, which served as a primary defence of the city of Coimbra (p196), is mostly 14th century, but it had previously been a Moorish stronghold, and the keep has fragments of Roman stonework. The church of Santa Maria de Alcáçova within its walls was founded in 1090. Restored in the 15th century, its naves and arches reflect the Manueline style.

Montemor was the birthplace of Fernão Mendes Pinto (1510–83), famous for his colourful accounts of his travels in the East. Another explorer, Diogo de Azambuja (died 1518), is buried here. Columbus is said to have sailed with Azambuja, who navigated along the West African coast. His tomb, by the Manueline master Diogo Pires, is in the Convento de Nossa Senhora dos Anjos in the square of the same name (the tourist office keeps the key). Its 17th-century façade hides an earlier, more lavish interior, with Manueline and Renaissance influences.

1️⃣1️⃣ Lousã

🅐 E3 🚗🚌 ℹ️ Rua João Luso; 239 990 040

The paper factory at Lousã, on the forested banks of the Arouce river, was opened in 1716 and is still working. Skilled papermakers imported from Italy and Germany by the Marquês de Pombal brought prosperity, still evident in the handsome 18th-century houses. Most elegant of these is the Palácio dos Salazares, now a hotel, located on Rua Viscondessa do Espinhal. Also notable is the Misericórdia, with a 1568 Renaissance portal, a few doors down.

Deep in a valley, just south of Lousã, is the Castelo de Arouce. Legend says it was built in the 11th century by a King Arunce, who took refuge in the valley when fleeing from raiders. To visit the castle, ask at the town hall. Near the castle are the three shrines of the Santuário de Nossa Senhora da Piedade.

A bell tower on the castle walls at
↓ Montemor-o-Velho

RABAÇAL CHEESE

The village of Rabaçal, 6 km (4 miles) west of Penela, is best known for its cheese of the same name. This regional speciality is made with a mixture of sheep's and goat's milk, which is aged for at least 20 days. Some villagers still mature the cheese rounds in darkened rooms in their homes.

The tortuous road south from here towards Castanheira de Pêra gives a splendid view across the valley. A turning east leads up to Alto do Trevim which, at 1,204 m (3,950 ft), is the highest point in the Serra de Lousã.

1️⃣2️⃣ Penela

🅐 E3 🚌 ℹ️ Praça do Município; 239 561 132

Penela's thick-set castle was built in 1087 by Sisinando, governor of Coimbra, as part of the line of defences of the Mondego valley. Its squat towers provide wonderful views over the village and, to the east, of the wooded Serra da Lousã. The church within the castle walls, São Miguel, dates back to the 16th century. Below, in Penela

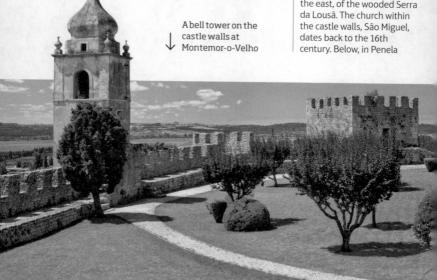

itself, Santa Eufémia, dated 1551 above its decorative doorway, has a Roman capital used as a font.

13

Conímbriga

A E3 **⏱** 2 km (1 mile)
S of Condeixa-a-Nova
☎ 239 941 177 (museum);
239 949 110 (tours) **🚌** From
Coimbra **⏰** 10am–6pm daily
(last adm 5:15pm) **⏱** 1 Jan,
Easter, 1 May, 24 Jul, 25 Dec

This, the largest and most extensively excavated Roman site in Portugal, was on the Roman road between Lisbon (Olisipo) and Braga (Bracara Augusta). There is evidence of Roman habitation here as early as the 2nd century BCE, but even before this time there was a Celtic settlement here. Under the Roman emperor Augustus, from about 25 BCE, Conímbriga became a substantial town: baths, a forum and the aqueduct have been uncovered from this era. The finest buildings, however, date from the 2nd and 3rd centuries CE, and they provide a vivid image of a prosperous city.

The site is approached along a section of Roman road that led into the city from the east. Just to the left cluster the outlines of shops, baths and two once-luxurious houses, both with exquisite mosaic floors.

At Conímbriga is one of the largest houses discovered in the western Roman Empire. This opulent villa, known as the Casa de Cantaber, is built around ornamental pools in colonnaded gardens, with its own bath complex and a sophisticated heating system. Some of the fine mosaics in the museum probably came from this huge residence.

The Casa das Fontes, dating from the early 2nd century, is under a protective cover but walkways provide good views. Its mosaics and fountains, rare survivals which give the house its name, form a strong image

Beautifully preserved central garden of Casa das Fontes in Conímbriga ↑

of the Roman taste for good living. The city's pools, and the baths and steam rooms of Trajan's thermae, were fed by a spring 3.5 km (2 miles) away via a mostly subterranean aqueduct.

Official excavation was begun here in 1912, but a considerable part of the 32-acre (13-ha) site has yet to be explored, including an amphitheatre north of the city. In the 3rd or early 4th century, buildings were plundered for stone as defensive walls were hastily raised against barbarian hordes. In a successful assault in 468 CE, the Suevi burned the city and murdered the inhabitants. Excavated skeletons may date from this episode.

An informative museum explains the history and layout of the site, and has exhibits of Roman busts, mosaics and coins alongside more ancient Celtic artifacts. There is also a restaurant and picnic site.

14

Luso

A E3 **🚌** **i** Rua Emídio
Navarro 136; 231 930 122

In the 11th century, Luso was just a village linked to a monastery at Vacariça, but it developed into a lively spa town in the 18th century as its hot-water springs became a

focus for tourism. The thermal waters, which originate from a spring below the Capela de São João, are promoted as being of therapeutic value in the treatment of a wide range of conditions, ranging from bad circulation and improving muscle tone to renal problems and rheumatism.

There are a number of grand, if somewhat faded, hotels here, and an elegant Art Nouveau lobby adorns the former casino, but the main reason for visiting the resort is to enjoy its spa facilities. An additional attraction of Luso is the proximity of the treasured national forest of Buçaco *(p202)*, which is a powerful presence above the town.

Nestled between Luso and Curia, Mealhada is an attractive small town in the heart of a region famous for *leitão*, suckling pig. This enormously popular dish is prominently advertised at numerous hotly competing restaurants in the area.

Did You Know?

Luso is one of the most popular brands of mineral water in Portugal.

⑮ Arganil

🅰E3 🚌 ℹ️ Avenida das Forças Armadas; 235 200 137

Tradition has it that this was a Roman city called Argos. In the 12th century, Dona Teresa, the mother of Afonso Henriques, gave the town to the bishopric of Coimbra, whose incumbent also acquired the title of Conde de Arganil. Most of the town's architecture is unremarkable, but the church of São Gens, the Igreja Matriz in Rua de Visconde de Frias, dates back perhaps to the 14th century.

One of the most curious local sights is kept in the sanctuary of Mont'Alto, 3 km (2 miles) above the town. Here, the Capela do Senhor da Ladeira harbours the Menino Jesus, a Christ Child figure in a bicorne hat (part of a full wardrobe). It is brought out for *festas* but you can ask to access the chapel at the tourist office.

The village of Piódão, blending into the Serra de Açor

⑯ Oliveira do Hospital

🅰E3 🚌 ☎️ 238 609 269

These lands once belonged to the Knights Hospitallers, a gift in 1120 from the mother of Afonso Henriques. The 13th-century Igreja Matriz in Largo Conselheiro Cabral Metelo houses a

magnificent reminder of the era of these warrior-monks. One of the founders of the town, Domingues Joanes, is buried beside his wife in the Capela dos Ferreiros. His large tomb is surmounted by a charming equestrian statue.

Today, this lively industrial town is perfectly situated for exploring the valleys of the Mondego and the Alva.

At Lourosa, 12 km (7 miles) to the southwest of Oliveira do Hospital, the simple 10th-century church of São Pedro reflects the changing fate of Portugal over the centuries. A cemetery excavated beneath the church dates from the Roman era; the porch is Visigothic, while inside are ten impressive Roman arches and an *ajimene* (Moorish window).

Statue in the church at Oliveira do Hospital

⑰ Piódão

🅰E3 🚌 From Coja, 20 km (12 miles) away ℹ️ Largo Cónego Manuel Fernandes Nogueira; 235 732 787

The Serra de Açor (Hills of the Goshawk) is a place of bleak beauty, where solitary villages cling to precipitous terraces. Piódão is the most striking of these dark schist and slate hamlets. Seemingly remote, Piódão was, until the 1800s, on the main commercial route from Coimbra to Covilhã, but with newer roads the village was forgotten. But Piódão is coming back to life: houses are being repainted and the bright white Igreja Matriz once again stands out against the surrounding dark stone.

⑱ Caramulo

🅰E3 🚌 ℹ️ Avenida Dr Jerónimo de Lacerda 750; 232 861 437

In a grassy rolling serra west of Viseu, this small town was once, with its clear mountain air, a centre for sanatoria. It is better known today for two very disparate museums.

In the **Museu do Caramulo**, the exhibits range from 16th-century Flemish tapestries, porcelain, silver and ivory to Egyptian bronzes from 1580 to 900 BCE. The paintings are as varied: from Portuguese primitives to the 20th century. One of Picasso's still lifes was donated by the artist in 1947.

The collection in the **Museu do Automóvel** is just as eclectic: Bugattis and Rolls-Royces, and a bulletproof 1938 Mercedes-Benz ordered for Salazar when he was prime minister but never used.

Museu do Caramulo and Museu do Automóvel
 ⌂Caramulo ⏰10am-1pm & 2-6pm Tue-Sun (Oct-Mar: to 5pm; Jul-mid-Sep: daily) ⌧1 Jan, Easter Sun, 24 & 25 Dec ⌨museudocaramulo.pt

---

⑲
Viseu
⓴E3 🚌 ⓘCasa do Adro, Adro da Sé; 232 420 950

The centre of the Dão wine-growing region, this city is also packed with history. On the western side of this regional capital's old town is the striking 15th-century Porta do Soar de Cima, a remnant of the original walls. In the Rossio, the main square, the 1887 town hall on the west side has a grand stairway and *azulejos* relating the history of Viseu.

Viseu's **Sé**, the town's cathedral, still retains a few Romanesque features, but it has been altered over the centuries in a variety of styles. The façade is a 17th-century replacement of a Manueline frontage that fell down in 1635. Inside, the vaulted roof is supported by 16th-century knotted ribs on 13th-century columns. In the north chapel are fine *azulejos* from the 18th century, while those in the two-storey cloister date from a century earlier. The cathedral's treasury, housed in the chapterhouse includes a 12th-century Gospel and a 13th-century Limoges coffer.

In the 16th-century former bishop's palace abutting the cathedral is the **Museu de Grão Vasco**, exhibiting the paintings of Vasco Fernandes (c.1475–1540) and his fellow artists of the Viseu School. On the top floor are the masterpieces that once adorned the cathedral's chancel altarpiece, including Grão Vasco's monumental *St Peter*.

Sé
⌂Largo da Sé ☎232 436 065 ⏰9am-1pm & 2-5:30pm Mon-Sat, 2-6:30pm Sun

Museu de Grão Vasco
◈ ⌂Largo da Sé ⏰Times vary, check website ⌨museu nacionalgraovasco.gov.pt

→ Woman resting in the cloisters, Viseu cathedral

Did You Know?

The local Serra cheese – made from ewe's milk – is at its tastiest when it turns runny.

20
Sernancelhe

 F2 ☎ 🛈 Town hall; 254 598 300

Whitewashed houses cluster around the granite heart of this modest Beira town. In Praça da República stands the Romanesque Igreja Matriz. The granite statues in its façade niches, survivors from the 12th century, flank a notable arched portal embellished by a semicircle of carved angels. The grandest house here is the Baroque Solar dos Carvalhos behind the church. Long and low, with carved granite portals against whitewashed walls, it is where the local noble family lived in the 18th century.

In the Serra da Lapa rising to the south of Sernancelhe, stands a shrine known as the

Santuário da Nossa Senhora da Lapa. The story tells of a mute shepherd girl, Joana, who found a statue of the Virgin Mary on a great boulder and took it home. Irritated, her mother threw it on the fire, at which moment the child miraculously spoke: "Don't burn it," she cried. "It is the Senhora da Lapa." A chapel was built to enshrine the boulder, and the image looks down from a recess.

The castle at Penedono is captivating. In the middle of this small town 17 km (11 miles) northeast of Sernancelhe, it has survived since at least the 10th century.

Santuário da Nossa Senhora da Lapa
🏠 Quintela da Lapa, 11 km (7 miles) SW of Sernancelhe ☎ 232 688 993 🕓 Daily

21
Celorico da Beira

 F3 🚉 ☎ 🛈 Rua Sacadura Cabral; 271 742 109

In the lee of the Serra da Estrela, the pastures around Celorico da Beira have long been a source of the region's

famous Serra cheese. The Solar do Queijo at Praça de Santa Maria sells this local delicacy and there is a cheese fair every February. Around Rua Fernão Pacheco, running from the main road up to the castle, is the old centre of Celorico, which is manifested in a cluster of granite houses with Manueline windows and Gothic doors.

Of the 10th-century castle, battered by a long succession of frontier disputes with Spain, only a tower and the outer walls remain. Its stark silhouette is less dramatic at close quarters. The Igreja Matriz, which was restored in the 18th century, has a painted coffered ceiling. During the Peninsular War,

A typical narrow street in the peaceful walled town of Trancoso ↑

the church served briefly as a makeshift hospital for the English forces.

Trancoso

🅰F2 🚍 🛈 Avenida Heróis de São Marcos 2; 271 811 147

When King Dinis married Isabel here in 1283, he gave her Trancoso as a wedding gift. He was also responsible for the walls that still encircle the town and, in 1304, established

←

The castle perched on rocks at Penedono, near Sernancelhe

here the first unrestricted fair in Portugal. Left in peace after 1385, the town became a lively commercial centre. Trancoso once had a large Jewish population; in the old Jewish quarter, houses survive with one broad and one narrow door, separating domestic life from commerce.

From the southern gate, Rua da Corredoura leads to São Pedro, restored after 1720. A tombstone in the church commemorates Gonçalo Anes, a local shoemaker who, in the 1580s, wrote the celebrated *Trovas* under the name of Bandarra. These stories prophesied the return of the young King Sebastião.

Almeida

🅰F2 🚍 🛈 Portas de São Francisco; 271 570 020

Formidable defences in the form of a 12-pointed star guard this small, delightfully preserved border town.

Almeida was recognized by Spain as Portuguese territory under the Alcañices Treaty on 12 September 1297, but this did not stop further incursions.

EAT

Retiro do Castiço
Inside Trancoso's medieval walls is this rustic tavern serving a mix of *petiscos* (Portuguese tapas) and regional desserts like a sardine-shaped sweet.

🅰F2 🏠 Rua de São João 24, Trancoso 📞919 188 129 🕐Sat

€€€

O Cortiço
A traditional restaurant serving a good range of tapas and hearty meat dishes, including duck with rice, which is best eaten with a Dão wine.

🅰E3 🏠 Rua Augusto Hilário 45, Viseu 📞916 461 576 🕐Sun D, Mon

€€€

The present Vauban-style stronghold was designed in 1641 by Antoine Deville after Spain's Philip IV, in post-Restoration rage, destroyed the earlier defences protecting the town and its castle.

From 1742 to 1743 Almeida was in Spanish hands again, and then during the Peninsular War was held in turn by the French under Masséna and the British under the Duke of Wellington. In 1810, a French shell lit a powder trail that destroyed the castle.

To breach the town's fortifications, cross a bridge and pass through a tunnel. The underground soldiers' barracks can be visited and an armoury in the main gateway, the Portas de São Francisco, holds further mementos of Almeida's military past. A walk around the grassy walls gives rewarding views of the town.

㉔ Guarda

AF3 🚌🚃 **ℹ**Praça Luís de Camões; 271 205 530

Spread over a bleak hill on the northeast flank of the Serra da Estrela, Guarda is the country's highest city, at 1,056 m (3,465 ft). Founded in 1199 by Sancho I, the city's original role as frontier guard explains its name and its rather forbidding countenance. Some of its arcaded streets and squares are lively, but the fortress-like Sé, with its flying buttresses, pinnacles and gargoyles, could never be described as lovely. Master architects who worked on the cathedral, begun in 1390 and completed in 1540, included Diogo Boitac (from 1504 to 1517) and the builders of Batalha (p172). The interior, by contrast, is light and graceful. The 100 carved figures high on the altarpiece

↓ Pedestrianized street close to the cathedral in Guarda

Did You Know?

The Portuguese named Brazil after the wood that they found there – Paubrasilia.

in the chancel were worked by Jean de Rouen in 1552.

Set out over two floors, the **Museu da Guarda** takes you on a trip through the history of the region from prehistory to the present day. On display are paintings, archaeological discoveries and a section on the city's own poet, Augusto Gil (1873–1929).

From the cathedral square, Rua do Comércio leads down to the 17th-century Misericórdia church. Inside the ornamental portal are Baroque altars and pulpits. Just north of the cathedral, in the historic town centre, is the 18th-century church of São Vicente, which has 16 elaborate *azulejo* panels depicting the life of Christ.

Guarda used to support a thriving Jewish community, which was founded at the beginning of the 13th century. History records that João I, on a visit to Guarda, was smitten by Inês Fernandes, the beautiful daughter of a Jewish shoemaker. From their liaison a son, Afonso, was born. In 1442 the title of first Duke of Bragança was bestowed on Afonso, and 200 years later his descendant would take the throne as João IV, first of the Bragança monarchs (p248).

Museu da Guarda

♿🚻 Rua Alves Roçadas 30 🕐9am–12:30pm & 2–5:30pm Tue–Sun 🚫1 Jan, Easter, 1 May, 25 Dec 🌐museu daguarda.pt

㉕ Belmonte

AF3 🚌🚃 **ℹ**Castelo de Belmonte; 275 911 488

Belmonte was for generations the fiefdom of the Cabral family. Pedro Álvares Cabral,

→ The stunning village of Sortelha, watched over by its castle

the first navigator to land in Brazil, had forebears who fought at Ceuta *(p44)* and Aljubarrota *(p173)*. Fernão, an earlier ancestor, was famed for his feats of strength. The family crest, incorporating a goat *(cabra)*, can be seen in the castle and adjacent chapel. The castle, begun in 1266, retains its keep and a Manueline window added later. The little church of São Tiago nearby has preserved its Romanesque simplicity: the frescoes above the altar and, in a tiny side chapel, a granite *pietà* date from the 13th century. Beside the church is the 15th-century Capela dos Cabrais, which holds the Cabral family tombs.

The modern Igreja da Sagrada Família (1940) is the repository for a treasured statue of Nossa Senhora da Esperança said to have accompanied Cabral on his voyage to Brazil. The **Museu Judaico de Belmonte** charts the development of the Jewish community in the region.

Northeast of Belmonte is the Roman Centum Cellas, also called Torre de Colmeal. It is not known what the role of this square, three-storeyed structure was – maybe a hostel or military base, a mansion or a temple.

Museu Judaico de Belmonte

🏠 Rua da Portela 4 📞 275 088 698 🕐 Tue–Sun

Sabugal

🅰F3 🚌 ℹ️ Inside the castle; 271 750 080

In 1296, when this small town beside the Côa river was confirmed as Portuguese in the Treaty of Alcañices, the castle was refortified by the ever-industrious King Dinis. Its imposing towered walls and unusual five-sided keep survive from this era, although the castle suffered in peacetime from villagers raiding it for building stone.

Peopled since prehistoric times, Sabugal still has part of its medieval walls, reinforced in the 17th century and now ringed by newer houses. In the Praça da República stands a granite clock tower, reconstructed in the 17th century.

Sortelha

🅰F3 ℹ️ Largo do Corro; 800 262 788

Wrapped in its ring of walls, Sortelha is enchanting. This beautifully preserved town sits on a granite outcrop and the views from the high keep of its gem of a 13th-century castle are stunning.

The castle has several Manueline features, including the coat of arms of Manuel I and armillary spheres. Parts of its walls were blown up by Napoleon's troops but later rebuilt.

In front of the castle entrance is a 16th-century pillory with an armillary sphere on top. In the tiny citadel are a school and stony lanes of granite houses.

Casa da Lagariça

With accommodation in one of Sortelha's attractive old stone houses, this 18th-century former grape store now offers three bedrooms, two bathrooms and a kitchen.

🅰F3 🏠 Calçada de Santo Antão 11, Sortelha casalagarica.com

€€€

Solar de Alarcão

This 17th-century manor house, with a serene atmosphere and filled with antiques, is right in the heart of Guarda, near the cathedral.

🅰F3 🏠 Rua Dom Miguel de Alarcão 25–27, Guarda solardealarcao.pt

€€€

Sortelha's old town is a short walk or drive from a newer town where you will find shops and restaurants.

The local fondness for bullfights is reflected in the names of nearby villages such as Vila do Touro. In a local variation of the controversial sport, the *capeia*, bulls were taunted into charging into a huge fork of branches.

28
Penamacor

 F3 🅿️🚌 ℹ️ **Largo Tenente Coronel Júlio R Silva; 277 394 106**

Fought over by successive waves of Romans, Visigoths and Moors, this frontier town was fortified in the 12th century by Gualdim Pais, Master of the Knights Templar (p176). Today the weatherbeaten castle walls rise above a quiet town at the heart of hardy, sparsely inhabited country where the main attraction is hunting.

From the main square, the road up to the old town passes beside the former town hall, built over a medieval archway. Beyond lie the restored castle keep and the 16th-century Igreja da Misericórdia.

29
Monsanto

 F3 🚌 ℹ️ **Rua Marquês da Graciosa; 277 314 642**

An odd fame hit Monsanto in 1938 when it was voted "most Portuguese village in Portugal". The village is at one with the granite hillside on which it perches: its lanes blend into the grey rock, the houses squeezed between massive boulders. Tiny gardens sprout from the granite and dogs drink from granite bowls.

The ruined castle began as a *castro*, a Lusitanian fortified settlement, and suffered a long history of sieges and battles for its commanding position. It was finally destroyed by a 19th-century gunpowder explosion. Cars cannot go beyond the village centre, but the view alone is worth the walk up to the ruined walls. Today, Monsanto's claim to fame has shifted, having been the fantasy setting for the acclaimed *House of the Dragon* (2022) series.

30
Idanha-a-Velha

 F3 🚌 ℹ️ **Rua do Lagar; 277 914 280**

This modest hamlet among the olive groves encapsulates the history of Portugal. Signposts in Portuguese, French and English guide visitors round the landmarks of this fascinating living museum.

Idanha-a-Velha was, it is said, the birthplace of the Visigothic King Wamba, and it had its own

bishop until 1199. The present appearance of the cathedral comes from early 16th-century restor-ation, but in the echoing interior are stacked inscribed and sculpted Roman stones.

In the middle of the village is a 17th-century pillory, the Renaissance Igreja Matriz and a ruined Torre dos Templários, a relic of the Templars. This order of religious knights held sway in Idanha until the 14th century.

31
Castelo Branco

 F4 🅿️🚌 ℹ️ **Avenida Nuno Álvares 30; 272 330 339**

This handsome, busy old city, overlooked by the vestiges of a Templar castle, is the most important in the Beira Baixa.

→ Monsanto's houses, dwarfed by immense granite boulders

The greatest attraction is the **Jardim Episcopal** beside the former bishop's palace. Created by Bishop João de Mendonça in the 18th century, the garden's layout is conventionally formal; its individuality lies in its dense population of statues. Baroque in style and often bizarre in character, stone saints and Apostles line the box-edged paths, lions peer at their reflections in pools and monarchs stand guard along the grand balustrades – the hated kings of the 60-year Spanish rule conspicuously half-size.

The 17th-century Paço Episcopal itself now houses the **Museu Francisco Tavares Proença Júnior**. Its wide-ranging collection includes archaeological finds, displays of 16th-century tapestries and Portuguese primitive art. Castelo Branco is also well known for its fine silk-embroidered bedspreads, called *colchas*, and examples of these are also exhibited in the museum.

Housed in two buildings (one old and one modern), the popular **Museu Cargaleiro** has a remarkable collection of rare paintings, tapestries and ceramics, donated by the Manuel Cargaleiro Foundation. Beside the road back towards

the town centre stands a 15th-century cross known as the Cruzeiro de São João.

Jardim Episcopal
⌖ 🏛Rua Bartolomeu da Costa ⏱Daily

Museu Francisco Tavares Proença Júnior
⌖ 🏛Largo Doutor José Lopes Dias 📞272 344 277 ⏱10am-1pm & 2-6pm Tue-Sun 🚫1 Jan, Easter, 25 Apr, 1 May, 25 Dec

Museu Cargaleiro
⌖ 🏛Rua dos Cavaleiros 23 ⏱10am-1pm, 2-6pm Tue-Sun 🚫1 Jan, Easter, 25 Apr, 1 May, 25 Dec 🌐fundacao manuelcargaleiro.pt

↑ Decorative pool in the Jardim Episcopal, Castelo Branco

EAT

Dom Sancho I
The open fireplace at this stone-walled restaurant in the old town is warm and welcoming. The menu includes local delicacies such as hare with rice, rabbit and wild boar.

🗺F3 🏛Largo do Corro, Sortelha 📞271 388 267 🚫Sun D, Mon

€€€

Pousada do Convento de Belmonte
A beautiful restaurant with original stone features and wonderful mountain views. The gourmet dishes on the tasting and à la carte menus are equally impressive.

🗺F3 🏛Serra da Esperança, Belmonte 🌐conventode belmonte.pt

€€€

A DRIVING TOUR
BORDER CASTLES

Length 115 km (72 miles) **Stopping-off points** Pinhel; Almeida **Terrain** The tour uses well-surfaced roads; short cuts are deceptive and not recommended

Defending Portugal's frontiers was a vital priority of the nation's early kings. All along the shakily held border, Spanish incursions were frequent and loyalties divided. Castles were constantly being assaulted, besieged and rebuilt, and the 20 that survived are a lasting reminder of this long period of dispute. Follow this route to visit five of these remaining fortified towns. Much of the terrain, especially in the Serra da Marofa, is bleak and rocky, but near Pinhel and beyond Castelo Mendo the scenic valley of the River Côa provides a dramatic backdrop.

Freixeda do Torrão

Penha de Águia

N221

Bizarri

Rio Côa

Quinta Nova

Vale de Madeira

Pinhel

Quintã dos Bernardos

N226

Gamelas

Malta

Vascoveiro

Pereiro

Manigoto

Carvalhal da Atalaia

Atalaia

N3

*Part of the region's defences since Roman times, **Pinhel** formed the fulcrum for a network of fortresses, and in the early 14th century King Dinis, who was responsible for the construction of many of Portugal's castles, built it up into an impressive citadel. Much of this ring of walls survives, as do two towers. The city has an abundance of cafés and restaurants, making it a good stopping off point.*

0 kilometres	4
0 miles	4

N ↑

Ribeira das Cabras

Freix

Amoreira

←

One of the two surviving towers that remain of the citadel at Pinhel

Just to the south of Figueira de Castelo Rodrigo, topped by a huge stone Christ the King, is the highest point of the **Serra da Marofa**, 977 m (3,205 ft).

The tiny fortified village of **Castelo Rodrigo** still has its encircling walls built by King Dinis in 1296, but the fine palace of its lord, the Spanish sympathizer Cristóvão de Moura, was burned down at the Restoration in 1640.

Locator Map
For more detail see p192

↑ Christ the King on the summit of the Serra da Marofa

Begin your tour at **Almeida,** where there are plenty of places to have breakfast or lunch. The town's star-shaped defences are a finely preserved example of the complex but effective style of fortifications developed by the French engineer, Vauban, in the 17th century.

Guarded by two stone boars, little survives of the castle at **Castelo Mendo**, but the distant views from the fort's remains make it the perfect place to end your drive.

Map labels:

N221, N332, N332, Figueira de Castelo Rodrigo, M607, N332, Castelo Rodrigo, Nave Redonda, Vilar Torpim, M604, Reigada, Cinco Vilas, GUARDA, Mangide, Rio Côa, N332, M604, N324, Vale Verde, START, Almeida, Vale da Mula, N340, N332, Junça, Aldeia Nova, Azinhal, Peva, Naves, São Pedro de Rio Seco, M566, N324, Senouras, M567, M561, Leomil, Mido, N332, Castelo Bom, Ribeira de Tourões, SPAIN, IP5, IP5, A25, Vilar Formoso, N620, FINISH, Castelo Mendo, M567, Freineda, Fuentes de Oñoro, N332, Mesquitela

Border Castles

THE BEIRAS

NORTHERN PORTUGAL

A vineyard on a hill in the Douro Valley

Viana do Bolo

San Martín
de Castañeda

Puebla de Sanabria

Rionegro del
Puente

A Gudiña

A Vilavella

Xinzo de Limia

Mahide

Vinhais

Bragança

Chaves

Alcañices

**DOURO AND
TRÁS-OS-MONTES**
p244

Valpaços

Vimioso

Macedo de
Cavaleiros

Miranda do
Douro

BRAGANÇA

Mirandela

Murça

Rio Tua

Alfândega
da Fé

Mogadouro

Alijó

Vila Flor

*Embalse de
Almendra*

Pinhão

Carrazeda de
Ansiães

Trabanca

Rio Douro

Torre de
Moncorvo

Rio Douro

Mieza

ão João da
Pesqueira

SPAIN

Rio Távora

Freixo de
Espada à Cinta

Penedono

Vila Nova
de Foz Côa

Vitigudino

Mêda

Cerralbo

Sernancelhe

EXPLORE
NORTHERN
PORTUGAL

aguiar da Beira

Trancoso

ornos de
lgodres

Celorico
da Beira

This section divides Northern Portugal into three
colour-coded sightseeing areas, as shown on
the map above. Find out more about each area
on the following pages.

Guarda

GETTING TO KNOW
NORTHERN
PORTUGAL

Beyond the cultivated valley of the Douro and the fertile Minho rises the remote and romantically named Trás-os-Montes ("Behind the Mountains"), with its tracts of wilderness and tiny medieval townships. Although seemingly rural, Northern Portugal was the birthplace of the nation and is where you'll find the country's most historic cities: Porto and Guimarães.

PORTO

PAGE 228

The country's second city, Porto has never sat in Lisbon's shadow. Its remarkable cityscape, wedged into the Douro Valley, has been granted UNESCO World Heritage status, while its range of museums, churches and port wine lodges have put it firmly on the city-break circuit. A foodie destination, its Michelin-starred restaurants rub shoulders with more traditional places serving the local speciality, tripe. Porto is also a hub for architecture and many of its once-crumbling mansions have been given a makeover, leaving an alluring mix of faded grandeur and sharp design.

Best for
A lively yet affordable city break

Home to
Ribeira, Vila Nova de Gaia

Experience
A boat cruise up the Douro river, stopping at port houses in Vila Nova de Gaia

PAGE 244

DOURO AND TRÁS-OS-MONTES

On its way to the Atlantic, the Douro or "Golden River" wends its scenic path through deep-cleft gorges, terraced with vineyards and home to prosperous *quintas* (wine estates) all dedicated to producing wine and port. To the east, untrammelled Trás-os-Montes remains a land of quiet stone villages amid fields of rye and moorland. Full of historic associations, its isolated capital Bragança lies on the edge of the wild Parque Natural de Montesinho, a great choice for hikers.

Best for
Getting off the beaten track

Home to
Bragança's Citadel, Casa de Mateus

Experience
A train ride on the scenic Linha do Douro from Porto to Pinhão

PAGE 266

MINHO

The Minho occupies the northwest corner of Portugal and is named after the river that marks its northern boundary with Spain. Outside the cities, the Minho's fertile farms have been handed down within families for centuries. So, too, have the traditions of carnivals and street markets, creating an interesting slice of Portuguese culture. Ox-drawn carts still carry the area's distinctive *vinhos verdes* or "green wines" to market in Barcelos. Walkers and wildlife enthusiasts should not miss the craggy peaks and untamed river valleys of Parque Nacional da Peneda-Gerês.

Best for
Diving into history and wild walks

Home to
Parque Nacional da Peneda-Gerês, Viana do Castelo, Braga, Bom Jesus do Monte

Experience
The traditional market at Barcelos, where local produce and handicrafts sit side by side

Although largely mountainous, Northern Portugal is well connected by fast roads and railway lines. Here is a suggestion of how to get the most from a visit to the region.

7 DAYS
In Northern Portugal

Day 1

Morning After arriving in Porto, explore Ribeira *(p232)*, the iconic riverside area with its warren of pastel-hued buildings. The Largo do Terreiro is a pretty spot for a coffee while you watch traditional *rabelo* boats floating down the Douro.

Afternoon Taste modern dishes at the Cantinho do Avillez, then climb the Torre dos Clérigos for amazing views *(p239)*. After taking in the view, stroll over to Livraria Lello bookshop, which has an ornate, Neo-Gothic interior *(p239)*. In the evening, catch an event at the innovative Casa da Música *(www.casadamusica.com)*.

Day 2

Morning Walk across the top of the Ponte de Dom Luís to Vila Nova de Gaia. The view from the circular Mosteiro da Serra do Pilar is simply stunning *(p234)*. Take the Teleférico de Gaia cable car *(p234)* along the riverside and lunch at one of the Douro-facing cafés. The Yeatman is ideal for a special occasion *(p237)*.

Afternoon The steep hillsides of Vila Nova de Gaia are punctuated by famous port wine lodges, each a perfect spot to sample the city's eponymous spirit. Return to Porto for the evening.

Day 3

Morning Peso da Régua is easily reached by car or by the Linha do Douro train, which winds through the valley *(p254)*. The town's Museu do Douro details the history of the river and the wine trade, making for an enlightening visit before you head to one of the *quintas* (wine estates).

Afternoon Take a boat ride on the river and then visit – or ideally stay the night at – one of the many vineyards that dot the surrounding hillsides. Our pick is Quinta Nova de Nossa Senhora do Carmo *(p255)*.

Day 4

Morning Drive to Guimarães via the A7 and explore the beautiful old town, which was the country's first capital *(p278)*.

1 The brightly coloured
buildings of the Ribeira. ↑

2 Cantinho do Avillez.

3 A lively street in Braga.

4 Bom Jesus do Monte.

5 Monte de Santa Luzia,
Viana do Castelo.

Afternoon Travel to Bom Jesus do Monte, a famous pilgrimage church (p276). The town of Braga, Portugal's religious capital, is surprisingly lively, making it a great place to spend the evening (p274). Try Livraria Mavy – a bookshop which has been converted into an art-festooned bar (p280).

Day 5

Morning A little under an hour's drive away, on the N103, is the Parque Nacional da Peneda-Gerês (p270). Inside the country's only national park, seek out the tranquil, alpine-esque spa town Caldas do Gerês.

Afternoon Spend the afternoon hiking one of the area's many trails. The Trilho da Cidade da Calcedónia walk starts and ends at Covide, and climbs to a fortified Iron Age village which offers amazing panoramic views.

Day 6

Morning The village of Soajo, in the northern section of the park, is known for its peculiar *espigueiros* (granaries).

You'll pass plenty of these strange tomb-like structures on the 4-km- (2.5-mile-) long Trilho de Ramil trail. Have a picnic lunch en route, stopping somewhere with a good view.

Afternoon After tiring yourself out exploring this ripe hiking territory, stay in one of the renovated village houses in Soajo.

Day 7

Morning It's a scenic drive back to Porto on the IC28 and N203 along the Lima valley via the handsome town of Ponte de Lima, which makes a good stop for a coffee (p281). We recommend Tasca das Fodinhas, a traditional café-bar (p280).

Afternoon Make a detour to stop for lunch in historic Viana do Castelo (p272). This picturesque town also has a fine local beach. The fast A28 motorway will take you back to Porto.

PORTO

Ever since the Romans built a fort here at their settlement of Portus, Porto has prospered from commerce. The city was quick to expel the Moors in the 11th century and to profit from provisioning Crusaders en route to the Holy Land. Porto also took advantage of the wealth generated by Portugal's extensive maritime explorations in the 15th and 16th centuries.

When Portugal lost the lucrative spice trade, as her former colonies were taken up by the Dutch or granted independence, Porto still thrived due to the precious drink to which the city gave its name: port. From its hillside, Porto looks across the Douro to the lodges that nurture this fortified wine, many of which bear the names of British companies such as Taylor's, Croft and Graham's. The trade with these foreign companies secured the city's fortunes.

Still a thriving industrial centre and Portugal's second-largest city, Porto, sometimes referred to as Oporto, blends industry with charm, cherishing its growing creative community while keeping traditions like textile-making and sardine-canning alive.

PORTO

Must Sees

1. Ribeira
2. Vila Nova de Gaia

Experience More

3. Sé
4. Paço Episcopal
5. Casa Guerra Junqueiro
6. World of Discoveries
7. Museu dos Transportes e Comunicações
8. São Bento Station
9. Palácio da Bolsa
10. Igreja de São Francisco
11. Museu da Misericórdia do Porto
12. Torre and Igreja de Clérigos
13. Livraria Lello
14. Igreja do Carmo and Carmelitas
15. Centro Português de Fotografia
16. Jardim do Palácio de Cristal
17. Museu Soares dos Reis

Eat

1. Cantinho do Avillez
2. The Yeatman

Drink

3. Dick's Bar
4. Terrace Lounge 360

Stay

5. 1872 River House
6. Oca Flores
7. The Yeatman

Shop

8. Chocolataria Equador
9. Fernandes Mattos & Co

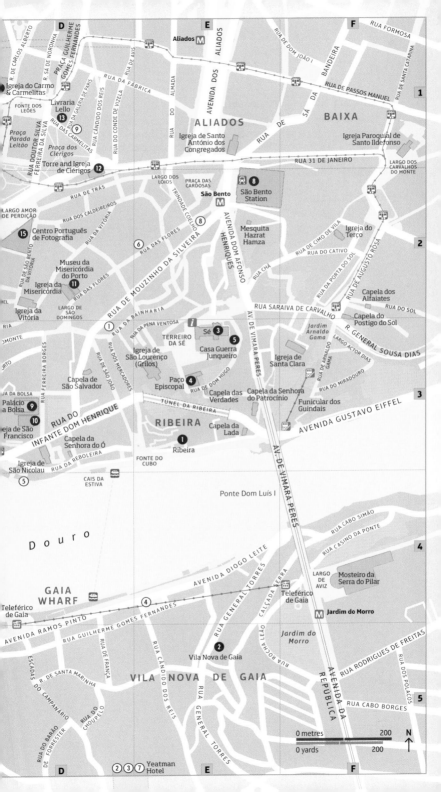

❶
RIBEIRA

📍E3 🚇1M, 500 🚏Infante 🚌Casa do Infante

The riverside quarter of Porto is a warren of narrow, twisting streets and shadowy arcades. Behind pastel-painted façades, many in faded glory, a working population earns its living, catches up through open windows and mixes in lively streets. As well as local life, Ribeira also offers plenty of trendy bars, cafés, boutiques and restaurants.

Ponte de Dom Luís I

The district is dominated at its eastern end by the Ponte de Dom Luís I, which connects the two cities of Porto and Vila Nova de Gaia. Constructed in 1886, it was designed by Theophile Seyrig – a business partner of Gustave Eiffel. Spanning 172 m (564 ft), it was the longest metal arch bridge in the world when it was first built. Although it no longer holds this accolade, it is still an impressive feat of engineering and offers amazing views of Ribeira from its upper tier.

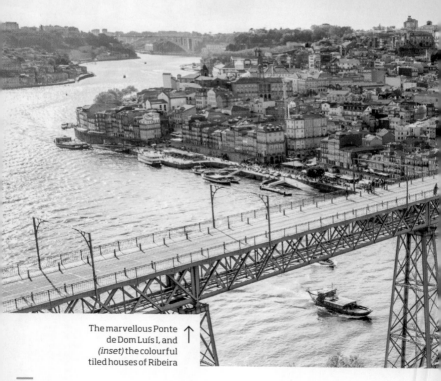

The marvellous Ponte de Dom Luís I, and *(inset)* the colourful tiled houses of Ribeira →

① Vila Nova de Gaia, on the other side of the Douro, is a good spot to take a photo of Ribeira.

② Linking Ribeira with the upper town, the Funicular dos Guindães saves a steep climb.

③ Largo do Terreiro, one of the district's main squares, is surrounded by colourful houses.

Did You Know?

Before the bridge was built, people used boats tied together to cross the Douro.

The expansive Mosteiro da Serra do Pilar, overlooking the city ↑

2

VILA NOVA DE GAIA

📍 E5 Ⓜ Jardim do Morro 🚌 10M, 900G, 901, 906 🚂 General Torres 🖥 ℹ️ Avenida de Diogo Leite 135; www.cm-gaia.pt

Despite its proximity to Porto, Vila Nova de Gaia is actually a separate city. Afonso III, in dispute with the bishop of Porto over shipping tolls, established a rival port here in the 12th century and Vila Nova de Gaia has been the centre of Portugal's port production ever since, with some 50 port lodges based here.

💬 INSIDER TIP
Teleférico de Gaia Tickets

If you only want to buy a one-way ticket on the Teleférico de Gaia cable car, choose to ride the ascent to save a steep uphill climb. The journey only takes five minutes but the photographs are well worth the ticket price and you'll disembark with plenty of energy to explore the upper level of the city.

①

Mosteiro da Serra do Pilar

🏛 Largo de Avis 📞 220 142 425 🕐 Apr-Oct: 10am-6:30pm Tue-Sun (Nov-Mar: to 5:30pm)

Sitting loftily on a hilltop above Vila Nova de Gaia, this remarkable circular monastery was built in the 16th century and reflects the architectural ideals of the

←

The Teleférico de Gaia cable car, hanging over traditional *rabelo* boats

Renaissance. The monastery's prime position, overlooking the city, the Douro and Porto, made it strategically important in the French invasions. Ironically, it was used by both the Duke of Wellington and Napoleon at different times to billet their troops and it was from its terrace that Wellington planned his surprise attack on the French in 1809.

The panorama from the terrace is impressive enough, taking in the port lodges below, the sweep of the Douro and the city of Porto on the far side, but you can climb up to the monastery's dome for even more far-reaching views.

③

Casa-Museu Teixeira Lopes

🏠 Rua de Teixeira Lopes 32 📞 22 374 2904 🕐 9am-12:30pm & 2-5:30pm Tue-Sun 🚫 1 Jan, Easter, 1 May, 24 Jun & 25 Dec

Dating from the 19th century, the former house and studio of Portuguese sculptor António Teixeira Lopes (1866–1942) has been beautifully renovated and restored to the state in which this fine example of regional architecture would have been when Lopes lived here. Displaying many of his personal effects, it also houses an impressive collection of his works. Some of his bronze and marble sculptures are found in the atmospheric courtyard, while others are on display in the Diogo de Macedo Galleries, which were built in 1975.

Don't miss the selection of art by his contemporary, the painter and sculptor Diogo de Macedo (1889–1959), plus paintings by the likes of Carlos Botelho (1899–1982) and Amadeo de Souza Cardoso (1887–1918).

DRINK

Dick's Bar
This swanky hotel bar offers some of the best views of the Douro river. There's a long drinks menu, including, of course, port-based cocktails.

📍 E5 🏠 The Yeatman, Rua do Choupelo 🌐 the-yeatman-hotel.com

Terrace Lounge 360
An open-air rooftop bar overlooking the river, Terrace Lounge 360 is a great spot for a sundowner. Order a glass of white port on a sweltering summer evening at this stylish bar, with a neutral colour scheme.

📍 E4 🏠 Espaço Porto Cruz, Largo Miguel Bombarda 23 📞 220 925 401 🚫 Mon

②

Jardim do Morro

🏠 Av da República 🚠 Teleférico de Gaia cable car: May-Sep: 10am-8pm daily; Apr & Oct: 10am-7pm daily; Nov-Mar: 10am-6pm daily 🌐 gaiacablecar.com

The design of the Jardim do Morro has little changed since it was built in 1927. The lake, bandstand and plants remain, including the 22 linden trees that line Avenida da República, and the rubbish and graffiti-scarred benches have been restored and tidied.

The pretty garden lies at the end of the top tier of the Ponte Dom Luís I, making it a great first stop in Vila Nova de Gaia. While away some time beneath the shady palms here, gazing over the city, the river and Porto below.

Once you've admired the view, use the upper station of the Teleférico de Gaia cable car to explore the rest of the city. As it makes its way between the Jardim do Morro and the port wine lodges down on the riverfront, this cable car gives its passengers sweeping views over the distinctive red-tiled rooftops of Vila de Gaia's port lodges.

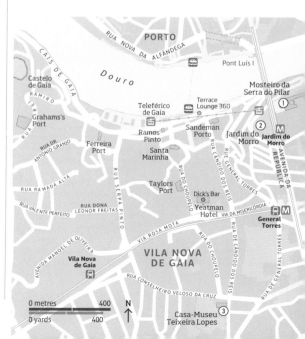

Pillory in Terreiro da Sé, with Porto's impressive Sé behind

EXPERIENCE MORE

3

Sé

⚑ E3 **⌂ Terreiro da Sé** **☎ 222 059 028** **⊙ Apr-Oct: 9am-6:30pm daily (Nov-Mar: to 5:30pm)**

Built as a fortress church in the 12th and 13th centuries, the cathedral has been modified several times. The beautiful rose window in the west front is an original element, dating from the 13th century. Don't miss the small chapel to the left of the chancel, which has a dazzling silver retable, saved from invading French troops in 1809 by a hastily raised plaster wall. The south

---

> **⊙ INSIDER TIP**
> **Barredo District**
>
> Explore the Barredo district – the area between the Sé and the riverfront – a maze of steep alleys lined with attractive bal-conied houses.

---

transept gives access to the 14th-century cloisters and the Capela de São Vicente. An 18th-century staircase leads to the upper levels, where *azulejo* panels depict the life of the Virgin and Ovid's *Metamorphoses*.

4

Paço Episcopal

⚑ E3 **⌂ Terreiro da Sé** **⊙ 9am-1pm & 2-6pm Mon-Sat** **🌐 diocese-porto.pt**

There has been a bishop's palace on this spot since the 13th century and the building has witnessed some momentous occasions in Portuguese history, including the coronation of the first king of Portugal. The Paço Episcopal was used as the residence of the city's bishops until the Siege of Porto in 1832 when the bishop fled the city. During this period of civil war, the palace was used by Pedro IV's troops as a stronghold in the battle

against Miguel I. The building also served as the seat of the Municipality of Porto between 1916 and 1956.

The building that you can visit today was first constructed in 1772 under Nicolau Nasoni (1691–1773), a highly influential Italian architect who helped to introduce Baroque styles to the Portuguese city. Subsequent alterations have left the palace with a mix-ture of architectural styles.

Tours, which run every half-hour for 30 minutes and should be booked in advance, take in a series of sumptuous rooms that give an insight into the lavish life-style of the bishops of Porto. The ornate interiors includes Indo-Portuguese cabinets and priceless paintings.

5

Casa Guerra Junqueiro

⚑ E3 **⌂ Rua de Dom Hugo 32** **☎ 222 003 689** **⊙ 10am-5:30pm Tue-Sun** **☒ Public hols**

Poet and Republican activist Guerra Junqueiro (1850–1923) is most widely known for penning the verses *Finis Patriae* (1890) and *Os Simples* (1892). His former home is an 18th-century Baroque gem, built by Nicolau Nasoni, whose buildings are found throughout the city.

Inside are items from the poet's private collection, which include rare ceramics, Portuguese furniture and a striking set of English alabaster sculptures. In the grand Dom João V Room is a colourful parade of Chinese dogs.

STAY

1872 River House
Charming old townhouse on the riverfront, with contemporary decor.

 D4 🏠 Rua do Infante Dom Henrique 133
🌐 1872riverhouse.com

€€€

Oca Flores
Behind the façade of a traditional townhouse lies a boutique hotel, with garden and pool.

 E2 🏠 Rua das Flores 139 🌐 ocahotels.com

€€€

The Yeatman
An exclusive hotel with sumptuous rooms and a top restaurant *(p241)*.

 E5 🏠 Rua do Choupelo, Vila Nova de Gaia 🌐 the-yeatman-hotel.com

€€€

6

World of Discoveries

📍 B2 🏠 Rua de Miragaia 106 🕐 10am–6pm Tue–Fri (to 7pm Sat & Sun) 🚫 1 Jan, 25 Dec 🌐 worldof discoveries.com

This family-friendly interactive museum is located in the heart of the city. The 20 themed areas recount Portugal's history, giving an unapologetic view of the country's colonial exploits during the 15th and 16th centuries.

7

Museu dos Transportes e Comunicações

📍 B2 🏠 Rua Nova da Alfândega, Edifício da Alfândega 🕐 10am–1pm, 2–6pm Tue–Fri, 3–7pm Sat & Sun 🚫 1 Jan, Easter, 24 Jun, 25 Dec 🌐 amtc.pt

Housed in a vast Neo-Classical building on the riverfront, this museum includes a permanent exhibition on the automobile and interactive exhibitions on media, science, new technologies and art.

8

São Bento Station

📍 E2 🏠 Praça Almeida Garrett Ⓜ São Bento

Porto's central railway station, São Bento, was built in Beaux-Arts style between 1900 and 1916. The soaring walls of the entrance hall are a feast of *azulejos*. The artist Jorge Colaço adorned the station with some 20,000 decorative tiles depicting scenes such as rural festivities, traditional modes of transport and historic events such as the Portuguese conquest of Ceuta. It's worth visiting the station for the entrance hall alone, although it's also the starting point of the Linha do Douro – a train ride up the Douro Valley past terraced vineyards.

The São Bento railway station, and *(inset)* a detail of an *azulejo* tile ↓

Palácio da Bolsa

D3 **Rua Ferreira Borges** **9am–6:30pm daily** **1 Jan, 25 Dec** **palaciodabolsa.com**

Where the monastery of São Francisco once stood, the city's merchants built the stock exchange, or Bolsa, in 1842. The Tribunal do Comércio, where the city's mercantile law was upheld, is full of historical interest.

Look out for the Pátio das Nações – the former trading floor – which is lined with the flags of all the countries the exchange once traded with. The stock exchange was in action until 1990, when it merged with the Lisbon stock exchange. The adjacent courtyard (which you can enter without a ticket) has a very smart restaurant, O Comercial. The glittering highlight is the Arabian Room. This galleried salon, its complex blue-and-gold arabesques inspired by Granada's Alhambra, makes a setting fit for Scheherazade – the heroine of *One Thousand and One Nights*.

Igreja de São Francisco

D3 **Rua do Infante Dom Henrique** **222 062 100** **9am–5:30pm daily (Mar–Jun & Oct: to 7pm; Jul–Sep: to 8pm)** **25 Dec**

The building of the Gothic Church of Saint Francis was begun in the 1300s, but it is the 18th-century Baroque interior that amazes visitors. Over 200 kg (450 lb) of gold encrusts the dazzling high altar, columns and pillars, wrought into cherubs and garlands, culminating with the Tree of Jesse on the north wall. Tours (which must be pre-booked) include the catacombs and treasures from the church's monastery, destroyed in 1832.

Did You Know?

Porto's staple, the *francesinha*, is a local take on the French *croque monsieur*.

Museu da Misericórdia do Porto

D2 **Rua das Flores 15** **Apr–Sep: 10am–6:30pm daily (Oct–Mar: to 5:30pm)** **1 Jan, 24 & 25 Dec** **mmipo.pt**

Santa Casa da Misericórdia was once the centre for Portugal's most important charitable organization, which was founded in 1499. Spread over four floors, it is now a museum that traces the fascinating history of the organization's philanthropic work, which included running hospitals, a medical school and an orphanage, as well as providing legal aid for prisoners.

The museum features an impressive collection of art, including evocative portraits of the organization's most important charitable donors, and religious artifacts

The Arabian Room, Palácio da Bolsa, and *(inset)* its exterior

that attest to the wealth of Santa Casa da Misericórdia. Look out for the stunning 18th-century ivory statue of the Crucifixion.

However, the museum's most precious possession is the *Fons Vitae* (Fountain of Life), donated by Manuel I in about 1520. It shows the king and his family kneeling before the crucified Christ. The artist's identity remains unproven, but both Van de Weyden and Holbein have been suggested.

The admission ticket also includes entry to the adjacent Igreja da Misericórdia. This church was originally built in the 16th century but was given an impressive Baroque makeover by famous Italian architect Nicolau Nasoni in the 18th century.

SHOP

Chocolataria Equador

Located on a lovely pedestrianized street, this boutique sells sublime artisan chocolates (including dark chocolate flavoured with port, a nod to the city's main industry), macaroons and bonbons.

📍E2 🏠Rua das Flores 298 🌐cacaoequador.pt

Fernandes Mattos & Co

This 19th-century fabric store may have kept its traditional fittings, including its wooden shelves, but it now sells games, toys, mugs and souvenirs.

📍D1 🏠Rua das Carmelitas 108-114 ☎222 005 568

↑ The beautiful interior of the popular bookshop Livraria Lello

12

Torre and Igreja dos Clérigos

📍D2 🏠Rua São Filipe de Nery 🕘9am-7pm daily 🌐torredosclerigos.pt

This unmistakable hilltop church was built in the 18th century by the Italian architect Nicolau Nasoni. The soaring Torre dos Clérigos with which the architect complemented his design is, at 75 m (246 ft), still one of the tallest buildings in Portugal. The dizzying 240-step climb is worth it for the superb views of the river, the coastline and the Douro Valley. During the climb you'll come across a large carillion, with 49 bells, that can give you quite a fright if you're in the bell tower when they ring.

13

Livraria Lello

📍D1 🏠Rua das Carmelitas 144 🕘9:30am-7pm daily (summer: to 8pm) 🕘Public hols 🌐livrarialello.pt

This beautiful bookshop was founded by the Lello brothers in 1906, who commissioned engineer Francisco Xavier Esteves to design a grand home for their limited edition books. Although it was always buzzing with local customers, Livraria Lello is now a popular attraction, largely because many believed it was here that author J K Rowling gained inspiration for *Harry Potter and the Philosopher's' Stone*. Though the Neo-Gothic interior, with its gallery, stained-glass roof panels and curving double staircase would not look out of place in Hogwarts, it has since been revealed that Rowling had never visited the bookshop before writing the book.

14

Igreja do Carmo and Carmelitas

📍 D1 🏛 Rua do Carmo
📞 222 078 400 🕐 9:30am-6pm daily (Nov-Mar: to 5pm)

Igreja do Carmo, a typically ornate example of Portuguese Baroque, was designed by the architect José Figueiredo Seixas. The church was constructed between 1750 and 1768, and one of its most remarkable features is the monumental white-and-blue *azulejo* panel that covers one of the outside walls. This was created by Silvestro Silvestri and depicts the legendary founding of the Carmelite order as a community of hermits on Mount Carmel, in Israel. Insider, there are seven lavish gilt altars, the work of sculptor Francisco

> 📷 PICTURE PERFECT
> **Stairway Shot**
>
> Walk down the very steep steps of Escada dos Guindais, alongside the Funicular dos Guindais, to snap the Ponte de Dom Luís I and Vila Nova de Gaia.

Pereira Campanhã, as well as a number of fine oil paintings.

The older Igreja das Carmelitas next door (meant for Carmelite nuns) was completed in 1628 in a combination of Classical and Baroque styles. It is now part of a barracks. The two churches are divided by a very narrow house, barely 1 m (40 in) wide, which prevented the monks and nuns sharing a party wall.

15

Centro Português de Fotografia

📍 D2 🏛 Largo Amor de Perdição 🕐 10am-6pm Tue-Fri, 3-7pm Sat & Sun 🚫 1 Jan, Easter, 1 May, 25 Dec 🌐 cpf.pt

This museum is one of Porto's most intriguing spaces. As well as displaying photography and temporary exhibitions, it also gives visitors a fascinating insight into the building's former incarnation as the city's tribunal and prison.

The prison opened in 1767 and was so large that it had its own hospital and residences for its guards. Prisoners were put on different floors

↑ Igreja do Carmo, noted for the white-and-blue *azulejos* on its exterior

depending on their crimes: serious offenders were in grim dungeons while "respectable" prisoners were allowed spacious cells on the top floor.

The former cells and communal spaces are now used as evocative backdrops for temporary photographic exhibitions. There is also a display of historic cameras and photographic equipment.

Jardim do Palácio de Cristal

⌖ A1 **Rua Dom Manuel II**
⌚ 8am–9pm daily (Oct–Mar: to 7pm)

Inspired by the Crystal Palace of London's Great Exhibition in 1851, Porto's own crystal palace was begun in 1861. The steel and glass structure of the original was replaced in the 1950s by the Pavilhão Rosa Mota, an ungainly shape dubbed "the half-orange".

The gardens themselves are the star attraction here. They are truly a lovely place to walk around, with peacocks roaming the lawns, avenues of lime trees, a rose garden with fountains and wonderful views of the river.

Concerts are occasionally held inside the palace, or in the open air, and the leisure gardens are enlivened by a fair at *festa* time.

Did You Know?

Porto's nickname is "Invicta" because it was never defeated during the War of the Two Brothers *(p46)*.

Museu Soares dos Reis

⌖ B1 **Rua Dom Manuel II**
⌚ 10am–6pm Tue–Sun
🌐 patrimoniocultural.gov.pt

The elegant Carrancas Palace, built in the 18th century, has been a Jewish textile workshop, a royal abode and a military headquarters. In 1809, Porto was in French hands, and Marshal Soult and his troops were quartered here. They were ousted in a surprise attack by Arthur Wellesley, later Duke of Wellington, who then calmly installed himself at the marshal's dinner table.

Today, the palace provides an appropriate setting for an outstanding museum, named after António Soares dos Reis, Portugal's leading 19th-century sculptor. Pride of place goes to the display of Portuguese art. This includes paintings by the 16th-century master Frey Carlos and the Impressionist Henrique Pousão. Also hung here are landscapes of Porto by the French artist Jean Pillement (1728–1808).

The star sculpture exhibit, *O Desterrado* (The Exile), is Soares dos Reis' own marvel of pensive tension in marble, completed in 1874. Further sections display Portuguese pottery, Limoges enamels, porcelain and decorative art. Historical exhibits include an appealing 15th-century silver bust of São Pantaleão, patron saint of Porto.

← Admiring a painting in the Museu Soares dos Reis

A SHORT WALK
PORTO'S CATHEDRAL DISTRICT

Distance 1.5 km (1 mile) **Nearest station**
São Bento metro **Time** 15 minutes

Archaeological excavations show that Penaventosa
Hill, now the site of Porto's cathedral, or Sé, was
inhabited as early as 3,000 years ago. Take a stroll
around this historic area, which, in its elevated
position, provides an excellent orientation point
while you explore the rest of the city. Pause halfway
at the broad Avenida de Vímara Peres, named after
the nobleman who expelled the Moors from the city
in 868 CE, which sweeps south past the Barredo's
steep alleys and stairways. The view to the north is
towards the extraordinarily embellished São Bento
station and the busy commercial heart of the city.

*Behind the traditional
shop-fronts in the Rua
das Flores are some of
the city's best jewellers
and goldsmiths.*

RUA DAS FLORES

R. MOUZINHO D. SILVEIRA

RUA ESCURA

CALÇADA DE VANDOM.

TERREIRO
DA SÉ

AV. DE VIMARA PER

↑ Gothic cloister of Porto's
Sé, adorned with blue-
and-white *azulejos*

*The broad open Terreiro da Sé
offers a wonderful panorama of
the city. In one corner stands a
stone pillory (pelourinho).*

*Although imposing and perhaps a
little forbidding from the outside,
inside Porto's Sé contains many
small-scale treasures (p236).*

Paço Episcopal

*The Casa Guerra Junqueiro
is a charming museum in a
house that once belonged to
the 19th-century poet (p236).*

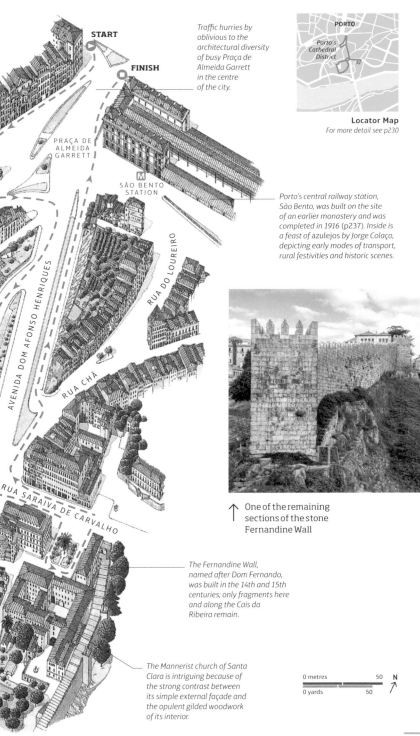

START

FINISH

Traffic hurries by oblivious to the architectural diversity of busy Praça de Almeida Garrett in the centre of the city.

PRAÇA DE ALMEIDA GARRETT

SÃO BENTO STATION

AVENIDA DOM AFONSO HENRIQUES

RUA DO LOUREIRO

RUA CHÃ

RUA SARAIVA DE CARVALHO

Porto's central railway station, São Bento, was built on the site of an earlier monastery and was completed in 1916 (p237). Inside is a feast of azulejos by Jorge Colaço, depicting early modes of transport, rural festivities and historic scenes.

↑ One of the remaining sections of the stone Fernandine Wall

The Fernandine Wall, named after Dom Fernando, was built in the 14th and 15th centuries; only fragments here and along the Cais da Ribeira remain.

The Mannerist church of Santa Clara is intriguing because of the strong contrast between its simple external façade and the opulent gilded woodwork of its interior.

PORTO

Porto's Cathedral District

Locator Map
For more detail see p230

| 0 metres | | 50 | N |
| 0 yards | | 50 | ↗ |

243

DOURO AND TRÁS-OS-MONTES

As early as the 9th century BCE, Phoenician merchants arrived in the Douro estuary to trade. The Romans later developed the settlements of Portus (modern-day Porto) and Cale on either side of the river, and the names subsequently united, as Portucale, to denote the region between the Minho and Douro rivers. This was the nucleus of the kingdom of Portugal.

The upper reaches of the Douro river are devoted to the cultivation of grapes for port, and the valley's landscape and history has been shaped by its endless vineyards and *quintas* (wine estates). Manuel I ordered the widening of fishing channels in the early 16th century in response to the growing demand for port during the Age of Discovery, as sailors requested barrel after barrel of the fortified wine to see them through long sea journeys. Between the 17th and 19th centuries, England became the main consumer of the wine grown in the region, resulting in the Methuen Treaty of 1703, which mutually abolished tariffs. In 1756, the Douro Valley became the first demarcated wine region in the world.

In contrast with the thriving Douro Valley, Trás-os-Montes is remote and untamed. It was a refuge in the past for religious and political exiles. The hard life and lack of opportunity to better it have depopulated the land; those who remain till the fields and herd their flocks in the unforgiving climate, according to the rhythm of the seasons.

DOURO AND TRÁS-OS-MONTES

Must Sees
1. Bragança
2. Casa de Mateus

Experience More
3. Santo Tirso
4. Penafiel
5. Cinfães
6. Amarante
7. Peso da Régua
8. Mesão Frio
9. Lamego
10. Vila Real
11. Serra do Barroso
12. Chaves
13. Mirandela
14. Murça
15. Parque Natural de Montesinho
16. Miranda do Douro
17. Mogadouro
18. Torre de Moncorvo
19. Freixo de Espada à Cinta
20. Pinhão
21. Parque Natural do Alvão

1 ⟨🔊⟩

BRAGANÇA

⬛F1 **ℹ** Rua Abílio Beça; www.turismo.
cm-braganca.pt

This town gave its name to Portugal's final royal
dynasty, descended from an illegitimate son of
João I who was created first duke of Bragança
in 1442. Dominated by an imposing citadel,
Bragança is shrouded in history and legend.

The Citadel

This strategic hilltop was the site of a succession of forts
before Fernão Mendes, brother-in-law of King Afonso
Henriques, built a walled citadel here in 1130 and kept
its historical name: Brigantia. Within the walls still stand
Sancho I's castle, built in 1187, with its watchtowers and
dungeons, and the pentagonal 12th-century Domus
Municipalis, beside the church of Santa Maria. The citadel
is closed on Mondays and public holidays.

The Town

By the 15th century, Bragança had expanded west along
the banks of the Fervença river. The Jewish quarter,
which centres around Rua dos Fornos, survives from this
era, when Jews from North Africa and Spain settled here
and founded the silk industry. Head to the lively covered
market, by the old cathedral, where delicacies such as
smoked hams and *alheiras* (chicken sausages) are sold.

*Porta de
Santo
António*
*Porta
da Vila*

1. The citadel dominates
the town of Bragança.

2. The Domus Municipalis is
the only surviving example of
Romanesque civic architecture
in Portugal. It served as a hall
where the *homens bons* ("good
men") settled disputes.

3. The castle's Torre da
Princesa, scene of many tragic
tales, was refuge to Dona
Sancha, unhappy wife of
Fernão Mendes, and prison
to other mistreated royal
wives kept in the citadel.

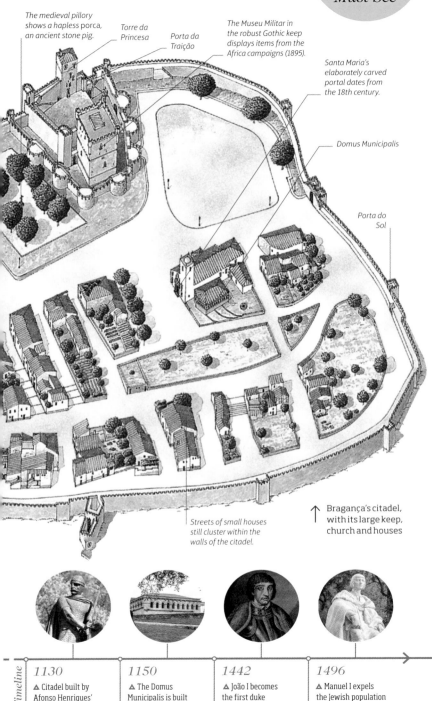

The medieval pillory shows a hapless porca, an ancient stone pig.

Torre da Princesa

Porta da Traição

The Museu Militar in the robust Gothic keep displays items from the Africa campaigns (1895).

Santa Maria's elaborately carved portal dates from the 18th century.

Domus Municipalis

Porta do Sol

↑ Bragança's citadel, with its large keep, church and houses

Streets of small houses still cluster within the walls of the citadel.

Timeline

1130
▲ Citadel built by Afonso Henriques' brother-in-law.

1150
▲ The Domus Municipalis is built to be a meeting place.

1442
▲ João I becomes the first duke of Bragança.

1496
▲ Manuel I expels the Jewish population from the town.

2 🏃 Ⓜ 🖥 🛍

CASA DE MATEUS

🄰 E2 🏠 Mateus, 3 km (2 miles) E of Vila Real 🚊 To Vila Real 🚌
🕘 Sep–Mar: 9am–5pm daily (to 5:30pm Sat & Sun); Apr–Oct:
9am–6:30pm daily 🌐 casademateus.com

The splendid manor house depicted on the labels of Mateus Rosé wine epitomizes the flamboyance of Baroque architecture in Portugal. Casa de Mateus was built in the early 18th century, probably by Nicolau Nasoni, for António José Botelho Mourão, whose descendants still live here.

Tours start in the first-floor entrance salon, a well-proportioned room graced by a pair of sedan chairs and with a magnificent wooden ceiling featuring family coats of arms. The Tea Salon has a 17th-century William and Mary cupboard and matching longcase clock from England, while the Salon of the Four Seasons gets its name from the large 18th-century paintings on its walls. The library, remodelled in the mid-20th century, contains volumes dating back to the 16th century, but the rarest book is in the small museum: an 1817 copy of *Os Lusíadas*, with engravings by leading artists. Also on display in the museum is family correspondence with famous historical figures, including Frederick the Great and Wellington.

Little remains of the original gardens planted by the 4th Morgado's uncle, who was an archdeacon in Rome, and the gardens that you can see today were laid out in the 1930s and 1940s. The style, however, is of an earlier romantic era and the complex parterres and formal beds edged with tightly clipped dwarf box hedges form a living tapestry that reflects perfectly the ornate symmetry of the house. In winter, the grand old camellias, relics from the 19th century, are a highlight of the gardens, but for most visitors the lasting memory is of the vast cedar tunnel, greatest among the many pieces of topiary here. Beyond the formal gardens lie the well-ordered orchards and fields of the estate.

↑ The grand manor house, and *(inset)* its formal gardens

THE CEDAR TUNNEL

This celebrated feature in the Casa de Mateus garden was formed from cedars planted in 1941. It is 35 m (115 ft) long and 7.5 m (25 ft) high, the tight-knit greenery providing an aromatic walk in summer. To keep the tunnel in shape, gardeners have to scale specially fashioned outsized ladders.

EXPERIENCE MORE

3

Santo Tirso

△E2 △▦ ℹLargo Coronel Batista Coelho 54; 252 830 411

Santo Tirso, a major textile centre, lies beside the Ave river. The town's most notable building is the former monastery of São Bento. Founded by the Benedictines in the 8th century, it was later rebuilt, then modified in the 17th century. The pairs of columns in the 14th-century Gothic cloister are graced with carved capitals.

The monastery, which is now an agricultural college, also houses the **Museu Abade Pedrosa**. The old monastery guesthouse and a modern extension converge to provide bright exhibition space for sculpture and local archaeological finds, including stone axes and bronze armlets.

At Roriz, 13 km (8 miles) east of Santo Tirso, the Romanesque church of São Pedro perches above the Vizela valley. A date of 1228 is carved in the porch, although there are claims that a church may have stood here as early as the 8th century. Above the portal is a noteworthy rose window. Set apart from the church are an attractive bell tower and the ruins of the monastic cloister.

Sanfins de Ferreira, 5 km (3 miles) further east, is the hilltop site of a *citânia*, an important Iron Age citadel, probably inhabited from around the 6th century BCE. Traces remain of a triple ring of defensive walls around about 100 huts, and there is also a small museum on the site.

Museu Abade Pedrosa
△ Rua Unisco Godiniz 100
🕒 9am–12:30pm & 2:30–5:30pm Tue-Fri, 2-7pm Sat & Sun 🔒 Public hols 🌐 mmap. cm-stirso.pt

Sanfins de Ferreira
△ Sanfins, signposted off N209 📞 255 963 643
🕒 10am-noon & 2-5pm Tue-Sun (Jun–Sep: to 6pm)

↑ The former monastery of São Bento at Santo Tirso, now a college and museum

The sanctuary of
Nossa Senhora da
Piedade in Penafiel ↑

1809

Portuguese soldiers
delayed Napoleon's
troops at Amarante.

At Tarouquela, around 16 km (10 miles) west of Cinfães, is the 12th-century church of Santa Maria Maior. Romanesque columns flank the portal, while later additions include the 14th-century Gothic mausoleum.

In the village of Cárquere, between Cinfães and Lamego, stands another church dedicated to the Virgin Mary. Legend tells how the sickly young Afonso Henriques, future king of Portugal, was healed at Cárquere by his devoted aide,

❹

Penafiel

🅰E2 🚌 🛈Largo Padre Américo; 255 710 722

The granite town of Penafiel stands on a hilltop above the Sousa river. Apart from an elegant Renaissance-style Igreja Matriz, there is also a sanctuary, Nossa Senhora da Piedade, built in 1908 in a curious medley of Neo-Gothic and Byzantine styles. Penafiel is chiefly known, however, as the regional centre for the production of *vinho verde*. One of the region's foremost estates producing *vinho verde* is **Quinta da Aveleda**, just north of Penafiel.

Boelhe, around 17 km (11 miles) south of Penafiel, merits a detour for the 12th-century church of São Gens. Only 10 m (33 ft) high, and a mere 7 m (23 ft) in width and length, it is claimed to be the smallest Romanesque church in the country. Its simple design enhances the aesthetic appeal.

In the 13th-century church of São Salvador at Paço de Sousa, 8 km (5 miles) south-west of Penafiel, is the tomb

of rich nobleman Egas Moniz. A figure of legendary loyalty, Moniz was counsellor to Afonso Henriques (1139–85), the first king of Portugal.

Quinta da Aveleda

🚭🚭 🅰Signposted from N15 🕒9am–6pm daily 🚫1 Jan, 1 May, 31 May, 25 Dec 🌐aveleda.pt

❺

Cinfães

🅰E2 🚌 🛈Rua Capitão Salgueiro Maia; 255 561 051

Cinfães lies just above the Douro river, tucked below the foothills of the Serra de Montemuro, whose peaks rise over 1,000 m (3,300 ft). The town is a gateway to bustling Lamego (*p254*) and the Upper Douro to the east, and is surrounded by verdant scenery. Cinfães is an agricultural centre and local handicrafts include weaving, lacework, basketry, and the production of miniature *rabelos*, the boats that used to ship port down the river to Porto.

Egas Moniz. In about 1110, guided by a dream, Moniz unearthed a buried statue of the Virgin and built a church for her. Miraculously, his young charge was cured overnight. The present church dates from the 14th or 15th century, but the finest of its treasures is a minute ivory carving of the Virgin, of unknown date.

Amarante

⚡E2 🅿️🚻 ℹ️Largo Conselheiro António Cândido; 255 420 246

The pretty riverside town of Amarante is one of the gems of Northern Portugal. Rows of 17th-century mansions with brightly painted wooden balconies line Amarante's narrow streets, and restaurants seat diners on terraces overhanging the river. The origins of the town are uncertain but the first settlement here was probably around

360 BCE. Much of the town was burned down in 1809, after a two-week siege by the French forces under Marshal Soult.

A recurring name in Amarante is that of São Gonçalo, who was born at the end of the 12th century. There are many stories of the dancing and festivities he organized to keep ladies from temptation by finding them husbands, and he has become associated with matchmaking and fertility. On the first weekend in June, the Festa de São Gonçalo begins with prayers for a marriage partner, followed by dancing, music and the giving of phallic-shaped São Gonçalo cakes.

When the old Roman bridge across the Tâmega collapsed during floods in the 13th century, it was São Gonçalo who was credited with replacing it. The present Ponte de São Gonçalo crosses to the 16th-century Igreja de São Gonçalo, where his memory lives on. In the chapel to the left of the chancel, the image on his tomb has been eroded

through the embraces of thousands of devotees.

The **Museu Amadeo de Souza-Cardoso** is housed in the old monastery cloister. One exhibit describes a fertility cult that predates São Gonçalo. The *diabo* and *diaba* are a pair of bawdy devils carved in black wood, and are 19th-century replacements for an older duo destroyed in the Peninsular War. They became the focus of a local fertility rite, and were threatened with burning by an outraged bishop of Braga; the *diabo* was "castrated" instead.

The museum's other prized possession is the collection of Cubist works by the artist after whom the museum is named, Amadeo de Souza-Cardoso (1887–1918).

Museu Amadeo de Souza-Cardoso
♿ 🏛️ Alameda Teixeira de Pascoães ⏰ Tue–Sun 🔒 Public hols 🌐 amadeo souza-cardoso.pt

Igreja de São Gonçalo's exterior, and *(inset)* its ornate details ↓

→

Grand stairway leading
to Nossa Senhora dos
Remédios, Lamego

INSIDER TIP
Grape Rails

Take one of Portugal's prettiest train rides from Peso da Régua to Pocinho. You'll pass along the banks of the Douro river and through some of the area's dramatically terraced vineyards.

7

Peso da Régua

 E2 🏠🚌 ℹ️ Av do Douro;
254 318 152

Developed from the villages of Peso and Régua in the 18th century, Peso da Régua is the major hub for rail and road connections in the region.

In 1756, Régua, as the town is invariably called, was chosen by the Marquês de Pombal as the centre of the demarcated region for port production. From here, *rabelos*, the traditional wooden sailing ships, transported the barrels of port through hazardous gorges to Vila Nova de Gaia *(p234)*. They continued to ply the river even after the advent of the Douro railway in the 1880s. Régua suffered frequently in the past from severe floods, and these are still a threat, although they have lessened since dams were built across the Douro in the 1970s and 1980s.

Many visitors to Régua often pause here only briefly on their way to explore the "port country", but budding connoisseurs shouldn't overlook Peso da Régua. The **Museu do Douro**, which is set in a beautifully designed contemporary building, is of particular interest. Well presented, it portrays the region's rich heritage through paintings, writings and other forms of local culture.

Set in the surrounding countryside are some beautiful *quintas*, country estates producing port. The **Quinta da Pacheca** is at Cambres, 4 km (2 miles) to the southwest. Dating from the 18th century, the estate also produces wine.

Museu do Douro

🏠 Rua Marquês de Pombal
🕙 10am-6pm daily (Nov-Feb: to 5:30pm) 🚫 1 Jan, 1 May, 25 Dec 🌐 museudodouro.pt

Quinta da Pacheca

🏠 Cambres 🕙 Tours by appt only 🌐 quintada
pacheca.com

8

Mesão Frio

 E2 🚌 ℹ️ Avenida
Conselheiro José Maria
Alpoim; 254 890 100

This scenic gateway to the port wine-growing region enjoys a fine setting above the Douro. Around it, the majestic tiers of the Serra do Marão rise to form a natural climatic shield for the vineyards to the east. Mesão Frio itself is known for its wickerwork and a culinary speciality, *falachas* – or chestnut cakes.

The Igreja Matriz of São Nicolau was rebuilt in 1877, but has retained its magnificent late-16th-century ceiling panels, each one bearing the portrait of a saint.

9

Lamego

 E2 🚌 ℹ️ Rua Regimento
de Infantaria 9; 254
099 000

An attractive town within the demarcated port area, Lamego also produces wines, including Raposeira, Portugal's premier sparkling wine. This fertile region is also known for its fruit and choice hams.

In its more illustrious past, Lamego claims to have been host in 1143 to the first *cortes*, or national assembly, which recognized Afonso Henriques as first king of Portugal. The town's later economic decline was halted in the 16th century, when it turned to wine and textile production, and handsome Baroque mansions from

←
Museu do Douro, set in a distinct modern building in Peso da Régua

STAY

Forte de São Francisco

Stay inside this 17th-century fortress in the heart of Chaves. It has been converted into a hotel, with its own bar, pool and restaurant.

 F1 Forte de São Francisco, Chaves fortesaofrancisco.com

€€€

Quinta Nova de Nossa Senhora do Carmo

This 18th-century manor house, in the heart of a wine estate, offers vineyard tours and wine tastings. There's a pool and terrific views towards the river.

 E2 Covas do Douro, Vila Real quintanova.com

€€€

---

this prosperous period are still a feature of the town. Today, the main focus of Lamego is as a pilgrimage town.

A small hilltop chapel, originally dedicated in 1391 to St Stephen, became the focus of pilgrims devoted to the Virgin, and in 1761 **Nossa Senhora dos Remédios** was built on the spectacular site. The church is reached via an awe-inspiring double stairway, similar to Braga's even larger Bom Jesus *(p276)*. Its 686 steps and nine terraces, embellished with *azulejos* and urns, rise to the Pátio dos Reis, a circle of noble granite figures beneath the twin-towered church. The church itself is of marginal interest, but there is a well-earned view across the town to the Douro and its tributaries.

In early September, pilgrims arrive in their thousands for Lamego's Romaria de Nossa Senhora dos Remédios, many of them climbing the steps on their knees.

Lamego's Gothic cathedral, founded in 1129, retains its original square tower, while the rest of the architecture reflects modifications between the 16th and 18th centuries, including a Renaissance cloister with a dozen arches.

The **Museu de Lamego** is housed in the former bishop's palace. Pride of place goes to the strikingly original *Criação dos Animais* (Creation of the Animals), part of a series of altar panels attributed to the great 16th-century Portuguese artist Grão Vasco.

At the foot of the valley 4 km (2 miles) east of Lamego, the Capela de São Pedro de Balsemão is said to be the oldest church in Portugal. Although much modified, the 7th-century sanctuary, of Visigothic origins, remains. Here, in an ornate tomb, lies Afonso Pires, a 14th-century bishop of Porto. A statue of Nossa Senhora do Ó, the pregnant Virgin, is from the 15th century.

The 12th-century monastery of **São João de Tarouca**, the first Cistercian house in Portugal, lies 16 km (10 miles) south of Lamego. The interior of the church has many fine 18th-century *azulejo* panels, notably those in the chancel depicting the founding of the monastery, and in the sacristy, where none of the 4,709 tiles has the same design. The church also contains a remarkable *St Peter* by Grão Vasco. The Count of Barcelos, bastard son of King Dinis, is buried here, his tomb adorned with hunting scenes.

Nossa Senhora dos Remédios

Monte de Santo Estêvão
Daily

Museu de Lamego

Largo de Camões
254 600 230 Daily
1 Jan, 1 May, Easter, 8 Sep, 25 Dec

São João de Tarouca

Signposted from N226
254 678 766 10am–1pm & 2–6pm Tue–Sun

Vila Real

E2 🚗🚌 **i** Av Carvalho Araújo 94; 259 308 170

Perched over a gorge cut by the confluence of the Cabril and Corgo rivers, Vila Real is a busy commercial centre. As the communications hub of the Upper Douro, it makes a convenient starting point from which to explore the valley of the Douro to the south and the Parque Natural do Alvão to the northwest. Vila Real also has a motor-racing circuit, which hosts major events each year during June and July.

Midway along the broad main street, Avenida Carvalho Araújo, is the 15th-century Sé. This fine Gothic cathedral was originally the church of a Dominican friary. The other monastic buildings burned down in suspicious circumstances in the mid-19th century.

At the southern end of the avenue, a plaque on the wall at No 19 marks the birthplace of Diogo Cão, the explorer who travelled to the mouth of the Congo in 1482.

The Igreja dos Clérigos, in nearby Rua dos Combatentes da Grande Guerra, is also known as Capela Nova. It has a Baroque façade attributed to Nicolau Nasoni and an interior of fine blue-and-white *azulejos*.

The small village of Bisalhães, 6 km (4 miles) to the west of Vila Real, is famed for its boldly designed black pottery. Examples can be seen displayed for sale at the annual Festa de São Pedro, celebrated in Vila Real each year on 28–29 June. Also seen at this time is the fine linen from nearby Agarez.

Serra do Barroso

E1 🚌 From Montalegre or Boticas **i** Terreiro do Açougue, Montalegre; 276 510 205

Just southeast of the Parque Nacional da Peneda-Gerês (p270) is the wild and remote Serra do Barroso. The landscape of heathery hillsides is split by the immense Barragem do Alto Rabagão, the largest of many reservoirs in the area created by the damming of rivers for hydro-electric power. Water is a mainstay of the local economy: a high rainfall enables farmers to eke out an existence on the poor soil, and the artificial lakes attract fishing and watersports enthusiasts. The source of one of the country's most popular bottled mineral waters is at Carvalhelhos.

Nearby, the village of Boticas produces a beverage with a more

 HIDDEN GEM

Santuário de Panóias

The Santuário de Panóias, east of Vila Real, was ordered to be built in the 2nd century by a Roman senator. The carved stones and ruins seen today were part of three temples. The large granite boulders were once the site of sacrifices to Serapis – the Greco-Egyptian god of life and death.

original claim to fame: *vinho dos mortos*. Bottles of wine are buried underground for up to two years – which is why they are called *mortos* ("dead") – a practice that originated to hide it from the invading enemy (p258).

The area's principal town is Montalegre, on a plateau to the north. Its most notable feature is the imposing keep, 27 m (88 ft) high, of the ruined 14th-century castle.

Oxen are bred in the Serra, and inter-village *chegas de bois* (ox fights) are a popular pastime. The contest is usually decided within half an hour, when the weaker ox takes to its heels.

↓ The bell tower of Vila Real's 15th-century Gothic cathedral

→

The historic centre of Chaves, the thermal spa town

Chaves

▲F1 🔲 **ℹ Paço dos Duques de Bragança; 276 348 180**

Beside the upper reaches of the Tâmega stands historic Chaves, attractively sited in the middle of a fertile plain.

Thermal springs and nearby gold deposits encouraged the Romans to establish Aquae Flaviae here in 78 CE. Its strategic position led to invasions and occupation by the Suevi, Visigoths and Moors, before the Portuguese gained final possession in 1160.

Today Chaves is renowned for its spa and historic centre, and for its smoked hams. The distinctive black pottery that is a curiosity of the north is made in nearby Nantes.

The old town centres on the Praça de Camões, where the

TOP 5 DOURO VALLEY VINEYARDS

Quinta da Pacheca
🆆 quintadapacheca.com
One of the valley's oldest vineyards.

Quinta de Vargellas
🆆 taylor.pt
This large vineyard is owned by Taylor's.

Quinta das Carvalhas
📞 254 738 050
As well as tastings, this estate has great views.

Quinta do Panascal
🆆 fonseca.pt
Produces the famed Fonseca port wines.

Quinta do Seixo
🆆 sandeman.com
Home to the famed Sandeman brand.

14th-century keep overlooking this pleasant medieval square is all that remains of the castle given to Nuno Álvares Pereira by João I. On the south side of the square stands the Igreja Matriz with its fine Romanesque portal. The Baroque Misericórdia church opposite has an exquisite interior lined with 18th-century *azulejos*. Attributed to Policarpo de Oliveira Bernardes, the huge panels depict scenes from the New Testament.

Within the castle keep is the **Museu Militar**, where suits of armour, uniforms and associated regalia are on display. Also exhibited are military memorabilia from the city's defence against the attack by Royalists from Spain in 1912. In the flower-filled garden surrounding the keep are a few archaeological finds from Chaves's long history, but most are to be found in the **Museu da Região Flaviense** behind the keep. Here, in the Paço dos Duques de Bragança, are displayed a variety of local archaeological discoveries. Items of interest include souvenirs of the Roman occupation, such as milestones and coins, alongside an oxcart.

The 16-arch Roman bridge across the Tâmega was completed around 100 CE, at the time of the Emperor Trajan. Its construction brought added importance to Chaves as a

staging post on the route between Braga and Astorga (in northwestern Spain). On the bridge are Roman milestones that record that funds to build it were raised locally.

A short walk from the city centre is one of the hottest **thermal springs** in Europe. Water here bubbles up at a temperature of 73°C (163°F) and the spa's facilities attract both holiday-makers and patients seeking treatment. Chaves water is said to alleviate ailments as diverse as rheumatism, hypertension and kidney problems.

Museu Militar and Museu da Região Flaviense
♿ ▲ Praça de Camões
📞 276 348 180 🕐 Apr-Sep: 10am-1pm & 2:30-6:30pm Tue-Sun; Oct-Mar: 9:30am-1pm & 2:30-6pm Tue-Sun
🚫 Public hols

Thermal Springs
▲ Largo da Caldas 🕐 Daily
🆆 termasdechaves.com

Did You Know?

Aquae Flaviae, Chaves' Roman name, was named after its patron, Emperor Titus Flavius Vespasianus.

Cityscape of Mirandela at twilight, from across the Tua river ↑

⑬
Mirandela

🅰F1 🚉 🛈 Rua Dom Afonso III; 278 203 143

Mirandela, at the end of the defunct Tua narrow-gauge railway line, has pretty gardens running down to the river and an elegant Roman bridge with 20 asymmetrical arches. Built for the deployment of troops and to aid the transport of ore from local mines, it was rebuilt in the 16th century and is now for pedestrians only.

Displayed in the **Museu Municipal Armindo Teixeira Lopes** are sculptures, prints and paintings, including views of Mirandela by the local 20th-century artist after whom the museum is named.

The 17th-century town hall once belonged to the Távoras,

but the family was accused of attempted regicide in 1759 and all trace of them was erased.

Museu Municipal Armindo Teixeira Lopes

🅰 Rua João Maria Sarmento Pimentel 📞 278 200 290 🕘 9am–12:30pm & 2–5:30pm Mon–Fri, 2:30–6pm Sat 🚫 Public hols

⑭
Murça

🅰F2 🚌 🛈 Parque Urbano; 259 510 139

The market town of Murça is famed for its honey, goat's cheese and sausage. Its major attraction, and the focal point of the garden in the main square, is its *porca*, an Iron Age granite pig with a substantial

girth of 2.8 m (9 ft). The role of *berrões*, as beasts such as these are called, is enigmatic, but they may have been linked to fertility cults. In more recent times the Murça *porca* has been pressed into service at elections, when the winning political parties would paint it in their colours.

The Misericórdia chapel is notable for its early Baroque façade, ornamented with designs of vines and grapes.

⑮
Parque Natural de Montesinho

🅰F1 🚌 From Rio de Onor & Vinhais 🛈 Parque Florestal, Bragança; 273 300 400

This wild reserve covers 700 sq km (270 sq miles) from Bragança to the Spanish border. The region, understandably, is known as Terra Fria (Cold Land). Bleak mountains rise to 1,481 m (4,859 ft) above heather and broom, descending to oak forests and valleys of alder and willow.

Amazing views of the park can be enjoyed from Vinhais, on its southern fringe, and the wilderness attracts walkers, bikers and horse riders.

The population clusters in farming communities on the lowlands, leaving much of the mountain range an undisturbed habitat for rare

---

LOCAL WINES

The granite pig in the town of Murça lends its name to the local Porca de Murça wine – one of the Douro's oldest wine brands. As well as trying this wine in local restaurants and bars, you should also ask for *vinho dos mortos* (wine of the dead). In 1809, locals buried their wine rather than have it fall into the hands of the invading French. When Napoleon's troops departed, the "dead" wine was retrieved and found to have improved. The practice continues to this day.

EAT

Adega do Faustino

This former wine merchant's store is lined with giant barrels. It offers a wide range of tasty *petiscos* (tapas), as well as grilled fish and meats, and of course wines, at bargain prices.

 F1 🚇 Travessa Cândido dos Reis, Chaves 🕒 Sun 🖥 adegafaustino.pt

€€€

Flor de Sal

This elegant, contemporary restaurant serves award-winning cuisine based on fresh local ingredients. Sit on the riverside deck.

🅰 F1 🚇 Parque Dr José Gama, Mirandela 🕒 Mon ☎ 278 203 063

€€€

 16

Miranda do Douro

🅰 G1 🚍 ℹ️ Largo do Menino Jesus da Cartolinha; 273 430 025

This medieval outpost stands on top of the Douro gorge, which here forms an abrupt border with Spain. Its key position and the establishment of a bishopric here in 1545 paved the way for the town's development into the cultural and religious centre of Trás-os-Montes. In 1762, during the Seven Years' War against France and Spain, the powder store exploded, claiming 400 lives and destroying the castle (only the keep remains). This mishap, compounded by the transfer of the bishopric to Bragança, led the town into a deep economic decline, only halted by trade links with the coast and Spain.

The twin-towered Sé was founded in the 16th century. The cathedral's most original feature is a wooden figure of the boy Jesus in the south transept. The *Menino Jesus da Cartolinha* represents a boy who, legend tells, appeared during a Spanish siege in 1711 to rally the demoralized Portuguese to miraculous victory. Devotees dressed the statue in 17th-century costume and later gave him a top hat (*cartolinha*).

The excellent **Museu da Terra de Miranda** houses an eclectic display of archaeological finds, folk costume and curious rural devices such as an inflated pig's-bladder cosh.

Just southwest of Miranda, the village of Duas Igrejas is famed for its stick dancers, or *pauliteiros*, who perform at local festivals and overseas.

Museu da Terra de Miranda

🎨 🏛 Largo Dom João III ☎ 273 417 288 🕒 Summer: 2–6pm Tue, 10am–1pm & 2–6pm Wed–Sun; Winter: 2–5:30pm Tue, 9:30am–1pm & 2–5:30pm Wed–Sun 🕒 1 Jan, Easter, 1 May, 10 Jul, 25 Dec

Local *pauliteiros* (stick dancers) performing in the village of Duas Igrejas ↑

---

species such as wolves and golden eagles.

Little changed from medieval times, villages such as França and Montesinho are typical in their stone houses, wooden balconies and cobbled streets. Ancient practices such as herbal cures and reverence for the supernatural linger.

Mogadouro

F2 **ℹ Avenida dos Comandos; 279 340 501**

Located on the Spanish border, Mogadouro can be traced back to prehistoric times. The town's history is evident in the number of Neolithic fortified settlements that dot the landscape.

Apart from the hilltop tower, little remains of the great castle founded here by King Dinis and presented to the Templars in 1297. From the top of the tower there are fine views over the little market town of Mogadouro, which is known for its handicrafts, particularly leather goods.

Mogadouro's 16th-century Igreja Matriz, rising on the north slope of the castle, features a 17th-century bell tower, while lavishly gilded retables from the 18th century decorate the altars.

> From the top of the tower there are fine views over the little market town of Mogadouro, which is known for its handicrafts, particularly leather goods.

Torre de Moncorvo

F2 **ℹ Rua dos Sapateiros 15; 279 252 289**

Famed for the white mantle of almond blossom that fleetingly covers the valleys in early spring (egg-shaped *amêndoas cobertas*, sugared almonds, are an Easter treat), Moncorvo offers an atmospheric stroll through its maze of medieval streets all year round. The town's name is variously attributed to a local nobleman, Mendo Curvo, or perhaps to his raven *(corvo)*.

The ponderous 16th-century Igreja Matriz, which is the largest in Trás-os-Montes, features a 17th-century altarpiece depicting scenes from the life of Christ.

The fate of the Côa valley, south of Moncorvo, was finally decided in 1996 when plans for a dam were dropped to preserve the world's largest

---

△ GREAT VIEW
Barragem de Miranda

Take a boat trip down the Douro from the quay near the Barragem de Miranda. This very pleasant 90-minute trip takes you along a dramatic gorge. Visit www.europarques.com for further details.

---

collection of open-air Stone Age rock art. Discovered in 1933 and estimated to be 20,000 years old, it features bulls, horses, fish and a naked man, the Homem de Pisco. Vila Nova de Foz Côa, Castelo Melhor and Muxagata offer several guided tours a day into the **Parque Arqueológico do Vale do Côa**, and visits must be booked in advance. The **Museu do Côa** houses some interesting art and archaeological exhibits on the Côa valley.

Parque Arqueológico do Vale do Côa/Museu do Côa
⊛ ⊛ △ Rua do Museu, Vila Nova de Foz Côa ◯ Daily ◯ 1 Jan, 1 May, Nov–Mar: Mon, 25 Dec ✉ arte-coa.pt

Did You Know?

The Portuguese word *oxalá*, meaning "if only", comes from the Arabic *insha'allah*, meaning "if Allah wishes it".

Freixo de Espada à Cinta

⚑F2 🚌 🛈 Praça Jorge Álvares; 279 653 480

Several stories try to explain the curious name of this remote border town. "Ash tree of the girt sword" may derive from the arms of a Spanish nobleman, or a Visigoth called Espadacinta, or from a tale that, when founding the town in the 14th century, King Dinis strapped his sword to an ash.

Dominating the skyline is the heptagonal **Torre do Galo**, a relic from the 14th-century defences. Views from the top are splendid, especially in spring when the almond blossom puts on a show, which attracts a great many visitors.

The cultivation of silkworms here is a revival of the 18th-century industry, and a visit to the **Museu da Seda e do Território** (Silk and Territory Museum) offers an insight into this tradition. This is the only place in Iberia producing entirely hand-crafted silk today; multimedia exhibits explain the process, and visitors can purchase handmade pieces. The museum also houses interesting ethnographic, archaeological and geological collections.

Museu Regional Casa Junqueiro, on Rua de São Francisco, occupies the home of José António Junqueiro,

father of the poet Guerra Junqueiro, and aims to highlight the importance of preserving rural life.

The intricate 16th-century portal of the Igreja Matriz leads into a splendid small-scale version of Belém's Mosteiro dos Jerónimos *(p108)*. Panels of the altarpiece, attributed to Grão Vasco, include a fine *Annunciation*.

Torre do Galo

📍 Praça Jorge Álvares
🕐 8am–5pm Mon–Sun

Museu da Seda e do Território

🖐 📍 Largo do Outeiro
📞 279 658 163 🕐 Apr–Sep: 9am–12:30pm & 2:30–6pm Mon–Sun; Oct–Mar: 9:30am–12:30pm & 2–5:30pm

↑ Rich interior of the Igreja Matriz, at Freixo de Espada à Cinta

THE DOVECOTES OF MONTESINHO

Doves, besides being sources of food, provide highly prized fertilizer through their droppings. In the Parque Natural de Montesinho *(p258)*, the traditional horseshoe-shaped dovecote or *pombal* is still a familiar sight. The birds nest in rough cells inside the whitewashed schist walls and enter through gaps in the roof. They are fed via a raised door at the front.

← The centre of Torre de Moncorvo, set in a lush green valley

THE STORY OF PORT

The "discovery" of port dates from the 17th century, when British merchants added brandy to the wine of the northern Douro region to prevent it souring in transit. They found that the stronger and sweeter the wine, the better flavour it acquired.

HOW PORT IS MADE

The climax of the Douro farmers' year comes in late September, when bands of pickers congregate to harvest the grapes. More than 40 varieties are used for making port, but there are five recommended varieties. The grapes are then either trodden in stone tanks (or *lagares*) to extract the juice or fermented in cement or steel tanks. Next comes the fortification process, where brandy – actually grape spirit – is added. This arrests the fermentation, leaving the wine naturally sweet.

↑ Testing port aged in oak barrels at the Symington estate

STYLES OF PORT

Tawny
Quality tawny port is matured in oak casks in port lodges. It may be a blend of red and white ports.

Ruby Port
Deep red in colour, this port has been aged for two or three years and should be full of lively fruit flavour.

White Port
Made from white grapes, this beverage may be sweet or not so sweet and is mainly drunk chilled.

Vintage
Made from wines of a single year, the liquid is blended and bottled after two years and left to mature.

Late Bottled Vintage
LBV is a wine of a single year, bottled between four and six years after the harvest.

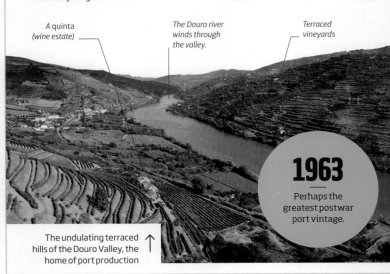

A quinta (wine estate)

The Douro river winds through the valley.

Terraced vineyards

1963
Perhaps the greatest postwar port vintage.

The undulating terraced hills of the Douro Valley, the home of port production ↑

↑ Striking river views from a restaurant terrace in Pinhão

 Pinhão

F2 **Pinhão**

Attractively set by a broad stretch of the Douro river, pretty Pinhão is a major stop for cruise boats. But don't let this put you off – this town is a gateway to port country. Close to some of the region's best port producers, this is the perfect place to pause if you are visiting a vineyard for a tour or staying at a *quinta* (wine-growing estate).

The wonderful Linha do Douro – one of the country's most spectacular rail routes – passes through Pinhão on its way from Porto. Even if you don't arrive by train, take a look at the town's pretty little station, which is decorated with 24 dazzling *azulejo* panels. These blue-and-white scenes depict local life, including the grape harvest.

Pinhão may be sleepy, but it does have a few restaurants and bars near the riverside promenade. Many of these restaurants have superb views of the steep terraced slopes where the vines are cultivated.

 Parque Natural do Alvão

E2 **From Ermelo via Campeã** **Largo dos Freitas, Parque Natural do Alvão; 259 302 830**

Within the 72 sq km (28 sq miles) of this nature reserve between the Corgo and Tâmega rivers, the scenery ranges dramatically from verdant, cultivated lowlands to bleak heights that reach 1,339 m (4,393 ft) at Alto das Caravelas. Despite hunters and habitat encroachment, hawks, dippers and otters can still be spotted here. Between the picturesque hamlets of Ermelo and Lamas de Olo, where maize is still kept in *espigueiros (p270)*, the Olo river drops in a spectacular cascade known as the Fisgas de Ermelo waterfalls. This area is one of the most stunning parts of the park.

From Alto do Velão, just southwest of the park, are splendid views west over the Tâmega valley.

→ The rugged, untouched landscape of the Parque Natural do Alvão

A DRIVING TOUR
PORT COUNTRY

Locator Map
For more detail see p246

Length 125 km (78 miles) **Stopping-off points** Peso da Régua; Pinhão; Sabrosa **Terrain** Beyond Pinhão, steep, narrow roads can make the going slow

The barrels of port maturing in the port lodges of Vila Nova de Gaia *(p234)* begin their life here, on the wine estates *(quintas)* of the Upper Douro. Centuries of toil on the poor schist have created thousands of terraces along the steep river banks, many no wider than a person's outstretched arms. Many vineyards have had their terraces widened to allow tractor access, but some of the oldest ones are protected as part of the cultural heritage. Many *quintas*, including those shown on the map, welcome visitors for port-tasting. Early autumn is the most rewarding time to tour; workers sing as they pick, and celebrate a good *vindima* or harvest.

DOURO AND
TRÁS-OS-MONTES
Port
Country

*The village of **Sabrosa**, which is set among vineyards, has a wealth of 15th-century houses, some of which are hotels. The explorer Magellan was born here in about 1480.*

*Begin your tour at **Peso da Régua** which has been an administrative centre for port since 1756. The rabelos moored here are a reminder of how port used to be transported.*

São Lourenço
Ribapinhão

N323

Souto
Maior

São
Martinho de
Anta

N322

Sabrosa

Quinta do Casal de Celeirós

Quinta do Portal
Quinta do Bucheiro

N32

*Agudo
729 m (2,392 ft)*

N322-2

Paços

Paradela de
Guiães

*Infantado
808 m (2,650 ft)*

Abaças

Provesend

Guiães

*São Domingos
863 m (2,831 ft)*

Vila Seca

Gouvães
Douro

Galafura

*São Leonardo
640 m (2,100 ft)*

Covas do Douro

Loureiro

Vilarinho dos
Freires

N322-2

Gouvinhas

A24

Poiares

Quinta do
Crasto

Ferrão

Godim

N2

START

Fontelas

Peso da Régua

Covelinhas

Douro

Quinta
São Luís

N222

N108

N2

D108

Folgosa

Adorigo

Quinta do
Panascal

Cambres

A24

N222

Parada do
Bispo

N313

*Seixo
565 m (1,853 ft)*

N3

Provesend

→
Terraced vineyards tumbling down the Douro Valley to the pretty village of Peso da Régua

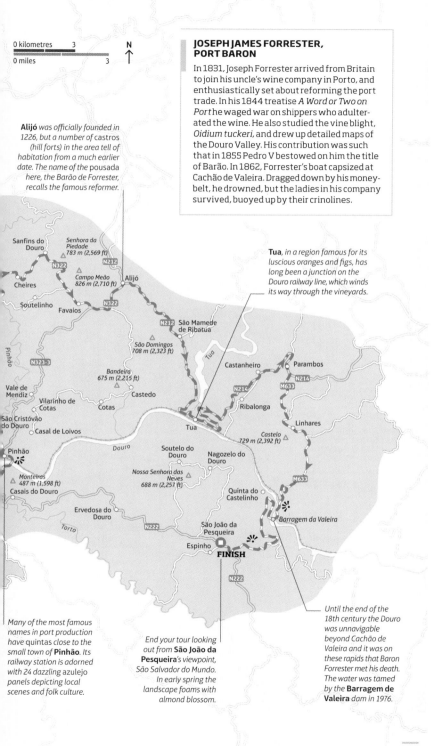

Alijó *was officially founded in 1226, but a number of castros (hill forts) in the area tell of habitation from a much earlier date. The name of the pousada here, the Barão de Forrester, recalls the famous reformer.*

JOSEPH JAMES FORRESTER, PORT BARON

In 1831, Joseph Forrester arrived from Britain to join his uncle's wine company in Porto, and enthusiastically set about reforming the port trade. In his 1844 treatise *A Word or Two on Port* he waged war on shippers who adulterated the wine. He also studied the vine blight, *Oidium tuckeri*, and drew up detailed maps of the Douro Valley. His contribution was such that in 1855 Pedro V bestowed on him the title of Barão. In 1862, Forrester's boat capsized at Cachão de Valeira. Dragged down by his money-belt, he drowned, but the ladies in his company survived, buoyed up by their crinolines.

Tua, *in a region famous for its luscious oranges and figs, has long been a junction on the Douro railway line, which winds its way through the vineyards.*

0 kilometres 3
0 miles 3

N

Sanfins do Douro
Senhora da Piedade 783 m (2,569 ft)
Cheires
Campo Meão 826 m (2,710 ft)
Alijó
Soutelinho
Favaios
N322
N212
N322
São Mamede de Ribatua
São Domingos 708 m (2,323 ft)
Castanheiro
Parambos
N214
Pinhão
N323-3
Bandeira 675 m (2,215 ft)
Castedo
Ribalonga
N214
M633
N214
Vale de Mendiz
Vilarinho de Cotas
Cotas
Tua
Castelo 729 m (2,392 ft)
Linhares
São Cristóvão do Douro
Casal de Loivos
Douro
Soutelo do Douro
Nagozelo do Douro
Pinhão
Monteiras 487 m (1,598 ft)
Casais do Douro
Nossa Senhora das Neves 688 m (2,257 ft)
M633
Quinta do Castelinho
Ervedosa do Douro
Torto
N222
São João da Pesqueira
Espinho
FINISH
Barragem da Valeira
N222

Many of the most famous names in port production have quintas close to the small town of **Pinhão**. *Its railway station is adorned with 24 dazzling azulejo panels depicting local scenes and folk culture.*

End your tour looking out from **São João da Pesqueira***'s viewpoint, São Salvador do Mundo. In early spring the landscape foams with almond blossom.*

Until the end of the 18th century the Douro was unnavigable beyond Cachão de Valeira and it was on these rapids that Baron Forrester met his death. The water was tamed by the **Barragem de Valeira** *dam in 1976.*

MINHO

The province of Minho occupies land between the Douro river in the south and the Minho river in the north. Fortified hilltop stone forts *(castros)* remain as evidence of the Neolithic history of the region. When Celtic peoples migrated into the area in the first millennium BCE, these sites developed into *citânias* (settlements) such as Briteiros.

In the 2nd century BCE, advancing Roman legions conquered the land, introduced vine-growing techniques and constructed a network of roads. When Christianity became the official religion of the Roman Empire in the 4th century CE, Braga became an important religious centre, a position it holds to this day. The Suevi swept aside the Romans in the 5th century, followed by the Visigoths, who were ousted in turn by the Moorish invasion of 711. The Minho was won back from the Moors in the 9th century. The region rose to prominence in the 1100s under Afonso Henriques, who proclaimed himself the first king of Portugal and chose Guimarães as his capital.

Since then, the Minho has been the territory of farmers and the region's fertile farms and estates have been handed down within families for centuries, each heir traditionally receiving a share of the land.

MINHO

Must Sees
❶ Parque Nacional da Peneda-Gerês
❷ Viana do Castelo
❸ Braga
❹ Bom Jesus do Monte

Experience More
❺ Guimarães
❻ Citânia de Briteiros
❼ Cabeceiras de Basto
❽ Barcelos
❾ Ponte de Lima
❿ Ponte da Barca
⓫ Caminha
⓬ Monção
⓭ Valença do Minho
⓮ Vila do Conde

1 ⊕

PARQUE NACIONAL DA PENEDA-GERÊS

🅰E1 🚍 From Braga to Caldas do Gerês; from Arcos de Valdevez to Soajo & Lindoso; from Melgaço to Castro Laboreiro & Lamas de Mouro 🛈 Caldas do Gerês: Avenida Dom João V (253 392 096); Lamas do Mouro: next to campsite; Arcos de Valdevez: Rua Professor Dr Mário Júlio Almeida Costa 🆆 natural.pt

Portugal's first national park, Parque Nacional da Peneda-Gerês preserves not just the country's precious flora and fauna, but also the unique way of life of the people who live in the 100 or so granite villages that pepper the landscape. Don't miss the tomb-like *espigueiros* (granaries).

Peneda-Gerês National Park, one of Portugal's greatest natural attractions, stretches from the Gerês mountains in the south to the Peneda range and the Spanish border in the north. Established in 1971, it extends over about 720 sq km (277 sq miles) of wild, dramatic scenery, with windswept rocky peaks and lush valleys of oak, pine and yew. It also hosts a rich variety of fauna, including rare wolves, deer and eagles. On top of these natural wonders, the park offers historic monasteries, good walking trails along a Roman road, and picturesque traditional villages. The park's long-distance footpath is well signposted (in parts); six sections are limited to groups of between 10 and 15 people.

> 💬 INSIDER TIP
> **Spa Break**
>
> Known since Roman times for its spa, Caldas do Gerês is a great place to recharge your batteries after hiking in the park. Our choice from the many options is the luxurious Águas do Gerês hotel *(www. aguasdogeres.pt)*.

Overlooking the Vilarinho das Furnas reservoir in the Parque Nacional da Peneda-Gerês, and *(inset)* one of its lovely waterfalls ↑

Did You Know?

Espigueiros are raised to keep grain and maize out of reach of rodents, and slatted for ventilation.

① The traditional village of Soajo, surrounded by terraced hillsides, is known for its collection of *espigueiros*. The village's local festival takes place in the middle of August.

② Sections of the old Roman road that ran from Braga to Astorga in Spain can still be seen at points along the Homem river valley.

③ Surrounded by massive rocks, Nossa Senhora da Peneda is an elaborate sanctuary. If it looks familiar, it is because it is a replica of Bom Jesus do Monte *(p276)*. The site is visited in early September by pilgrims from all over the region.

HIDDEN GEM
Anciet Ruins

Behind the Pousada Monte de Santa Luzia, at the top of the hill, you'll find traces of a Celtiberian settlement (*citânia*), dating from the 4th century BCE. Wander along the boardwalk, admiring the ancient stones.

Did You Know?

The Templo do Sagrado Coração de Jesus was modelled on Paris's Sacré Coeur.

The striking Templo do Sagrado Coração de Jesus atop Monte de Santa Luzia

❷
VIANA DO CASTELO

🅰D1 🚉 Largo da Estação 🛈 Viana Welcome Centre, Praça do Eixo-Atlântico;
www.cm-viana-castelo.pt

With winding streets and intimate squares, Viana do Castelo is an appealing destination. Both a busy fishing port and a holiday resort, the town is also the capital of Minho folk culture, hosting lively festivals and supporting a thriving handicrafts industry. The main attraction in Viana do Castelo, however, is Monte de Santa Luzia, whose peak overlooks the town.

Viana do Castelo lies in a beautiful setting on the Lima estuary. This 13th-century town gained prominence as a fishing centre in the 1400s; later it provided ships and seafarers for Portugal's era of colonial expansion in the 16th century *(p44)*. From here, João Velho set off to explore the Congo, and João Álvares Fagundes charted the rich fishing grounds of Newfoundland. Wealth derived from trade with Europe and Brazil funded the town's many opulent mansions built in Manueline, Renaissance and Baroque styles.

Monte de Santa Luzia

To enjoy exceptional views, take the zigzag road to Monte de Santa Luzia, 5 km (3 miles) north of the town centre. Perched on the mountain is the Templo do Sagrado Coração de Jesus, an extravagant Neo-Byzantine basilica completed in 1926. The steep climb to the top of its graffiti-scrawled dome is rewarded by superb panoramas. Behind the church you can wander along woodland paths or visit the Pousada Monte de Santa Luzia.

← *Caramuru* by José Rodrigues (2008) in Praça da República

1 Praça da República, Viana's main square, is full of café tables and overlooked by the Paços do Concelho, which was once the town hall.

2 Around late August of each year, people process through the streets of Viana do Castelo during the Nossa Senhora da Agonia Festival.

3 Monte de Santa Luzia is the perfect place to go for a beautiful sunset panorama.

Garden in the middle
of the Romanesque
Sé's cloisters ↑

3

BRAGA

🅰 E1 **🚆 Largo da Estacão** **🚌 Praça da Galiza** **ℹ Avenida da Liberdade 1; 253 262 550**

Churches, grand 18th-century houses and pretty gardens characterize Braga's centre. The city hosts some of Portugal's most colourful festivals. Semana Santa is celebrated with dramatic, solemn processions, while the festival of São João in June is a lively affair.

①

Sé

🏠 Rua Dom Paio Mendes
🕐 Museu de Arte Sacra:
253 263 317 **🕐 9:30am-**
12:30pm & 2:30-6:30pm
daily (winter: to 5:30pm)

Braga's cathedral, the oldest in Portugal, was begun in the 11th century, when Henry of Burgundy decided to build on the site of an older church, destroyed in the 6th century. Since then the Romanesque building has seen many changes, including the addition of a graceful galilee (porch) in the late 15th century. Outstanding features include the chapel to the right, just inside the west door, housing the ornate 15th-century tomb of the first-born son of João I,

Dom Afonso, who died as a child. The cathedral also houses the Treasury or Museu de Arte Sacra, which contains a rich collection of ecclesiastical treasures as well as statues, carvings and *azulejo* tiles.

Several chapels can be seen in the courtyard and cloister. The Capela dos Reis houses the tombs of the founders, Henry of Burgundy and his wife Dona Teresa, as well as the preserved body of the 14th-century archbishop Dom Lourenço Vicente.

After admiring the interior of the cathedral, walk around the outside of the building to Rua de São João. Here, on the cathedral's wall, is a statue of Nossa Senhora do Leite (Our Lady of the Milk), symbol of the city of Braga, sheltered under an ornate Gothic canopy.

②

Palácio dos Biscainhos

🏠 Rua dos Biscainhos **🕐 253 204 650** **🕐 10am-12:30pm & 2-5:30pm Tue-Sun**

To the west of the city centre is the Palácio dos Biscainhos. Built in the 16th century and modified over the centuries, it is adorned by painted blue-

---

DRINK

Café Brasileira
Sip drip-brewed coffee at historic Brasileira. Furnished in 19th-century salon style, this café opened in 1907 as a wholesale coffee shop where patrons were offered a cup of steaming coffee with their purchase of coffee beans.

🏠 Largo do Barão de São Martinho 17
🕐 253 262 104

↑ The Jardim de Santa Bárbara in the shadow of the Antigo Paço Episcopal

and-white *azulejos* depicting hunting scenes. An unusual detail is the ribbed, paved ground floor, designed to allow carriages inside the building to deposit guests and drive on to the stables beyond.

This imposing aristocratic mansion now houses the city's Museu Etnográfico e Artístico (Ethnography and Arts Museum), with fascinating displays of Roman relics as well as furniture dating from the 17th to 19th centuries.

③
Antigo Paço Episcopal

🏛 Praça Municipal
🚫 To the public

Near the Sé you'll find the former archbishop's palace. The façades of this once grand building date from the 14th, 17th and 18th centuries, but a major fire destroyed the interior in the 18th century. The palace is now used as a private library and archives.

Beside it are the immaculate gardens of the Jardim de Santa Bárbara. Landscaped in 1955, its design reflects the romanticism of the *Estado Novo* period (p46). The gardens are laid out in geometric patterns, with box hedges, topiary and a statue of its namesake, St Barbara, at its centre. One particularly striking feature is the broken ruins of an arcade which once ran along the exterior of the palace.

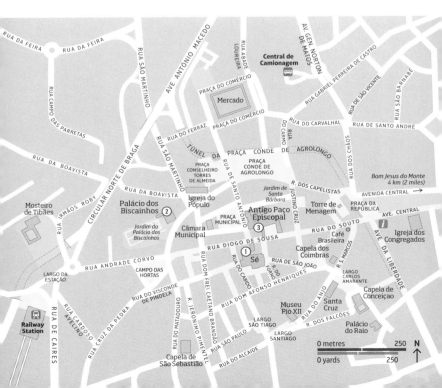

4 🍴 ☕

BOM JESUS DO MONTE

577

The number of steps on the Escadaria.

🗺 E1 🚗 5 km (3 miles) E of Braga 🚌 From Braga 🚠 To the top
📅 Daily 🌐 bomjesus.pt

On a forested slope east of Braga stands Portugal's most spectacular religious sanctuary. Ascend the zigzagging staircases, passing tiny chapels on the way, to the church of Bom Jesus.

In 1722, the archbishop of Braga devised the giant Baroque Escadaria (stairway) of Bom Jesus as the approach to a small existing 15th-century shrine. The stairway and the church of Bom Jesus were completed by Carlos Amarante in 1811. The lower section features a steep Sacred Way with chapels showing the 14 Stations of the Cross, the scenes leading up to Christ's crucifixion. The Escadório dos Cinco Sentidos, in the middle section, depicts the five senses with ingenious wall fountains and statues of biblical, mythological and symbolic figures. This is followed by the similarly allegorical Staircase of the Three Virtues.

At the summit, an esplanade provides superb views and access to the church. Close by are several hotels, a café and a boating lake hidden among the trees. Both a pilgrimage site and tourist attraction, the sanctuary attracts large festive crowds at weekends.

← The exterior of Bom Jesus, with its two bell towers, at the top of the Escadaria

↑ The hydraulically operated funicular, which dates back to 1882, on the ascent to the church

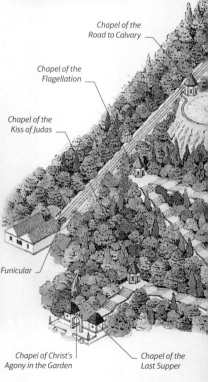

Chapel of the Road to Calvary

Chapel of the Flagellation

Chapel of the Kiss of Judas

Funicular

Chapel of Christ's Agony in the Garden

Chapel of the Last Supper

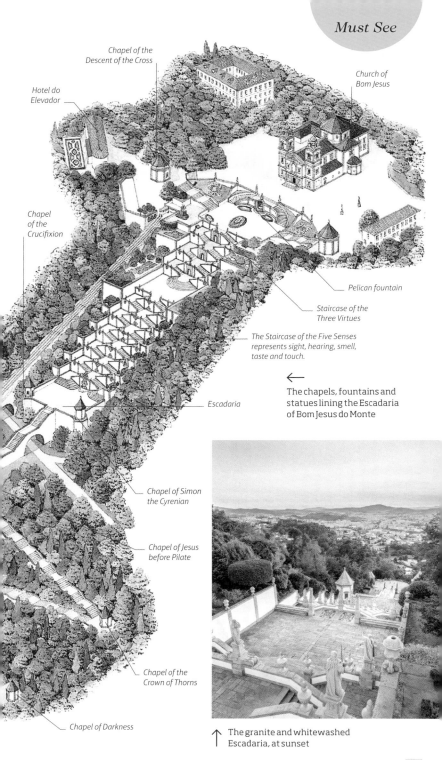

Chapel of the Descent of the Cross

Church of Bom Jesus

Hotel do Elevador

Chapel of the Crucifixion

Pelican fountain

Staircase of the Three Virtues

The Staircase of the Five Senses represents sight, hearing, smell, taste and touch.

←

The chapels, fountains and statues lining the Escadaria of Bom Jesus do Monte

Escadaria

Chapel of Simon the Cyrenian

Chapel of Jesus before Pilate

Chapel of the Crown of Thorns

Chapel of Darkness

↑ The granite and whitewashed Escadaria, at sunset

EXPERIENCE MORE

⑤ Guimarães

🅰E1 🚉 Avenida Dom João IV 🚌 Alameda Mariano Felgueiras 🛈 Praça de São Tiago; www.visit guimaraes.travel

A UNESCO World Heritage Site, the town of Guimarães is celebrated as the birthplace of the nation. When Afonso Henriques proclaimed himself the first king of Portugal in 1139 (p43), he chose Guimarães as his capital, and the distinctive outline of its proud castle appears on the Portuguese coat of arms.

The narrow streets of the medieval quarter are ideal for exploration on foot. The cobbled Rua de Santa Maria, lined with old townhouses embellished with ornate statuary, leads up from the main square, the Largo da Oliveira, past the Paço dos Duques to the **Castelo de Guimarães**. The castle's huge square keep, encircled by eight crenellated towers, dominates the skyline. First built to deter attacks by Moors and Normans in the 10th century, Henry of Burgundy extended it two centuries

↑ Stately Largo do Toural in Guimarães, dating from the 18th century

later and, according to legend, it was the birthplace of Afonso Henriques. The font where he was said to have been baptized is kept in the tiny Romanesque chapel of São Miguel, situated at the western end of the castle.

Constructed in the 15th century by Dom Afonso (first duke of Bragança), the Burgundian style of the **Paço dos Duques** reflects Dom Afonso's taste, acquired on his travels through Europe. The palace fell into disuse when the Bragança family moved to Vila Viçosa (p300). In 1933, under Salazar's dictatorship (p46), it was renovated as an official presidential residence.

The **Museu de Alberto Sampaio**, housed in the Romanesque cloister and adjoining rooms of Nossa Senhora da Oliveira, displays some outstanding religious art, azulejos and ceramics, all from local churches. The star exhibits, donated to the church by João I, are his tunic worn at the battle of Aljubarrota in 1385 (p173), and a 14th-century silver altarpiece, comprising a triptych of the Visitation, Annunciation and Nativity, reportedly taken from the defeated Spanish king. The former monastery (**Nossa Senhora da Oliveira**) lies on the square's east side.

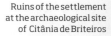

→ Ruins of the settlement at the archaeological site of Citânia de Briteiros

Founded by Afonso Henriques, the church was restored by João I in gratitude to Our Lady of the Olive Tree for his victory at Aljubarrota.

Named after the famous archaeologist, the **Museu Martins Sarmento** is housed in the Gothic cloister of the 14th-century convent of São Domingos. Specializing in finds from excavated sites, some dating from the Stone Age, the museum contains a wealth of archaeological, ethnological and numismatic exhibits. These include a rare pair of Lusitanian granite warriors (p42).

Built in 1400 in Gothic style, the elegant church of **São Francisco** was reconstructed in the 18th century. The interior of the church features a chancel covered in magnificent 18th-century azulejos with scenes from the life of St Anthony.

The former monastery of Santa Marinha da Costa is one of Portugal's top pousadas. It stands 5 km (3 miles) south-east of Guimarães, and was founded in 1154. The gardens and chapel are open to the public.

Castelo de Guimarães
⊗ 🅰 Rua Conde Dom Henrique 📞 253 412 273 🕙 10am–6pm daily 🚫 1 Jan, Easter, 1 May, 25 Dec

Paço dos Duques

⌖ 🏠 Rua Conde Dom Henrique ⏰ Daily 🚫 1 Jan, Easter, 1 May, 25 Dec ⊕ pacodosduques.gov.pt

Museu de Alberto Sampaio

⌖ 🏠 Rua Alfredo Guimarães ⏰ 10am-6pm Tue-Sun 🚫 1 Jan, Easter, 1 May, 25 Dec ⊕ museualberto sampaio.gov.pt

Nossa Senhora da Oliveira

🏠 Largo da Oliveira 📞 253 416144 ⏰ Daily

Museu Martins Sarmento

⌖ 🏠 Rua Paio Galvão ⏰ Tue-Sun 🚫 Public hols ⊕ msarmento.org

São Francisco

🏠 Largo de São Francisco 📞 253 439850 ⏰ Tue-Sun

💬 **INSIDER TIP**
Game Time

Get tickets to see a football match at the Estádio Dom Afonso Henriques. Vitória de Guimarães are the home team and regularly take on Portugal's top football clubs, including Benfica and Porto.

6
Citânia de Briteiros

🗺 E1 🏠 15 km (9 miles) N of Guimarães, off N101 📞 253 415969 🚌 From Guimarães & Braga ⏰ Apr-Oct: 9:30am-12:30pm & 2-6pm daily (Nov-Mar: to 5pm Tue-Sun)

This Iron Age settlement is one of Portugal's most impressive archaeological sites. It was excavated by Martins Sarmento (1833–99), who devoted his life to the study of Iron Age sites. Here, you'll find the foundations of 150 stone dwellings; many have since been reconstructed.

From about the 4th century BCE to the 4th century CE, the site was inhabited by Celtiberians, but was most probably under Roman rule from c.20 BCE. A network of paths leads past paved streets, subterranean cisterns, sewers and water supply ducts. The Museu Martins Sarmento in Guimarães displays excavated artifacts.

7
Cabeceiras de Basto

🗺 E1 🚌 ⓘ Praça da República; 253 669100

The Terras de Basto, once a region of refuge from Moorish

STAY

Casa do Cruzeiro do Outeiro

Just northwest of Ponte de Lima *(p281)*, this 18th-century manor house is named after a century-old cross erected nearby. It has three bedrooms and a spacious garden with an outdoor pool.

🗺 E1 🏠 Rua do Senhor da Fortuna, Arcozelo ⊕ solaresdeportugal.pt

€ € €

---

invasion, lies east of Guimarães among mountains and forests. Statues known as *bastos*, believed to represent Celtic warriors, are found in various parts of the Terras de Basto, where they served as territorial markers. In the main town, Cabeceiras de Basto, the prime attraction is the Baroque Mosteiro de Refojos, with its splendid dome surrounded by statues of the Apostles and topped by the Archangel Michael.

The town also owns the best of the *basto* statues, albeit with a French head; it was changed by troops as a joke during the Napoleonic Wars.

Igreja do Senhor da Cruz, overlooking the central square in Barcelos

da Cruz, built around 1705 on the site where two centuries earlier João Pires, a cobbler, had a miraculous vision of a cross etched into the ground. The Festa das Cruzes (Festival of Crosses), the town's most spectacular event, is held at the beginning of May to celebrate the vision. During the celebrations thousands of flowers are laid on the streets to welcome a procession to the church, and events include displays of local folk costumes, dancing and fireworks.

Other historic attractions in the town cluster beside the 15th-century granite bridge that crosses over the Cávado river. The privately owned Solar dos Pinheiros is an attractive mansion on Rua Duques de Bragança, built in 1448. The sculpted figure plucking his beard on the south tower is known as Barbadão, the "bearded one". So incensed was this Jew when his daughter bore a child to a gentile (King João I) that he vowed never to shave again, hence his nickname.

A rich Gothic pillory stands in front of the ruined Count's Palace or Paço dos Condes, destroyed by the earthquake of 1755. The ruins provide an open-air setting for the **Museu Arqueológico**, which displays stone crosses, sculpted blazons, sarcophagi, and its famous exhibit, the Cruzeiro do Senhor do Galo, a cross paying tribute to the Barcelos cock. Next to the palace, the Igreja Matriz is Romanesque with Gothic influences, and dates from the 13th century.

DRINK

Coconuts
This buzzy café-bar has outdoor tables laid out on one of Guimarães's loveliest squares.

🅰 E1 🏠 Largo da Oliveira 1, Guimarães
📞 253 047 207 🕔 Mon

Quinta de Soalheiro
At this rural estate near Monção, visitors can tour the grounds - where aromatic herbs and vines thrive - and participate in tea and wine tastings.

🅰 E1 🏠 Lugar da Charneca, Alvaredo
🌐 soalheiro.com

Tasca das Fodinhas
This old-time bar is decked out with lots of interesting knick-knacks, and is an ideal place to partake of *vinho verde* in ceramic bowls.

🅰 E1 🏠 Rua do Rosário 28, Ponte de Lima
🌐 tascadas fodinhas.com

⑧
Barcelos

🅰 D1 🚉🚌 **i** Largo Dr José Novais 27; 253 811 882

A pleasant riverside town, Barcelos is most famous as the origin of the legendary cock that has become Portugal's national symbol. It is also famed as the country's leading ceramics and crafts market.

From its origins as a settlement in Roman times, the town of Barcelos developed into a flourishing agricultural centre and achieved political importance during the 15th century as the seat of the first duke of Bragança. The town's star attraction is the Feira de Barcelos, a huge weekly market held on Campo da República. Anything from clothes to livestock can be bought here.

North of the square stands Nossa Senhora do Terço, the 18th-century church of a former Benedictine nunnery. In contrast to its plain exterior, the interior is beautifully decorated with panels of *azulejos* illustrating St Benedict's life.

In the southwest corner of the square, a graceful cupola crowns the Igreja do Senhor

> **A pleasant riverside town, Barcelos is most famous as the source of the legendary cock that has become Portugal's national symbol.**

There are 18th-century *azulejos* inside as well as an impressive rose window.

Museu Arqueológico

 Paços dos Condes
253 809 600 Daily

9

Ponte de Lima

E1 Passeio 25 de Abril, Torre da Cadeia Velha; 258 240 208

This riverside town takes its name from the ancient bridge over the Lima river. During the Middle Ages, the town played a pivotal role in the defence of the Minho against the Moors. The Roman bridge has only five of its original stone arches; the rest were rebuilt in the 14th and 15th centuries. The 15th-century church of Santo António houses the **Museu dos Terceiros**, a museum of sacred art. The Centro de Interpretação do Território has antique farming equipment, a regional kitchen and gardens.

Ponte de Lima's remaining medieval fortifications include the 15th-century Palácio dos Marqueses de Ponte de Lima.

The town's market, dating from 1125, takes place every two weeks on Monday and in mid-September crowds gather in the town to celebrate the Feiras Novas (New Fairs), a religious festival and folkloric market.

Museu dos Terceiros

Avenida 5 de Outubro
258 240 220 10am–12:30pm & 2–6pm Tue–Sun

10

Ponte da Barca

E1 Rua Conselheiro Rocha Peixoto 9; 258 455 246

The town of Ponte da Barca derives its name from the graceful 15th-century bridge that replaced the boat once used to ferry pilgrims across the Lima river (*ponte* means bridge, and *barca* means boat). A stroll through the tranquil town centre leads past the pillory, graceful

VINHO VERDE

Ponte da Barca and Ponte de Lima are well known for their young sparkling white wine - *vinho verde* (green wine). You can buy it on tap, and it is still served in ceramic bowls in some bars. Perfect for hot summer days, *vinho verde* is fairly low in alcohol content (about 10 or 11 per cent). A weightier version is produced from the Alvarinho grape, which is cultivated around Monção *(p282)*. *Vinho verde* made from red grapes is also available.

arcades and noble mansions from the 16th and 17th centuries. The Jardim dos Poetas (Poets' Garden) and riverside parks are ideal for picnics, and there is a huge open-air market along the river.

Some of Portugal's finest Romanesque carvings are on the 13th-century church at Bravães, 4 km (2 miles) west of Ponte da Barca. Sculpted monkeys, oxen and birds of prey decorate the columns of its main portal; the tympanum shows Christ in majesty flanked by two angels.

↓ Striking bronze statue dedicated to rural people in Ponte de Lima

⓫ Caminha

🅐D1 🚂🚌🚢 *ⓘ*Praça Conselheiro Silva Torres; 258 921 952

This ancient fortress town perches beside the Minho with fine views across the river to Spain. Occupied in Celtic and Roman times for its strategic position, Caminha developed into a major port until the diversion of its trade to Viana do Castelo in the 16th century. Today it is a small port, with a daily ferry connection to A Guarda in Spain.

On the main square is the 13th-century Torre do Relógio clock tower, once a gateway in the medieval defensive walls, and the 16th-century Paços do Concelho with its attractive loggia supported by pillars. Cross to the other side of the square, past the Renaissance fountain, to admire the seven Manueline windows on the upper storey of the Solar dos Pitas mansion (17th century).

The Rua Ricardo Joaquim de Sousa leads to the Gothic Igreja Matriz. Begun in the late 15th century, it has a superb inlaid ceiling of panels carved in Mudéjar (Moorish) style. Renaissance carvings above the side doors depict the Apostles, the Virgin, and several figures in daring poses, including one man with his posterior bared towards Spain.

Foz do Minho, the mouth of the Minho, lies 5 km (3 miles) southwest of Caminha. From here local fishers will take groups (by prior arrangement) to the ruined island fortress of Forte da Ínsua.

The small walled town of Vila Nova de Cerveira, 12 km (7 miles) northeast of Caminha on the road to Valença, is ideal for a stroll. Either meander in narrow streets lined with 17th- and 18th-century mansions, or wander along the river.

⓬ Monção

🅐E1 🚌 *ⓘ*Praça Deu la Deu, Casa do Curro; 251 649 013

A remote and charming town, Monção once formed part of the string of fortified border posts standing sentinel on the Minho river. Both the town's main squares are lined with old houses, and decorated with chestnut trees, flowerbeds and mosaic paths.

The 13th-century Igreja Matriz in Rua João de Pinho features an outstanding Romanesque doorway of sculpted acanthus flowers. Inside to the right of the transept is the cenotaph of the valiant Deu-la-Deu Martins. This baker used the last of the town's flour to bake rolls that she then flung at the Spanish during the siege of 1368. The troops soon retreated.

A colourful element in the June Corpus Christi festival is the Festa da Coca, when St George engages the dragon (*coca*) in comic ritual combat before giving the final blow.

The countryside around Monção produces excellent *vinho verde (p281)*; one of the best-known estates is the Palácio da Brejoeira, 5 km (3 miles) south of town.

About 5 km (3 miles) southeast of Monção, the monastery of São João de Longos Vales was built in Romanesque style in the 12th century. The exterior capitals and interior apse have fantastical sculpted figures, including serpents and monkeys. Visits are arranged by the tourist office in Monção.

Did You Know?

Monção's coat of arms show a brave baker who threw rolls at besieging Spanish troops in 1368.

→ Rua Direita, one of Caminha's attractive narrow streets

Valença do Minho

🅰 D1 🚉🚌 ℹ Portas do Sol; 251 823 329

Set in a commanding position on a hilltop overlooking the Minho, Valença is an attractive border town. Valença do Minho's old quarter is set in the narrow confines of two double-walled forts, shaped like crowns and linked by a causeway. During the reign of Sancho I (1185– 1211), the town was named *Contrasta*, due to its position facing the Spanish town of Tui.

The forts date from the 17th and 18th centuries and were designed according to the principles of the French architect Vauban. There are fine views from the ramparts across the river into Galicia. Although the town was briefly captured by Napoleonic troops in 1807, its formidable bastions resisted subsequent shelling and attacks from across the river in 1809.

Lining the cobbled alleys of the old quarter are shops full of linen, wickerwork, pottery and handicrafts to tempt the thousands of Spanish visitors who stroll across the bridge to shop. South of the ramparts is the newer part of town. In Largo São Teotónio, Casa do Eirado (1448) has a crenellated roof and a late Gothic window, adorned with the builder's signature. The 18th-century

↑ Old Portuguese galleon docked in the harbour at Vila do Conde

Casa do Poço presents symmetrical windows and wrought-iron balconies.

The Convento de Ganfei, 5 km (3 miles) east of Valença on the N101, was reconstructed in the 11th century by a Norman priest. The convent retains exceptional Romanesque features, including ornamental animal and plant motifs and vestiges of medieval frescoes. To visit the chapel, call ahead (251 822 421).

Vila do Conde

🅰 D2 🚉🚌 ℹ Rua 25 de Abril 103; 252 248 473

This small town enjoyed its boom years as a shipbuilding centre in the Age of Discovery (p44); today it is a quiet fishing port. In the historic centre, the main attraction is the Mosteiro de Santa Clara, founded in 1318. The Gothic church contains the tombs of the nunnery's founders, Dom Afonso Sanches (son of King Dinis) and his wife Dona Teresa Martins. The entire building is closed for redevelopment. By the Mosteiro de Santa Clara are parts of the imposing 5-km (3-mile) aqueduct, built in 1705–14, with 999 arches.

EAT

Aloha Surf Bar
Choose to sit on the terrace facing the fine beach at Vila do Conde, or in the contemporary interior. There is a good-value lunchtime buffet, as well as à la carte dishes such as mixed meat grills.

🅰 D2 🏠 Via Pedonal Manuel de Barros, Vila do Conde ☎ 252 618 886 🚫 Mon

Design & Wine
This chic, modern restaurant serves a good range of *petiscos* (Portuguese tapas) and a mixture of Portuguese and international dishes, which are all served with excellent local wines.

🅰 D1 🏠 Praça do Conselheiro Silva Torres 8, Caminha 🌐 designwinehotel.com

The Praça Vasco da Gama has a pillory in the shape of an arm with a thrusting sword – a vivid warning to wrongdoers. Bordering the square is the 16th-century Igreja Matriz, with its Manueline portico, attributed to João de Castilho.

The town is a centre for lacemaking. Visitors can buy samples and see the skills at the **Escola de Rendas** (lace-making school). The same building houses the Museu de Rendas (Lace Museum).

Escola de Rendas
🏠 Rua de São Bento 70
☎ 252 248 468 🕐 Tue-Sun
🚫 Public hols

SOUTHERN PORTUGAL

Beautiful Praia do Camilo, near Lagos in the Algarve

EXPLORE
SOUTHERN
PORTUGAL

This section divides Southern Portugal into
two colour-coded sightseeing areas, as shown
on this map. Find out more about each area on
the following pages.

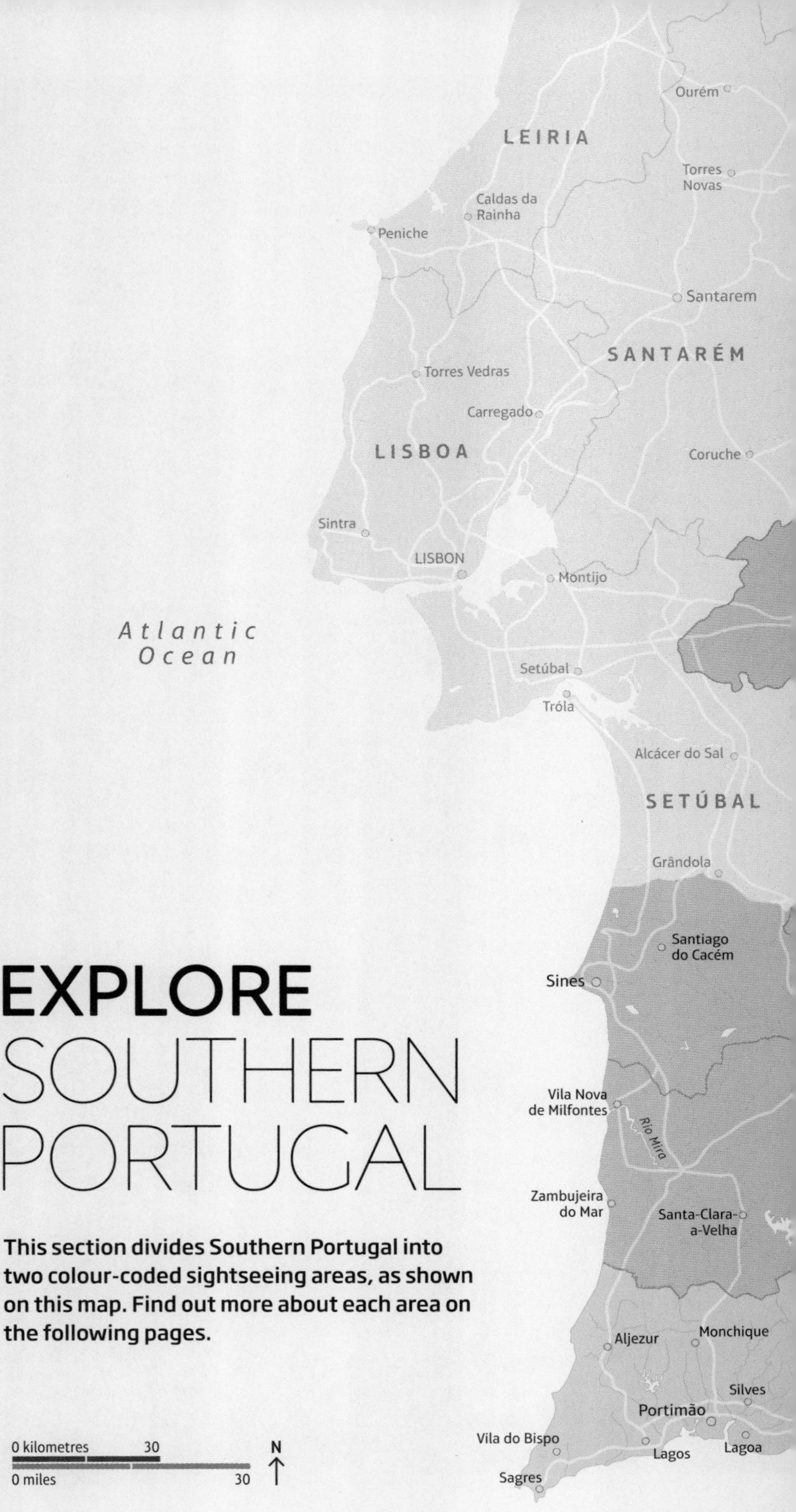

LEIRIA

Ourém

Torres
Novas

Caldas da
Rainha

Peniche

Santarem

SANTARÉM

Torres Vedras

Carregado

Coruche

LISBOA

Sintra

LISBON

Montijo

*Atlantic
Ocean*

Setúbal

Tróla

Alcácer do Sal

SETÚBAL

Grândola

Santiago
do Cacém

Sines

Vila Nova
de Milfontes

Rio Mira

Zambujeira
do Mar

Santa-Clara-
a-Velha

Aljezur

Monchique

Silves

Portimão

Vila do Bispo

Lagoa

Lagos

Sagres

| 0 kilometres | 30 |
| 0 miles | 30 |

N
↑

GETTING TO KNOW
SOUTHERN
PORTUGAL

Most people imagine manicured golf courses, smart resort hotels and water parks when they think of Southern Portugal. But a short journey inland reveals vast rolling plains of golden wheat and silver olive trees, vineyards, and pretty whitewashed villages. Home to storks nesting in spring and fields still tended by horse and cart, this bucolic region is also rich in history, from Neolithic dolmens to Roman temples and medieval castles.

PAGE 292

ALENTEJO

The sun-baked Alentejo occupies nearly one-third of Portugal, between the Tagus and the Algarve. Its capital, Évora, is home to Stone Age relics and a well-preserved Roman temple, as well as the lively Praça do Giraldo. To the southeast, the labyrinthine white towns of Serpa and Mértola interrupt the largely rural terrain while, nearer the Spanish frontier, massive fortifications still shelter Castelo de Vide and Monsaraz. To the west of the Alentejo's southern plains, surfers flock to windswept beaches, and small former fishing villages such as Vila Nova de Milfontes make great low-key destinations.

Best for
Castles and countryside

Home to
Évora, Paço Ducal

Experience
A walk along the Rota Vicentina, specifically the Trilho dos Pescadores, a long-distance hike made up of former fishers' paths along the coast

PAGE 318

ALGARVE

Enclosed by hilly ranges to the north, the stunning coastline and year-round mild weather of the Algarve make it one of the most popular holiday destinations in southern Europe. Central Algarve is where you'll find all the action – upmarket resorts, golf courses, water parks, smart shopping centres, Michelin-starred restaurants and lively late-night bars. Head west of Lagos, however, and you'll find a rural hinterland and wild, windswept beaches. In the east is a series of offshore spits, which can only be accessed by boat, making them calmer than the crowded resorts in the centre.

Best for
*Family-friendly resorts
and fantastic beaches*

Home to
Faro

Experience
*A short boat trip out to the
beaches of Ilha da Tavira*

There's so much more to Southern Portugal than the sunny beaches of the Algarve. Here we show you how to make the most of a week in the south of the country.

7 DAYS
In Southern Portugal

Day 1

Morning Fly into Faro, capital of the Algarve, to explore its attractive walled old town *(p322)*. Inside, cobbled streets lead to the elegant Largo da Sé. Ascend the Sé's bell tower for fantastic views over the water. Pedestrianized streets bustling with shops and cafés lead off the attractive waterfront square, making it easy to find a spot for lunch.

Afternoon Join a sightseeing cruise around the protected Parque Natural da Ria Formosa *(p335)*, looking out for the myriad birds that call the park home. Back in the city, you'll find that the liveliest nightlife revolves around the harbour.

Day 2

Morning Drive north on the IP2 to Beja for a wander round its historic streets and a coffee break *(p312)*. Suitably refreshed, continue on to the whitewashed town of Évora *(p296)*. Begin your exploration of the town at the Roman temple, before heading to the 12th-century cathedral.

Afternoon Momentos serves up a daily-changing organic menu *(p299)*. Later, take the cobbled alleys to the bustling Praça do Giraldo, then down Rua da República. End the day at the macabre Capela dos Ossos, inside the church of São Francisco.

Day 3

Morning Leave Évora for the fortified towns of Estremoz and Elvas. Medieval Estremoz has a remarkable 13th-century marble keep, overlooking the surrounding cork and olive groves *(p306)*. Come lunch time, A Cadeia Quinhentista *(p304)*, a quirky former prison, is a welcoming spot.

Afternoon Continue on the N4 or A6 to the impressive fortifications of Elvas *(p304)*. On your way back to Évora, drop in at the marble town of Vila Viçosa to visit the vast Paço Ducal *(p300)*.

Day 4

Morning and afternoon It's time to leave the historic towns behind and hit the beach. It's a long drive to the bustling

1 Purple jacaranda trees
blooming in Faro. ↑

2 Évora's 12th-century Sé.

3 A rocky cove near Lagos.

4 Admiring the lighthouse
at Cabo de São Vicente.

town of Lagos *(p329)*, but you'll be rewarded by some of the prettiest coves in the Algarve, surrounded by towering cliffs and offshore rock formations.

Evening After freshening up after a day spent on the sand, enjoy a sundowner on the waterfront.

Day 5

Morning Follow the N125 through the Parque Natural da Costa Vicentina, which clings to the Algarve's western tip, all the way to Sagres. Roam the windblown Cabo de São Vicente *(p328)*, which juts into the Atlantic Ocean, with its landmark lighthouse.

Afternoon Back in Sagres *(p328)*, take a dip in the refreshing shallow waters off nearby Martinhal beach. The restaurants lining the sheltered bay tempt with just-caught seafood menus.

Day 6

Morning Drive east on the A22 to Tavira, a pretty riverside town with a Roman bridge and lively market *(p336)*. Browse

the vibrant stalls before selecting some fresh produce for lunch on the waterfront.

Afternoon Clamber the ancient walls of the Moorish castle for wonderful town views, then head to the former convent of Nossa Senhora da Graça, now a *pousada* *(p329)*. Non-guests can visit the bar, which displays Moorish street foundations unearthed here during refurbishment.

Day 7

Morning In summer you can get a boat over to the Ilha de Tavira: a sandbar beach. Out of season, you'll need to drive to nearby Quatro Águas and take a ferry. Bring a picnic and walk along the long, sandy stretch to find a restful spot.

Afternoon You can soak up the sun and paddle in the sea here until late in the afternoon – it's only a short drive back to Faro on the A22.

Brightly coloured bunting outside a church in Redondo

ALENTEJO

Stone circles, dolmens and other relics of
Stone Age life pepper the Alentejan plain,
particularly around Évora, a historic gem of
a city at the region's geographical centre. Évora,
like Beja, Elvas and Alter do Chão, was founded
by the Romans, who valued this land beyond the
Tagus – *além Tejo* – for its wheatfields. Introducing
irrigation systems to overcome the soil's aridity,
they established enormous farms to grow grain
for the Empire. Worked by peasant farmers, these
huge estates, or *latifúndios*, still exist.

Vineyards across the region have long produced
powerful wines, and some areas are classified at
the Denominação de Origem Controlada (DOC)
level. Since 1986, Portugal's membership of
the European Union has increased the rate
of investment and modernization in the region,
although it is still sparsely populated, supporting
only 10 per cent of the population. Land tenure
has always been a concern here, and Communism
has a strong appeal – the Alentejans were solid
supporters of the 1974 revolution *(p47)*. The
amiable *alentejanos* are widely admired for their
singing, handicrafts, gastronomy and wines.

ALENTEJO

Sitting in the plant-lined Praça do Giraldo, Évora's expansive main square ↑

①

ÉVORA

 ⑧ *Aqueduto da Água de Prata*

⑨ *Walls*

ⒶE5 🚉Largo da Estação 🚌Avenida Túlio Espanca ℹ️Praça do Giraldo; 266 777 071

Rising out of the Alentejan plain is the enchanting walled city of Évora. It rose to prominence under the Romans and flourished throughout the Middle Ages as a centre of learning and the arts. Students throng Évora's streets, joined by visitors who come to discover its many historic sites and enjoy the atmosphere of the old town, with its evocatively named streets, including the Alley of the Unshaven Man and Street of the Countess's Tailor.

The historic centre ↑
of Évora around the
Roman temple and Sé

①

Sé

ⒶLargo do Marquês de Marialva 🕐Daily (museum: Tue–Sun) 🚫1 Jan, 24 Dec pm, 25 Dec 🌐evoracathedral.com

Although building began in 1186, and it was consecrated in 1204, the granite cathedral of Santa Maria was completed in 1250. Romanesque melds with Gothic in this castle-like cathedral whose towers, one turreted, one topped by a blue cone, give the façade an odd asymmetry. Flanking the portal between them are superb 14th-century sculpted Apostles. The 18th-century high altar and marble chancel are by J F Ludwig, the architect of the Palácio de Mafra (p156), while a Renaissance portal in the north transept is by Nicolau Chanterène. In the cloisters, which date from about 1325, statues of the Apostles stand watch.

A glittering treasury houses sacred art. The most intriguing exhibit here is a 13th-century ivory Virgin whose body opens out to become a triptych of tiny carved scenes: her life in nine episodes.

Did You Know?

The Roman temple has been used as an armoury, theatre and slaughterhouse.

> 💬 **INSIDER TIP**
> ### Get Crafty
>
> If you're on the lookout for a quality souvenir, head straight for Rua 5 de Outubro. The shops along this street sell curios and handicrafts, from painted chairs to colourful ceramics, as well as anything you could ever imagine being made from cork.

↑ One of the ornate, gilded side chapels in the city's imposing Sé

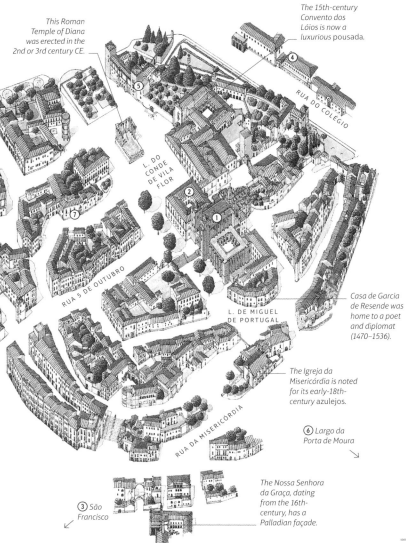

This Roman Temple of Diana was erected in the 2nd or 3rd century CE.

The 15th-century Convento dos Lóios is now a luxurious pousada.

④

RUA DO COLÉGIO

⑤

L. DO CONDE DE VILA FLOR

②

①

⑦

RUA 5 DE OUTUBRO

L. DE MIGUEL DE PORTUGAL

Casa de Garcia de Resende was home to a poet and diplomat (1470–1536).

The Igreja da Misericórdia is noted for its early-18th-century azulejos.

RUA DA MISERICÓRDIA

⑥ *Largo da Porta de Moura*
↘

③ *São Francisco*
↙

The Nossa Senhora da Graça, dating from the 16th-century, has a Palladian façade.

The interior of the Capela dos Ossos in the church of São Francisco ↑

Did You Know?

Évora was named Ebora by the Celts, meaning "of the yew trees".

②
Museu de Évora

🏠 Largo do Conde de Vila Flor 📞 266 730 480 🕐 Apr-Oct: 10am–1pm & 2–6pm Tue-Sun; Nov-Mar: 9:30am–1pm & 2–5:30pm Tue-Sun 🗙 Public hols

This 16th-century palace, once the residence of governors and bishops, is now the regional museum. Évora's history is all here, from Roman columns to modern sculpture in local marble. Don't miss *The Life of the Virgin*, a 16th-century Flemish polyptych in 13 panels.

③
São Francisco

🏠 Praça 1° de Maio 📞 266 704 521 🕐 Daily 🗙 1 Jan, Easter, 24 Dec pm, 25 Dec 🌐 igrejadesaofrancisco.pt

The main attraction of this 15th-century church is its Capela dos Ossos, a gruesome chapel of bones created in the 17th century from the remains of 5,000 monks. Two leathery corpses, one of a child, dangle from a chain, and a mordant reminder at the entrance reads: *Nós ossos que aqui estamos, pelos vossos esperamos* ("We bones that are here await yours").

④
University

🏠 Largo dos Colegiais 2 📞 266 740 800 🕐 Mon-Sat 🗙 Public hols

With the establishment of the Jesuits' Colégio do Espírito Santo, Évora, already noted for its architecture and sacred art, became a seat of learning.

←

An 18th-century monstrance on display in the Museu de Évora

The school flourished for 200 years but was closed in 1759 when the reforming Marquês de Pombal banished the Jesuits from Portugal.

Today part of the University of Évora, the school still has a graceful cloister and notable *azulejos* – in the classrooms they depict suitably studious themes such as Plato lecturing to his disciples (1744–9). The 18th-century Baroque chapel, now the Sala dos Actos, is used in graduation season.

⑤
Palácio dos Duques de Cadaval

🏠 Rua Augusto Filipe Simões 🕐 Tue-Sun 🌐 palaciocadaval.com

The Palace of the Dukes of Cadaval, on the site of the city's former castle, dates from the 14th century. The façade is noted for its unusual pentagonal tower. Tickets provide access to regular art exhibits and the nearby church of Lóios, with its blue-and-white tiled interior.

Largo da Porta de Moura

The western entrance to this square is guarded by the vestiges of a Moorish gateway. Both the domed Casa Soure and the double arches of the belvedere on Casa Cordovil at the opposite end, show the Arab influence on architecture in Évora. The central fountain, looking like some futuristic orb, surprisingly dates back to 1556.

Fundação Eugénio de Almeida

📍 Páteo de São Miguel
🕙 10am-1pm & 2-7pm Tue-Sun (Oct-Apr: to 6pm)
🚫 Public hols 🌐 fea.pt

This avant-garde modern exhibition space plays host to local and national artists and the occasional international name, such as Marcel Duchamp. It also promotes the performing arts, staging regular concerts and recitals. The building provides access to the Carriage Museum, and tours to the nearby Cartuxa winery can be booked here.

Aqueduto da Água de Prata

Évora's aqueduct was built between 1531 and 1537 by the city's own eminent architect, Francisco de Arruda. The construction was regarded with wonder, and is even described in *Os Lusíadas*, the epic by Luís de Camões *(p184)*. It originally carried water as far as the Praça do Giraldo. It was damaged in the 17th century during the Restoration War with Spain, but visitors can

→

Évora's walls, bathed in a gloriously golden evening light

follow a trail for 8.3 km (5 miles) along a surviving 9-km- (6-mile-) long stretch.

Walls

The fortifications that have protected Évora down the centuries form two incomplete concentric circles. The inner ring, of which only fragments are discernible, is Roman, from perhaps as early as the 1st century CE, with Moorish and medieval additions – the two stubby towers that give the Largo da Porta de Moura its name mark an Arab gate.

In the 14th century, new walls were built to encompass the growing town. Completed under Fernando I, these had 40 towers and 10 gates, including the Porta de Alconchel, which still faces the Lisbon road.

When João IV was defiantly declared king in 1640 *(p45)*, major fortifications were erected in anticipation of Spanish attack, and it is these 17th-century walls which are most evident today. The walls withstood much battering from the besieging Spanish in 1663.

② 🏛️ 🗺️

PAÇO DUCAL

A F5 🏛️ Terreiro do Paço, Vila Viçosa 🚌 🕐 Jun–Sep: 2–6pm Tue,
10am–1pm, 2–6pm Wed–Sun; Oct–May: 2–5pm Tue, 10am–1pm,
2–5pm Wed–Sun 🚫 Public hols, 16 Aug 🌐 fcbraganca.pt

The dukes of Bragança owned vast estates, but this lavish palace at Vila
Viçosa, begun by Dom Jaime in 1501, became their favoured residence.
The palace is set in a pretty hillside town, which was named Val Viçosa –
"fertile valley" – after the expulsion of the Moors in 1226. Substantial
houses, built from the local white marble, reflect Vila Vicosa's prosperous
royal past and the town is full of reminders of the Braganças. Dominating
the west side of the Terreiro do Paço is the long façade of the Paço Ducal,
which stretches for 110 m (360 ft).

The Royal House of Bragança

Afonso, illegitimate son of João I, was created
duke of Bragança in 1442, first of an influential
but bloodstained dynasty. Fernando, the 3rd
duke, was executed in 1483 by his cousin, João
II, who feared his power. Jaime, the unstable
4th duke, locked up his wife in Bragança castle
(p248), then killed her at Vila Viçosa. It was Dom
Jaime who initiated the building of the palace
at Vila Viçosa, an ambitious work embellished
by later dukes to reflect their aspirations and
affluence. The 8th duke was very reluctant to
relinquish a life of music and hunting here
to take up the throne (p45).

Exploring the Palace

When the 8th duke became king in 1640, many
of the furnishings accompanied him to Lisbon,
but the long suite of first-floor rooms is still
splendid, from the Sala da Cabra-Cega, where
royal parties played blind man's buff, to the
grand Sala de Hércules. More intimate are the
rooms of King Carlos and his wife, which are
much as the king left them the day before his
assassination in 1908.

Guided tours, which last about an hour, take
in the royal rooms ranged along the first floor
and ground-floor areas such as the kitchen
and the treasury. Entry to the coach
museum, on the north side
of the palace, and armoury
is by separate tickets.
From time to time
areas may be closed
for restoration and
rooms can be shut
off without notice.

1910

The year the
last monarch,
Manuel II, fled into
exile after 270 years
of Bragança rule.

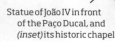

→ Statue of João IV in front
of the Paço Ducal, and
(inset) its historic chapel

↑ The Paço Ducal dominating the whitewashed houses of Vila Viçosa

TOP 5 ROOMS TO VISIT

Sala dos Duques
Lining the ceiling of the Room of the Dukes are portraits of all the dukes of Bragança by Domenico Dupra (1689–1770).

Kitchen
The vast kitchen gleams with over 600 copper pots and pans, some large enough to bathe in.

Chapel
Despite later additions, the chapel has retained its coffered ceiling from the early 16th century.

Armouries
A series of vaulted rooms, displaying swords, crossbows, halberds and suits of armour.

The Library
Home to precious early works collected by King Manuel II while in exile.

EXPERIENCE MORE

③

Serra de São Mamede

 F4 🚌 From Portalegre
ℹ️ Rua Guilherme Gomes
Fernandes 22, Portalegre;
245 307 445

The diverse geology and capricious climate of this remote mountain range, which could be on the Mediterranean rather than the Atlantic Ocean, encourage a fascinating range of flora and fauna. In 1989, 320 sq km (120 sq miles) of the Serra were designated a Nature Park, as classified by the EUROPARC Federation. Red deer, wild boar and the cat-like genet live among the sweet chestnut trees and holm oaks, and streams attract otters and amphibians, such as the Iberian midwife toad. Look out, too, for griffon vultures and Bonelli's eagles soaring overhead, as well as bats from one of Europe's largest colonies.

The Serra's apparent emptiness is deceptive: megaliths suggest that it was settled in prehistoric times, and rock paintings survive in the Serra de Cavaleiros and Serra dos Louções. Below Marvão is the Roman town of Ammaia, and the Roman network of roads still winds among the trim white villages, offering grand views.

From Portalegre, the road climbs for 15 km (9 miles) to the Pico de São Mamede at 1,025 m (3,363 ft). A minor road leads south to Alegrete, a fortified village crowned by its ruined 14th-century castle.

④

Marvão

 F4 🚗🚌 ℹ️ Rua de Baixo;
245 909 131

This serene medieval hamlet is dramatically set at 862 m (2,828 ft) on a spectacular escarpment facing Spain. Its 13th-century walls and 17th-century buttresses blend seamlessly into the granite of the mountains, making it an impregnable stronghold. The Romans, who called the outcrop Herminius Minor, were followed by the Moors (the name may have come from Marvan, a Moorish leader), whom the Christians evicted with difficulty only in 1166.

The walls completely enclose the little collection of whitewashed houses, a *pousada* and the 15th-century Igreja Matriz. Rua do Espírito Santo leads past the former governor's house (now a bank) with its 17th-century iron balcony, and a Baroque fountain, up towards the castle.

Built by King Dinis in about 1299, the castle dominates the village. Its walls enclose two cisterns and a keep. The castle offers spectacular views south and west towards the Serra de São Mamede and east to the Spanish frontier.

The **Museu Municipal**, in the former church of Santa Maria, retains the main altar, and has an exhibition of traditional remedies and local archaeological finds from Palaeolithic to Roman times.

Museu Municipal

 🏛️ Largo de Santa Maria
📞 245 909 132 🕐 10am–
12:30pm & 1:30–5pm daily

> 💬 INSIDER TIP
> ## Take a Dip
>
> Head to the little village of Portagem, below Marvão, and cool off in the Praia Fluvial de Portagem, which is a shallow, but very refreshing river beach.

← The castle at Marvão, set impressively among granite mountains

↑ Fonte da Vila, a 16th-century stone fountain located in the Jewish Quarter of Castelo de Vide

---

⑤

Castelo de Vide

🅰F4 🏠🚌 ℹ️ Praça Dom Pedro V; 245 908 227

Sprawled out on a lush green slope of the Serra de São Mamede, the pretty spa town of Castelo de Vide, enjoyed by the Romans, has worn well. It is fringed by modern development but the lower town, around Praça Dom Pedro V, retains its Baroque church of Santa Maria, the 18th-century town hall and pillory, and handsome mansions from the same era. In the Largo Frederico Laranjo is one of several sources of the town's curative waters: the Fonte da Vila, a carved stone fountain with a pillared canopy. Just above is the maze-like Judiaria, where small white houses sprout vivid pots of geraniums. Its cobbled alleys are lined with fine Gothic doorways and conceal a 13th-century synagogue housing a

> **Sprawled out on a lush green slope of the Serra de São Mamede, the pretty spa town of Castelo de Vide, enjoyed by the Romans, has worn well.**

small museum. The town's oldest chapel, dating from the same time, Salvador do Mundo on the Estrada de Circunvalação, has a much admired depiction of the Holy Family's flight into Egypt by an unknown 18th-century artist.

In the upper town, the tiny Nossa Senhora da Alegria offers a feast of 17th-century floral tiles. It stands within the walls of the castle that gave the town its name. This was rebuilt in 1310 by King Dinis, who negotiated here to marry Isabel of Aragon. Inside the castle is the Casa da Cidadania Salgueiro Maia, a museum dedicated to the Portuguese army officer who played a leading role in Portugal's Carnation Revolution (p47).

---

⑥

Crato

🅰F4 🏠🚌 ℹ️ Mosteiro de Santa Maria de Flor da Rosa, inside the pousada; 245 997 341

Modest houses under outsize chimneys give no hint of Crato's past eminence. Part of a gift from Sancho II to the powerful crusading Order of Hospitallers, Crato was the Order's headquarters by 1350. Its prestige was such that Manuel I and João III were both married here.

In 1662, the town's fortunes changed as invading Spanish forces sacked and burned the town, which never recovered. The Hospitallers' castle remains, in ruins, and in Praça do Município the 15th-century Varanda do Grão-Prior marks the entrance to what was the Grand Prior's residence.

Rua de Santa Maria leads, via an avenue of orange trees, to the Igreja Matriz, much altered since its 13th-century origins. In the chancel, 18th-century *azulejos* depict fishing, hunting and travelling scenes.

Did You Know?

Most Lusitano horses, Portugal's national breed, are grey – but Alter Real are brown.

7

Alter do Chão

△E4 🚌 ℹ️ Palácio do Álamo; 245 610 004

The Romans founded Civitas Abelterium in 204 BCE, but razed it under the Emperor Hadrian after the inhabitants were accused of disloyalty. The town was re-established in the 13th century.

Dominating the town centre is the five-towered **Castelo de Alter do Chão** with a Gothic portal built in 1359 by Pedro I. The flower-filled market square, the Largo Doze Melhores de Alter, is at its feet.

Alter is best known for the **Coudelaria de Alter**, which was founded in 1748 to breed the Alter Real. King José I (1750–77) yearned for a quality Portuguese-bred horse. He imported a stock of Andalusian mares, which were known for their prowess in war, to breed with local horses. From these Spanish pure-breds came the gracious and nimble Alter Real ("*real*" means royal). The stud prospered until the Napoleonic Wars (1807–15), when stealing and erratic breeding sent the Alter into decline. By 1930, the royal horse was nearly extinct, but years of dedication have ultimately revived this classic breed. The stud is set around attractive stables painted in the royal livery of white and ochre. Accommodation is available here.

Spanning the Seda river 12 km (7 miles) west along the N369 is the robust six-arched Ponte de Vila Formosa. This bridge carried the Roman road from Lisbon to Mérida in Spain.

Castelo de Alter do Chão

🏛 🚪 Largo Barreto Caldeira
🕐 Apr–Sep: 10am–1pm & 2:30–6:30pm Tue–Sun; Oct–Mar: 9am–12:30pm & 1:30–5pm Tue–Sun

Coudelaria de Alter

🏛 🚪 3 km (2 miles) NW of town 🕐 Tue–Sun 🚫 1 Jan, 24 & 25 Dec alterreal.pt

8

Elvas

△F5 🚌🚌 ℹ️ Praça da República; 268 622 236

Only 12 km (7 miles) from the Spanish border, Elvas feels like a frontier town. The old town's fortifications are among the best preserved in Europe. Within the walls, a few architectural features and many of the street names are reminders that for 500 years the town was in Moorish hands.

Elvas was liberated from the Moors in 1230, but for another 600 years its fate was to swing between periodic attacks from Spain.

Romano-Moorish in origin, the **Castelo de Elvas** was rebuilt for Sancho II in 1226. It underwent further remodelling

EAT

A Cadeia Quinhentista

It's not often that you can dine in a former 16th-century prison. This stylish conversion serves Alentejan specialities.

△F5 🚪 Rua Rainha Santa Isabel, Estremoz 📞 268 323 400

€€€

Flor da Rosa

This restaurant inside a former monastery has a menu that favours regional cuisine.

△F4 🚪 Rua do Mosteiro da Flor da Rosa 10, Crato pousadas.pt

€€€

over the years, notably in the late 15th century under João II. The king's coat of arms, incorporating a pelican, is seen above the entrance.

→ Arches of the great aqueduct that once brought water to Elvas

Until the late 16th century the castle was the residence of Elvas's mayors.

Until 1882, Nossa Senhora da Assunção was the cathedral of Elvas. Built in the early 16th century, its architect was Francisco de Arruda, who also designed the town's impressive aqueduct. His Manueline south portal survives, but much of the church has been modified. The *azulejos* in the nave date from the early 17th century.

The engaging **Museu Municipal de Fotografia João Carpinteiro** is divided into the History of Photography Room, with numerous black-and-white images documenting life in the region, and the Collector's Room, featuring rare and valuable vintage cameras and photographic equipment.

The **Museu de Arte Contemporânea de Elvas**, the only national museum displaying exclusively contemporary Portuguese art, occupies a former hospital. The collection includes works by artists such as Adriana Molder, André Gomes and Joana Vasconcelos.

A plain exterior belies the wealth within the walls of Nossa Senhora dos Aflitos. This little 16th-century church

FORTIFICATIONS OF ELVAS

Using the principles of the French military architect the Marquis de Vauban, a series of pentagonal bastions and freestanding angled ravelins form a multifaceted star, protecting the walls from every angle. What survives dates mostly from the 17th century, when the defences held off Spanish troops in the War of Restoration. Two surviving satellite forts indicate the strategic importance of Elvas: to the southeast lies the military fort and museum of Forte de Santa Luzia (1641-87), and 2 km (1 mile) north is the carefully restored 18th-century Forte de Graça.

has fine marble columns and spectacular *azulejos* added in the 17th century. These line the walls and reach up into the cupola. Just behind the church is the archway of the Arab Porta da Alcáçova, a vestige of Elvas's Moorish fortifications.

Castelo de Elvas
⊛ ⌂ Parada do Castelo
☏ 268 626 403 ◷ 9:30am-1pm & 2-5:30pm Tue-Sat
☒ 1 & 14 Jan, Easter Sun, 1 May, 25 Dec

Museu Municipal de Fotografia João Carpinteiro
⊛ ⌂ Largo Luís de Camões
☏ 268 636 470 ◷ Apr-Sep: 10am-1pm & 3-7pm Tue-Sun; Oct-Mar: 10am-1pm & 2-5pm Tue-Sun

Museu de Arte Contemporânea de Elvas
⊛ ⌂ Rua da Cadeia ☏ 268 626 218 ◷ Apr-Sep: 3-6pm Tue, 10am-1pm & 3-6pm Wed-Sun; Oct-Mar: 2-5pm Tue, 10am-1pm & 2-5pm Wed-Sun

Festival decorations
in the streets of
Campo Maior

9

Campo Maior

F5 **Largo dos Carvajais; 268 680 319**

According to legend, this peaceful town got its name when three peasant families settled in the *campo maior*, the "bigger field". King Dinis fortified the town in 1310 and the monumental Porta da Vila was added in 1646.

In 1732, a gunpowder magazine, ignited by lightning, destroyed the citadel and killed 1,500 people. It seems likely that after a period, the victims provided the material for the morbid **Capela dos Ossos**, entirely faced in human bones. Dated 1766, it bears an inscription on mortality spelt out in collar bones.

The **Centro de Ciência do Café** charts the history of coffee with exhibits such as rare antique grinders. A barista shows visitors how to make different kinds of coffees.

Capela dos Ossos

Largo Dr Regala 6 268 686 168 For renovations

Centro de Ciência do Café

Delta Coffee, Herdade das Argamassas 10am–6pm Mon–Fri, 10am–2pm Sat & Sun Public hols centro cienciacafe.com

10

Estremoz

F5 **Rossio Marquês de Pombal; 268 339 227**

A key stronghold in the War of Restoration and then in the War of the Two Brothers, Estremoz looks out from its hilltop over groves of gnarled olive trees.

The medieval upper town, set within stout ramparts, is dominated by a 13th-century marble keep, rising to 27 m (89 ft). The adjoining castle and palace complex, built for Dona Isabel, is now a *pousada*. The saintly Isabel, wife of King Dinis, died here in 1336 and the **Capela da Rainha Santa** dedicated to her is lined with *azulejos* recording her life. In the lower side of town is the **Museu Berardo Estremoz**, which contains one of the world's biggest private tile collections. The visit ends with a wine tasting at the museum's courtyard.

On Saturdays, visit the bustling weekly market in the Rossio, the city's main square, where you can purchase fresh produce from local farmers. Across the square are the remains of King Dinis's once-fine palace and the town's **Museu Municipal**. The museum is over two floors and displays such things as archaeological finds, restored living rooms and a parade of *bonecos*, the charming pottery figurines for which Estremoz is famous.

ALENTEJO'S WHITE GOLD

Portugal is the second-largest exporter of marble, and even Italy, the biggest producer, buys its quality stone. Around 90 per cent - over 500,000 tonnes a year - is quarried around Estremoz. The marble from Estremoz and nearby Borba and Vila Viçosa is white or pink, while the quarries at Viana do Alentejo yield green stone. Marble has been used for construction since Roman times and in towns such as Évora (*p296*) and Vila Viçosa (*p300*), palaces and humble doorsteps alike gleam with the stone known as "white gold".

SANTA ISABEL

Capela da Rainha Santa
Largo Dom Dinis (access via adjacent Design Gallery)
🚪Ask at the Igreja de Santa Maria, on Largo Dom Dinis

Museu Berardo Estremoz
Palácio Tocha, Largo Dragões de Olivença 100
🕐May-Sep: 10am-7pm Tue-Sun; Oct-Apr: 9am-5:30pm Tue-Sun 🌐museuberardo estremoz.pt

Museu Municipal de Estremoz Professor Joaquim Vermelho
⌖ Largo Dom Dinis 📞268 339219 🕐9am-12:30pm & 2-5:30pm Tue-Sun 🚫Public hols

⑪
Alandroal
🗺F5 🚌 ℹ️Praça da República; 268 440 045

Surrounded by groves of cork oaks, the town of Alandroal, wrapped tidily around its castle ruins, was built by the Knights of Avis, who settled here from 1220. Little remains inside the castle, but a surviving inscription shows it was completed in 1298. The Igreja Matriz within its walls dates from the 16th century. The Misericórdia church near the castle walls contains beautiful *azulejos* reputed to be the work of Policarpo de Oliveira Bernardes (1695–1778).

Terena, 10 km (6 miles) south of Alandroal, is well known for its pottery. The 14th-century sanctuary of Nossa Senhora de Boa Nova has frescoes covering its walls and ceiling; dating from 1706, these depict saints and Portuguese kings. For access ask at the tourist office.

⑫
Redondo
🗺F5 🚌 ℹ️Praça da República; 266 909 100

As with much of the Alentejo, Redondo is known for its wines; however, this medieval town is

---

1497
—
Manuel I welcomed Vasco da Gama at Estremoz castle, shortly before his voyage to India.

---

also famous for its pottery. Roman-style water jugs, casserole dishes and bowls painted with humorous folk-art motifs are sold from the tiny white houses leading up to the ruins of the castle founded by King Dinis.

The Convento de São Paulo in the Serra de Ossa, 10 km (6 miles) north of Redondo, was built in 1376; Catherine of Bragança stayed here on her return home in 1692 after the death of her husband, King Charles II of England. It has now been converted into a luxury hotel, but retains its 16th- to 18th-century *azulejos*.

⑬
Évoramonte
🗺E5 🚌 ℹ️Rua Santa Maria; 268 959 227

The village is entered through a grand portal in the walls. Above the doorway of No 41, along Évoramonte's single street, is a historic plaque. It records that here, on 26 May 1834, Dom Miguel ceded the throne, ending the conflict with his older brother *(p46)*.

The eye-catching **Castelo de Évoramonte**, its walls bound by bold stone "ropes", largely replaced an earlier castle that fell in an earthquake in 1531. The 16th-century walls have been restored and an exhibition explains the castle's history.

Castelo de Évoramonte
⌖ 🕐9am-12:30pm & 2-5:30pm Tue-Sun 🚫Last weekend of month

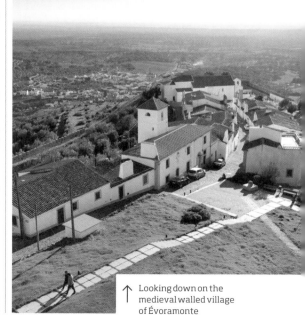

↑ Looking down on the medieval walled village of Évoramonte

Honrado Vineyards

Around Vidigueira, many wineries, such as this one, still produce *vinho de talha*, a type of wine aged in clay amphorae, following ancient Roman methods. Combine your visit with a traditional lunch at the upstairs restaurant.

⚑E6 ⌂Rua General Humberto Delgado 17, Vidigueira ⊞honrado.pt

Esporão

This vineyard dates back to the 13th century. The 1,730 acres (700 ha) of vineyards are home to more than 40 grape varieties.

⚑F5 ⌂Apartado 31, Reguengos de Monsaraz ⊞esporao.com

L'And Vineyards

A wine resort that offers wine courses and has its own luxury restaurant.

⚑E5 ⌂Herdade das Valadas, Estrada Nacional 4, Montemor-o-Novo ⊞l-and.com

---

⑭ Montemor-o-Novo

⚑E5 ⎙ ℹLargo Calouste Gulbenkian; 266 898103

Montemor was fortified by the Romans and then by the Moors – the Arab warrior Al-Mansur is remembered in the name of the Almançor river. The town, regained from the Moors in the reign of Sancho I, was awarded its first charter in 1203. The castle, re-built in the late 13th century, is now a ruin crowning the hill.

Montemor's 17th-century Igreja Matriz stands in Largo São João de Deus, named after the saint who was born nearby in 1495. The Order of Brothers Hospitallers that St John of God founded evolved from his care for the sick. He notably looked after foundlings and prisoners.

 Montemor-o-Novo's ruined castle, watching over the town below

A former convent in the upper town now houses the **Museu de Arqueologia**, displaying local archaeological finds and antique farming tools.

Museu de Arqueologia

⊛ ⌂Convento de São Domingos, Largo Professor Dr Banha de Andrade ☏266 890 235 ⊙Tue–Sun ⌂Public hols

⑮ Monsaraz

⚑F5 ⎙ ℹRua Direita; 266 508 177

The tiny medieval walled town of Monsaraz perches above the Guadiana river on the frontier with Spain. Now a pretty backwater, it has known more turbulent times. Regained from the Moors in 1167 by the intrepid adventurer Geraldo Sem-Pavor (the Fearless), the town was handed over to the militant Knights Templar. It continued to suffer from Spanish attack, but in 1381 assault came from an unexpected quarter. Troops of the Earl of Cambridge, Portugal's ally, were enraged by lack of pay and the annulment of the earl's betrothal to Fernando I's daughter, and unleashed their wrath on Monsaraz.

Principal access to the town is through the massive Porta da Vila. Rua Direita, the main street, leads up to the castle. Built by Afonso III and Dinis in the 13th century as part of the border defences, it was reinforced in the 17th century. The keep commands glorious views and at its foot is the garrison courtyard, which today serves on occasion as a bullring.

The 16th-century Igreja Matriz in Rua Direita is worth visiting for its tall gilded altars and painted pillars. The 17th- and 18th-century houses along here display coats of arms. In the Gothic Paços da Audiência, now the **Museu do Fresco**, is a fine fresco and temporary exhibition space. Its earlier role as a law court is reflected in an unusual secular fresco: *O Bom e o Mau Juiz* (The Good and Bad Judge).

Surrounded by vineyards, Reguengos de Monsaraz, 16 km (10 miles) west, lies at the heart of one of the region's demarcated wine areas. São Pedro do Corval, 5 km (3 miles) east of Reguengos de Monsaraz, is one of Portugal's greatest centres for pottery.

 GREAT VIEW
Castle Keep
Climb to the top of the keep of Monsaraz's castle for glorious views of olive groves in one direction and the stunning, sparkling waters of the Barragem de Alqueva in the other.

Near Monsaraz are a number of striking megaliths. The spectacular Menhir of Outeiro, standing 5.6 m (18 ft) tall, and the strangely inscribed Menhir of Belhoa are both signposted in Telheiro, just to the north of Monsaraz.

Museu do Fresco
◈ ⌂ Largo Dom Nuno Álvares Pereira ☎ 927 997 316 ◷ Tue-Sun

16
Arraiolos
🅰 E5 🚌 ℹ️ Praça do Município; 266 490 254

The foundation of Arraiolos is attributed either to Celts or perhaps to local tribes in about 300 BCE. Its 14th-century castle seems overwhelmed by the town walls and looming 16th-century Igreja do Salvador. Typically, houses in Arraiolos are low and white, and are painted with a blue trim to ward off the devil.

The principal sight, however, is of locals stitching their bright wool rugs in shadowy rooms behind the main street. Carpets have been woven in Arraiolos since the 13th century and decorate countless manor houses and palaces throughout Portugal. The craft may have begun with the Moors, but floral designs of the 18th century are thought to be the finest. As well as browsing the town's carpet shops, you can visit the **Centro Interpretativo do Tapete** to discover more about this craft.

Centro Interpretativo do Tapete
⌂ Praça do Município 19 ◷ 10am-1pm & 2-6pm Tue-Sun 🌐 tapetedearraiolos.pt

Did You Know?
The design of Arraiolos rugs was inspired by Persian carpets.

Embroidered wool rugs hung up in the streets of Arraiolos →

⓱ Serpa

🅰F6 🚌 *i* Rua dos Cavalos 19; 284 544 727

Serpa is a quiet agricultural town known for its cheese. Pleasing squares and streets of whitewashed houses are overlooked by a Moorish castle, rebuilt in the late 13th century. Serpa's stout walls are topped by an arched aqueduct. Beside the monumental Porta de Beja is a *nora*, or Arab water wheel. Won from the Moors in 1232, Serpa successfully resisted foreign control until a brief Spanish occupation in 1707.

The **Watch Museum**, occupying 10 rooms of the 16th-century Convento do Mosteirinho, has a collection of more than 2,300 watches and clocks, all of them mechanical and some dating from the 17th century.

Serpa is just 35 km (22 miles) from the Spanish border. The Moors, and later Spain, fought for control of the region, which was finally ceded to Portugal in 1295. Continued disputes have left the legacy of a chain of watch-towers and a peppering of fortresses across these hills. One of the most remote, the deserted fort at Noudar (for which you follow a dirt road to get to), was built in 1346, but even in this isolated

↑ The great historic walls and arched aqueduct at Serpa

corner, evidence of pre-Roman habitation has been uncovered.

On the border at Barrancos, 76 km (47 miles) northeast of Serpa, an idiosyncratic mix of Spanish and Portuguese is spoken. A speciality produced here is the dry-cured *barrancos* ham, which is made from the local black pigs.

Watch Museum

📍 Convento do Mosteirinho 🕐 2–5:30pm Tue–Fri, 10am–12:30pm & 2–5:30pm Sat & Sun 🔲 museudorelogio.com

⓲ Vidigueira

🅰E6 🚌 *i* Edifício das Piscinas Municipais; 284 437 410

Fine wines make Vidigueira a leading centre of wine production in the Alentejo region. Less well known is the fact that the explorer Vasco da Gama was the count of Vidigueira (*p114*). His remains, now in the Mosteiro dos Jerónimos (*p108*), lay from 1539 to 1898 in the Quinta do Carmo, now private property. A modern statue of the town's most famous son stands in the flowery square named after him. The main features of this little town are a Misericórdia church dated 1620, and a clock tower from Vasco da Gama's time.

One of Portugal's most notable Roman sites, São Cucufate, named after a later monastery, lies 4 km (2.5 miles) west of Vidigueira. The vaulting belonged to a 4th-century villa, but excavations have revealed the baths of a 2nd-century house, whose wine presses, reservoir and temple indicate a sumptuous Roman residence.

Nestled against the slopes of the Serra do Mendro, the Cortes de Cima winery is close by and can be visited for tours and wine tasting (*www.vinhos doalentejo.pt*).

 The traditional Moita-Viana do Alentejo Horse Pilgrimage ↑

> ### Did You Know?
> —
> Most of Portugal's strategic castles were ordered to be built by King Dinis (1279–1325).

⓳ Viana do Alentejo

🅰E6 🚌 *i* Inside the castle; 266 930 012

Viana do Alentejo's castle, begun in 1313, was built to the design of King Dinis, the height of the outer wall exactly calculated to protect soldiers from attacking lancers. The unusual cylindrical towers show a Moorish influence and much of the later remodelling dates from João II, who held a *cortes* here in 1481–2.

Mirroring the castle walls are the crenellations and pinnacles of the adjacent

16th-century Igreja Matriz. The highly carved Manueline entrance to this fortified church leads into a majestic triple-naved interior.

Twenty minutes' walk east of the town stands the pilgrimage church of Nossa Senhora de Aires, rebuilt in the 1700s. The chancel's golden canopy contrasts with pilgrims' humble *ex votos*. Every April, hundreds of people participate in the Moita-Viana do Alentejo Horse Pilgrimage. Originally of a religious nature, the event today has become more of a festival.

The Moorish-style castle at Alvito, 10 km (6 miles) south of Viana, was built in 1482; it is now a *pousada*.

Moura

⚑F6 🚌 *ℹ* **Inside the castle; 285 251 375**

Legend mingles with history in this quiet town nestled among oak and olive trees. Salúquia, daughter of a Moorish governor, is said to have thrown herself from the castle tower on learning that her lover had been killed. From this tragedy, the town acquired its name – Moura, the Moorish girl. The town's old Moorish quarter is a tangle of narrow streets.

Even after the Reconquest in the 12th century, Moura's frontier position left it open to attack. A siege in 1657, during the War of Restoration, levelled much of it. The 13th-century castle survived, only to be blown up by the Spanish in 1707 – just a skeletal keep and wall remain.

The **Lagar de Varas do Fojo**, a former 19th-century olive press, is now home to a small museum. On display is a number of traditional wooden and stone-wheel presses, some dating from the 14th century.

Lagar de Varas do Fojo
⚑ Rua São João de Deus
📞 285 253 978 🕐 Tue–Sun

STAY

Casa do Adro
This charming family home in the centre of the old town has neatly decorated guest rooms, some with terraces or balconies. The owner plies her guests with homemade cakes and juices.

⚑D6 ⚑ **Rua Diário de Notícias 10, Vila Nova de Milfontes**
🌐 **casadoadro.com.pt**

Casa da Muralha
Right by the town walls of historic Serpa, this wonderfully traditional guesthouse has its own pretty courtyard garden.

⚑F6 ⚑ **Rua das Portas de Beja 43, Serpa**
📞 **284 543 150**

↑ Stone cross in front of the Igreja Matriz at Santiago do Cacém

㉑
Santiago do Cacém

🅰D6 🚌 🛈 Parque da Quinta do Chafariz; 269 826 696

Santiago do Cacém's Moorish castle was rebuilt in 1157 by the Templars (p176). Its walls, which enclose the cemetery of the adjacent 13th-century Igreja Matriz, afford great views of the Serra de Grândola. The church is the starting point of the 350-km (217-mile) Rota Vicentina footpath to

Cabo de São Vicente (www. rotavicentina.com). The main square is enhanced by elegant 18th-century mansions.

The **Museu Municipal** still retains some cells from its days as a Salazarist prison. Exhibits include Roman finds from nearby Miróbriga.

On a hill just to the east of Santiago do Cacém lies the site of the Roman city of **Miróbriga**. Excavations have uncovered a forum, two temples, thermal baths and a circus that had seating for 25,000 spectators.

Museu Municipal

🏠 Praça do Município 🕻 269 827 375 🕘 10am-noon & 2-4:30pm Tue-Fri, noon-6pm Sat 🚫 Public hols

> 🔍 HIDDEN GEM
> **Lagoa de Santo André**
>
> The warm shallow waters of the Lagoa de Santo André, 15 km (9 miles) northwest of Santiago do Cacém, offer a safe place for swimming compared to the beaches on the Atlantic Ocean.

Miróbriga

 🏠 Signposted off N121 🕻 269 818 460 🕘 9am-12:30pm & 2-5:30pm Tue-Sat, 9am-noon & 2-5:30pm Sun 🚫 1 Jan, Easter, 1 May, 25 Dec

㉒
Beja

🅰E6 🚊🚌 🛈 Castle; 284 311 913

Capital of the Baixo (lower) Alentejo, Beja is a city of historic importance. It is also a major centre for the production of wines and the harvesting of olives and cork, which are grown on the Bejan plains.

The city became a regional capital under Julius Caesar, who called it Pax Julia after the peace made here with the Lusitanians (p42). The Praça da República marks the site of the Roman forum. The Moors arrived in 711 CE, giving the town its present name and a city, poetic culture until they were forced out in 1162.

Beja has been the scene of struggles against oppressive regimes. In 1808, occupying French troops massacred inhabitants and sacked the city, and in 1962, during the

Medieval walls of the ↑
city of Sines, and
(inset) its castle

Salazar regime, General Delgado led an unsuccessful uprising at Beja.

Beja's old town, an area of narrow, often cobbled, streets, stretches from the castle keep southeast to the 13th-century convent of São Francisco, now a superb *pousada*. The former Convento de Nossa Senhora da Conceição (now a regional museum) is a remarkable blend of architectural styles, with a Gothic church portal, Manueline windows and a dazzling Baroque chapel.

㉓
Sines

 D6 🚌🚆 ℹ️ Inside the castle; 269 860 095

The birthplace of Vasco da Gama *(p114)* is now a major industrial port and tanker terminal ringed with refinery pipelines. Once past this heavy industrial zone, visitors reach the old town with its

←

Chapter room of the Convento de Nossa Senhora da Conceição at Beja

popular sandy beach, but it is not always possible to escape the haze of pollution.

A landmark above the beach is the modest medieval castle, restored in the 16th century by King Manuel. It was here that Vasco da Gama, son of the *alcaide-mor*, or mayor, is reputed to have been born in 1469. A multimedia museum dedicated to the navigator, the **Casa Vasco da Gama**, is housed in the castle keep. A statue of Vasco da Gama looks out over the bay.

Particularly appealing are two sea-blue lagoons, the Lagoa de Santo André and Lagoa de Melides nature reserves, set in a long stretch of sandy coast about 20 km (12 miles) north of Sines. Camping within the reserves is prohibited and the area is patrolled by park rangers.

Casa Vasco da Gama
🏛️ Castelo de Sines 📞 269 860 095 🕐 10am–1pm & 2–5pm Tue–Sun (summer: to 6pm) 🚫 Public hols

> ### LOVE LETTERS OF A HEARTSICK NUN
>
> *Lettres Portugaises*, published in French in 1669, are celebrated for their lyric beauty. They are the poignant letters of a nun whose French lover left her: she was Mariana Alcoforado, born in Beja in 1640; he was the Comte de Saint-Léger, later Marquis de Chamilly, fighting in the Restoration Wars with Spain. The true authorship of the five letters may be in doubt, but the story of the lovelorn nun endures – Matisse even painted her imaginary portrait. Sentimental visitors to the Convento de Nossa Senhora da Conceição in Beja still sigh over "Mariana's window".

㉔
Vila Nova de Milfontes

⊞D6 **☷** **𝒊** Rua António Mantas; 283 996 599

One of the loveliest places on Portugal's west coast is found where the Mira river meets the sea. The popular resort of Vila Nova de Milfontes, which is located on the sleepy estuary, is delightfully low key and unassuming, but offers many places to stay. Its small castle overlooking the bay once had an important role defending the coast from pirates. In contrast to the quiet river are the pretty beaches with their crashing waves, a major summer attraction, especially with surfers.

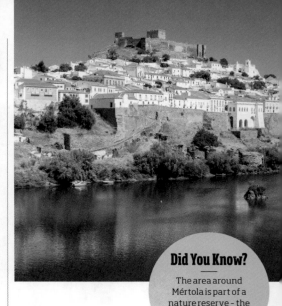

EAT

Adega 25 de Abril
Bare brickwork and giant terracotta urns create a rustic backdrop for typical Alentejan fare, including giant pork steaks and amazing homemade desserts.

⊞E6 **⌂** Rua da Moeda 23, Beja **☎** 284 325 960 **☍** Sun D, Mon

€€€

Marquês
This classy *marisqueira* is the place to sample the local fishers' catch. It's a lovely tiled restaurant, with outdoor seats facing an attractive square.

⊞D6 **⌂** Largo Marquês de Pombal 10, Porto Covo **☍** Tue **🖥** marques cervejaria.com

€€€

㉕
Mértola

⊞F6 **☷** **𝒊** Rua da Igreja 31; 286 610 109 **☉** 9:15am-12:30pm & 2-5:30pm daily **☍** 1 Jan, 1 May & 25 Dec

Pretty whitewashed Mértola is of historical interest as this small town is a *vila museu*, a museum site. It has various discoveries from different eras exhibited in *núcleos*, or areas where lots of treasures from a particular period can be found. The tourist office has details of each *núcleo*.

Mértola dates back to the Phoenicians, who created a thriving inland port here, later enjoyed by the Romans and the Moors. Roman artifacts can be seen at the Museu de Mértola. The post-Roman period is on display in the Núcleo Visigótico and in an early Christian basilica whose ruins adjoin the Roman road to Beja (p312). The influence bestowed by several centuries of Moorish domination is seen in the museum's Núcleo Islâmico, which houses one of the country's best collections of Portuguese Islamic art. The Igreja Matriz below the Moorish walls was formerly a mosque, with a

Did You Know?

The area around Mértola is part of a nature reserve - the Parque Natural do Vale do Guadiana.

five-nave layout, four horseshoe arches and a *mihrab* or prayer niche.

Overlooking the town is a ruined hilltop castle, with its keep of 1292. The Alcácova do Castelo, the excavated ruins of a Moorish village and earlier Roman cistern, are within the grounds.

Mértola's castle, high above the town and Guadiana river

The copper mines at Minas de São Domingos, 16 km (10 miles) to the east, were the main employer in the area from 1858 to 1965, when the mine was exhausted. An English company ran the site under the harshest conditions, with miners' families living in one windowless room. The village's population is about 700, and the ghost-town atmosphere is relieved only by a reservoir and surrounding lush greenery.

26
Zambujeira do Mar

A D7 **B** **i** Rua da Escola; 283 961 144 **W** sudoeste. meo.pt

A narrow strip of sheltered land divides the Alentejo plains from the Atlantic. Here lies the solitary village of Zambujeira do Mar, the whiteness of its gorgeous beach enhanced by the dark backdrop of high basalt cliffs. The annual Festival Meo Sudoeste, usually held in the second week in August at Herdade da Casa Branca, just outside the village, draws music lovers from all over Europe.

27
Porto Covo

A D6 **Q** 10 km (6 miles) south of Sines

Small but bustling, Porto Covo is one of the most attractive resorts on the Alentejo coast. Its tiny main square is ringed by traditional whitewashed houses that are trimmed with blue. The coast to the north and west of the village is made up of a series of beaches, linked by a scenic road and clifftop paths. The coves soften the impact of the Atlantic waves, creating safe swimming areas.

South from Porto Covo it's a short drive along a coastal track to the lovely beach at Ilha do Pessegueiro. The beach is protected by a little island of the same name, which has its own ruined sea fort. Fishing boats often offer trips around the island from Porto Covo.

THE VERSATILITY OF CORK

Groves of evergreen cork oak *(Quercus suber)* provide the Alentejo with a thriving industry. Portugal, the world's largest cork producer, has almost 7,000 sq km (2,700 sq miles) under cultivation and turns out some 30 million corks a day. In rural areas, this versatile bark is fashioned into waterproof, heat-proof food containers and these decorated boxes are a traditional craft of the Alentejo.

↑ Praia da Ilha do Pessegueiro, over-looking Porto Covo

A DRIVING TOUR
MEGALITHS TOUR

Length 80 km (50 miles) **Stopping-off points** Évora;
Grutas do Escoural **Terrain** Access roads to the sites are
often no more than tracks, and signposting can be erratic

Archaeologists date the *pedras talhas*, hewn stones, near Évora to
between 4000 and 2000 BCE. Their symbolism remains mysterious.
Dolmens are thought to be where Neolithic communities buried
their dead, together with their possessions – more than 130 have
been found in the region. Tall phallic menhirs jutting from olive
groves immediately suggest fertility rites, while cromlechs – carved
stones standing in regulated groups – probably had religious
significance. This tour includes examples of each; more can be found
further east, near Monsaraz and Reguengos de Monsaraz, and the
museum in Castelo de Vide (p303) has finds related to the area.

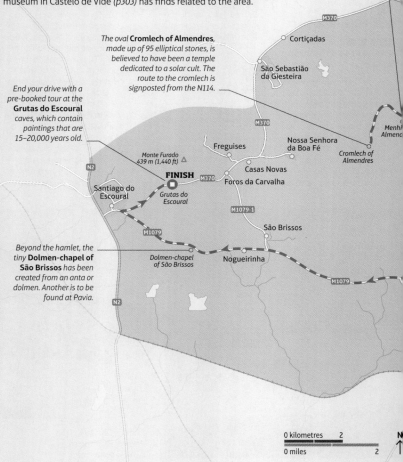

*Standing 2.5 m (8 ft)
tall, the solitary stone
Menhir of Almendres
is located away from
the cromlech, in an
olive grove behind a
row of tall storage bins.*

*The oval **Cromlech of Almendres**,
made up of 95 elliptical stones, is
believed to have been a temple
dedicated to a solar cult. The
route to the cromlech is
signposted from the N114.*

*End your drive with a
pre-booked tour at the
Grutas do Escoural
caves, which contain
paintings that are
15–20,000 years old.*

*Beyond the hamlet, the
tiny **Dolmen-chapel of
São Brissos** has been
created from an anta or
dolmen. Another is to be
found at Pavia.*

Cortiçadas

São Sebastião
da Giesteira

Menhir
Almend...

Freguises

Nossa Senhora
da Boa Fé

Cromlech of
Almendres

Monte Furado
439 m (1,440 ft) △

FINISH
*Grutas do
Escoural*

Casas Novas
Foros da Carvalha

Santiago do
Escoural

São Brissos

*Dolmen-chapel
of São Brissos*

Nogueirinha

0 kilometres   2

0 miles   2

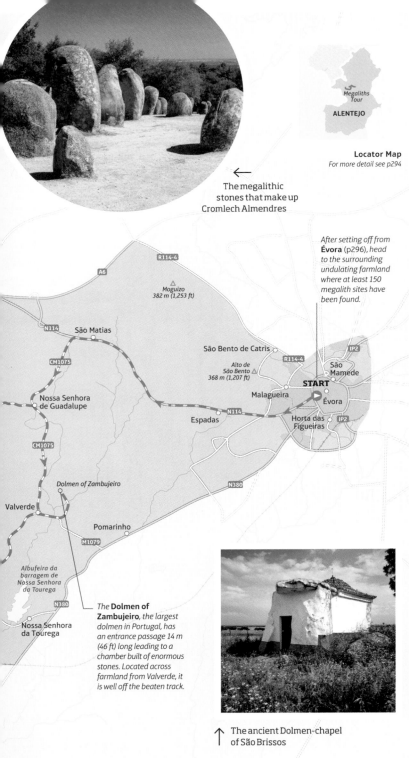

The megalithic
stones that make up
Cromlech Almendres

←

Locator Map
For more detail see p294

After setting off from
Évora (p296), *head
to the surrounding
undulating farmland
where at least 150
megalith sites have
been found.*

Megaliths
Tour

ALENTEJO

R114-4

A6

Moguizo
382 m (1,253 ft)

N114   São Matias

São Bento de Catris

R114-4

Alto de
São Bento
368 m (1,207 ft)

IP2

São
Mamede

CM1075

START

Malagueira

Évora

Nossa Senhora
de Guadalupe

N114

CM1075

Espadas

Horta das
Figueiras

IP2

Dolmen of Zambujeiro

Valverde

N380

Pomarinho

M1079

Albufeira da
barragem de
Nossa Senhora
da Tourega

N380

Nossa Senhora
da Tourega

The **Dolmen of
Zambujeiro,** *the largest
dolmen in Portugal, has
an entrance passage 14 m
(46 ft) long leading to a
chamber built of enormous
stones. Located across
farmland from Valverde, it
is well off the beaten track.*

↑   The ancient Dolmen-chapel
of São Brissos

ALGARVE

The Algarve's fertile soil and strategic headlands and rivers have attracted visitors since the time of the Phoenicians. Five centuries of Arab rule, from 711 CE, left a legacy that is still visible in the region's architecture, lattice chimneys, *azulejos*, orange groves and almond trees. Place names beginning with Al are also of Moorish origin; Al-Gharb ("the West") denoted the western edge of the Islamic empire. When the Algarve was reclaimed by the Christians in 1249, the Portuguese rulers designated themselves kings "of Portugal and of the Algarves", emphasizing the region's separateness from the rest of the country. It was the Algarve, however, that shot Portugal to prominence in the 15th century, when Henry the Navigator is said to have set up a school of navigation at Sagres, and launched the age of exploration from these southern shores. Three centuries later the region was struck a devastating blow by the earthquake of 1755, which destroyed or damaged virtually all of the towns and villages.

Since the 1960s, when Faro airport was opened, international tourism has replaced agriculture and fishing as the region's main industry. Nonetheless, in places such as the pretty whitewashed village of Alte or the border town of Alcoutim, the Algarve's rural way of life continues virtually uninterrupted.

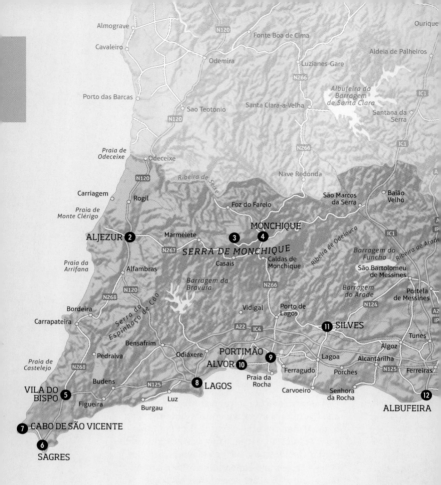

Almograve

Cavaleiro

Ourique

Fonte Boa de Cima

Aldeia de Palheiros

N120

Porto das Barcas

Odemira

Luzianes-Gare

N266

Albufeira da
Barragem
de Santa Clara

IC1

N120

Santa Clara-a-Velha

Santana da
Serra

Sao Teotónio

Praia de
Odeceixe

Odeceixe

IC1

Ribeira de Seixe

N120

Nave Redonda

Carriagem

Rogil

São Marcos
da Serra

Baião
Velho

Foz do Farelo

Praia de
Monte Clérigo

MONCHIQUE

ALJEZUR ❷

Marmelete

❸

❹

IC1

Praia da
Arrifana

SERRA DE MONCHIQUE

N267

Casais

Caldas de
Monchique

Ribeira de Odelouca

Barragem do
Funcho

Barragem da
Arade

Alfambras

São Bartolomeu
de Messines

Bordeira

N268

N120

*Serra de
Espinhaço de Cão*

Barragem da
Bravura

N266

Portela
de Messines

A2

IP

Carrapateira

Vidigal

Porto de
Lagos

N124

Praia de
Castelejo

Bensafrim

A22   IC4

❶❶ **SILVES**

Tunes

Pedralva

Odiáxere

PORTIMÃO

❾

Lagoa

Álgoz

Alcantarilha

Ferreiras

N268

ALVOR ❿

Ferragudo

Porches

N125

Budens

N125

❽ **LAGOS**

Praia da
Rocha

**VILA DO
BISPO ❺**

Figueira

Luz

Burgau

Carvoeiro

Senhora
da Rocha

❶❷

ALBUFEIRA

❼ **CABO DE SÃO VICENTE**

❻

SAGRES

Atlantic Ocean

ALGARVE

0 kilometres   10

0 miles   10

N

ALGARVE

Must See
1 Faro

Experience More
2 Aljezur
3 Serra de Monchique
4 Monchique
5 Vila do Bispo
6 Sagres
7 Cabo de São Vicente
8 Lagos
9 Portimão
10 Alvor
11 Silves
12 Albufeira
13 Vilamoura
14 Almancil
15 Olhão
16 Loulé
17 Parque Natural da Ria Formosa
18 Tavira
19 Alte
20 Estoi
21 Vila Real de Santo António
22 Cacela Velha
23 Castro Marim
24 Alcoutim

Faro's marina, lined with palm trees, bathed in a warm evening glow ↑

❶

FARO

🅰E7 ✈5 km (3 miles) SW 🚉Largo da Estação 🚌Avenida da República 🛈Rua da Misericórdia; 289 803 604

Often overlooked by visitors, this city is more than just a gateway to the beaches. Capital of the Algarve since 1756, Faro has been reborn several times over the centuries – following invasion, fire and earthquake. Captured from the Moors in 1249 by Afonso III, Faro prospered until 1596, when it was sacked and burned by the Earl of Essex. A new city rose from the ashes, only to be damaged in the earthquake of 1755 *(p45)*.

①
Sé

🅰Largo da Sé 📞289 823 018 🕙10am-6pm Mon-Fri (Dec-Jan: to 5:30pm), 9:30am-4pm Sat 🚫Public hols

The first Christian church here, built on the site of a mosque, was all but destroyed in the attack by the English in 1596. The base of the bell tower, its medieval doorway and two chapels survived, and long-term reconstruction resulted in a mixture of styles.

By the 1640s, a grander building had emerged, which included a chancel decorated with *azulejos* and the Capela de Nossa Senhora dos Prazeres, adorned with ornate gilded woodcarving.

One of the cathedral's most eccentric features is the large 18th-century organ decorated with Chinese motifs. Its range includes an echoing horn and a nightingale's song, and it has often been used by leading European organists.

The cathedral is free to enter, but you must purchase a ticket to ascend the bell tower.

②
Museu Municipal

🅰Largo Dom Afonso III 📞289 870 827 🕙10am-6pm Tue-Fri, 10:30am-5pm Sat & Sun (last adm 30 min before closing) 🚫Public hols

The city's museum is housed in the former convent of Nossa Senhora da Assunção, which was founded for the Poor Clares by Dona Leonor, sister of Manuel I. Look for her emblem, a fishing net, which adorns the portico.

Under the Romans, Faro became an important port and administrative centre, named Ossonoba. A variety of fascinating local archaeological finds from the city's Roman heyday, including busts of Emperor Hadrian and Agrippina, are displayed in the Museu Municipal. The museum is partly housed in the lovely two-storey Renaissance cloister, built by Afonso Pires in 1540. The collection also contains medieval and Manueline stone carvings and statuary. However, the most attractive exhibit is a huge Roman floor mosaic featuring a magnificently executed head of the god Neptune (3rd century CE), which was found near the city's railway station.

> 💬 INSIDER TIP
> **Set Your Alarm**
>
> Get up early and head straight for the morning market on Largo Dr Francisco Sá Carneiro to beat the crowds. The bustling stalls offer fresh local produce, as well as clothing and local crafts.

EXPLORING THE OLD CITY

At Faro's heart, the Largo da Sé is a peaceful square, lined with orange trees and flanked by the elegant Paço Episcopal (bishop's palace). Venture beyond the old city walls to the *azulejo*-decked church of São Francisco. Further north is the 17th-century Nossa Senhora do Pé da Cruz with fanciful oil panels of stories from Genesis.

③ ✏

Museu Regional

🏛 Praça da Liberdade 2
📞 289 870 893 🕐 10am-6pm Tue-Fri (to 4:30pm Sat) 🚫 Public hols

This ethnographic museum takes a nostalgic look at the Algarve's traditional way of life, displaying ceramics, looms and horse tack. Old photographs document peasant farming techniques, with their heavy reliance on manpower, donkeys and oxen. The most charming exhibit is the cart used by the last waterseller in Olhão, in operation until 1974.

Did You Know?

Portugal's first printed book, *The Faro Pentatuch*, was produced in Faro's Jewish quarter in 1487.

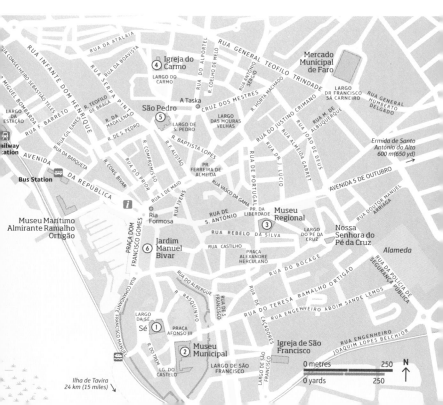

④

Igreja do Carmo

⌂ Largo do Carmo ☎ 289 824 490 ⌚ 9am–6pm Mon–Fri (winter: to 5pm), 9am–1pm Sat

The impressive façade of this church was begun in 1713. The 1755 Lisbon earthquake proved disastrous for the construction, and the structure that you see today, with its delicate twin bell towers, was designed by Diogo Tavares (1711–1765) after the earthquake. While the exterior of the church was not completed until 1878, the finishing touches were made to the lavish interior 150 years earlier.

Inside the Igreja do Carmo, the decoration is Baroque run wild, with every scroll and barley-sugar twist covered in precious Brazilian gold leaf. In sombre contrast, the Capela dos Ossos (Chapel of Bones) has walls lined with skulls and bones. It was built in 1816, using remains from the friars' cemetery. Similarly to the chapel found in Évora's São Francisco (p298), it was designed to be a stark reminder of the transience of human life. Unlike the church, you must buy a ticket to visit the chapel.

→

Pretty purple jacaranda trees blooming in front of the whitewashed São Pedro church

⑤

São Pedro

⌂ Largo de São Pedro ☎ 930 542 698 ⌚ 9am–1pm & 3–5pm Mon–Fri

The parish church of Faro is dedicated to St Peter, patron saint of fishers. Though restored with Italianate columns after the earthquake of 1755, much of the original Baroque decoration in the tri-nave church has survived, including the main altarpiece, dating from 1689.

Highlights include the chapel of the Santíssimo Sacramento, with a dazzling altarpiece (c.1745) featuring a bas-relief of the Last Supper, and a sculpture of St Anne teaching the young Virgin Mary to read. Be sure not to miss the altar of the Capela das Almas, which is surrounded by stunning *azulejos* (c.1730) showing the Virgin and other saints pulling souls out of purgatory. The church also has some lovely stained-glass windows, which bathe the floor in light.

EAT

A Taska
The *xarém* (thick cornmeal soup with clams and bacon) is a speciality at this rustic restaurant. Look out for the dish of the day and the codfish dishes.

⌂ Rua do Alportel 38 ☎ 969 441 381

€€€

Ria Formosa
This lounge bar and restaurant on the roof of the Hotel Faro offers amazing views. It is a great spot to watch the sunset with a cocktail.

⌂ Hotel Faro, Praça Dom Francisco Gomes 2 🌐 hotelfaro.pt

€€€

↑ The macabre interior of the Capela dos Ossos in Igreja do Carmo

⑥
Jardim Manuel Bívar

📍 Praça Dom Francisco Gomes 12

Erected in the 19th century, this central garden was once called the Jardim do Bacalhau due to its codfish shape. It sits across from the marina, sandwiched between historical buildings such as Igreja da Misericórdia, a 16th-century church, and the Banco de Portugal, a Moorish-style building housing a bank. It's a delightful place to relax, glimpsing the boats arriving at the harbour, admiring the nearby buildings and, on the second and fourth Saturdays of each month, browsing the craft fair held here. The garden is also a key stop along the Ecovia do Litoral, a cycling route crossing the Algarve coast.

Erected in the 19th century, the central garden, the Jardim Manuel Bívar, was once called the Jardim do Bacalhau due to its codfish shape.

→

The beautiful garden Jardim Manuel Bívar with a view of Arco da Vila

EXPERIENCE MORE

EAT

Ocean

Overseen by German chef Hans Neuner, Ocean has two Michelin stars thanks to the chef's creative cooking of local ingredients. The menu features quail, prawns and the catch of the day.

🅰E7 **🏠Hotel Vila Vita Parc, Rua Anneliese Pohl, Alporchinhos, Porches** **🕐Wed-Sun L, Mon & Tue** **🌐restaurante ocean.com**

€€€

Rei das Praias

A sublime beachside restaurant built on stilts above a charming cove. The daily specials feature fresh fish and seafood.

🅰E7 **🏠Praia dos Caneiros, Ferragudo** **🕐Mon** **🌐restaurantereidas praias.com**

€€€

2

Aljezur

🅰D7 **🚌** **ℹ️Rua 25 de Abril 62; 282 998 229**

The small village of Aljezur is overlooked by a 10th-century Moorish castle, which is reached via the old quarter. Although in ruins, a cistern and towers remain, and there are splendid views towards the Serra de Monchique.

Aljezur's Igreja Matriz, much rebuilt after the earthquake of 1755, has a fine Neo-Classical altarpiece. Dating from about 1809, it was probably executed in the workshop of José da Costa of Faro.

From Aljezur, the wild and deserted beaches of the Algarve's west coast are easily explored, although a car is essential. Open to the strong currents of the Atlantic, Praia da Arrifana, 10 km (6 miles) southwest, and Praia de Monte Clérigo, 8 km (5 miles) northwest, are sandy, sweeping beaches backed by cliffs. On the Alentejo border, Praia de Odeceixe has a stunning beach, and the sheltered cove is popular with surfers.

3

Serra de Monchique

🅰E7 **🚌Monchique** **ℹ️Monchique; 282 911 189**

Providing shelter from the north, this volcanic mountain range helps to ensure the mild southern climate of the Algarve. The highest point is Fóia at 902 m (2,959 ft). This, however, is less pleasantly wooded than Picota, which at 773 m (2,536 ft) is the second-highest peak. An impressive 4-km (2.5-mile) walk to this peak from Monchique passes among chestnut trees and fields of wild flowers. A spectacular panorama sweeps down to the Ponta de Sagres (p328) and there are stunning views of the rest of the range.

The 30-km (19-mile) drive along the N267 from Nave, just below Monchique, to Aljezur in the west, leads through a beautiful part of the Serra. The landscape is a mixture of woods and moorland. The cork oak trees that grow here are home to the tiny nuthatch and lesser-spotted woodpecker.

→ The pretty main square in the spa town of Monchique

There is a wonderful variety of vegetation to enjoy in the Serra, including mimosa, rhododendron, chestnut, pine and cork oak. The fast-growing eucalyptus trees, however, have given cause for concern. This highly flammable species is one of the reasons for the serious fires that break out all too often in the Serra.

---

❹

Monchique

⚑E7 🚌 ℹ️Largo de São Sebastião; 282 911 189

The small market town of Monchique is primarily famous for its altitude, 458 m (1,500 ft),

300
—
The number of days of sunshine per year enjoyed in the Algarve.

and consequently spectacular views. It is also known for its wooden handicrafts, particularly the folding chairs which date back to Roman times.

The 16th-century Igreja Matriz, on the cobbled Rua da Igreja behind the main square, has an impressive Manueline doorway whose knotted columns end in unusual pinnacles. Above the town is the ruined monastery of Nossa Senhora do Desterro. This Franciscan house, founded in 1632 by Dom Pero da Silva, is now only a shell but it is worth visiting for the stunning views across to the peak of Picota.

A delightful spa 6 km (4 miles) south of Monchique, Caldas de Monchique is set in the foothills of the Serra in wooded surroundings. The hot, curative waters have attracted the ailing since Roman times, and even though João II died soon after taking them in 1495, their reputation has remained undiminished. In the summer, people come to be treated for skin, digestive and rheumatic complaints. As well as the spring water, the bars here offer local firewater, *medronho*.

The shady main square has a large, attractive handicraft centre and there are some pretty walks in the woods.

← The sweet village of Aljezur, surrounded by fertile land

❺

Vila do Bispo

⚑D7 🚌 ℹ️Sagres; 282 624 873

The grand name of "The Bishop's Town" today refers to a peaceful village, rather remote in feel. It acquired its name in the 17th century when it was donated to the bishop of Faro. The town's parish church, Nossa Senhora da Conceição, has a delightful interior decorated with 18th-century *azulejos* from the floor up to the painted ceiling, and an altarpiece dating from 1715.

The beaches in the area are remote and unspoiled. Praia do Castelejo, 5 km (3 miles) to the west, is accessible by a dirt road that winds up from the village. The intrepid can turn off this track for the 6-km (4-mile) journey to Torre de Aspa, an obelisk at 156 m (512 ft) marking the spot for spectacular views over the ocean. The road is quite rough, so it's best to walk the last 2 km (1 mile).

 HIDDEN GEM
Fóia

From Monchique, it is an easy drive to the top of Fóia, the highest point of the Algarve. From here, there are wonderful vistas over the coast and across the hills of the Serra de Monchique.

↑ Promontory of Cabo de São Vicente jutting into the Atlantic Ocean

6 Sagres

 D7 🚌 ℹ Rua Comandante Matoso; 282 624 873

The small town of Sagres has little to offer except a picturesque harbour, but it is a good base from which to explore the superb beaches and isolated peninsula west of the town. Henry the Navigator built a fortress on this wind-swept promontory and, according to tradition, a school of navigation and a shipyard. From here he realized his

↑ Interior of Nossa Senhora da Graça in Sagres

dream "to see what lay beyond the Canaries and Cape Bojador… and attempt the discovery of things hidden from men". From 1419 to 1460, he poured his energy and the revenues of the Order of Christ (p176), of which he was master, into building caravels and sending his fear-stricken sailors into unknown waters.

In 1434, Gil Eanes of Lagos was the first sailor to round the dreaded Cape Bojador, in the region of Western Sahara. With this feat, the west coast of Africa was opened up for exploitation and Portugal's empire expanded.

Little remains of Prince Henry's original fortress: the walls that can be seen today are part of a 17th-century fort. Still visible is the giant pebble wind compass, the Rosa dos Ventos, 43 m (141 ft) in diameter, said to have been used by Henry. The simple chapel of Nossa Senhora da Graça was also built by him. The whole site, looking across to Cabo de São Vicente and out towards the open Atlantic, is exhilarating and atmospheric.

The town is within easy reach of superb beaches, such as family-friendly Martinhal and Telheiro, which is perfect for surfing and bodyboarding.

7 Cabo de São Vicente

D7 🚌 To Sagres then taxi ℹ Sagres; 282 624 873

In the Middle Ages, this wind-blown cape at the extreme southwest of Europe was believed to be the end of the world. Today, with its 60-m- (200-ft-) tall cliffs, it still presents an awe-inspiring aspect. The ocean waves have created long, sandy beaches and carved deep caves.

HENRY THE NAVIGATOR

Although he didn't sail himself, Henry (1394–1460), the third son of João I, laid the foundations for Portugal's maritime expansion that were built upon by João II and Manuel I. As master of the rich Order of Christ and governor of the Algarve, Henry could finance voyages to the African coast, instigating Portugal's trade of enslaved people. By the time he died he had a monopoly on all trade south of Cape Bojador.

Since the 15th century, Cabo de São Vicente has been an important reference point for shipping, and its present lighthouse has a 95-km (60-mile) range, said to be the most powerful in Europe. It has long had religious associations, and its name arises from the legend that the body of St Vincent was washed ashore here in the 4th century.

Since 1988, the coast from Sines in the north *(p313)* to Burgau in the east has been made a nature reserve, providing important nesting grounds for Bonelli's eagle, kestrel, white stork, heron and numerous other bird species. There is also a colony of sea otters.

8

Lagos

🗺 D7 🚆🚌 🛈 Praça Gil Eanes; 282 763 031

Set on a large bay, Lagos is an attractive, bustling town. In the 8th century it was taken over by the Moors, who left behind fortifications. A well-preserved section and archway can be seen near Rua do Castelo dos Governadores, where there is a monument to the navigator Gil Eanes.

The breakthroughs of the 15th century, pioneered by Henry the Navigator, whose statue gazes out to sea, turned Lagos into an important naval centre. At the same time a most deplorable period of history began, with the first enslaved people brought back from the Sahara in 1441 by Henry's explorer Nuno Tristão. The site of the first market of enslaved people in Europe is marked by a plaque under the arcades on Rua da Senhora da Graça.

Extensive damage was caused by the earthquake of 1755, so today the centre consists primarily of pretty 18th- and 19th-century buildings. The citizens of Lagos continue to make their living from fishing, which helps the town to retain a character independent of the tourist trade. The smart marina on the east side of town is the first safe place for anchorage on the south coast for boats coming in from the Atlantic.

On the seafront stands the 17th-century fortress which defended the entrance to the harbour. Its imposing ramparts afford far-reaching views over the town and the bay.

The 18th-century church of **Santo António** is an Algarvian jewel. The lower section of the

$\rightarrow$
Café-lined street leading up to Santo António

walls is covered in blue-and-white *azulejos*, the rest in carved, gilded and painted woodwork, an inspirational and riotous example of Baroque carving. Cherubs, beasts, flowers and scenes of hunting and fishing surround eight panel paintings of miracles performed by St Anthony. Near the altar is the grave of Hugh Beatty, an Irish colonel who commanded the Lagos regiment during the 17th-century wars with Spain. He died here in 1709 and his motto *Non vi sed arte* ("Not with force but with skill") adorns the tomb. The church forms part of the neighbouring museum, Museu Municipal Dr José Formosinho.

Santo António

🏠 Rua General Alberto Silveira 📞 282 762 301 🕐 10am–12:30pm & 2–5:30pm Tue–Sun 🚫 Public hols

⑨ Portimão

🅐E7 🚉🚌 🚹Teatro Municipal de Portimão, Largo 1° de Dezembro; 282 402 487

The Algarve's second-largest city, Portimão has plenty of character and a long history as a port. The Romans settled here, attracted by the natural harbour on the estuary of the Rio Arade.

Portimão's northern outskirts consist of commercial and residential areas. Further into the municipality is the historic 18th-century town centre, which has plenty of excellent shopping options, as well as a large, bustling market. The picturesque riverfront is nearby.

The centre lies around the pedestrianized Rua Vasco da Gama, with shops specializing in leather goods. Along Rua da Igreja, the church of Nossa Senhora da Conceição occupies a low hill. Rebuilt after being damaged in the earthquake of 1755 *(p45)*, its 14th-century origins are still visible in the portico, with its carved capitals. Inside, there are 17th- and 18th-century *azulejo* panels.

The waterfront is lively and many of the restaurants serve the fresh catch of the day. Portimão has a long fishing tradition that developed between the 19th and 20th centuries with the advent of the canning industry. The award-winning **Museu de Portimão**, housed in a former canning factory, is located on the southern end of the esplanade. The museum pays homage to the local people, and the town that for centuries has lived exclusively off the sea.

Just 3 km (2 miles) south lies Portimão's touristic neighbour, Praia da Rocha, a series of sandy coves among protruding red and ochre rocks. At its east end is the 16th-century Fortaleza de Santa Catarina, with superb beach views, and below is Portimão Marina.

For a thrilling experience, head to the Autódromo Internacional do Algarve racing circuit located 20 km (12 miles) north of the city centre.

Museu de Portimão

🏠Rua Dom Carlos, Zona Ribeirinha 🕐Aug: 3–11pm Wed–Sun (from 7:30pm Tue & 3pm Sun); Sep–Jul: 10am–6pm Wed–Sun (from 2:30pm Tue) 🌐museudeportimao.pt

↑ Beautiful little church of Divino Salvador in the centre of Alvor

⑩ Alvor

🅐E7 🚉🚌 🚹Rua Dr Afonso Costa 51; 282 457 540

This pretty fishing town of white houses is popular with holiday-makers, so visit during the low season. It was a Roman port, and later the Moorish town of Al-Bur. By the 16th century it was again a prosperous town, but it was damaged in the earthquake of 1755. The town was rebuilt with stone from the Moorish castle, so little of that remains.

↑ A life-size exhibit at the Museu de Portimão demonstrating the life of a local worker

→

Statues in an ornamental pool in Praça al Mutamid, Silves

At the top of the town the 16th-century church, Divino Salvador, has a Manueline portal carved with foliage, lions and dragons. The outermost arch is an octopus tentacle.

11

Silves

E7 Parque das Merendas; 282 098 927

Silves' commanding position made it the ideal fortified settlement. The Romans built a castle here, but it was under the Arabs that the city flourished, becoming the Moorish capital, Xelb. In the mid-12th century the Arab geographer Idrisi praised its beauty and its "delicious, magnificent" figs. Silves was renowned as a centre of culture in Moorish Al-Gharb until the Knights of Santiago took the city in 1242.

Today, the red walls of the castle stand out against the skyline. The nearby **Casa da Cultura Islâmica e Mediterrânica** hosts local exhibitions and events.

The red sandstone **Castelo de Silves** dates back mainly to Moorish times, though it has done duty as a Christian fortress and a jail. It was the site of the Palace of the Verandahs, abode of Al-Mu'tamid from 1053 when he was ruler of Seville and Wali of Al-Gharb.

There are superb views of the city and countryside from the massive, polygonal ramparts. Inside, there are gardens and the impressive vaulted Moorish Cisterna da Moura Encantada (Cistern of the Enchanted Moorish Girl).

Built on the site of a mosque, the **Sé** dates from the 13th century. In the chancel, light falls from lovely double windows with stained-glass borders on a jasper statue of Nossa Senhora da Conceição, believed to date from the 14th century.

Opposite the Sé, the 16th-century Misericórdia church has a Manueline side door and a Renaissance altarpiece.

Downhill from the cathedral, the **Museu Arqueológico** was opened in 1990. Its exhibits include Stone and Iron Age tools, sculpted Roman capitals, surgical instruments from the 5th–7th centuries and items of 18th-century ceramics. The museum is built around a large Arab well-cistern that was uncovered in 1980. The staircase built into the structure descends 15 m (49 ft) to the bottom of the well.

Did You Know?

Sancho I (1185-1211) styled himself as king of Silves from 1189 to 1191.

One kilometre (half a mile) east of Silves is the Cruz de Portugal, an ornate 16th-century granite cross, carved with the Crucifixion. This may have been given to the city by Manuel I, when João II's body was transferred from Silves to Batalha *(p172)*.

Casa da Cultura Islâmica e Mediterrânica

Largo da República 282 440 895 Times vary, call ahead

Castelo de Silves

Rua do Castelo 282 440 837 Jan-Mar: 9am-5:30pm daily (Apr & Jun: to 8pm; Jul & Aug: to 10pm; Sep & Oct: to 8pm; Nov & Dec: to 5:30pm)

Sé

Rua da Sé 10am-1pm & 2-6pm Mon-Fri Public hols

Museu Arqueológico

Rua das Portas de Loulé 14 282 440 838 10am-6pm daily

← Rocky coastline at Praia de São Rafael, just outside Albufeira

high-rise hotels. Vilamoura is a prime example of this kind of development. Its 16 sq km (6 sq miles) encompass four golf courses, tennis courts, a riding school, fishing and shooting facilities, and sports complexes. There is even a landing strip. Its many hotels and apartment blocks are still on the rise, and the already well-established complex is still under construction.

The focal point is the large marina, which bristles with powerboats and is fronted by restaurants, cafés and shops frequented by Portugal's jet set. The nearby Roman ruins of **Cerro da Vila**, dating from

EAT

A Barquinha
What this local joint lacks in glamour, it makes up for with its fantastic seafood dishes.

⛰F7 🍴Rua José Pires Padinha 142, Tavira
📞281 322 843 🚫Wed

€€€

Bon Bon
Although it occupies an unassuming location, Chef José Lopes delivers delicately crafted cuisine at this Michelin-starred restaurant.

⛰E7 🍴Urb Cabeço de Pias, Carvoeiro 🚫Tue & Wed; Thu & Fri L
🌐bonbon.pt

€€€

Veneza
Shelves stacked with wine bottles surround the walls of this traditional restaurant, which serves the likes of Iberian black pork and veal loin.

⛰E7 🍴Estrada de Paderne, Albufeira 🚫Tue 🌐restaurant eveneza.com

€€€

 12

Albufeira

⛰E7 🚆🚌 ℹ️Rua 5 de Outubro; 289 585 279

Once a charming fishing town Albufeira is now the tourist capital of the Algarve. The town's name originates from the Arabic Al-Buhar (The Castle on the Sea). It was a prosperous town under the Moors, profiting from trade with North Africa. One of the town's main attractions is the **Museu Arqueológico** which houses a captivating collection of Stone Age, Roman and Moorish artifacts, with the Islamic-era silo as its highlight. Rua 5 de Outubro leads through a tunnel to the beach, east of which is the Praia dos Barcos where the fishers ply their trade. From Praia de São Rafael, 2 km (1 mile) west of Albufeira, to Praia da Oura due east, the area is punctuated by small sandy coves.

Museu Arqueológico
🏛Praca da Republica 1 📞289 599 508 🕐9:30am-5:30pm Wed-Fri, 9:30am-12:30pm & 1:30-5:30pm Tue, Sat & Sun

---

13

Vilamoura

⛰E7 🚌 ℹ️Praça do Mar, Quarteira; 289 389 209

The coast between Faro and Lagos has effectively become a strip of villa complexes and the 1st century CE, include a bath complex and a house with mosaics depicting fish. Not far from here is one of the Algarve's many LGBTQ+-friendly beaches, Praia do Cavalo Preto.

Cerro da Vila

◈ ⊞ Avenida Cerro da Vila
☎ 289 312 153 ◷ 9:30am–12:30pm & 2–6pm Mon–Fri

Almancil

⬛E7 ⊞⊞ ❼ Rua Manuel dos Santos Vaquinha; 289 400 887

East of the undistinguished town of Almancil lies one of the Algarve's gems, the 18th-century Igreja Matriz de São Lourenço. Commissioned by local inhabitants in gratitude to St Laurence, who appeared to have answered their desperate prayers for water, the church's interior is a masterpiece of decoration in *azulejo* panels, probably designed by master crafters in Lisbon and shipped down. They cover the cupola, the walls of the chancel, nave and nave vault, to stunning effect. The wall panels depict episodes from the life of St Laurence; on one side of the altar the saint is shown healing two blind men, and on the other, giving money to the poor. The nave arches show the saint conversing with Pope Sixtus II; arguing for his Christian belief with the Roman Emperor Valerian; and refusing to give up his faith.

The story culminates in his martyrdom. In the last panel on the right, in which the saint is placed on a gridiron to be burned, an angel comforts him. The nave vault depicts the *Coronation of St Laurence*, and the cupola has decorative, trompe-l'oeil effects of exceptional quality. The last tiles were put in place in 1730. The altarpiece, dating from around 1735, was the work of sculptor Manuel Martins and was gilded by leading local painters.

←
Azulejos on the interior of Igreja Matriz de São Lourenço, and *(inset)* its exterior

↑ The 17th-century parish church in Olhão, with its bell tower

15

Olhão

🅐E7 🚇🚌 *i* Largo Sebastião Martins Mestre 8A; 289 713 936

Olhão has been involved in fishing since the Middle Ages, and today is one of the largest fishing ports and tuna- and sardine-canning centres in the Algarve. In 1808 the village was elevated to the status of town after 17 of its fishers crossed the Atlantic Ocean to Rio de Janeiro, without charts, to bring the exiled King João VI the news that Napoleon's troops had been forced out of the country.

Olhão's square, whitewashed houses with their flat roof terraces and box-like chimneys are reminiscent of Moorish architecture. The best view is from the top of the bell tower of the parish church Nossa Senhora do Rosário, on Praça da Restauração, built between 1681 and 1698 with donations from the local fishers. They were extremely devout because of the dangers they faced at sea, particularly in summertime when North African pirates often sailed off the coast. The custodian lets visitors through the locked door leading from the nave. At the rear of the church is the external chapel of Nossa Senhora dos Aflitos, where families pray for the fishers' safety in stormy weather.

The narrow, pedestrianized streets of the old town wind down from here to the waterfront, the scene of one of the region's most lively and picturesque markets. The noisy, covered fish market sells the morning's catch, while on Saturdays, outside stalls line the quay, with local farmers selling an array of seasonal produce, including fruit, nuts, honey and live chickens.

At the eastern end of the quay, beyond the market, boats take you out to the islands of Armona (15 min), Culatra (30 min) and Farol (45 min). These flat, narrow bars of sand provide shelter to the town, and excellent sandy beaches for visitors, particularly on the ocean side. The islands are in the Parque Natural da Ria Formosa *(p335)*.

Centro de Educaçáo Ambiental de Marim, about 3 km (2 miles) east of Olhão, is an environmental education centre. Its 148 acres (60 ha) of dune and pinewoods are home to a restored farmhouse, a tidal mill and a centre for injured birds, as well as exhibitions and aquariums.

Centro de Educaçâo Ambiental de Marim

⊛♿🚫🅿 🅓Quelfes 📞289 700 210 🕐9am–noon & 2–5pm Mon–Fri 🗙1 Jan, 25 Dec

16

Loulé

🅐E7 🚇🚌 *i* Avenida 25 de Abril; 289 463 900

Loulé is an attractive market town and thriving craft centre. Its Moorish origins are still visible in the bell tower of the church of São Clemente. The castle, on the north side of town, is also Moorish in origin, rebuilt in the 13th century. Remnants of the walls behind the castle afford fine views over Loulé.

The heart of the town lies immediately south of Praça da República and encompasses the busy market. On Saturdays, the area is

The pink domed building that houses ↓ Loulé's indoor market

PICTURE PERFECT
Boat Trip

Departing from Faro or Olhão, boat trips on the Ria Formosa offer plenty of opportunities to snap photos of local wildlife. The vessels follow the marshy waterways beside the picturesque islands.

particularly lively with outdoor markets running alongside the indoor market. From Rua 9 de Abril to the Igreja Matriz you can watch handicrafts workers carving wood, weaving hats, making lace, decorating horse tackle and painting pottery and tiles.

The 13th-century church of São Clemente, on Largo da Silva, was badly damaged in three earthquakes but its triple nave, defined by Gothic arches, has been conserved. There are two beautiful side chapels dating from the early 16th century. The Capela de Nossa Senhora da Consolação is decorated from floor to vault with superb blue-and-white *azulejo* panels, while the Capela de São Brás has a Manueline arch and a blue-and-gold Baroque altarpiece.

Another religious building of note is the chapel of Nossa Senhora da Conceição, close to Praça da República. Here, the Baroque altarpiece (1745) is complemented by scenes in the ubiquitous blue-and-white *azulejos*.

 A wooden boardwalk in the Parque Natural da Ria Formosa

17

Parque Natural da Ria Formosa

🅰 E7 🛈 Centro de Educação Ambiental de Marim, Quelfes 🚌 East of Olhão on N125 🚆 From Faro, Olhão, Tavira 🕐 8am–8pm daily

Stretching from Praia de Faro to Cacela Velha (p338), this nature reserve follows 60 km (37 miles) of coastline. It was created in 1987 to protect the ecosystem of the area, which was under threat from building, sand extraction and pollution, all by-products of the massive rise in tourism. The lagoon area of marshes, saltpans, islets and channels is sheltered from the open sea by a chain of barrier islands – actually sand dunes. Inlets between the islands allow the tide to ebb and flow into the lagoon.

These waters are rich in shellfish, such as oysters, cockles and clams: bred here, they make up 80 per cent of the nation's mollusc exports. The fish life and warm climate attract many wildfowl and waders; snakes and chameleons also live here. Apart from fish and shellfish farming and salt-panning, all other human activities that might encroach on the park's ecosystem are strictly controlled or forbidden.

TOP 5 BIRDS IN RIA FORMOSA

Purple Gallinule
A rarity, the gallinule is the symbol of the park.

Cattle Egret
These birds feed on insects and flies off the backs of cattle.

Red-Crested Pochard
A brightly coloured duck originally from Central Europe.

Purple Heron
This slender bird has a darker plumage than the more common grey heron.

Kentish Plover
You'll find this tiny white and brown bird on the shoreline.

↑ Cafés in Tavira, and
(inset) the scenic
riverside town

⑱
Tavira

**Ⓐ F7 🚍 🚌 ⓘ Praça da
República 5; 281 322 511**

The pretty town of Tavira, full
of historic churches and fine
mansions with filigree balconies, lies along both sides
of the Gilão river, linked by a
bridge of Roman origin. This
was part of the coastal Roman
road between Castro Marim
(p338) and Faro *(p322)*.

Tavira's early ascendancy
began with the Moors, who
saw it as one of their most
important settlements in the
Algarve, along with Silves and
Faro. It was deafeated in 1242
by Dom Paio Peres Correia,
who was outraged at the mur-
der of seven of his knights
by the Moors during a truce.

Tavira flourished until the
16th century, after which a
slow decline set in, aggravated
by a severe plague (1645–6)
and the silting up of the
harbour. The town now
welcomes tourists, without

compromising either its
looks or its atmosphere.

The best view of the town is
from the walls of the Moorish
castle in the old Arab quarter
on top of the hill. From here
the distinctive four-sided
roofs of the houses that line
Rua da Liberdade are clearly
visible. These pyramid-like
roofs possibly evolved to
allow the sudden torrential
rain of the Algarve to run off
easily. From the castle walls,
the nearby clock tower of
the church of Santa Maria
do Castelo also acts as a
landmark. The church itself
occupies the site of what was
once the biggest mosque in
the Algarve. Its façade retains
a Gothic doorway and win-
dows, and its interior, restored
in the 19th century, houses
the tombs of Dom Paio Peres
Correia and his seven knights.
Santa Maria do Castelo and
Igreja da Misericórdia are
the only two of Tavira's 21
churches to be open outside
service hours. Below the
castle is the 1569 convent of
Nossa Senhora da Graça.

Renaissance architecture
was pioneered in the town by
André Pilarte and can be seen
on the way up to the castle, in

the Igreja da Misericórdia
(1541–51), with its lovely doorway topped by saints Peter
and Paul, and in the nearby
Palácio da Galeria. The fascinating Núcleo Islâmico on
Praça da República showcases
Moorish artifacts, including an
11th-century figurative vase.

Seeking some beach time?
The sandy, offshore Ilha de
Tavira provides excellent
swimming. A popular resort
in summer, you can reach it
by ferry from Quatro Águas.

---

⑲
Alte

**Ⓐ E7 🚍 🚌 ⓘ Rua Condes de
Alte; 289 478 060**

Perched on a hill, Alte is one
of the prettiest villages of the
Algarve. The approach from
the east is the most picturesque, with sweeping views
of rolling hills. The focus of
this steep, white village is the
16th-century Nossa Senhora
da Assunção, which has a
Manueline doorway and
baptismal fonts, and a fine
gilded altarpiece celebrating
the Assumption. The little
chapel of São Sebastião has
beautiful, rare 16th-century
Sevillian *azulejos*.

A short walk from the church,
and signposted, is the Alte
river, overhung with trees, and

Perched on a hill, Alte is one of the prettiest villages of the Algarve. The approach from the east is the most picturesque, with sweeping views of rolling hills.

a water source known as the Fonte Grande. This leafy setting is ideal for picnicking. On the steep slopes, about 700 m (half a mile) from the village, is a mill (now a restaurant) and a 5-m- (16-ft-) high waterfall, Queda do Vigário.

Estoi

🅰E7 🚌 𝒊Faro; 289 803 604

The quiet village of Estoi has two notable sights, separated by a short distance and about 1,800 years. Just off the main square is the Pousada Palácio de Estoi, an unashamedly pretty Rococo pastiche. The palace was the brainchild of a local nobleman, who died soon after work was begun in the mid-1840s. Another wealthy local later acquired the palace, and completed it in 1909. For the vast amount of money and energy he expended on his new home, he was made viscount of Estoi. The work was supervised by the architect Domingos da Silva Meira, whose interest in sculpture is evident everywhere. The palace interior, a feast of pastel and stucco, is now a *pousada*, but the gardens can be visited daily by non-guests. Dotted with orange trees and palms, they continue the joyful Rococo spirit of the palace. The lower terrace features a blue-and-white tiled pavilion, inside which is a copy of Canova's *Three Graces*. The walled terrace above,

the Patamar da Casa do Presépio, has a large pavilion with stained-glass windows, fountains adorned with nymphs and tiled niches.

A walk downhill from the other end of the main square leads to the second major sight in Estoi: the Roman ruins of **Milreu**, a complex that dates from the 1st or 2nd century CE. The buildings probably began as a large farmhouse, which was converted in the 3rd century into a luxurious villa, built around a courtyard.

Well-preserved mosaics of fish and other marine creatures still adorn the walls and floor of the baths, located alongside the living quarters; however, most portable archaeological finds from this complex are now housed in the Museu Municipal in Faro *(p322)*. The importance of the villa is indicated by the remains of a temple overlooking the site.

Milreu

🏠N2-6 ☎289 997 823 🕐May–Sep: 10am–6pm Tue–Sun; Oct–Apr: 9am–5pm Tue–Sun 🔒1 Jan, Easter Sun, 1 May, 7 Sep, 25 Dec

DRINK

O Postigo
In a corner of the old town, this lively bar serves a tasty selection of *petiscos* (Portuguese tapas), coffee and wine all day.

🅰E7 🏠Rua 9 de Abril, Loulé ☎289 075 571 🔒Sun

Rei das Praias
Sit back and relax while sipping a cocktail at this beach restaurant on stilts, with views of a lovely cove.

🅰E7 🏠Praia dos Caneiros, Ferragudo ☎282 461 006

Ofélia Cocktail & Art Bar
A stylish cocktail bar with occasional live music just steps away from Tavira's picturesque riverfront.

🅰F7 🏠Rua José Pires Padinha 164 🔒Tue 🌐ofeliadetavira.com

→ Grand Rococo-style stairs at the Pousada Palácio de Estoi

Cyclist on a cobbled street in Vila Real de Santo António ↑

Vila Real de Santo António

🅰F7 🚆🚌 ℹ️ Avenida Marginal, Monte Gordo; 281 544 495

Built to a plan by the Marquês de Pombal in 1774, Vila Real de Santo António is a little like a miniature version of Lisbon's Baixa (p74), rebuilt after the 1755 earthquake also under the auspices of Pombal. The symmetrical grid of fairly wide streets, and the equal-sized blocks

INSIDER TIP
Head to Spain

Take the 20-minute ferry trip from Vila Real de Santo António, which crosses the Rio Guadiana, to Ayamonte in Spain for lunch. Remember to change your watch – Spain is one hour ahead of Portugal.

with similar façades, all speak of Pombal's practical and political ideals (p45).

Today, the town is one of the most important fishing ports on the Algarve coast, as well as a border town, with its markets geared towards visiting Spaniards. The Igreja Matriz is famous for its stained glass. The town's centre now seems too grand for its size, all of which makes it an interesting place to drop in on.

Cacela Velha

🅰F7 ℹ️ Avenida Marginal, Monte Gordo; 281 544 495

This coastal hamlet lies in the Parque Natural da Ria Formosa and grew primarily during the 17th century, when it formed part of the coastal defensive system. Perching on a clifftop, it is reached via a landscape of fields and olive trees.

Cacela Velha has remained untouched by mass tourism

and retains a peaceful atmosphere. Charming blue-and-white fishers' houses cluster around the remains of an 18th-century fort (closed to the public) and a white-washed 18th-century church.

The beach is sheltered by a long spit of sand, and fishing boats are dotted about. The Phoenicians and Moors used this protected site until it was taken over by the Knights of Santiago in 1240.

Castro Marim

🅰D7 🚌 ℹ️ Rua de São Sebastião; 281 531 232

The Phoenicians, Greeks and Romans all made use of Castro Marim's commanding location above the Rio Guadiana. It was the gateway to the Moorish Al-Gharb and for centuries it was a sanctuary for fugitives from the Inquisition. The castle above the town is of Moorish origin, the outlying walls a 13th-century addition, and sits beside the 17th-century Misericórdia church.

The town was also a centre for salt production, and the surrounding *salinas* are now home to the Reserva Natural do Sapal. Extending for 21 sq km (8 sq miles) south and east of town, this is an area of saltpans and marshes with a large variety of bird species including flamingos, avocets and black-winged stilts, symbol of the reserve. Individuals don't need to book, but group tours should book on 281 531 257.

24

Alcoutim

 F7 **i** Rua 1° de Maio; 281 546 179

The tiny, gem-like, unspoiled village of Alcoutim lies 15 km (9 miles) from the border with the Alentejo, and on the natural border with Spain, the Rio Guadiana. The drive there along the N122-2, a rough, winding road which sometimes runs alongside the Guadiana, provides stunning views of the countryside and across the river to Sanlúcar in Spain.

The size of Alcoutim belies its history. As a strategic location and river port, it was seized on by the Phoenicians, Greeks, Romans and, of course, the Moors, who stayed until the Reconquest in 1240. Here, in

→

Inside the castle housing the Archaeological Museum of Alcoutim

1371, on flower-decked boats midway between Alcoutim and its Spanish counterpart, Sanlúcar de Guadiana, King Fernando I of Portugal signed the peace of Alcoutim with Enrique II of Castile. By the late 17th century, when its political importance had waned, the town had acquired a new reputation – for smuggling tobacco and snuff from Spain.

Alcoutim today is a town of cobbled streets, small squares and a paved promenade along the riverfront. A few cafés and restaurants overlook the river, making them ideal spots from which to watch boats go by. The nearby church originates from the 16th century, but has been rebuilt. Over the porch are the arms of the marquises of Vila Real and counts of Alcoutim. The walls of the 14th-century castle give an excellent view over the small village and its idyllic setting. The castle houses a small archaeological museum exhibiting artifacts from the Iron Age.

Alcoutim's most unique visitor attraction is an exhilarating cross-border zip line (p31), set over the river that divides Spain and Portugal.

(p31)

SHOP

Casa das Portas
This well-stocked gift shop is located near the Roman bridge. Inside is a collection of books, soaps and other home decor items, including photos of the town's picturesque windows and doorways.

F7 Rua Dr. Augusto da Silva Carvalho 3, Tavira **281 321 025** Sun

---

Mercado Municipal
Olhão's municipal market is the best in the region. It is set in two buildings – one for fresh fish, the other for fruit and vegetables.

E7 Avenida 5 de Outubro, Olhão 7am-2pm Mon-Sat

PORTUGAL'S ISLANDS

Bottlenose dolphins swimming near the island of Madeira

Corvo

Flores

Graciosa

Faial   Terceira

São Jorge

Pico

São Miguel

THE AZORES
p364

Santa Maria

EXPLORE
PORTUGAL'S
ISLANDS

**This section divides Portugal's Islands into two colour-coded
sightseeing areas, as shown on the map below. Find out
more about each area on the following pages.**

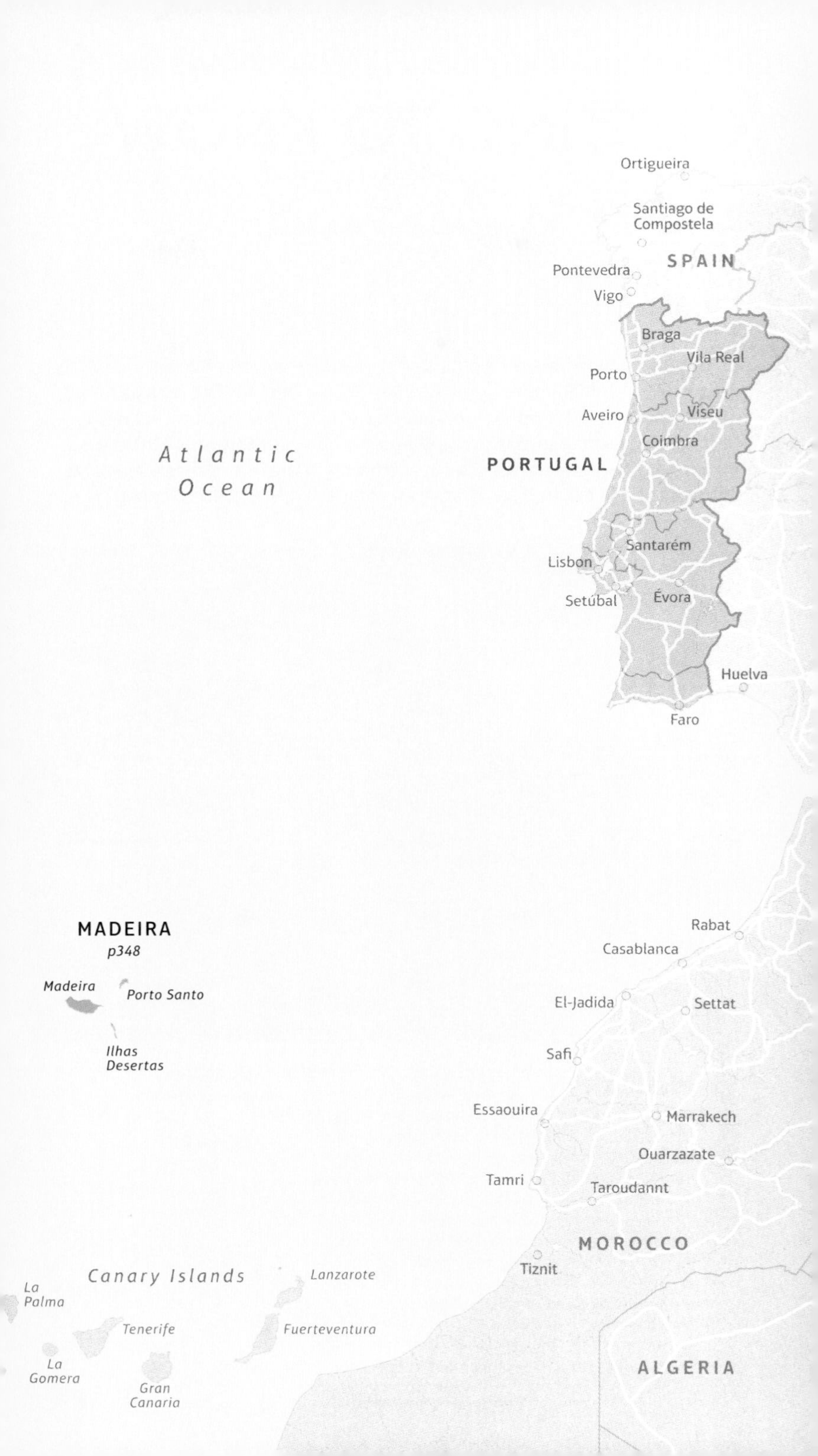

Ortigueira

Santiago de
Compostela

SPAIN

Pontevedra

Vigo

Braga

Vila Real

Porto

Viseu

Aveiro

Coimbra

*Atlantic
Ocean*

PORTUGAL

Santarém

Lisbon

Setúbal

Évora

Huelva

Faro

MADEIRA
p348

Rabat

Casablanca

Madeira   *Porto Santo*

El-Jadida

Settat

*Ilhas
Desertas*

Safi

Essaouira

Marrakech

Ouarzazate

Tamri

Taroudannt

MOROCCO

Canary Islands   *Lanzarote*

Tiznit

*La
Palma*

Tenerife   *Fuerteventura*

*La
Gomera*

*Gran
Canaria*

ALGERIA

GETTING TO KNOW
PORTUGAL'S
ISLANDS

Once remote maritime outposts, today Madeira and the Azores are easily accessible by air. Madeira, lying 600 km (375 miles) off the African coast, offers a beguiling blend of Portuguese culture and semitropical beauty. Further west, the Azorean archipelago, spread over 650 km (400 miles), is close to the Mid-Atlantic Ridge. The balmy climate and recently active volcanoes have created an alluring mix of lush valleys and collapsed craters.

PAGE 348

MADEIRA

Madeira's handsome historical capital, Funchal, is often called "Little Lisbon" because of its resemblance to the Portuguese capital. The rest of the island, however, has a completely different character to the Portuguese mainland. Much of its mountainous interior is covered in lauraceous forests so ancient that they have been awarded UNESCO World Heritage status. The network of irrigation canals called *levadas* attracts keen walkers to this compact island, while the surrounding seas draw watersports enthusiasts, and those hoping to spot whales and dolphins.

Best for
Year-round warm weather and alluring scenery

Home to
Funchal

Experience
The infamous Monte Toboggan, a hair-raising 2-km (1-mile) descent in a wicker basket on runners

THE AZORES

With few beaches, a capricious climate and no large-scale resorts, the Azores has escaped mass tourism. Come here to explore green mountains decked with blue hydrangeas, swim in waters brimming with marine creatures and relax in quiet ports where the pace of life is refreshingly civil and unhurried. The largest settlements are São Miguel's Ponta Delgada – the regional capital – and the charming, historic town of Angra do Heroísmo on Terceira. But to get firmly off-grid, where better than Pico, a towering 2,350-m (7,700-ft) volcanic peak.

Best for
Getting away from it all

Home to
São Miguel

Experience
The majesty of some of the ocean's largest creatures aboard a whale-watching trip from either Faial, Pico, Graciosa, Terceira or São Miguel

From whale-watching trips to walking along volcanic craters, the Azores is packed with things to see and do. Here we select some of the highlights to help you plan a week's stay.

7 DAYS

In the Azores

Day 1

Morning Explore Ponta Delgada, the capital of São Miguel *(p368)*. Start off at the Portas da Cidade, the iconic city gate in the main square, then walk along the harbour front, with its outdoor cafés and ocean views.

Afternoon The greenhouses of Arruda Açores Pineapple Plantation are found 3 km (2 miles) from the city centre. Take the tour, and be sure to buy some of the fruit, then return to Ponte Delgada for a reasonably priced steak dinner at Alcides *(p373)*.

Day 2

Morning Spend the day chilling out. Head east to the spa resort of Furnas, famed for its geothermal activity *(p369)*. Bathing in natural hot springs and indulging in modern spa treatments makes for a relaxing start to the day.

Afternoon The beautiful Parque Terra Nostra has some wonderful warm swimming pools for an afternoon dip. Be sure to order *cozido das Furnas* for dinner at

O Miroma *(p373)*. After eating your fill, head to bed at the luxurious Terra Nostra Garden Hotel *(p375)*.

Day 3

Morning In the northwest of the island is the Lagoa das Sete Cidades *(p368)*, the legendary twin blue and green lakes that fill a dormant volcanic crater. Walk along the path that traverses the circumference of the crater, pausing at the Miradouro da Vista do Rei to admire the view of the lakes below.

Afternoon Hire a bike to explore the stunning scenery around the small village of Sete Cidades, which sits in the crater. Its Neo-Gothic church is well worth a visit.

Day 4

Morning Take a flight to the island of Terceira and visit Angra do Heroísmo, the island's historic and strikingly unspoiled capital *(p370)*. The top of Monte Brasil, which overlooks the harbour, is our choice for the perfect picnic spot.

1 The Portas da Cidade gate in Ponta Delgada at dusk.

2 Lagoa das Sete Cidades.

3 Angra do Heroísmo harbour.

4 Orcas off the Azores.

5 The cloud-shrouded peak of Pico, seen in the distance.

Afternoon Curated with considerable flair, the Museu de Angra do Heroísmo traces Terceira's evolution from the arrival of the Portuguese in the 13th century to 19th-century industrialization. Spend the afternoon here learning about the island.

Day 5

Morning Hire a car to explore the volcanic interior of Terceira. Visit the Caldeira de Guilherme Moniz, a massive crater with impressive lava caves and crystal-clear springs, and the Algar do Carvão, an ancient volcanic vent. A little further north, roam the island's protected laurel forests on foot.

Afternoon Head north to Biscoitos and learn about wine production at the Museu do Vinho dos Biscoitos, stopping off for a swim at one of the nearby sea pools.

Day 6

Morning Fly to Pico, whose volcanic peak is the highest point in Portugal (p373). Make your way to the tiny town of Lajes

do Pico, which runs whale-watching trips in summer: there's a good chance you'll see some of the 28 species of cetaceans that pass through these waters.

Afternoon Back on dry land, the Museu dos Baleeiros charts the history of whaling in the Azores. Spend the night at Aldeia da Fonte, a small, eco-friendly resort with its own sea pool (p375).

Day 7

Morning Return to São Miguel and spend your last morning visiting the Museu Carlos Machado in Ponta Delgada to learn about Azorean island life.

Afternoon Fly to the mainland, or home, from São Miguel, feeling satisfied that you've experienced the highlights of these spectacular islands.

MADEIRA

Madeira is a mere dot in the Atlantic Ocean, 600 km (375 miles) from Morocco and nearly 1,000 km (620 miles) from Lisbon. Despite this, Madeira and Porto Santo, its sister island, appear on a Genoese map of 1351. They remained unclaimed, however, until 1418, when João Gonçalves Zarco was blown out into the Atlantic by violent storms while exploring the coast of Africa. Zarco found safe harbour in Porto Santo, returning on a voyage sponsored by Henry the Navigator. Early in 1420, after a winter on Porto Santo, he set sail for the mist-shrouded land on the horizon. He found a beautiful, thickly wooded island (*madeira* means wood), with abundant fresh water. Within seven years, the island had attracted a pioneer colony and the early settlers exploited the fertile soil and warm climate to grow sugar cane. The islanders grew rich on this, and enslaved people were brought in to work the land and create the terraced fields and irrigation channels (*levadas*) that still cling to the steep hillsides to this day.

Despite the gradients, Madeirans make use of every spare patch of land – growing bananas, flowers and grapes – although tourism is the main industry. The island's Laurisilva, or laurel forest, is a UNESCO World Heritage Site.

MADEIRA

Must See

1 Funchal

Experience More

2 Monte
3 Quinta do Palheiro Ferreiro
4 Camacha
5 Machico
6 Caniçal
7 Santana
8 Ribeiro Frio

9 Pico do Arieiro
10 Pico Ruivo
11 Paúl de Serra
12 Curral das Freiras
13 São Vicente
14 Porto Moniz
15 Calheta
16 Ribeira Brava
17 Câmara de Lobos
18 Porto Santo

PORTO SANTO ⑱

Ilhéu da Fonte
da Areia

Ilhéu
das Cenouras

Camacha

Serra de Dentro

Ponta
do Varadouro

Farrobo

Serra de
Fora

Porto Santo
Airport

Tanqué

Ponta
dos Ferreiros

Campo de Cima

Vila
Baleira

Ponta da Galé

Ilhéu
de Cima

Ilhéu
de Ferro

Cabeço da Ponta

Zimbralinho

Ponta

Ponta
da Calheta

Ilhéu de Baixo
ou da Cal

↓ Funchal
75 km (46 miles)

Ponta de
São Jorge

São Jorge

Ponta de Santana

Ribeira
Funda

Achada da Cruz

⑦ SANTANA

Ilha

Faial

Achada
do Marques

Queimadas

R101

Pico Canário
△ 1,592 m (5,223 ft)

R116

Porto da Cruz

Achada do
Teixeira

R103

Cruzinhas

Ponta do
Espigão Amarelo

Ponta de
São Lourenço

⑩ PICO RUIVO

Refeita

Maiatá

△ Pico da Coroa
738 m (2,421 ft)

Prainha

Pico das Torres
△ 1,851 m
(6,073 ft)

Balcões
860 m △
(2,822 ft)

Portela

Maroços

R109

⑥

Ilhéu
da Cevada

⑧ RIBEIRO
FRIO

Ribeira
de Machico

Ribeira Seca

CANIÇAL

Ilhéu
do Farol

⑨ PICO DO
ARIEIRO

R202

R202

R102

Santo António
da Serra

⑤ MACHICO

Esteios
1,346 m △
(4,416 ft)

Passo de Poiso
1,400 m (4,593 ft)

R203

João Ferino

Água de Pena

Porto Santo
75 km (46 miles) →

Pico Alto
1,129 m (3,704 ft)

Choupana

Águas
Mansas

Terra

R107

R103

② MONTE

R102

④ CAMACHA

Cristiano Ronaldo
International Airport

Santo
António

São João
de Latão

Gaula

Santa Cruz

R101

São
Gonçalo

③ QUINTA DO
PALHEIRO FERREIRO

R101

São
Martinho

① FUNCHAL

Caniço

Garajau

Caniço de Baixo

Ponta da Oliveira

MADEIRA

0 kilometres   5

0 miles   5

N
↑

The yellow façades of buildings on the front of Funchal's harbour ↑

❶ FUNCHAL

🅰B7 ✈Cristiano Ronaldo International Airport, 18 km (11 miles) NE 🚌Avenida do Mar 🚢 ℹAvenida Arriaga 16; 291 145 305

The deep natural harbour of Madeira's capital, Funchal, attracted early settlers in the 15th century. The city's historic core still overlooks the harbour and has an air of grandeur, with its stately 18th-century houses.

① Sé

🅰Largo da Sé 📞291 228 155 🕐7:15am–6:30pm Mon–Fri, 7:15am–noon & 4–7pm Sat, 7:30am–noon & 4:15–7pm Sun

The cathedral is one of the few buildings in Madeira to have survived virtually untouched since the early days of the island's colonization. In the 1490s, King Manuel I sent the architect Pêro Anes from the mainland to work on the Sé and it was finally completed in 1514.

Highlights of the building are the ceiling and the choir stalls, though neither is easy to see in the dark interior. The ceiling of inlaid wood is best seen from the south transept, where enough light filters in to illuminate the intricate patterning. The choir stalls depict saints, prophets and Apostles in 16th-century costume.

② Museu de Arte Sacra

🅰Rua do Bispo 21 📞291 228 900 🕐10am–5:30pm Mon–Fri (to 1:30pm Sat) 🚫Public hols

Madeiran merchants sought to secure their salvation by commissioning works of art, embroidered vestments and illuminated hymn books for their churches. Hundreds of examples now fill this museum, which is housed in the 17th-century bishop's palace. There are some masterpieces in the collection, such as the late-Gothic processional cross donated by King Manuel I, and paintings by major Flemish artists of the 15th and 16th centuries. Some works include portraits of the dignitaries who commissioned them. For example, *Saints Philip and James* shows Simão Gonçalves de Câmara.

$\rightarrow$
Manueline-style window frame in the gardens of the Museu Quinta das Cruzes

③

Museu Quinta das Cruzes

🏛 Calçada do Pico 1
🕐 10am–5:30pm Tue–Sat
🚫 Public hols 🌐 mqc.
madeira.gov.pt

It is said that Zarco, the man who claimed Madeira for Portugal, built his house where the Quinta das Cruzes now stands. The elegant 19th-century mansion is now the Museum of Decorative Arts, and it is furnished as a wealthy Madeiran sugar merchant's house with Indian silk wall hangings, Regency sideboards and Eastern carpets. On the ground floor, look out for the examples of furniture made from mahogany packing cases. In the 17th century, these would have been used for shipping sugar before being turned into charming chests and cupboards when the sugar trade moved to Brazil in the 18th century.

The romantic garden is dotted with ancient tombstones and architectural fragments. These include two window frames from 1507 carved with rope motifs, acrobatic figures and man-eating lions in a Madeiran version of the Manueline style of architecture (*p19*).

Did You Know?

Funchal is named after the fennel (*funcho* in Portuguese) which grew in abundance on the island.

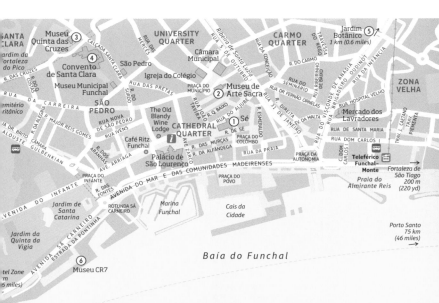

0 metres   250
0 yards   250

N ↑

The interior of the Convento de Santa Clara, with its beautiful *azulejos*

SHOP

Mercado dos Lavradores

Full of the colour and bustle of island life, the Mercado dos Lavradores attracts flower-growers, basket-weavers, farmers and fishers from all over Madeira. Stallholders offer slices of mango to punters and marble tables are draped with great slabs of tuna and black-skinned scabbard fish, with huge eyes and razor-sharp teeth.

🏠 Largo dos Lavradores
📞 291 214 080 🕐 Mon-Sat 🚫 Public hols

---

④

Convento de Santa Clara

🏠 Calçada de Santa Clara
📞 291 742 602 🕐 For renovations

The Convento de Santa Clara was founded in 1496 by João Gonçalves de Câmara, one of Zarco's grandsons. Zarco himself is buried under the high altar, and Martim Mendes Vasconcelos, his son-in-law, has a tomb at the rear of the church. Precious 17th-century *azulejo* tiles cover the walls.

⑤

Jardim Botânico

🏠 Quinta do Bom Sucesso, Caminho do Meio 📞 291 211 200 🕐 Daily

Established in 1960, the Botanical Gardens display plants from all over the world. Desert cactuses, rainforest orchids and South African proteas are all represented here, as well as Madeiran dragon trees. There are contrasting sections: formal areas of bedding plants, which form a pink-and-yellow chessboard, quiet carp ponds and wild wooded parts.

→ The colourful, geometric flowerbeds in the Jardim Botânico

⑥ Museu CR7

🏠 Avenida Sá Carneiro, Praça do Mar 27
🕐 10am-5pm Mon-Fri
🌐 museucr7.com

You'll be greeted at this museum dedicated to Madeira's most famous son by a bronze statue of the footballer Cristiano Ronaldo (thankfully it's a lot more lifelike than the bust at Funchal's airport). Proclaimed as the best football player of the 21st century by some, Ronaldo has impressed the footballing world while representing Sporting Lisbon, Manchester United and Real Madrid. Here, he is most respected for his captaincy of the Portuguese team.

The museum houses more than 150 of Ronaldo's trophies, although many are replicas. You can admire various signed shirts, read gushing fan mail, and watch recordings of some of his greatest goals on an interactive timeline of his career.

⑦ Design Centre Nini Andrade Silva

🏠 Estrada da Pontinha, Forte de Nossa Senhora da Conceição 🕐 11am-7pm daily 🌐 niniandrade silva.com

Dedicated to one of the world's most renowned interior designers, this beautifully curated space showcases Nini Andrade Silva's highly original work. The Funchal-born artist has been awarded many national and international awards for her designs and her hotel interiors are often featured in glossy magazines.

As well as the permanent exhibition of Silva's work, the centre also hosts a dynamic

↑ Replica trophies on display in the Museu CR7

programme of temporary exhibitions by other cutting-edge designers.

Futuristic chairs and atmospheric lighting enhance the Design Centre's historic setting. Accessed via a lift, the centre sits atop the Forte de Nossa Senhora da Conceição – a seafort which was once home to Gonçalves Zarco. The views across the harbour from the fort, which was built on a rocky islet, are spectacular. Take advantage of the vistas by heading up to the DC Lounge Cafeteria or Restaurant DC Atelier for drinks or dinner once you've explored the exhibitions.

FUNCHAL'S LIDOS

There are plenty of swimming opportunities in Madeira's capital. Locals tend to swim in the small Barreirinha Lido, next to the Fortaleza de São Tiago, or in the sea here. If the thought of swimming in the Atlantic makes you shiver, head to the municipal lido in the hotel zone, which has an Olympic-sized seawater pool, as well as slides and pools for kids. There are similar facilities to be found at the Complexo Balnear da Ponta Gorda.

EXPERIENCE MORE

❷ Monte

 B7 🚌 🚕 🛈 Avenida Arriaga 16, Funchal; 291 145 305

Monte has been a favourite destination for visitors since the late 19th century, when a rack-and-pinion railway was built to haul cruise liner passengers up the hillside from Funchal (now replaced by a *teleférico, p352*). Coming down, they would take the famous Monte Toboggan ride.

Toboggan-drivers in straw hats wait for passengers every day on the corner of Caminho do Monte, and they run (for a fee) to Livramento. From the church steps, past the drivers' corner, a left turn signposted "Old Monte Gardens" leads to the **Monte Palace Tropical Gardens**. These gardens feature areas devoted to Madeiran flora and plants from Japan and China, as well as azaleas, camellias and orchids. The museum exhibits precious stones and minerals, as well as contemporary Zimbabwean sculpture.

To reach the gardens, you pass the twin-towered church of Nossa Senhora do Monte. The Virgin of Monte is Madeira's patron saint and this church is the focal point of the pilgrimage that takes place on 15 August (when penitents climb the church's steps on their knees).

Monte Palace Tropical Gardens
⊛ 🕐 9:30am–6pm daily; museum: 10am–4:30pm 🚫 25 Dec 🌐 montepalace.com

---

GREAT VIEW
A Cable Car with a View

Accessed from the top end of Funchal's Jardim Botânico, this cable car passes high over the forested João Gomes river valley to hilltop Monte in just 10 minutes.

---

❸ Quinta do Palheiro Ferreiro

🅰 B7 🏠 Rua do Balançal, São Gonçalo 🚌 🕐 9am–5pm daily 🚫 1 Jan, 25 Dec 🌐 palheirogardens.com

A French landscape architect laid out the Quinta do Palheiro Ferreiro – Madeira's finest gardens – in the 18th century for the wealthy Count of Carvalhal, who built the elegant mansion (not open to visitors) and the Baroque chapel in the garden.

The estate was acquired in 1885 by the Anglo-Madeiran Blandy family, hence its English name: Blandy's Gardens. New species were introduced from South Africa, Australia and China, resulting in a garden that combines the clipped formality of late-18th-century layout with the profusion of English-style herbaceous borders, as well as tropical and temperate climate varieties.

↑ Viaduct that now forms part of the luxuriant Monte Palace Tropical Gardens

→ The 15th-century church on Machico's main square

STAY

Quinta do Furão
Surrounded by vineyards, this luxurious hotel offers a traditional restaurant, two pools and a spa.

🅰B7 🏠Estrada da Quinta do Furão 6, Santanal 🌐quintadofurao.com

€€€

Quinta da Casa Branca
A Modernist boutique hotel set in its own semitropical grounds, with a fabulous health centre and restaurant.

🅰B7 🏠Rua da Casa Branca 7, Funchal 🌐quintacasabranca.com

€€€

④
Camacha

🅰B7 *i* Avenida Arriaga 16, Funchal; 291 145 305

A monument in the centre of Camacha declares that Portugal's first-ever game of football was played here in 1875. Aside from that, the town is famous for its wicker basket industry, and you can still see occasional demonstrations of this traditional craft on the streets. A few walking trails pass through here, including the Levada dos Tornos and the Levada do Caniço.

Around October, the town hosts the Festa da Maçã (Apple Festival), which includes displays of traditional apple crushing to make cider, alongside concerts and a lively parade starting at the parish church.

---

⑤
Machico

🅰B7 *i* Avenida Arriaga 16, Funchal; 291 145 305

Legend has it that Machico was named after Robert Machim, a merchant from Bristol, who eloped with the aristocratic Anne of Hertford and set sail for Portugal. Caught in a storm and shipwrecked on Madeira, the two lovers died from exposure. The rest of the crew repaired the boat and sailed to Lisbon, where their story inspired Prince Henry the Navigator (*p328*) to send João Gonçalves Zarco in search of this mysterious wooded island.

Machico has been Madeira's second most important town since the first settlements. Funchal's superior location and harbour ensured that it developed as the capital of Madeira while Machico became a sleepy agricultural town.

The Igreja Matriz on Alameda Dr António Jardim d'Oliveira, dates from the 15th century. Across the water stream is the Capela dos Milagres (Chapel of the Miracles). The present structure dates from 1815, but it stands on the site of Madeira's first church. The earlier church of 1420 was destroyed in a flood in 1803, but the 15th-century crucifix was found floating out at sea. Machico celebrates the return of its cross with a procession on 8 October.

MONTE TOBOGGAN

Originally developed in the 1850s to transport produce to market, the toboggan now takes tourists on a thrilling 2-km (1-mile) descent from hilltop Monte to Livramento. The wicker baskets are steered by *carreiros* (toboggan-drivers) who control the speedy descent with their rubber-soled boots.

Did You Know?

Villages on the north coast of Madeira have sea-water pools for cooling dips.

6
Caniçal

 B7 🚌 ℹ️ Avenida Arriaga 16, Funchal; 291 145 305

Caniçal was once the centre of Madeira's whaling industry: the whaling scenes for John Huston's film version of *Moby Dick* (1956) were shot here. Whaling ceased in June 1981, and since then the waters around Madeira have been declared a marine mammal sanctuary – killing whales, dolphins and seals is now forbidden. Fishers who once hunted whales now help marine biologists at the Society for the Protection of Sea Mammals understand whale migrations.

The modern **Museu da Baleia** (Whaling Museum) illustrates the history of the island's whaling industry through hunting tools, artifacts and vintage photographs. There are also several life-like models of whales.

Museu da Baleia

⊘ 🏠 Rua Garcia Moniz 1 🕐 Tue–Sun 🔒 1 Jan, Easter Sun, 24, 25 & 26 Dec 🌐 museudabaleia.org

7
Santana

 B7 🚌 ℹ️ Rua do Sacristão, Sítio do Serrado; 291 575 162

Named after St Anne, mother of the Virgin Mary, Santana has more than 100 thatched triangular houses, several of which can be visited. The surrounding hillsides are also dotted with thatched byres. The **Parque Temático da Madeira** has a maze, a water mill and exhibits on various aspects of Madeira.

Santana valley is farmed for fruit and vegetables, and for osiers – the willow branches that provide the raw material for the wicker-workers of Camacha (*p357*).

THE TRIANGULAR HOUSES OF SANTANA

Constructed using two A-shaped timber frames, with a thatched roof, these triangular houses are unique to Madeira. The doors and windows are brightly painted and the interiors are surprisingly spacious.

Whale models hanging from the ceiling in the Museu da Baleia, Caniçal

and steep drops. Easier is the 45-minute walk on the left signposted to Balcões, which grants panoramic views across the Ametade water stream.

 9

Pico do Arieiro

🅰B7 🚌 To Camacha, then taxi

From Funchal it is about a 30-minute drive up the Pico do Arieiro, Madeira's third-highest mountain at 1,810 m (5,938 ft). The route leads through steep hillsides cloaked in eucalyptus and bay laurel. At the top, the spectacular view is of clouds in the valleys and dramatic mountain ridges with knife-edge peaks. On especially clear days you may be able to see the neighbouring island of Porto Santo.

 10

Pico Ruivo

🅰B7 🚌 To Santana or Faial, then taxi to Achada do Teixeira, then walk

Madeira's highest mountain at 1,861 m (6,105 ft), Pico Ruivo is only accessible on foot. The easiest way to scale its heights

EAT

Quinta do Furão
The terrace views here will take your breath away. The menu has a good range of fish, meat and vegetarian options.

🅰B7 🏠 Achada do Gramacho, near Santana quintadofurao.com

€€€

Vila do Peixe
Overlooking the harbour, this contemporary space serves sublime grilled fish from the daily catch.

🅰A7 🏠 Rua Dr João Abel de Freitas, Câmara de Lobos viladopeixe.com

€€€

is via a footpath that begins at the village of Achada do Teixeira and leads you on a 1.5 hour walk to the top.

Alternatively, follow the challenging route from the top of Pico do Arieiro, which involves negotiating narrow ridges with sheer drops on either side. Awe-inspiring mountain scenery and glorious views can be enjoyed all along the 10-km (6-mile) walk.

Parque Temático da Madeira
⊘ 🏠 Fonte da Pedra 🕐 Apr-Oct: 10am-7pm Tue-Sun (Nov-Mar: 9am-6pm) parque tematicodamadeira.pt

8

Ribeiro Frio

🅰B7 🚌 From Funchal

Ribeiro Frio is a pretty spot consisting of a couple of restaurants, shops and a trout farm, fed by the "cold stream" after which the place is named.

Surrounding the trout farm is an attractive garden full of native trees and shrubs. This is the starting point for two of the island's best *levada* walks *(p362)*. The 12-km (7-mile) path signposted to Portela (on the right past the restaurants) passes through dramatic mountain scenery but is best left to experienced walkers because of the long tunnels

Walking the trail along the red peaks at the summit of Pico Ruivo ↑

Steep road twisting and turning on the way up to the Paúl da Serra ↑

⑪
Paúl da Serra

 A7 ☐ To Canhas, then taxi

The Paúl da Serra (literally meaning "high moorland") is a large, boggy plateau, extending 17 km (11 miles) in length and 6 km (4 miles) in width. The plain contrasts dramatically with the jagged mountains that characterize the rest of Madeira.

Electricity for the north of the island is generated here by wind turbines. Only gorse and grass grow on the thin soil, and the sponge-like volcanic substrata act as a natural reservoir for rainfall. Water filters through the rock to emerge as springs which then feed the island's *levada* system (p362).

⑫
Curral das Freiras

 B7 ☐ ℹ Avenida Arriga 16, Funchal; 291 145 305

Curral das Freiras means "Nuns' Refuge" and the name refers to the nuns of the Santa Clara convent who fled to this idyllic spot when pirates attacked Funchal in 1566. The nuns have left now, but the village remains. Visitors first glimpse Curral das Freiras from a viewpoint known as the Eira do Serrado, perched some 800 m (2,625 ft) above the village.

The valley is surrounded on all sides by jagged mountain peaks. Until 1959, the only access to the village was by a steep zigzagging path, but road tunnels now make the journey much easier and allow local people to transport their produce to the capital. Television arrived in 1986.

The sweet chestnuts that grow in profusion around the village are turned into sweet chestnut bread, best eaten still warm from the oven, and *licor de castanha*, a chestnut-flavoured liqueur. Both can be sampled in local bars.

MADEIRA WINE

In the 16th century, ships stopping at Funchal would take on barrels of local wine. This unfortified Madeira often spoiled during the voyage, so shippers started adding spirit to preserve it. The wine then seemed to improve after a long, hot voyage, and quality Madeira began to be sent on round trips as an alternative to maturing it in Funchal's lodges. This expensive method was replaced with the *estufa* system, still very much in use today. Large volumes of wine are heated to between 30 and 50°C (86 and 122°F) for a period of three months to a year. The effect is to hurry up the ageing process: the best wines are "cooked" more gently and slowly. The finest Madeirans are heated by the sun, maturing slowly in the attics of the wine lodges. Most Madeira is made from the Tinta Negra Mole grape, often blended with either Sercial, Bual, Verdelho or Malmsey.

coast. To see how the village looked before development began, visit the Igreja Matriz, which was built in the 17th century, and look at the ceiling painting of St Vincent blessing the town. He appears again over the elaborately carved main altar, blessing a ship.

Around the church, cobbled traffic-free streets are lined with boutiques, bars and shops selling sweet cakes, including the popular Madeiran speciality *bolo de mel*, the so-called "honey cake" (actually made with molasses and fruit).

Nearly 20 m (65 ft) below the ground is a network of caves, the **Grutas e Centro do Vulcanismo de São Vicente**, which formed 850,000 years ago during a volcanic eruption. Visitors can walk the 1-km (0.6-mile) trail of excavated lava channels dripping with stalactites. By the caves' entrance is the Volcanism Centre. Inside, the centre presents audio-visual shows recreating the geological evolution of the caves, the eruption of a volcano and the birth of the Madeira archipelago.

Around 8 km (5 miles) northwest is Seixal. Despite the storms that batter the coast, this village occupies a remarkably sheltered spot, where vineyards cling to the hillside terraces, producing excellent wine.

⑬
São Vicente

🅐 A7 🚌 🛈 Avenida Arriaga 16, Funchal; 291 145 305

The agricultural town of São Vicente grew prosperous by tempting travellers to break their journeys here as they explored Madeira's northern

> **The agricultural town of São Vicente grew prosperous by tempting travellers to break their journeys here as they explored Madeira's northern coast.**

Grutas e Centro do Vulcanismo de São Vicente

🅐 Sitio do Pé do Passo
🕒 Until further notice, check website for details
🌐 grutasecentrodovulcanismosaovicente.com

The beautifully
↓ decorated interior of
São Vicente's church

⑭ Porto Moniz

A7 🚌 ℹ Rua dos Emigrantes, Vila do Porto Moniz; 291 853 075

It is only a 50-km (31-mile) journey to this remote coastal village, on the northwest tip of Madeira, from Funchal.

Porto Moniz is surrounded by a patchwork pattern of tiny fields that are protected by fences made from tree heather, a necessary precaution against the heavy, salt-laden air that blows in off the Atlantic. Apart from its picturesque charm, the main attraction at Porto Moniz is the series of natural rock pools on the foreshore, where you can swim in sun-warmed water.

⑮ Calheta

A7 🚌 ℹ Avenida Arriaga 16, Funchal; 291 145 305

Calheta sits at the centre of what sugar-cane production survives in Madeira. The smell of cane syrup being extracted and turned into rum hangs

THE LEVADAS OF MADEIRA

Madeira possesses a unique irrigation system that enables the plentiful rainfall of the north of the island to be distributed to the drier south. Rainfall is stored in reservoirs and lakes, or channelled from natural springs, and fed into the network of *levadas* that ring the island. These narrow channels carry water long distances to banana groves, vineyards and market gardens. There are 1,500 km (932 miles) of canals, some dating back to the 1500s.

1772
—
The date of the oldest surviving bottle of Madeira.

around the village from the factory. The **MUDAS. Museu de Arte Contemporânea da Madeira** provides a more contemporary setting. Picasso is among the artists whose work is exhibited here.

The Igreja Matriz looks modern but dates from 1430 and contains a large ebony and silver tabernacle donated by Manuel I. There is also a fine wooden ceiling.

Calheta's main attraction is its beach, being one of the only beaches with golden sands. In fact, the sand is imported from Africa and locals complain that it is only borrowed, as winter storms often wash it back to the continent again. This yearly loss doesn't stop hundreds of families descending on this sheltered beach.

MUDAS. Museu de Arte Contemporânea da Madeira

 ♿ 🅰 Estrada Simão Gonçalves da Câmara 37, Calheta 🕒 9:30am–1pm & 2–5:30pm Tue–Sat 🔒 Public hols 🌐 cultura.madeira.gov.pt

⑯ Ribeira Brava

A7 🚌 ℹ Forte de São Bento; 291 951 675

Ribeira Brava is a resort town, situated on the south coast of Madeira. It has a pebble beach and a fishing harbour, which is reached through a tunnel to the east of the main town.

Overlooking the principal square, São Bento is one of the Madeira's most unspoiled

churches. Despite restoration and reconstruction, several of its 16th-century features are still intact. These include a stone-carved font and an ornate pulpit decorated with wild beasts such as wolves, and the Flemish painting of the Nativity in the side chapel.

The engaging **Museu Etnográfico da Madeira** has exhibits illustrating Madeiran culture and society.

Museu Etnográfico da Madeira

🅰 Rua São Francisco 24 🕒 9:30am–5pm Tue–Fri, 10am–12:30pm & 1:30–5:30pm Sat 🔒 Public hols 🌐 cultura.madeira.gov.pt

⑰ Câmara de Lobos

A7 🚌 ℹ Avenida Arriaga 16, Funchal; 291 145 305

This pretty fishing village was painted by Winston Churchill, who often visited Madeira in the 1950s. Bars and restaurants are named in his honour and a plaque marks the spot on the main road, east of the harbour,

São Bento church with a charming clock tower, Ribeira Brava ↑

where the British statesman set up his easels. This is one of Madeira's main centres for catching scabbard fish *(peixe espada)*, which feature on every local menu. Long lines are baited with octopus to catch these fish that dwell at depths of between 800 m (2,600 ft) and 1,600 m (5,250 ft). The fishers live in dwellings along the harbour front, and their tiny chapel dates from the 15th century, but was rebuilt in 1723. The chapel is dedicated to St Nicholas, the patron saint of seafarers, and is decorated with scenes from the saint's life, as well as vivid portrayals of drownings and shipwrecks.

HIDDEN GEM
Jardim do Mar

Near Calheta, you'll find one of Madeira's most delightful villages. Sitting below cliffs, Jardim do Mar befits its name, "Garden by the Sea". Take a stroll down its seafront promenade or through its twisting-turning alleyways.

18
Porto Santo

🅰C6 ➡️🚢 *i* Avenida Dr Manuel Gregório Pestana Júnior; 291 985 244

Porto Santo, an island 37 km (23 miles) northeast of Madeira, is smaller, flatter and drier than its sister island. It possesses something that Madeira lacks: a natural beach of golden sand, running the entire length of the island's south coast. There is a daily ferry between Funchal and Porto Santo, which takes 2 hours and 30 minutes. There are also daily flights that take just 15 minutes.

↑ Part of Porto Santo's splendid 9-km (5.5-mile) sandy beach

Porto Santo is a popular holiday destination, with hotels and holiday resorts of villas and apartments. Snorkelling is good and bicycles can be hired.

The **Casa de Colombo** (House of Christopher Columbus) is built from rough stone, and contains exhibits that tell Columbus's story.

Casa de Colombo

🏠 Travessa da Sacristia 2, Vila Baleira 📞 291 983 405 🕙 10am–12:30pm & 2–5:30pm Tue–Sat (Jul–Sep: to 7pm), 10am–1pm Sun

THE AZORES

Santa Maria was the first of the nine islands of the Azores where the Portuguese landed (in 1427), beginning a wave of settlement in the 15th and 16th centuries by colonists from Portugal and Flanders. The archipelago was named after the buzzards the early explorers saw flying overhead and mistook for goshawks *(açores)*.

The Azores have profited from their far-flung position in the Atlantic. Between 1580 and 1640, when Portugal came under Spanish rule, the ports of Angra do Heroísmo on Terceira and Ponta Delgada on São Miguel prospered from the trade with the Americas. In the 19th century, the islands were a regular port of call for American whaling ships, and during the 20th century they benefited from their use as stations for transatlantic cable companies, meteorological observatories and military air bases.

Today, the majority of islanders are involved in either dairy farming or fishing, and close links are maintained with both mainland Portugal and the sizeable communities of emigrant Azoreans in the United States and Canada. Once a brave new world of pioneer communities, the Azores are now an autonomous region of Portugal and a distinctive corner of the European Union.

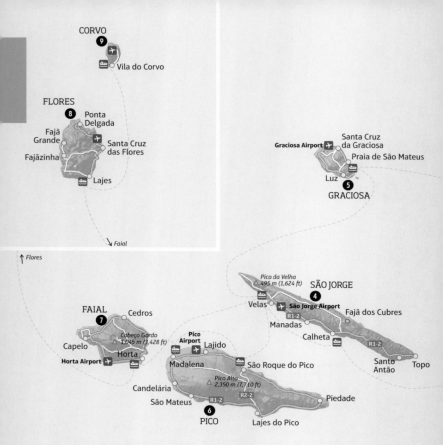

THE AZORES

Must See

1 São Miguel

Experience More

2 Santa Maria
3 Terceira
4 São Jorge
5 Graciosa
6 Pico
7 Faial
8 Flores
9 Corvo

0 kilometres   20

0 miles   20

N

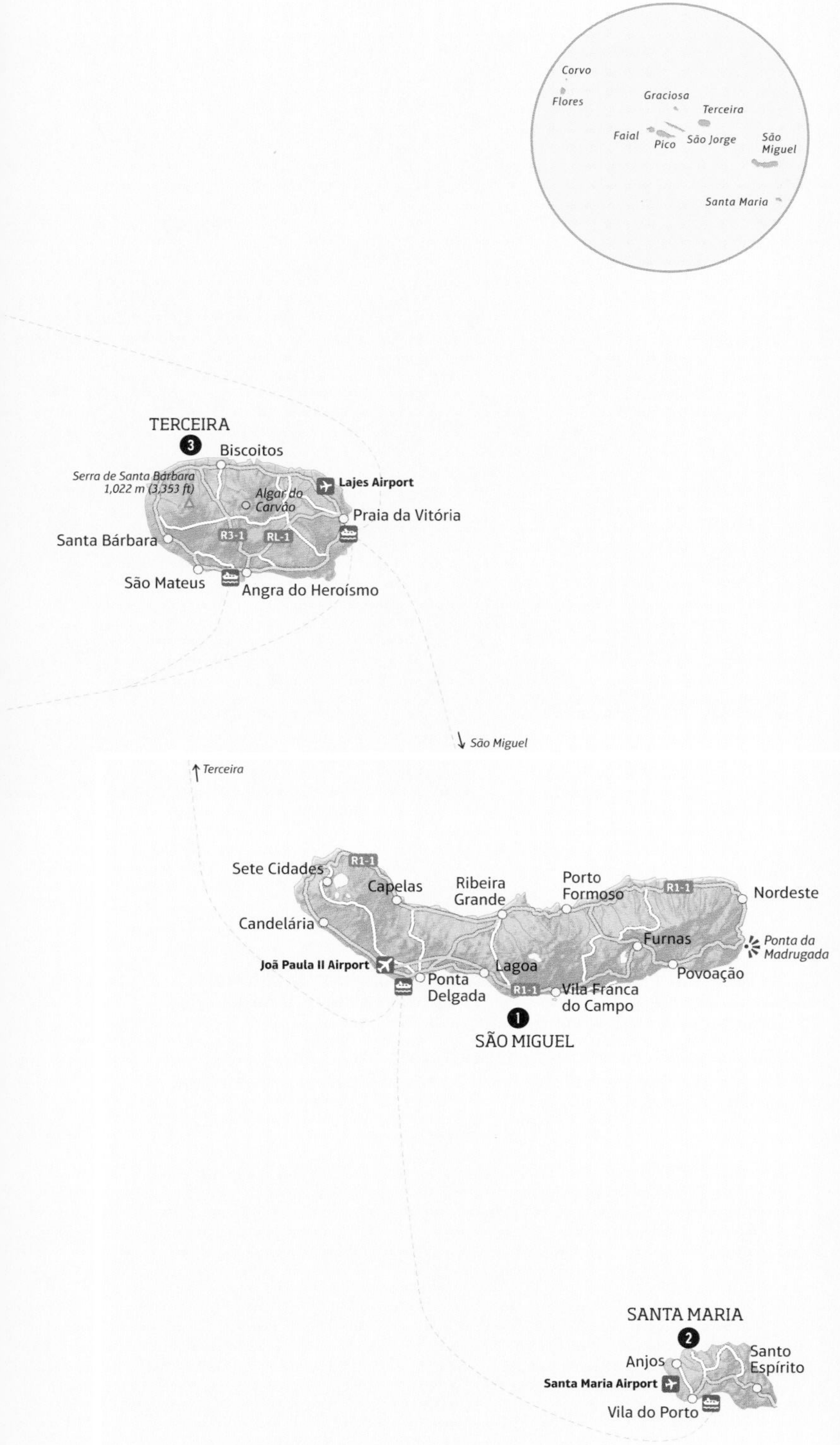

TERCEIRA

❸ Biscoitos

Serra de Santa Bárbara
1,022 m (3,353 ft)

Algar do Carvão

✈ **Lajes Airport**

Praia da Vitória

Santa Bárbara

`R3-1` `RL-1`

São Mateus

Angra do Heroísmo

↓ *São Miguel*

↑ *Terceira*

Sete Cidades

`R1-1`

Capelas

Ribeira Grande

Porto Formoso

`R1-1`

Nordeste

Candelária

Furnas

☀ *Ponta da Madrugada*

Joã Paula II Airport ✈

Ponta Delgada

Lagoa

`R1-1`

Vila Franca do Campo

Povoação

❶

SÃO MIGUEL

SANTA MARIA

❷

Anjos

Santo Espírito

Santa Maria Airport ✈

Vila do Porto

The turquoise water of the majestic Lagoa das Sete Cidades ↑

❶ SÃO MIGUEL

🅰C5 🚗3 km (2 miles) W of Ponta Delgada 🚢Ponta Delgada 🚌Avenida Infante Dom Henrique, Ponta Delgada 🛈Avenida Infante Dom Henrique, Ponta Delgada; visitazores.com

With its historic maritime capital, rich green fields and dramatic volcanic scenery, beautiful São Miguel island provides a rewarding introduction to the Azores.

The largest and most populated of the archipelago's nine islands, São Miguel is 65 km (40 miles) long. The capital, Ponta Delgada, is a good base from which to make day tours of São Miguel's rugged coast or visit the volcanic crater lakes and steaming thermal springs in the interior of the island. Lined with many impressive churches, convents and trim white houses, the cobbled streets of the Azorean capital recall the wealthy days when the port was a crucial staging post between Europe and the Americas.

Northwest of Ponta Delgada, the west of the island is punctured by a giant volcanic crater, Lagoa das Sete Cidades, with a 12-km (7-mile) circumference. In places, its sheer walls drop like green curtains for 300 m (1,000 ft).

To the city's east, the Lagoa do Fogo, "Lake of Fire", was formed in the island's central mountains by a volcanic eruption in 1563. On sunny days its remote sandy beach is a tranquil picnic spot. On the island's east coast, the Miradouro da Ponta da Madrugada is a popular spot for watching the sunrise.

GREAT VIEW
Lake Vistas

When not obscured by cloud, the Lagoa das Sete Cidades is best seen from the Vista do Rei. After admiring the turquoise crater from this viewpoint, follow the 12-km (7-mile) trail around its rim.

Did You Know?

São Miguel is often called *Ilha Verde* (the green island).

① Porto Formoso, on the north coast of the island, is renowned for its tea plantations, which tumble down to the sea.

② Scattered around the town of Furnas are the Caldeiras das Furnas. These hot bubbling springs provide the therapeutic mud and mineral water used for the town's spa treatments.

③ In front of the 17th-century façade of Ponta Delgada's town hall, you'll find a statue of St Michael the Archangel, the island's patron saint.

EXPERIENCE MORE

❷ Santa Maria

🅰C6 ✈3 km (2 miles) NW of Vila do Porto 🚌Vila do Porto 🚏Rua Dr Luís Bettencourt, Vila do Porto 🛈 Aeroporto de Santa Maria, Vila do Porto; 296 886 355

Santa Maria lies 55 km (34 miles) south of São Miguel. Though only 17 km (11 miles) long, it has great scenic variety and features sandy beaches, tranquil countryside and the warmest climate in the Azores.

The island's capital, Vila do Porto, is on the south coast and consists of a long main street that runs down to a small harbour. The west of the island is a dry, flat plateau with a vast airstrip built in World War II. To the north lies the fishing town of Anjos, where a statue commemorates a visit made by Christopher Columbus in 1493 on his return from the Americas. Next to it, the small, whitewashed chapel of Nossa Senhora dos Anjos is the oldest in the Azores.

The highest point of Santa Maria is the central Pico Alto, 590 m (1,935 ft) above sea level, which on a clear day offers fine views over the green and hilly east side of the island. Towards the east coast, the village of Santo Espírito is worth visiting for the white Baroque façade of its church of Nossa Senhora da Purificação, adorned with black lava decoration, while the vine-covered half-crater of Baía de São Lourenço, north of here, is a delightful summer beach resort.

❸ Terceira

🅰B5 ✈3 km (2 miles) NW of Praia da Vitória 🚌Angra do Heroísmo, Praia da Vitória 🚏Avenida 1° de Maio, Angra do Heroísmo 🛈 Rua Direita 70–74 Angra do Heroísmo, 295 404 810; Praia da Vitória Aerogare Civil das Lajes, 295 513 140

Terceira is the most developed of the five central islands and is known for the brightly painted chapels (impérios) devoted to the cult of the Holy Spirit. The large, oval-shaped island's interior mainly consists of gentle green pastureland and laurel forest, while the coast has barren areas of black lava.

1983

Angra do Heroísmo is classified as a World Heritage Site by UNESCO.

For over three centuries, the city of Angra do Heroísmo was a stopover point on the routes between Europe, America and Africa, and in the early 17th century its harbour glittered with Spanish fleets returning laden with treasure from the Americas. The city's wealthy past is reflected in the pretty streets lined with balconied houses. In 1983, the historic centre of the city was classified as a World Heritage Site by UNESCO.

The most spectacular view of the harbour is from Monte Brasil, a volcanic crater on the western side of the bay. Beside this popular picnic spot stands the fort, Fortaleza de São João Baptista, built during Spain's annexation of Portugal (p44) as a treasure store, and still in military use. A second rewarding viewpoint is from the Alto da Memória at the south end of Rua São João de Deus, from where the twin towers of the 16th-century Sé are easily seen. A path leads down into the Jardim Duque da Terceira, the city's restful public gardens. These once formed part of the 15th-century Convento de São Francisco, which now houses the **Museu de Angra do Heroísmo**. The museum's exhibits reflect the history

Pretty windmill standing on the outskirts of Vila do Porto, Santa Maria

of the Azores and the city, and include armour, maps, paintings and sculptures. Away from the capital, the island's centre bears witness to its volcanic origins: the Caldeira de Guilherme Moniz is an eroded crater 3 km (2 miles) wide and one of the largest in the Azores. Nearby, the **Algar do Carvão** is a dramatic volcanic blast-hole, thick with dripping moss, where visitors can tour a huge subterranean cave. West of here, the Furnas do Enxofre are hot steaming fumaroles where the sulphur vapours crystallize into coloured formations.

Two viewpoints overlooking the island can be reached by car: in the west, a road bordered with blue hydrangeas winds up through the Serra de Santa Bárbara to a vast lonely crater, while the eastern Serra do Cume overlooks the airport and Praia da Vitória. This port has a large bay with a sandy beach. On the north coast, Biscoitos (which means "biscuits") takes its name from the rubble of biscuit-like lava spread along the shore. Exhilarating swimming pools have been created among the

↑ Looking over Angra do Heroísmo, Terceira's capital

rocks. The area is also known for its wine, and the land is covered in a chessboard of stone-walled pens built to shelter vines. The **Museu do Vinho** explains the simple production methods used to produce the rich Verdelho wine that was once exported to the Russian court, and offers the chance to taste and purchase today's vintages.

Museu de Angra do Heroísmo
🏠 Ladeira de São Francisco 🕐 Apr–Sep: 10am–5:30pm Tue–Sun; Oct–Mar: 9:30am–5pm Tue–Sun 🚫 Public hols 🌐 museu-angra.azores.gov.pt

Algar do Carvão
♿ 🏠 Off R5-2 🕐 Times vary, check website 🌐 montanheiros.com/algarCarvao

Museu do Vinho
🏠 Canada do Caldeiro 3 📞 965 667 324 🕐 1:30–4pm Tue–Sat

DRINK

Kalema Bar
Facing the beach, this laid-back bar offers affordable drinks, a games room and the occasional live music act.

🅰 B5 🏠 Estrada Gaspar Corte-Real, Angra do Heroísmo, Terceira 📞 2960 161 938 🕐 Mon

Cella Bar
Chic wine bar and restaurant that has won awards for its striking curved wooden extension, with porthole windows and a terrace offering awesome views of the coast.

🅰 B5 🏠 Lugar da Barca, Madalena, Pico 📞 292 623 654

④ São Jorge

⚠ B5 **➡ 7 km (4 miles) E of Velas** 🚢 **Velas & Calheta**
ℹ **Rua Conselheiro Dr José Pereira 1, Velas; 295 412 440**

São Jorge is a mountainous island that stretches for 55 km (34 miles) but is only 8 km (5 miles) wide. On its north coast, sheer cliffs drop to the sea. Over the centuries these cliffs have collapsed in places, creating tongues of land known as *fajãs* – UNESCO-recognized as Biosphere Reserves.

Today, many islanders on São Jorge are engaged in the production of a cured cheese, *queijo de São Jorge*. The pace of life is leisurely, and most visitors come to walk along the paths that climb between the *fajãs*. The most popular route is from Topo, on the east coast of the island, 10 km (6 miles) down to Fajã dos Cubres.

Most of the settlements lie along the gentler south coast, including the capital, Velas, and Calheta, where the **Museu Francisco de Lacerda** displays objects of local history such as the ornate breads baked for the Holy Spirit festival, a honey press, agricultural utensils and religious sculptures. West of Calheta, in the pretty parish of Manadas, the 18th-century church of Santa Bárbara has an atmospheric carved and painted interior.

Museu Francisco de Lacerda

⊛ 🏛 **Rua das Alcaçarias, Calheta** 🕐 **Apr–Sep: 10am–5:30pm Tue–Sun; Oct–Mar: 9:30am–5pm Tue–Sun**
🚫 **Public hols** 🌐 **museu-fran ciscolacerda.azores.gov.pt**

⑤ Graciosa

⚠ B5 **➡ 2 km (1 mile) W of Santa Cruz da Graciosa** 🚢 **Praia de São Mateus**
ℹ **Rua Dom João IV 28, Santa Cruz; 295 712 430**

Graciosa Island is one of the most peaceful places in the Azores, classified by UNESCO as a biosphere reserve. Only 12.5 km (8 miles) long, most of its low-lying land is given over to farms and vineyards where ox-drawn carts and ploughs are still in use. The capital, Santa Cruz da Graciosa, on the north coast, has a simple quayside backed by rows of stark, two-storey, whitewashed houses with wrought-iron balconies and oval windows. The **Museu da Graciosa** recalls life on this sleepy island with a homely miscellany of toys, sea chests, kitchenware, wine presses, furniture and mementos sent back by emigrants to North America. A building next door houses a whaling boat.

The picturesque Monte da Ajuda that rises behind the town is capped by a 16th-century fortified chapel, Nossa Senhora da Ajuda, decorated with 18th-century tiles.

In the southeast lies the **Furna do Enxofre**, where visitors can descend flights of steps into the bowels of a volcanic crater. At the bottom is a huge cave with a deep, sulphurous lake and peep-holes where bubbling brews of evil grey liquid can be spied beneath the rocks.

Above the cave, at Furna Maria Encantada, a natural tunnel leads to the edge of the crater, offering stunning views over the island. Treatments using the island's geothermal waters are available at the resort of Carapacho, at the foot of the volcano.

←

A pretty street leading to the church in Velas, on the island of São Jorge

← Walking along the lush and dramatic coastline of Pico

Museu da Graciosa

 🏠 Largo Conde de Simas 17, Santa Cruz 🕐 Apr-Sep: 10am-5:30pm Tue-Sun; Oct-Mar: 9:30am-5pm Tue-Sun 🚫 Public hols 🌐 museu-graciosa.azores.gov.pt

Furna do Enxofre

🏠 2 km (1 mile) E of Luz, follow signs to Caldeira 🕐 9am-12:30pm & 1:30-5pm Tue-Sat (Apr-Oct: daily)

---

❻
Pico

🅰 B5 ✈ 8 km (5 miles) E of Madalena 🚢 Madalena 🚌 Avenida Machado Serpa, Madalena 🛈 Gare Marítima, Madalena; 292 623 524

The majesty of Pico, the highest mountain in Portugal, becomes apparent when it is seen from the neighbouring central islands. Only then does one realize how gracefully this volcanic peak soars out of the Atlantic, shooting up 2,350 m (7,700 ft) to form the summit of the longest mountain range in the world, the Mid-Atlantic Ridge.

The island's largest town, Madalena, is a relaxed port that lies opposite Faial's capital, Horta. A regular ferry service crosses the 8 km (5 miles) between the two islands.

Many people come to Pico to climb its eponymous peak.

It is a strenuous climb, best done alongside a guide, and advance permission is needed.

Another draw in summer is whale-watching. From Lajes do Pico, groups are taken out in boats for 3-hour trips. The history of Azorean whaling is recalled at the **Museu dos Baleeiros**, also in Lajes. The whales were processed at a vast factory (closed down in 1984) on the north side of the island that now houses the **Museu da Indústria Baleeira**.

Minor eruptions have covered parts of the island's landscape with black mole-hills of lava that the islanders christened *mistérios* (mysteries). The black lava has been used to build houses and grids of stone walls that enclose fields or shelter vines. In some places, the eroded lava has formed curious arches in the sea.

The island's vineyards are a UNESCO World Heritage Site. A visitor's centre at Lajido explains Pico's viniculture, featuring the Verdelho wine.

Museu dos Baleeiros

 🏠 Rua dos Baleeiros 13, Lajes 📞 292 679 340 🕐 Apr-Sep: 10am-5:30pm Tue-Sun; Oct-Mar: 9:30am-5pm

Museu da Indústria Baleeira

 🏠 Rua do Poço, São Roque do Pico 📞 292 679 349 🕐 Apr-Sep: 10am-5:30pm Tue-Sun; Oct-Mar: 9:30am-5pm

---

EAT

O Petisca
Limpets, barnacles and tuna are among the specialities at this seafood restaurant.

🅰 B5 🏠 Avenida Padre Nunes da Rosa 9950, Madalena, Pico 📞 292 622 357 🚫 Wed L, Sun

 €€€

Restaurante Costa Sol
Close to the natural pools of Calheta, this place serves a mix of burgers and steaks.

🅰 B5 🏠 Largo da Calheta, Santa Cruz da Graciosa, Graciosa 📞 295 712 694 🚫 Sun

 €€€

Sal & Pico
Found inside the 16th-century Forte da Horta, this pleasant restaurant specializes in regional cuisine.

🅰 B5 🏠 Rua Vasco da Gama, Horta, Faial 🌐 pousadas.pt

 €€€

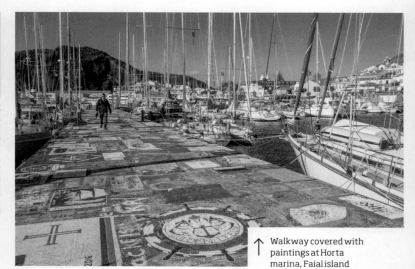

↑ Walkway covered with paintings at Horta marina, Faial island

❼ Faial

 B5 ✈ 10 km (6 miles) SW of Horta 🚢 Horta 🚌 Rua Vasco da Gama, Horta ℹ Rua Vasco da Gama, Horta; 292 292 237

Faial was settled by Flemish farmers in the 15th century and prospered with the development of Horta harbour as a stopover for ships and – more recently – flying boats crossing the Atlantic. Today it is a fertile island with a mild climate. It is known around the world as a yachting destination, and for the endless rows of colourful hydrangeas that bloom in June and July.

Stretching around a wide bay, Faial's capital Horta has been a convenient anchorage for caravels, clippers and sea

Did You Know?

Hydrangeas have blue flowers when grown in acidic soil, but produce pink blooms in alkaline conditions.

planes over the centuries. Today, visiting crews crossing between the Caribbean and Mediterranean paint a calling card on the quayside and celebrate their safe passage in Peter's Café Sport, which overlooks the harbour. In the upstairs rooms of the café, the **Museu de Scrimshaw** exhibits engraved whales' bones and teeth dating back to 1884. In the **Museu da Horta**, displays of antique furniture, portraits, nautical memorabilia and nostalgic photographs of the island's port are upstaged by miniature sculptures of liners and scenes of daily life, painstakingly carved from the white pith of fig trees.

Two viewpoints overlook Horta: to its south rises the volcanic peak of Monte da Guia, while the northern Miradouro da Espalamaca is guarded by a huge statue of Nossa Senhora da Conceição. Faial's other spectacular natural sight is the Vulcão dos Capelinhos in the far west of the island. A volcano erupted here in 1957–8, smothering a lighthouse that can now be seen buried in ash. Around it lies a scorched and barren landscape. The story of the eruption is told in the nearby

Centro de Interpretação do Vulcão dos Capelinhos, where multimedia displays trace the area's geological activity.

Museu de Scrimshaw

⊗ 🅰 Peter's Café Sport, Rua José Azevedo 9, Horta ☎ 292 292 327 🕒 Mon-Sat

Museu da Horta

⊗ 🅰 Largo Duque D'Ávila e Bolama ☎ 292 202 581 🕒 Apr-Sep: 10am-5:30pm Tue-Sun; Oct-Mar: 9:30am-5pm Tue-Sun 🗙 Public hols

Centro de Interpretação do Vulcão dos Capelinhos

⊗ 🅰 Farol dos Capelinhos ☎ 292 200 470 🕒 Apr-Oct: 9am-6pm daily; Nov-Mar: 9am-5pm Tue-Sat

❽ Flores

 A5 ✈ 1km (half a mile) N of Santa Cruz 🚢 Lajes 🚌 Centro de Saúde, Santa Cruz ℹ Rua Dr Armas da Silveira 1, Santa Cruz; 292 592 369

The island of "Flowers" is a romantic outpost that was not permanently settled until the

STAY

Aldeia da Fonte
An eco-friendly resort, with six rustic stone houses set in lush gardens, and its own sea pools.

B5 ☐ Caminho de Baixo 2, Lajes do Pico, Pico ☑ aldeia dafonte.com

€€€

Quinta das Buganvilias
This family-run estate offers charming rooms and apartments. Check out the bar in the old mill house.

B5 ☐ Castelo Branco, Horta, Faial ☑ quintadas buganvilias.com

€€€

Aldeia da Cuada
This abandoned village turned rural retreat is home to traditional stone houses, ranging from one to six bedrooms.

A5 ☐ Fajã Grande, Lajes das Flores, Flores ☑ aldeiadacuada.com

€€€

---

as fishing rods and a guitar made from whalebone.

The deep, verdant valleys of the south are punctuated with dramatic peaks, volcanic crater lakes and caves. The tranquil Lagoa Funda, 25 km (16 miles) southwest of Santa Cruz, is a lake at the base of a mountain.

The winding road continues northwards over the mountains and, as it descends towards the west coast, there are stunning views of the green valley and village of Fajãzinha. The resort of Fajã Grande, ringed by cliffs, is a popular base for walkers and impressive waterfalls plunge into the sea from the high cliffs. A short walk north from the town is the Cascata da Ribeira Grande, a towering jet of water that divides into smaller waterfalls before collecting in a still pool.

Museu da Fábrica da Baleia do Boqueirão
Rua do Boqueirão, Santa Cruz 292 542 932 Apr-Sep: 10am-5:30pm Tue-Sun; Oct-Mar: 9:30am-5pm Tue-Sun

Museu das Flores
 Edificio do Convento de São Boaventura 292 592 159 10am-5:30pm Tue-Sun & public hols; Oct-Mar: 9:30am-5pm Tue, Sun & public hols 1 Jan & 25 Dec

---

⑨
Corvo

A5 ☑ Vila do Corvo ☐ Rua da Matriz, Vila do Corvo ☐ Caminho dos Moinhos; 292 596 227

Corvo lies 24 km (15 miles) northeast of Flores. The smallest island in the Azores, it has just one settlement, Vila do Corvo, and is blissfully undeveloped, with only one hotel and a few restaurants. The entire island is the blown top of a marine volcano. A green crater, the Lagoa do Caldeirão, squats at its northern end. Its rim can be reached by road, after which there is a steep descent down to the crater floor 300 m (984 ft) below. In its centre, the crater is dotted with serene lakes and islands.

16th century. This western-most island of the Azores is a UNESCO listed biosphere reserve, where an abundance of flowers grow in its ravines.

The capital, Santa Cruz, is enlivened by the **Museu da Fábrica da Baleia do Boqueirão**, a museum dedicated to the island's whaling heritage, and the **Museu das Flores**, housed in a former Franciscan convent. Its displays include shipwreck finds, Azorean pottery, furniture and agricultural tools, as well

Lagoa Funda with hydrangeas growing in the foreground, Flores ↑

NEED TO KNOW

Tram 28 trundling through Lisbon

BEFORE YOU GO

Things change, so plan ahead to make the most of your trip. Be prepared for all eventualities by considering the following points before you travel.

AT A GLANCE

CURRENCY
Euro (EUR)

AVERAGE DAILY SPEND

SAVE
€35

SPEND
€70

SPLURGE
€150+

BOTTLED WATER
€0.80

COFFEE
€1

BEER
€3

DINNER FOR TWO
€45

ESSENTIAL PHRASES

Hello	Olá
Goodbye	Adeus
Please	Por favor
Thank you	Obrigado/Obrigada
Do you speak English?	Fala inglês?
I don't understand	Não compreendo

ELECTRICITY SUPPLY

Power sockets are type F, fitting a two-prong, round-pin plug. Standard voltage is 220–240v.

Passports and Visas

For entry requirements, including visas, consult your nearest Portuguese embassy or check the Portuguese **Ministry of Foreign Affairs**. Citizens of the UK, US, Canada, Australia and New Zealand do not need a visa for stays of up to three months but, from late 2023, must apply in advance for the European Travel Information and Authorization System **(ETIAS)**. EU nationals do not need a visa or an ETIAS. Non-EU nationals must have passports valid for at least three months beyond their planned departure date.
ETIAS
🔳 etiasvisa.com
Ministry of Foreign Affairs
🔳 vistos.mne.gov.pt

Government Advice

Now more than ever, it is important to consult both your and the Portuguese government's advice before travelling. The **UK Foreign, Commonwealth & Development Office (FCDO)**, the **US State Department**, the **Australian Department of Foreign Affairs and Trade** and the **Câmara Municipal de Lisboa** offer the latest information on security, health and local regulations.
AUS
🔳 smartraveller.gov.au
Câmara Municipal de Lisboa
🔳 visitar.lisboa.pt
UK Foreign, Commonwealth & Development Office (FCDO)
🔳 gov.uk/foreign-travel-advice
US
🔳 travel.state.gov

Customs Information

You can find information on the laws relating to goods and currency taken in or out of Portugal on the **Visit Portugal** website.
Visit Portugal
 visitportugal.com

Insurance

We recommend taking out a comprehensive insurance policy covering theft, loss of belongings, medical care, cancellations and delays, and read the small print carefully. UK citizens are eligible for free emergency medical care in Portugal provided they have a valid EHIC (European Health Insurance Card) or **GHIC** (UK Global Health Insurance Card).

GHIC
w ghic.org.uk

Vaccinations

No inoculations are necessary for Portugal.

Money

Most urban establishments accept major credit and debit cards. Contactless payments are becoming more common, but it is a good idea to carry cash for smaller items.

Tipping around 10 per cent is normal when dining out or travelling by taxi; hotel porters and house-keeping will expect €1-2 per bag or day.

Booking Accommodation

Portugal offers a range of accommodation. During the summer lodgings fill up and prices become inflated, so book in advance. Lisbon and Porto are popular for city-breaks; avoid last-minute weekend bookings even in the low season (Dec–Mar). In some cities, and in the Algarve, a tourist tax will be charged on top of the room price (€1–2 per person per night). Hotels are required by law to share details of foreign visitors with local authorities.

Travellers with Specific Requirements

Portugal can be a challenge for visitors with reduced mobility and for those travelling with prams or buggies. Facilities have improved, with increased wheelchair access, adapted toilets and reserved car parking. There are ramps and lifts in public places and on public transport. Most sights offer audio guides for the visually impaired and audio induction loops for the hard of hearing.

Tourism For All offers specialist holiday packages tailored to travellers' needs, while

Accessible Portugal gives useful advice on travelling in Portugal with limited mobility.
Accessible Portugal
w accessibleportugal.com
Tourism For All
w tourism-for-all.com

Language

Portuguese is the official language. English is widely spoken in most towns, cities and tourist resorts, but it is less prevalent in rural areas.

Opening Hours

> The COVID-19 pandemic proved that situations can change suddenly. Always check before visiting attractions and hospitality venues for up-to-date hours and booking requirements.

Monday State-run museums, public buildings and monuments are closed all day.
Sunday Churches and cathedrals are closed to tourists during Mass. Some public transport runs less frequently.
Public holidays Most museums, public buildings and many shops are closed early or for the day.

PUBLIC HOLIDAYS

1 Jan	New Year's Day
Mar/Apr	Good Friday
Mar/Apr	Easter Sunday
25 Apr	Freedom Day
1 May	Labour Day
May/Jun	Corpus Christi
10 Jun	Portugal Day
13 Jun	Feast of St Anthony (Lisbon)
24 Jun	Feast of St John the Baptist (Porto)
15 Aug	Assumption Day
5 Oct	Republic Day
1 Nov	All Saints' Day
1 Dec	Restoration of Independence
8 Dec	Immaculate Conception Day
25 Dec	Christmas Day

GETTING
AROUND

Whether you are visiting for a short city break or rural country retreat, discover how best to reach your destination and travel like a pro.

AT A GLANCE

PUBLIC TRANSPORT COSTS

LISBON

€6.50

24-hr ticket
Metro, bus, tram

PORTO

€4.20

24-hr ticket (zone 2)
Metro, bus, tram

COIMBRA

€3.50

Day ticket
Bus

TOP TIP
Always try to buy a travel pass, rather than paying for individual journeys.

SPEED LIMIT

MOTORWAY

120
km/h
(75 mph)

DUAL CARRIAGEWAY

100
km/h
(60 mph)

SECONDARY ROAD

90
km/h
(55 mph)

URBAN AREAS

50
km/h
(30 mph)

Arriving by Air

Lisbon, Porto and Faro are the main airports for long-haul flights into Portugal, while European budget airlines fly to cities across Portugal year-round at very reasonable prices. These European companies also offer very good rates on regular internal flights.

For information on getting to and from Portugal's main airports, see the table opposite.

Driving

Although Portuguese roads are renowned for being accident-prone, with the country suffering the highest road fatality rate in Europe in 2000, in 2015, the World Economic Forum pronounced the road network itself to be the best in the continent. A comprehensive motorway system allows for speedy travel between major cities, although some less-travelled rural roads may be in need of repair. Make sure you are familiar with the rules of the road and carry all necessary documentation with you at all times.

Driving to Portugal

The quickest route into the country is to cross the French–Spanish border at Irun, then take the E80 motorway to Vilar Formoso on the Portuguese border. Southern Spain connects to the Algarve's main artery, the A22, which intersects the E1 (Portugal's north–south lifeline) near Albufeira.

Most of the main motorways in Portugal are toll roads which are paid electronically. The easiest system to use is **EasyToll**, which matches your credit card to your licence plate and automatically deducts the necessary funds. Payments and details can be managed on its website.

If you bring your own foreign-registered car, you must carry a valid driver's licence, proof of ownership, insurance and address, as well as an up-to-date MOT certificate. After 183 days, the car must either be registered in Portugal or taken to another country.

EasyToll
W portugaltolls.com

GETTING TO AND FROM THE AIRPORT

Airport	Distance to city	Taxi fare	Public transport	Journey time
Faro (Algarve)	4 km (2.5 miles)	€20	Bus	20 mins
Lisbon (Humberto Delgado)	7 km (4 miles)	€20	Metro	25 mins
Madeira (Funchal)	13 km (8 miles)	€23	Bus	45 mins
Porto (Francisco Sá Carneiro)	11 km (7 miles)	€25	Metro	35 mins
Ponta Delgada (João Paulo II)	2 km (1 mile)	€10	Bus	10 mins

CAR JOURNEY PLANNER

Plotting the main driving routes according to journey time, this map is a handy reference for travelling between Portugal's main cities by car. The times given reflect the fastest and most direct routes available. Tolls apply on most motorways.

Faro to Albufeira	45 mins
Faro to Évora	2.5 hrs
Faro to Lagos	1 hr
Faro to Lisbon	2.75 hrs
Lisbon to Coimbra	2 hrs
Lisbon to Évora	1.5 hrs
Lisbon to Lagos	2.75 hrs
Porto to Braga	45 mins
Porto to Lisbon	3 hrs

Braga
Porto
Coimbra
Lisbon
Évora
Lagos
Albufeira
Faro

••• Direct car routes

Car Rental

Car hire agencies can be found in main towns and at airports. To rent a car in Portugal you must be over 18 and have held a valid driver's licence for at least one year, although those under 25 usually need to pay a surcharge. Prices drop considerably in the low season and some companies offer special off-peak and weekend deals. As Portuguese drivers are infamously erratic, it is sensible to arrange third-party insurance beforehand or take the pricier "no excess" insurance deals offered upon pick-up. Most car hire companies give the option to pay all road toll fees upon the vehicle's return.

Rules of the Road

When using a car in Portugal, drive on the right and use the left lane only for passing other vehicles. The wearing of seat belts are required for all passengers and heavy fines are incurred for using a mobile phone while driving. Drivers are required to stop at pedestrian crossings. The blood-alcohol concentration (BAC) limit is 0.5mg/ml and is very strictly enforced. Dashboard cameras are illegal in Portugal, as they contravene privacy laws.

Always carry your passport, licence and insurance details. In the event of an accident or breakdown, the driver and passengers must don a fluorescent yellow safety vest and erect a collapsible warning triangle 50 m (164 ft) behind the vehicle. Both of these items must be stored in the trunk at all times. Driver's licences issued by any EU member state are valid throughout the EU, including Portugal. If visiting from outside the EU, you may need to apply for an International Driving Permit (IDP).

The local motoring association, the **ACP** (Automóvel Club de Portugal), has a reciprocal breakdown service with most other international motoring organizations. To qualify, drivers should take out European cover with their own organization. Should you be involved in a road accident, the emergency services number is 112. If you have simply broken down, call the ACP or, if driving a hired car, check the instructions supplied by your chosen company.

ACP
☎ 808 222 222
🅦 acp.pt

Train Travel

International Train Travel

There are two main routes into Portugal by train: the Sud Express and the Lusitânia, with connections from Paris and Madrid. Both services were cut off at the start of the COVID-19 pandemic, and have yet to return. Currently, air travel, driving and international buses are the only way to enter the country.

Domestic Train Travel

Portugal's national rail operator is **CP** (Comboios de Portugal). Most of the country is served by rail, although some of the more remote lines have been made obsolete by new road links. CP runs two types of train service, with routes spanning from north of Braga to Faro, some of which take in Lisbon, Coimbra and Porto. The new Alfa Pendular trains are faster, more comfortable and have free Wi-Fi, while Intercidades trains are older, cheaper and stop regularly. Trains should be pre-booked, either online or at the station, except for journeys on urban rail networks (*urbanas*), such as Lisbon's Sintra and Cascais lines. A conductor will validate tickets on-board and will often ask for ID. Tickets for *urbanas* can be bought at the station prior to departure and should be validated at the ticket machines on the platform before boarding.

CP
🅦 cp.pt

Long-Distance Bus Travel

Travelling to Portugal by coach is cheap but time consuming. **Flixbus** offers routes into Portugal from destinations across Western Europe including Paris, Madrid and Geneva. Buses depart from the Sete Rios or the Oriente station in Lisbon.

National coach travel is far more convenient. Coach companies in Portugal are competitive and offer efficient, comfortable services. **Rede Expressos** covers most of Portugal, linking Braga, Porto, Lisbon and Faro. As a rule, you can no longer buy tickets on-board for long distance trips and there are discounts for booking early.

Tickets for shorter trips can be bought at the station or from the driver. **EVA** covers the Algarve particularly well, with discounted ticket deals, and **Rodonorte** focuses on the extreme north.

Organized coach tours are plentiful, especially from major cities and in the Algarve. Tourist offices, hotels and travel agencies can advise on which company might best suit your needs.

EVA
🅦 eva-bus.com
Flixbus
🅦 flixbus.com
Rede Expressos
🅦 rede-expressos.pt/en/
Rodonorte
🅦 rodonorte.pt

Public Transport

In most cities and towns, bus services suffice as the sole means of public transport. However, larger cities operate multiple services including trains, buses, trams and metro systems. Major transport authorities include Coimbra's **SMTUC** (Serviços Municipalizados de Transportes Urbanos de Coimbra); Porto's **STCP** (Sociedade de Transportes Colectivos do Porto); and **Carris** in Lisbon. In the Algarve, buses are run privately and several companies operate between cities. Safety and hygiene measures, timetables, ticket information, transport maps, and more can be obtained from their respective offices or online.

Carris
🅦 carris.pt/en
SMTUC
🅦 smtuc.pt
STCP
🅦 stcp.pt/en/travel

Lisbon and Porto

Portugal's two largest cities have extensive public transport networks comprising buses, metro systems, trams and funiculars. The metro runs until 1am and is the most convenient way to travel, while trams and funiculars are pleasant, but generally less practical. Buses go just about everywhere and some services run through the night on a reduced schedule.

The price of a single ticket varies for each method of transport. Both cities offer travel cards that allow comprehensive access to networks at a discounted rate. Travel cards (Lisbon's Navegante and Porto's Andante) can be bought in the main metro and train stations. There is a small charge (€0.50/€0.60) to purchase the card itself and each traveller must have their own. Cards can be topped up in advance or loaded with a 24-hour pass.

In Lisbon, a basic 24-hour pass (€6.45) allows unlimited travel on the metro, buses, trams and funiculars. Advanced passes either include access to Lisbon's urban rail network (Cascais, Sintra, Estoril) or to ferry services across the Tagus. In Porto, the price is graded by distance, according to the city's zone system, and can be used on the metro, buses and urban trains. A 2-zone pass (€4.20) covers most areas of interest, while 4-zone tickets include the airport.

Taxis

Taxis in Portugal are relatively inexpensive compared to the rest of Europe and can work out as being cheaper than public transport for large groups travelling together. Most taxi drivers only accept cash and can be hailed in the street and at taxi ranks.

In cities, always take an official, metered taxi. A green light indicates that the taxi is available and two green lights mean a higher rate of charge. Ensure that the meter is on, suggest agreeing on a price for longer routes and always check the extra cost for luggage before setting off. The average starting rate for a taxi is €3.25 by day, although rates differ between companies and are usually 20 per cent higher between 10pm and 6am. In smaller towns, taxis can usually be found at ranks in the centre and several local firms may operate in each area. In the Algarve, many visitors choose private hire cars or mini buses, as taxi rank queues are often long in peak season and taxis can rarely be booked in advance. It is common to tip by rounding up the fare.

Cycle and Scooter Hire

Portugal's historic city centres are ill-equipped for bicycles, but popular cycling routes exist on the flatter fringes and you can rent bicycles in most towns and cities. Long-distance journeys are best attempted during the milder shoulder seasons when the roads are quieter. In Lisbon, a growing number of companies, including **Lisbon Bike Rentals**, now offer electric bikes.

Scooters are suitable for short journeys and are a more popular choice; inter-city travel really requires a motorcycle. Most rental companies require a deposit and ask you to leave your passport at the rental shop. You must have a driver's licence valid for your desired bike category. 50cc vehicles are forbidden on motorways and riders must wear helmets by law, which can be rented from most hire shops.

Lisbon Bike Rentals
ⓦ lisbonbikerentals.com

Walking and Hiking

Most of Portugal's historic town and city centres, including Lisbon and Porto, are fairly compact and can easily be covered on foot. Note that some streets are notoriously steep, especially in Lisbon, and can get slippery in the rain.

Beyond the cities, Portugal is a fantastic destination for walkers and hikers, but planning and good preparation are essential. Ensure you have good walking boots, suitable clothing and plenty of water, especially if you plan to hike in the heat of the day. Always tell someone where you're going and when you plan to return.

Islands and Ferries

Several national airlines run daily direct flights to Madeira and the Azores from Lisbon and Porto. Flights between islands are the fastest way to get around. **TAP** flies several times a day between Funchal and Porto Santo in the Madeira group; on the Azores, flights are operated by **SATA**. Flights to Flores and Corvo are often disrupted by bad weather, so it is a good idea to insure against delays.

A network of passenger ferries operated by **Atlânticoline** links all the islands of the Azores, allowing visitors to explore the archipelago by sea. Journey times range from 30 minutes to 18 hours, and as a rule, shorter services run more frequently. **Azores Islands Travel** offers a special three-in-one ticket between the islands of Pico, Faial and São Jorge.

Atlânticoline
ⓦ atlanticoline.pt
Azores Islands Travel
ⓦ azoresislands.travel
SATA
ⓦ sata.pt
TAP
ⓦ flytap.com

PRACTICAL
INFORMATION

A little local know-how goes a long way in Portugal. Here is all the essential advice and information you will need during your stay.

AT A GLANCE

EMERGENCY NUMBERS

GENERAL EMERGENCY

112

TIME ZONE
CET/CEST: Central European Summer time (CEST) runs from the last Sun in Mar to the last Sun in Oct.

TAP WATER
Unless stated otherwise, tap water in Portugal is safe to drink.

WEBSITES AND APPS

VisitPortugal
Check out www.visitportugal.com, the website of Portugal's tourism board.
Odisseias
Visit www.odisseias.com for deals in Lisbon and Porto.
Street Art Cities
Locate street art in the capital with this cool app.
VisitAzores
This app is essential for anyone travelling in the Azores.
WalkMe
For information on Madeira's hiking trails, including offline maps, check out this app.

Personal Security

While crime in Portugal is very low, pickpockets are fairly common in major cities. Take care in crowded tourist areas and aboard Lisbon's trams, particularly the 28 and 15. Keep your valuables in a safe place when in your accommodation and with you at all times.

If you have anything stolen, report the crime within 24 hours to the nearest police station and take ID with you. Get a copy of the crime report to make an insurance claim. Contact your embassy if you have your passport stolen, or in the event of a serious crime or accident. The number to dial in an emergency is 112. Ask for the required service – *polícia* (police), *ambulância* (ambulance) or *bombeiros* (fire brigade). In Lisbon visitors can report assaults, thefts and lost property to the **Lisbon Tourist Police**.

The Portuguese are generally accepting of all people, regardless of their race, gender or sexuality. Homosexuality was legalized in 1982 and in 2010, Portugal became the eighth country in the world to recognize same-sex marriage. Portugal prides itself on being a tolerant country; homophobic attitudes are very much the exception, not the norm. Having said this, some rural areas remain conservatively Catholic, and public displays of affection may be met with hostility. If you do feel unsafe, the **Safe Space Alliance** pinpoints your nearest point of refuge.

Women may receive unwanted attention, especially around tourist areas. If you feel threatened, head straight for the nearest police station.
Lisbon Tourist Police
C 213 421 623
Safe Space Alliance
W safespacealliance.com

Health

Portugal has a world-class health system. Emergency medical care in Portugal is free for all EU citizens. If you have an EHIC or GHIC *(p379)*, be sure to present this as soon as possible. You may have to pay after treatment and reclaim the money on your insurance later. For visitors

coming from outside the EU, payment of hospital and other medical expenses is the patient's responsibility, so it is important to arrange comprehensive medical insurance before travelling.

Seek medicinal supplies and advice for minor ailments from pharmacies (*farmácias*), identifiable by a green cross. Pharmacists can dispense a range of drugs that would normally be available only on prescription in many other countries. Each pharmacy displays a card in the window showing the address of the nearest all-night pharmacy.

Smoking, Alcohol and Drugs

Smoking is banned in most enclosed public spaces and is a fineable offence, although some bars still allow it.

Portugal has a high alcohol consumption rate; however, it is frowned upon to be openly drunk. In cities it is common to drink on the street outside the bar of purchase.

All drugs have been decriminalized in Portugal since 2001, but possession of even small quantities is considered a public health issue and will result in a warning or small fine. Be aware of drug dealers brazenly plying their wares in city centres.

ID

By law you must carry identification with you at all times in Portugal. A photocopy of your passport should suffice. If stopped by the police you may be asked to report to a police station with the original document.

Local Customs

As the pressure of tourism grows in Portugal's cities, small efforts to integrate are appreciated. Try to use simple Portuguese phrases and greetings appropriate to the time of day.

A much-loved aspect of Portugal is the slow pace of life. Avoid impatience as a pedestrian, at events and when making social engagements.

Visiting Places of Worship

Most churches and cathedrals will not permit visitors during Sunday Mass. Generally, entrance to churches is free; however a fee may apply to enter special areas, like cloisters.

Portugal retains a strong Catholic identity. When visiting religious buildings dress modestly, with your knees and shoulders covered.

Mobile Phones and Wi-Fi

Free Wi-Fi can be found in most cafés, restaurants and bars.

Visitors travelling to Portugal with EU tariffs are able to use their devices abroad without being affected by roaming charges. Users will be charged the same rates for data, calls and texts as at home.

Post

The postal service is run by **CTT** (Correios de Portugal), which offers a wide range of services at prices lower than the European average. Stamps are sold in post offices, newsagents and on the CTT website.
CTT
w ctt.pt

Taxes and Refunds

VAT is usually 23 per cent. Under certain conditions, non-EU citizens can claim a rebate. Either claim the rebate before you buy (show your passport to the shop assistant and complete a form) or present a customs officer with your receipts as you leave.

Discount Cards

Most major cities offer a visitor's pass or tourist discount card for exhibitions, events and museum entry. Some, like the **Lisboa Card** and the **Porto Card**, even cover the cost of public transport within the city for a set number of days. These cards are not free, and though they may often seem like a bargain, it is worth carefully considering how many of the offers you are likely to take advantage of before purchasing one for the duration of your stay.
Lisboa Card
w shop.visitlisboa.com
Porto Card
w visitporto.travel

INDEX

N

PHRASE BOOK

IN EMERGENCY

Help!	Socorro!	soo-**koh**-roo
Stop!	Pare!	pahr'
Call a doctor!	Chame um médico!	shahm' ooñ **meh**-dee-koo
Call an ambulance!	Chame uma ambulância!	shahm' oo-muh añ-boo-**lañ**-see-uh
Call the police!	Chame a polícia!	shahm'uh poo-**lee**-see-uh
Call the fire brigade!	Chame os bombeiros!	shahm' oosh bom-**bay**-roosh
Where is the nearest telephone?	Há um telefone aqui perto?	ah ooñ te-le-**fon'** uh-**keepehr**-too
Where is the nearest hospital?	Onde é o hospital mais próximo?	ond' eh oo ohsh-pee-**tahl'** mysh **pro**-see-moo

COMMUNICATION ESSENTIALS

Yes	Sim	seeñ
No	Não	nowñ
Please	Por favor/ Faz favor	poor fuh-**vor** fash fuh-**vor**
Thank you	Obrigado/da	o-bree-**gah**-doo/duh
Excuse me	Desculpe	dish-**koolp'**
Hello	Olá	oh-**lah**
Goodbye	Adeus	a-**deh**-oosh
Good morning	Bom dia	boñ **dee**-uh
Good afternoon	Boa tarde	boh-uh **tard'**
Good night	Boa noite	boh-uh **noyt'**
Yesterday	Ontem	oñ-**tayñ**
Today	Hoje	ohj'
Tomorrow	Amanhã	ah-mañ-**yañ**
Here	Aqui	uh-**kee**
There	Ali	uh-**lee**
What?	O quê?	oo keh
Which?	Qual?	kwahl'
When?	Quando?	**kwañ**-doo
Why?	Porquê?	poor-**keh**
Where?	Onde?	oñd'

USEFUL PHRASES

How are you?	Como está?	koh-moo shtah
Very well, thank you.	Bem, obrigado/da.	bayñ o-bree-**gah**-doo/duh
Pleased to meet you.	Prazer.	pra-**ser**
See you soon.	Até logo.	uh-**teh loh**-goo
That's fine.	Está bem.	shtah bayñ
Where is/are ...?	Onde está/estão ...?	ond' shtah/ shtowñ
How far is it to ...?	A que distância fica ...?	uh kee dish-**tañ**-see-uh **fee**-kuh
Which way to ...?	Como se vai para ...?	koh-moo seh vy puh-ruh
Do you speak English?	Fala inglês?	**fah**-luh eeñ-**glehsh**
I don't understand.	Não compreendo.	nowñ kom-pree-**eñ**-doo
Could you speak more slowly please?	Pode falar mais devagar por favor?	pohd' fuh-**lar** mysh d'-va-**gar** poor fuh-**vor**
I'm sorry.	Desculpe.	dish-**koolp'**

USEFUL WORDS

big	grande	grañd'
small	pequeno	pe-**keh**-noo
hot	quente	keñt'
cold	frio	**free**-oo
good	bom	boñ
bad	mau	**mah**-oo
quite a lot/enough	bastante	bash-**tañt'**
well	bem	bayñ
open	aberto	a-**behr**-too
closed	fechado	fe-**shah**-doo
left	esquerda	shkehr'-duh
right	direita	dee-**ray**-tuh
straight on	em frente	ayñ freñt'
near	perto	**pehr**-too
far	longe	loñj'
up	para cima	pur-ruh **see**-muh
down	para baixo	pur-ruh **buy**-shoo
early	cedo	**seh**-doo
late	tarde	tard'
entrance	entrada	eñ-**trah**-duh
exit	saída	sa-**ee**-duh
toilets	casa de banho	**kah**-zuh d' **bañ**-yoo
more	mais	mysh
less	menos	**meh**-noosh

MAKING A TELEPHONE CALL

I'd like to place an international call.	Queria fazer uma chamada internacional.	**kree**-uh fuh-**zehr** oo-muh sha-**mah**-duh in-ter-na-see-oo-**nahl'**
a local call.	uma chamada local.	oo-muh sha-**mah**-duh loo-**kahl'**
Can I leave a message?	Posso deixar uma mensagem?	**poh**-soo day-**shar** oo-muh meñ-**sah**-jayñ

SHOPPING

How much does this cost?	Quanto custa isto?	**kwañ**-too koosh-tuh **eesh**-too
I would like ...	Queria ...	**kree**-uh
I'm just looking.	Estou só a ver obrigado/a.	shtoh sohuh vehr o-bree-**gah**-doo/uh
Do you take credit cards?	Aceita cartões de crédito?	uh-**say**-tuh kar-**toiñsh** de **kreh**-dee-too
What time do you open?	A que horas abre?	uh **kee** oh-rash **ah**-bre
What time do you close?	A que horas fecha?	uh **kee** oh-rash **fay**-shuh
This one	Este	ehst'
That one	Esse	ehss'
expensive	caro	**kah**-roo
cheap	barato	buh-**rah**-too
size (clothes/shoes)	tamanho	ta-**man**-yoo
white	branco	**brañ**-koo
black	preto	**preh**-too
red	vermelho	ver-**mehl'**-yoo
yellow	amarelo	uh-muh-**reh**-loo
green	verde	vehrd'
blue	azul	uh-**zool'**

TYPES OF SHOP

antique shop	loja de antiguidades	**loh**-juh de añ-tee-gwee-**dahd'sh**
bakery	padaria	pah-duh-**ree**-uh
bank	banco	**bañ**-koo
bookshop	livraria	lee-vruh-**ree**-uh
butcher	talho	**tah**-lyoo
cake shop	pastelaria	pash-te-luh-**ree**-uh
chemist	farmácia	far-**mah**-see-uh
fishmonger	peixaria	pay-shuh-**ree**-uh
hairdresser	cabeleireiro	kab'-lay-ray-roo
market	mercado	mehr-**kah**-doo
newsagent	quiosque	kee-**yohsk'**
post office	correios	koo-**ray**-oosh
shoe shop	sapataria	suh-puh-tuh-**ree**-uh
supermarket	supermercado	soo-pehr-mer-**kah**-doo
tobacconist	tabacaria	tuh-buh-kuh-**ree**-uh
travel agency	agência de viagens	uh-**jen**-see-uh de vee-**ah**-jayñsh

SIGHTSEEING

cathedral	sé	seh
church	igreja	ee-**gray**-juh
garden	jardim	jar-**deeñ**
library	biblioteca	bee-blee-oo-**teh**-kuh
museum	museu	moo-**zeh**-oo
tourist information office	posto de turismo	**posh**-too d' too-**reesh**-moo
closed for holidays	fechado para férias	fe-**sha**-doo puh-ruh **feh**-ree-ash
bus station	estação de autocarros	shta-**sowñ** d' oh-too-kah-**roosh**
railway station	estação de comboios	shta-**sowñ** d' koñ-**boy**-oosh

STAYING IN A HOTEL

Do you have a vacant room?	Tem um quarto livre?	tayñ ooñ **kwar**-too **leevr'**
room with a bath	um quarto com casa de banho	ooñ **kwar**-too koñ kah-zuh d' **bañ**-yoo
shower	duche	doosh
single room	quarto individual	**kwar**-too een-dee-vee-doo-**ahl'**
double room	quarto de casal	**kwar**-too d' kuh-**zahl'**
twin room	quarto com duas camas	**kwar**-too koñ **doo**-ash kah-mash
porter	porteiro	poor-**tay**-roo
key	chave	shahv'
I have a reservation.	Tenho um quarto reservado.	**tayñ**-yoo ooñ **kwar**-too-re-ser-**vah**-doo

EATING OUT

Have you got a table for ...?	Tem uma mesa para ...?	tayñ oo-muh meh-zuh puh-ruh

English	Portuguese	Pronunciation
I want to reserve a table.	Quero reservar uma mesa.	keh-roo re-zehr-var oo-muh meh-zuh
The bill please.	A conta por favor/ faz favor.	uh kohn-tuh poor fuh-vor/ fash fuh-vor
I am a vegetarian.	Sou vegetariano/a.	Soh ve-je-tuh-ree-ah-noo/uh
Waiter!	Por favor!/ Faz favor!	poor fuh-vor fash fuh-vor
the menu	a lista	uh leesh-tuh
fixed-price menu	a ementa turística	uh ee-mehñ-tuh too-reesh-tee-kuh
wine list	a lista de vinhos	uh leesh-tuh de veeñ-yoosh
glass	um copo	ooñ koh-poo
bottle	uma garrafa	oo-muh guh-rah-fuh
half bottle	meia-garrafa	may-uh guh-rah-fuh
knife	uma faca	oo-muh fah-kuh
fork	um garfo	ooñ gar-foo
spoon	uma colher	oo-muh kool-yair
plate	um prato	ooñ prah-too
napkin	um guardanapo	ooñgoo-ar-duh-nah-poo
breakfast	pequeno-almoço	pe-keh-noo-ahl-moh-soo
lunch	almoço	ahl-moh-soo
dinner	jantar	jan-tar
cover	couvert	koo-vehr
starter	entrada	eñ-trah-duh
main course	prato principal	prah-too prin-see-pahl'
dish of the day	prato do dia	prah-too doo dee-uh
set dish	combinado	koñ-bee-nah-doo
half portion	meia-dose	may-uh doh-se
dessert	sobremesa	soh-bre-meh-zuh
rare	mal passado	mahl'puh-sah-doo
medium	médio	meh-dee-oo
well done	bem passado	bayñ puh-sah-doo

MENU DECODER

abacate	uh-buh-kaht'	avocado
açorda	uh-sor-duh	bread-based stew (often seafood)
açúcar	uh-soo-kar	sugar
água mineral	ah-gwuh mee-ne-rahl'	mineral water
(com gás)	koñ gas	sparkling
(sem gás)	sayñ gas	still
alho	al'-yoo	garlic
alperce	ahl'-pehrce	apricot
amêijoas	uh-may-joo-ash	clams
ananás	uh-nuh-nahsh	pineapple
arroz	uh-rohsh	rice
assado	uh-sah-doo	baked
atum	uh-tooñ	tuna
aves	ah-vesh	poultry
azeite	uh-zayt'	olive oil
azeitonas	uh-zay-toh-nash	olives
bacalhau	buh-kuh-lyow	dried, salted cod
banana	buh-nah-nuh	banana
batatas	buh-tah-tash	potatoes
batatas fritas	buh-tah-tash free-tash	french fries
batido	buh-tee-doo	milk-shake
bife	beef	steak
bolacha	boo-lah-shuh	biscuit
bolo	boh-loo	cake
borrego	boo-reh-goo	lamb
caça	kah-ssuh	game
café	kuh-feh	coffee
camarões	kuh-muh-roysh	shrimp
caracóis	kuh-ruh-koysh	snails
caranguejo	kuh-rañ-gay-joo	crab
carne	karn'	meat
cataplana	kuh-tuh-plah-nuh	sealed wok used to steam dishes
cebola	se-boh-luh	onion
cerveja	sehr-vay-juh	beer
chá	shah	tea
cherne	shern'	stone bass
chocolate	shoh-koh-laht'	chocolate
chocos	shoh-koosh	cuttlefish
chouriço	shoh-ree-soo	red, spicy sausage on the spit
churrasco	shoo-rash-coo	
cogumelos	koo-goo-meh-loosh	mushrooms
cozido	koo-zee-doo	boiled
enguias	eñ-gee-ash	eels
fiambre	fee-añbr'	ham
fígado	fee-guh-doo	liver
frango	frañ-goo	chicken
frito	free-too	fried
fruta	froo-tuh	fruit
gambas	gam-bash	prawns
gelado	je-lah-doo	ice cream

gelo	jeh-loo	ice
goraz	goo-rash	bream
grelhado	grel-yah-doo	grilled
iscas	eesh-kash	marinated liver
lagosta	luh-gohsh-tuh	lobster
laranja	luh-rañ-juh	orange
leite	layt'	milk
limão	lee-mowñ	lemon
limonada	lee-moo-nah-duh	lemonade
linguado	leeñ-gwah-doo	sole
lulas	loo-lash	squid
maçã	muh-sañ	apple
manteiga	mañ-tay-guh	butter
marisco	muh-reesh-koosh	seafood
meia-de-leite	may-uh-d' layt'	white coffee
ostras	osh-trash	oysters
ovos	oh-voosh	eggs
pão	powñ	bread
pastel	pash-tehl'	cake
pato	pah-too	duck
paysh	paysh'	fish
peixe-espada	paysh'-shpah-duh	scabbard fish
pimenta	pee-meñ-tuh	pepper
polvo	pohl'-voo	octopus
porco	por-coo	pork
queijo	kay-joo	cheese
sal	sahl'	salt
salada	suh-lah-duh	salad
salsichas	sahl-see-shash	sausages
sandes	sañ-desh	sandwich
santola	sañ-toh-luh	spider crab
sopa	soh-puh	soup
sumo	soo-moo	juice
tamboril	tañ-boo-ril'	monkfish
tarte	tart'	pie/cake
tomate	too-maht'	tomato
torrada	too-rah-duh	toast
tosta	tohsh-tuh	toasted sandwich
vinagre	vee-nah-gre	vinegar
vinho branco	veeñ-yoo brañ-koo	white wine
vinho tinto	veeñ-yoo teeñ-too	red wine
vitela	vee-teh-luh	veal

NUMBERS

0	zero	zeh-roo
1	um	ooñ
2	dois	doysh
3	três	tresh
4	quatro	kwa-troo
5	cinco	seeñ-koo
6	seis	saysh
7	sete	set'
8	oito	oy-too
9	nove	nov'
10	dez	desh
11	onze	oñz'
12	doze	doz'
13	treze	trez'
14	catorze	ka-torz'
15	quinze	keeñz'
16	dezasseis	de-zuh-saysh
17	dezassete	de-zuh-set'
18	dezoito	de-zoy-too
19	dezanove	de-zuh-nov'
20	vinte	veent'
21	vinte e um	veen-tee-ooñ
30	trinta	treeñ-tuh
40	quarenta	kwa-reñ-tuh
50	cinquenta	seen-kweñ-tuh
60	sessenta	se-señ-tuh
70	setenta	se-teñ-tuh
80	oitenta	oy-teñ-tuh
90	noventa	noo-veñ-tuh
100	cem	sayñ
101	cento e um	señ-too-ee-ooñ
102	cento e dois	señ-too ee doysh
200	duzentos	doo-zeñ-toosh
300	trezentos	tre-zeñ-toosh
400	quatrocentos	kwa-troo-señ-toosh
500	quinhentos	kee-nyeñ-toosh
700	setecentos	set'-señ-toosh
900	novecentos	nov'-señ-toosh
1,000	mil	meel'

TIME

one minute	um minuto	ooñ mee-noo-too
one hour	uma hora	oo-muh oh-ruh
half an hour	meia-hora	may-uh-oh-ruh
Monday	segunda-feira	se-goon-duh-fay-ruh
Tuesday	terça-feira	ter-sa-fay-ruh
Wednesday	quarta-feira	kwar-ta-fay-ruh
Thursday	quinta-feira	keen-ta-fay-ruh
Friday	sexta-feira	say-shta-fay-ruh
Saturday	sábado	sah-ba-doo
Sunday	domingo	doo-meen-go

ACKNOWLEDGMENTS

DK would like to thank the following for their contribution to the previous edition: Matthew Hancock and Mandy Tomlin, Andy Gregory, Martin Symington, Helen Peters.

The publisher would like to thank the following for their kind permission to reproduce their photographs:

Key: a-above; b-below/bottom; c-centre; f-far; l-left; r-right; t-top

123RF.com: ermess 40cla; manganganath 96b; Sean Pavone 83cla; seregalsv 111tl, 164bl; Michael Spring 133bl; sytnik 40cra.

4Corners: Gnter Grfenhain 325br

Alamy Stock Photo: Mauricio Abreu 41cr, 81br, 85b, 259br, 262b, 271tr, 271cra, 313cra; agefotostock 19c, 182tl, 218bl, / Paulo Amorim 32-3t, / Juanma Aparicio 151ca, / Danuta Hyniewska 180t, / Ken Welsh 127clb; Archive PL 122cl; Arco Images GmbH 332-3b; ART Collection 249br; Sergio Azenha 27cl, 197tr, 206tr, 226tr; John Baran 128br; Paul Bernhardt 323tr, Bildagentur-online / McPhoto-Boyungs 79tc, Schoening 113tl; Bildarchiv Monheim GmbH / Markus Bassler 251clb; Brazil Photo Press 41tl; Michael Brooks 39br, 55bl, 88–9, 124cl, 127bl, 255t; Sean Burke 317br; Jan Butchofsky 41clb; Nuno Campos 23tl; Julian Castle 17tr; Classic Image 44br; David Coleman 114tr; Fernando Cruz 209tr; Roger Day 260b; Xavier Dealbert 156-57x; dbimages 24bl, 177cra, 305tr; Education & Exploration 1 79tr; Luis Elvas 70tr; Giulio Ercolani 16tl; Evgeni Fabisuk 346-7t; Faraway Photos 125tr; Jose Pedro Fernandes 258bc, 300bc; Stuart Forster 254bl; Robert Fried 203tl; Manfred Gottschalk 328t; Jeff Greenberg 122-3b; Jeffrey Isaac Greenberg 11, 20-21b; Emile Haydon 117t; Hemis 20bl, 240-1b, 253crb, 335tl; Hemis.fr / Pierre Jacques 111br; Peter Herbert 54, 60-1; Marc Hill 187b; Historical Images Archive 45tr; homydesign 252tl; Peter Horree 210bl, 262cl; Chris Howes / Wild Places Photography 330tr; Hufton+Crow-VIEW 18-9b; imageBROKER / Christian Handl 353cra; imageimage 119tl; Ingram Publishing 58crb; INTERFOTO 45bc, 116tc; Ivoha 272; Jose Elias / StockPhotosArt - Mafra National Palace 19br; Art Kowalsky 38-9b, 127crb; kpzfoto 234-5t, 273bl; Leuntje 143tr; Ian Littlewood 302b; LOOK Die Bildagentur der Fotografen GmbH / Thomas Peter Widmann 205crb, / Thomas Stankiewicz 300-1b; Jon Lovette 203tr; M.Sobreira 21bl, 58cr, 98t, 153br; Cro Magnon 13t, 40bl, 140, 144-5, 227tr, 270cl, 280tl, 310bl, 339br; Tina Manley 180cra; Martin Thomas Photography 12-3b; Benny Marty 274t; Mauritius images GmbH 162-3t; Aliaksandr Mazurkevich 237b; Mikehoward 1 86bl, 329br; Mikehoward 2 317tl, 326–7b; Mikehoward 3 332tl; Mikel Bilbao Gorostiaga- Travels 32br, 358-9t; Rolandas Misius 313t; Jonathan Mitchell 175tr; Mito Images Gmbh 28tl; Eric Murphy 31crb; ilpo musto 17cla, 22-3b; Nature Picture Library 27tr; Niday Picture Library 44cla; Alexander Nikiforov 359br; nobleIMAGES 8-9; Pacific Press 273cr; Sofia Pereira / StockPhotosArt - Urban Landscape 186tr; Roman Pesarenko 134tl; Luke Peters 172bc; photolocation 2 208b, 324-5t, 336t; Photolocation 3 37cl, 202cl, 314-5b; Photolocation ltd 69t, 160b, 301tl, 303tl, 333cr; Pictorial Press Ltd 45br; Pictures Colour Library 102bl; Norman Pogson 58bl; Alex Ramsay 135cr; Simon Reddy 22bc; Dirk Renckhoff 31t; Vítor Ribeiro 142-3ca, 334tl; Mieneke Andeweg-van Rijn 151cla; robertharding / Stuart Forster 172bl; Michael Robertson 212-3b; RosalreneBetancourt 3 38-9t; RossHelen editorial 23cr; Boaz Rottem 47tr; Roussel Photography 45cr; Sagaphoto.com / Forget-Gautier 36tl, / Stephane Gautier 126-7t; scenicireland.com / Christopher Hill Photographic 22tr; shoults 372–3t; Witold Skrypczak 35br; Kumar Sriskandan 328bl; Stockimo / karrot 205cb; StockPhotosArt / Oporto / Porto / Jose Elias 242cl; Jonathan Sumpton 369bc; The Picture Art Collection 171br; travelstock44 39clb; UtCon Collection 130bc; Ivan Vdovin 177tr; Alvaro German Vilela 201cra; VWPics 40cl; Westend61 Gmbh 30b; Charlotte Wilkins 347ca; Rob Wilkinson 240t; Jan Wlodarczyk 28-9b, 30t, 35t, 78-9b, 360-1t; Dudley Wood 99b, 189bl; Rawdon Wyatt 291tr; Xinhua 21tr.

AWL Images: Mauricio Abreu 10clb, 25cb, 202-3b, 217tr, 257tr, 261tr, 298t, 299br, 304-5b, 307br, 310-1t, 370bl, 375br; Walter Bibikow 345, 346tl, 364-5; Shaun Egan 136-7; Neil Farrin 337br; Franck Guiziou 374t, 26-7t; Karol Kozlowski 372bl, 376-7; Sabine Lubenow 290tl; Alex Robinson 327tr.

Bridgeman Images: Look and Learn 42crb; Tarker 43clb.

© Calouste Gulbenkian Foundation, Lisbon: Carlos Azevedo 123cla, 124tr; Founder's Collection / Catarina Gomes Ferreira 123tr.

Depositphotos Inc: ccaetano 273crb; pkazmierczak 10-1b; sepavone 6-7.

Doclisboa: Gonçalo Castelo Soares 40crb

Dorling Kindersley: Clive Streeter 360br; Peter Wilson 70bc; Francesca Yorke 312tl.

Dreamstime.com: A1977 196br; Ahfotobox 264br; Aldorado10 362-3b; Allard1 57, 120; Steve Allen 271tc; Altezza 34tl; Leonid Andronov 108clb; Anitasstudio 356b; Anyaivanova 336cla; Arenaphotouk 331tr; Myoung Bae 131br; Bennymarty 155tc, 155tr, 165tl, 176bl, 201cla, 234bl, 275tr; Biathlonua 276cra; Ettore Bordieri 152bc; Boule13 2-3; Christophe Cappelli 312b; Joaquin Ossorio Castillo 142tl; Caviarliu 18tr; Wessel Cirkel 204bl; Clickos 357br; Luis Costa 283tl; Phil Darby 84tl; Debu55y 79cra; Devy 290-1ca; Pierre Jean Durieu 151tl; Artem Evdokimov 8cla; Evgeniy Fesenko 233cla; Anton Foltin 34br; Fosterss 290-1t; Freesurf69 216-7b; Dan Grytsku 148br, 334b; Mikalai Holubau 226-7ca; Homydesign 281b; Izabog 12clb; Jmammapac 25br; Jorisvo 198bl; Joyfull 289, 318-9; García Juan 306tr; Brenda Kean 357tr; Vichaya Kiatying-Angsulee 158tc; Vladimir Korostyshevskiy 115b; Mihai-bogdan Lazar 87cra; Martin Lehmann 224c, 228-9; Lejoch 181b; Emanuele Leoni 178tr, 249fbl; Luisafonso 363tr; Mapics 130t; Meinzahn 109cla; Milosk50 251br, 256b; Juan Moyano 97tl; Roland Nagy 94-5t; Carlos Neto 26bl, 237crb; Alexander Nikiforov 11cr; Nunocarreira 184br; Paop 369br; Sean Pavone 10ca, 11t, 48-9, 58t, 148t, 150bl; Peek Creative Collective 65br; Carlos Sanchez Pereyra 67bl; William Perry 71cl, 132t, 182crb, 182-3b; Photogolfer 30cra; Presse750 239tr, 330b; Antonio Ribeiro 112b; Vítor Ribeiro 210tr, 219cra, 243cr, 278-9t; Ricardo Rocha 142-3t; Mauro Rodrigues 43br; Rosshelen 13br, 101b, 315tr; Saiko3p 68br, 82bl, 198tr, 238clb, 238b, 278bl, 297tr; Rui G. Santos 134-5b; Sohadiszno 80-1t, 83t; Jacek Sopotnicki 13cr; Nikolai Sorokin 24-5t; Jose I. Soto 155cra; Taiga 158tl; TasFoto 233tr; Miguel Angel Morales Hermo 111cl; Stefano Valeri 81cl; Venemama 253b; Wastesoul 100tl; Anne M. Fearon-wood 250cr; Zts 66-7t, 84bl, 116b, 123tc, 156b, 161t, 174bl, 232cra, 236tl.

Eduardo Teixeira de Sousa: 282b.

Getty Images: Mauricio Abreu 50-1, 92-3b, 185t, 188tl, 207b, 248clb, 306br; AFP 46br, / Eric Feferberg 47bc, / Francisco Leong 41tr; Alex Robinson Photography 29tr; J.M.F. Almeida 41br; Apic / Retired 46cr; AWL Images / Mauricio Abreu 204-5t, / Alan Copson 273cra; Jose A. Bernat Bacete 346-7ca; Carlos Carvalho 29br; Corbis / Julianne Eggers 73tl, / Horacio Villalobos 40cr, 47br; Culture Club 184tc; DAE / G. Dagli Orti 44tl, 44-5t; DEA Picture Library 46bl; Reinhard Dirscherl 33br; Shaun Egan 211b; Terry Eggers 8clb; Herve Gloaguen 46-7ca; Pedro Gomes 41cl; Historic Map Works LLC and Osher Map Library 42t; Maya Karkalicheva 35cla; Moment / Rui Almeida Fotografia 203cla; MyLoupe 64bc; NurPhoto 36-7b; Octavio Passos 355tr; PHAS 42bc; Photo Enthusiast 308tl; ptlapse .pt 263br; Hans Georg Roth 163bl; Sylvain Sonnet 66bl, 71b, 72bl; Alexander Spatari 8cl; Hubert Stadler 361b; ullstein bild Dtl. 46-7t; Universal History Archive 43cla, 44bc; UniversalImagesGroup 43tr, / Jeff Greenberg 37br; Santiago Urquijo 215tr; Vertigo3d 33cl; Moritz Wolf 64bl.

Grupo José Avillez: Boa Onda 100bc.

iStockphoto.com: 101ArtStudio 16-7t; Acnakelsy 16-7ca, 194t; Aitormmfoto 314tr; alxpin 174-5t; borchee 340-1; CBCK-Christine 338t; diatrezor 64clb; e55evu 56, 104-5; Estellez 43tl; font83 371t; Freeartist 171tl; gkuna 171tr; Gregobagel 158-9b; hsvrs 129t; jacquesvandinteren 205br; LeoPatrizi 226tl; LordRunar 55t, 74-5; LucVi 277br; LuisPortugal 220-1; luniversa 109tr; Onfokus 11br; peeterv 12t; Fabricio Rezende 171cra; ribeiroantonio 189tr, 250-1t; Ruibento 258-9t; rusm 177tl; Juergen Sack 344, 348-9; sack 3 69crb; saiko3p 195tr; SeanPavonePhoto 152cb; simonbradfield 4; Sohadiszno 172clb; soniabonet 103cr; StockPhotosArt 173tl; Thegift777 225bl, 227tl, 232-3b, 233tl, 266-7, 276bl; Borut Trdina 27b; urf 39cra, 109tl, 324bl; ~User2afd53ea_709 354tl; Nuno Valadas 143tl; vector99 213tl; VickySP 368-9t; Visual_Intermezzo 19cb; VladimirGerasimov 263t; wundervisuals 29cl; zodebala 179b, 347tr.

Limitezero: 31cl.

© Museu Nacional de Arte Antiga, Lisboa Instituto dos Museus e da Conservação - MC: Paulo Alexandrino 92clb, 93tl, 93tr, 93cla, 94bl, 95tr, 95clb.

Museu da Marioneta: Andre é Boto 98bc.

Museu de Arte Sacra do Funchal: Arquivo MASF / Our Lady of "Amparo" Attributed to Jan Gossart named Mabuse and his followers, Flanders, Antwerp, 1543, Oil painting on oak wood, provenance: Chapel of Nossa Senhora do Amparo – Cathedral of Funchal 21cr.

Museu do Fado: José Frade / EGEAC 68tl.

Picfair.com: Alberto Novo 270-1b; Carlos Sanchez Pereyra 225t, 244-5; Inácio Joaquim Martins Pires 288, 292-3; Tiago Sousa 196t; Pedro Venâncio 141t, 166-7.

Robert Harding Picture Library: Neale Clark 354-5b; Neil Farrin 322-3t; Frank Fell 352-3t; G&M Therin-Weise 37tr; Andre Goncalves 309b; Oliver Wintzen 284-5.

This editon updated by
Contributor Joana Taborda
Senior Editors Dipika Dasgupta, Alison McGill, Zoë Rutland
Senior Designers Laura O'Brien, Stuti Tiwari
Project Editors Alex Pathe, Anuroop Sanwalia
Assistant Editor Tavleen Kaur
Assistant Art Editor Divyanshi Shreyaskar
Picture Research Administrator Vagisha Pushp
Manager Picture Research Taiyaba Khatoon
Publishing Assistant Halima Mohammed
Jacket Designer Jordan Lambley
Cartographer Ashif
Cartography Manager Suresh Kumar
DTP Designer Rohit Rojal
Senior Production Editor Jason Little
Production Controller Kariss Ainsworth
Managing Editors Shikha Kulkarni, Beverly Smart, Hollie Teague
Managing Art Editor Sarah Snelling
Senior Managing Art Editor Priyanka Thakur
Art Director Maxine Pedliham
Publishing Director Georgina Dee

First edition 1997

Published in Great Britain by Dorling Kindersley Limited, DK, One Embassy Gardens, 8 Viaduct Gardens, London SW11 7BW, UK

The authorised representative in the EEA is Dorling Kindersley Verlag GmbH. Arnulfstr. 124, 80636 Munich, Germany

Published in the United States by DK Publishing, 1745 Broadway, 20th Floor, New York, NY 10019

A CIP catalogue record for this book is available from the British Library.

A catalogue record for this book is available from the Library of Congress.

ISSN: 1542 1554
ISBN: 978 0 2416 1598 0

Printed and bound in China.

www.dk.com

A NOTE FROM DK EYEWITNESS
The rapid rate at which the world is changing is constantly keeping the DK Eyewitness team on our toes. While we've worked hard to ensure that this edition of Portugal is accurate and up-to-date, we know that opening hours alter, standards shift, prices fluctuate, places close and new ones pop up in their stead. So, if you notice we've got something wrong or left something out, we want to hear about it. Please get in touch at travelguides@dk.com